T0190478

Lecture Notes in Artificial Intelligence 12177

Subseries of Lecture Notes in Computer Science

Series Editors

Randy Goebel
University of Alberta, Edmonton, Canada
Yuzuru Tanaka
Hokkaido University, Sapporo, Japan
Wolfgang Wahlster
DFKI and Saarland University, Saarbrücken, Germany

Founding Editor

Jörg Siekmann
DFKI and Saarland University, Saarbrücken, Germany

Ben Goertzel · Aleksandr I. Panov ·
Alexey Potapov · Roman Yampolskiy (Eds.)

Artificial General Intelligence

13th International Conference, AGI 2020
St. Petersburg, Russia, September 16–19, 2020
Proceedings

Springer

Editors
Ben Goertzel (iD)
SingularityNET Foundation
Amsterdam, The Netherlands

Aleksandr I. Panov (iD)
Moscow Institute of Physics and Technology
Dolgoprudny, Russia

Alexey Potapov (iD)
SingularityNET Foundation
Amsterdam, The Netherlands

Roman Yampolskiy (iD)
University of Louisville
Louisville, KY, USA

ISSN 0302-9743   ISSN 1611-3349 (electronic)
Lecture Notes in Artificial Intelligence
ISBN 978-3-030-52151-6   ISBN 978-3-030-52152-3 (eBook)
https://doi.org/10.1007/978-3-030-52152-3

LNCS Sublibrary: SL7 – Artificial Intelligence

This Springer imprint is published by the registered company Springer Nature Switzerland AG
The registered company address is: Gewerbestrasse 11, 6330 Cham, Switzerland

Preface

This volume contains the papers presented at the 13th Conference on Artificial Intelligence (AGI 2020), held virtually during June 23–26, 2020, and physically at Saint Petersburg during September 16–19, 2020. The choice of venue was not accidental, it is in Russia that a lot of attention is being paid to AGI topics and new leading research groups are emerging with promising results. Continuing the tradition of enhanced engagement and fruitful discussion between European, American, and Chinese researchers during AGI 2019, AGI 2020 brought together researchers from around the globe, resulting in the exchange of experience and ideas.

This volume contains the contributed talks presented at AGI 2020. There were 60 submissions. The Program Committee decided to accept 22 long papers (37% acceptance) for oral presentation and 17 papers for a poster presentation. The topics covered proved to be very diverse. There are papers covering AGI architectures, papers discussing artificial creativity and AI safety, papers developing ideas from psychology and hyperdimensional representations, papers on transfer learning, papers on AI unification and benchmarks for AGI, and a host of other papers covering a wide-ranging array of additional relevant topics. In addition, the AGI 2020 conference featured tutorials and workshops on the Non-Axiomatic Reasoning System (NARS), on the Next Generation of AGI Architectures, on social AI agents and OpenCog Architecture. We thank all the Program Committee members for their dedicated service to the review process. We thank all of our contributors, participants, and tutorial, workshop, and panel session organizers, without whom the conference would not exist.

May 2020

Ben Goertzel
Aleksandr I. Panov
Alexey Potapov
Roman Yampolskiy

Organization

Program Committee

Joscha Bach	AI Foundation, USA
Jordi Bieger	Reykjavik University, Iceland
Cristiano Castelfranchi	Institute of Cognitive Sciences and Technologies, Italy
Antonio Chella	Università di Palermo, Italy
Madalina Croitoru	LIRMM, Montpellier 2 University, France
Deborah Duong	SingularityNET, USA
Aaron Eberhart	Kansas State University, USA
Kasim Ebrahim Ebrahim	iCog-Labs, Ethopia
Arthur Franz	Odessa Competence Center for Artificial Intelligence and Machine Learning (OCCAM), Ukraine
Nil Geisweiller	OpenCog, SingularityNET, Novamente LLC, USA
Ben Goertzel	SingularityNET, USA
Patrick Hammer	Temple University, USA
Jose Hernandez-Orallo	Universitat Politècnica de València, Spain
Marcus Hutter	The Australian National University, Australia
Matt Iklé	SingularityNET, USA
Peter Isaev	Temple University, USA
Cliff Joslyn	Pacific Northwest National Laboratory, USA
Garrett Katz	Syracuse University, USA
Randal Koene	Boston University, USA
Oliver Kutz	Free University of Bozen-Bolzano, Italy
Christian Lebiere	Carnegie Mellon University, USA
John Licato	Indiana University and Purdue University, USA
Maricarmen Martinez	Universidad de los Andes, Colombia
Amedeo Napoli	LORIA, CNRS, INRIA, Universite de Lorraine, France
Eray Ozkural	Bilkent University, Turkey
Guenther Palm	Ulm University, Germany
Alexander Panov	Russian Academy of Sciences, Russia
Wiebke Petersen	University of Düsseldorf, Germany
Maxim Peterson	ITMO University, Russia
Alexey Potapov	SingularityNET, USA
Vladimir Redko	SRISA, Italy
Rafal Rzepka	Hokkaido University, Japan
Ricardo Sanz	Universidad Politécnica de Madrid, Spain
Oleg Scherbakov	ITMO University, Russia
Ute Schmid	University of Bamberg, Germany
Leslie Smith	University of Stirling, UK
Bas Steunebrink	NNAISENSE, Switzerland

Contents

AGI and the Knight-Darwin Law: Why Idealized AGI Reproduction Requires Collaboration

Samuel Allen Alexander$^{(\boxtimes)}$ (iD)

The U.S. Securities and Exchange Commission, New York, USA
samuelallenalexander@gmail.com
https://philpeople.org/profiles/samuel-alexander/publications

Abstract. Can an AGI create a more intelligent AGI? Under idealized assumptions, for a certain theoretical type of intelligence, our answer is: "Not without outside help". This is a paper on the mathematical structure of AGI populations when parent AGIs create child AGIs. We argue that such populations satisfy a certain biological law. Motivated by observations of sexual reproduction in seemingly-asexual species, the Knight-Darwin Law states that it is impossible for one organism to asexually produce another, which asexually produces another, and so on forever: that any sequence of organisms (each one a child of the previous) must contain occasional multi-parent organisms, or must terminate. By proving that a certain measure (arguably an intelligence measure) decreases when an idealized parent AGI single-handedly creates a child AGI, we argue that a similar Law holds for AGIs.

Keywords: Intelligence measurement · Knight-Darwin Law · Ordinal Notations · Intelligence explosion

1 Introduction

It is difficult to reason about agents with Artificial General Intelligence (AGIs) programming AGIs[1]. To get our hands on something solid, we have attempted to find structures that abstractly capture the core essence of AGIs programming AGIs. This led us to discover what we call the *Intuitive Ordinal Notation System* (presented in Sect. 2), an ordinal notation system that gets directly at the heart of AGIs creating AGIs.

---

[1] Our approach to AGI is what Goertzel [11] describes as the Universalist Approach: we consider "...an idealized case of AGI, similar to assumptions like the frictionless plane in physics", with the hope that by understanding this "simplified special case, we can use the understanding we've gained to address more realistic cases."

© Springer Nature Switzerland AG 2020
B. Goertzel et al. (Eds.): AGI 2020, LNAI 12177, pp. 1–11, 2020.
https://doi.org/10.1007/978-3-030-52152-3_1

We call an AGI *truthful* if the things it knows are true[2]. In [4], we argued that if a truthful AGI X creates (without external help) a truthful AGI Y in such a way that X knows the truthfulness of Y, then X must be more intelligent than Y in a certain formal sense. The argument is based on the key assumption that if X creates Y, without external help, then X necessarily knows Y's source code.

Iterating the above argument, suppose $X_1, X_2, \ldots$ are truthful AGIs such that each X_i creates, and knows the truthfulness and the code of, X_{i+1}. Assuming the previous paragraph, X_1 would be more intelligent than X_2, which would be more intelligent than X_3, and so on (in our certain formal sense). In Sect. 3 we will argue that this implies it is impossible for such a list $X_1, X_2, \ldots$ to go on forever: it would have to stop after finitely many elements[3].

At first glance, the above results might seem to suggest skepticism regarding the singularity—regarding what Hutter [15] calls *intelligence explosion*, the idea of AGIs creating better AGIs, which create even better AGIs, and so on. But there is a loophole (discussed further in Sect. 4). Suppose AGIs X and X' collaborate to create Y. Suppose X does part of the programming work, but keeps the code secret from X', and suppose X' does another part of the programming work, but keeps the code secret from X. Then neither X nor X' knows Y's full source code, and yet if X and X' trust each other, then both X and X' should be able to trust Y, so the above-mentioned argument breaks down.

Darwin and his contemporaries observed that even seemingly asexual plant species occasionally reproduce sexually. For example, a plant in which pollen is ordinarily isolated, might release pollen into the air if a storm damages the part of the plant that would otherwise shield the pollen[4]. The Knight-Darwin Law [8], named after Charles Darwin and Andrew Knight, is the principle (rephrased in modern language) that there cannot be an infinite sequence $X_1, X_2, \ldots$ of biological organisms such that each X_i asexually parents X_{i+1}. In other words, if $X_1, X_2, \ldots$ is any infinite list of organisms such that each X_i is a biological parent of X_{i+1}, then some of the X_i would need to be multi-parent organisms. The reader will immediately notice a striking parallel between this principle and the discussion in the previous two paragraphs.

In Sect. 2 we present the Intuitive Ordinal Notation System.

---

[2] Knowledge and truth are formally treated in [4] but here we aim at a more general audience. For the purposes of this paper, an AGI can be thought of as knowing a fact if and only if the AGI would list that fact if commanded to spend eternity listing all the facts that it knows. We assume such knowledge is closed under deduction, an assumption which is ubiquitous in modal logic, where it often appears in a form like $K(\phi \to \psi) \to (K(\phi) \to K(\psi))$. Of course, it is only in the idealized context of this paper that one should assume AGIs satisfy such closure.

[3] This may initially seem to contradict some mathematical constructions [18,22] of infinite descending chains of theories. But those constructions only work for weaker languages, making them inapplicable to AGIs which comprehend linguistically strong second-order predicates.

[4] Even prokaryotes can be considered to occasionally have multiple parents, if lateral gene transfer is taken into account.

In Sect. 3 we argue[5] that if truthful AGI X creates truthful AGI Y, such that X knows the code and truthfulness of Y, then, in a certain formal sense, Y is less intelligent than X.

In Sect. 4 we adapt the Knight-Darwin Law from biology to AGI and speculate about what it might mean for AGI.

In Sect. 5 we address some anticipated objections.

Sections 2 and 3 are not new (except for new motivation and discussion). Their content appeared in [4], and was more rigorously formalized there. Sections 4 and 5 contain this paper's new material. Of this, some was hinted at in [4], and some appeared (weaker and less approachably) in the author's dissertation [2].

2   The Intuitive Ordinal Notation System

If humans can write AGIs, and AGIs are at least as smart as humans, then AGIs should be capable of writing AGIs. Based on the conviction that an AGI should be capable of writing AGIs, we would like to come up with a more concrete structure, easier to reason about, which we can use to better understand AGIs.

To capture the essence of an AGI's AGI-programming capability, one might try: "computer program that prints computer programs." But this only captures the AGI's capability to write *computer programs*, not to write *AGIs*.

How about: "computer program that prints computer programs that print computer programs"? This second attempt seems to capture an AGI's ability to write *program-writing programs*, not to write *AGIs*.

Likewise, "computer program that prints computer programs that print computer programs that print computer programs" captures the ability to write *program-writing-program-writing programs*, not *AGIs*.

We need to short-circuit the above process. We need to come up with a notion X which is equivalent to "computer program that prints members of X".

Definition 1 *(See the following examples). We define the Intuitive Ordinal Notations to be the smallest set $\mathcal{P}$ of computer programs such that:*

– *Each computer program p is in $\mathcal{P}$ iff all of p's outputs are also in $\mathcal{P}$.*

Example 2 *(Some simple examples)*

1. *Let P_0 be "End", a program which immediately stops without any outputs. Vacuously, all of P_0's outputs are in $\mathcal{P}$ (there are no such outputs). So P_0 is an Intuitive Ordinal Notation.*
2. *Let P_1 be "Print('End')", a program which outputs "End" and then stops. By (1), all of P_1's outputs are Intuitive Ordinal Notations, therefore, so is P_1.*
3. *Let P_2 be "Print('Print('End')')", which outputs "Print('End')" and then stops. By (2), all of P_2's outputs are Intuitive Ordinal Notations, therefore, so is P_2.*

---

[5] This argument appeared in a fully rigorous form in [4], but in this paper we attempt to make it more approachable.

Example 3 *(A more interesting example). Let P_ω be the program:*

Let X = 'End'; While(True) {Print(X); X = "Print('" + X + "')";}

When executed, P_ω outputs "End", "Print('End')", "Print('Print('End')')", and so on forever. As in Example 2, all of these are Intuitive Ordinal Notations. Therefore, P_ω is an Intuitive Ordinal Notation.

To make Definition 1 fully rigorous, one would need to work in a formal model of computation; see [4] (Section 3) where we do exactly that. Examples 2 and 3 are reminiscent of Franz's approach of "head[ing] for general algorithms at low complexity levels and fill[ing] the task cup from the bottom up" [9]. For a much larger collection of examples, see [3]. A different type of example will be sketched in the proof of Theorem 7 below.

Definition 4. *For any Intuitive Ordinal Notation x, we define an ordinal $|x|$ inductively as follows: $|x|$ is the smallest ordinal α such that $\alpha > |y|$ for every output y of x.*

Example 5. – *Since P_0 (from Example 2) has no outputs, it follows that $|P_0| = 0$, the smallest ordinal.*
- *Likewise, $|P_1| = 1$ and $|P_2| = 2$.*
- *Likewise, P_ω (from Example 3) has outputs noting $0, 1, 2, \ldots$ —all the finite natural numbers. It follows that $|P_\omega| = \omega$, the smallest infinite ordinal.*
- *Let $P_{\omega+1}$ be the program "Print(P_ω)", where P_ω is as in Example 3. It follows that $|P_{\omega+1}| = \omega + 1$, the next ordinal after ω.*

The Intuitive Ordinal Notation System is a more intuitive simplification of an ordinal notation system known as Kleene's $\mathcal{O}$.

3   Intuitive Ordinal Intelligence

Whatever an AGI is, an AGI should know certain mathematical facts. The following is a universal notion of an AGI's intelligence based solely on said facts. In [4] we argue that this notion captures key components of intelligence such as pattern recognition, creativity, and the ability or generalize. We will give further justification in Sect. 5. Even if the reader refuses to accept this as a genuine intelligence measure, that is merely a name we have chosen for it: we could give it any other name without compromising this paper's structural results.

Definition 6. *The* Intuitive Ordinal Intelligence *of a truthful AGI X is the smallest ordinal $|X|$ such that $|X| > |p|$ for every Intuitive Ordinal Notation p such that X knows that p is an Intuitive Ordinal Notation.*

The following theorem provides a relationship[6] between Intuitive Ordinal Intelligence and AGI creation of AGI. Here, we give an informal version of the proof; for a version spelled out in complete formal detail, see [4].

---

[6] Possibly formalizing a relationship implied offhandedly by Chaitin, who suggests ordinal computation as a mathematical challenge intended to encourage evolution, "and the larger the ordinal, the fitter the organism" [7].

Theorem 7. *Suppose X is a truthful AGI, and X creates a truthful AGI Y in such a way that X knows Y's code and truthfulness. Then $|X| > |Y|$.*

Proof. Suppose Y were commanded to spend eternity enumerating the biggest Intuitive Ordinal Notations Y could think of. This would result in some list L of Intuitive Ordinal Notations enumerated by Y. Since Y is an AGI, L must be computable. Thus, there is some computer program P whose outputs are exactly L. Since X knows Y's code, and as an AGI, X is capable of reasoning about code, it follows that X can infer a program P that[7] lists L. Having constructed P this way, X knows: "P outputs L, the list of things Y would output if Y were commanded to spend eternity trying to enumerate large Intuitive Ordinal Notations". Since X knows Y is truthful, X knows that L contains nothing except Intuitive Ordinal Notations, thus X knows that P's outputs are Intuitive Ordinal Notations, and so X knows that P is an Intuitive Ordinal Notation. So $|X| > |P|$. But $|P|$ is the least ordinal $> |Q|$ for all Q output by L, in other words, $|P| = |Y|$. □

Theorem 7 is mainly intended for the situation where parent X creates independent child Y, but can also be applied in case X self-modifies, viewing the original X as being replaced by the new self-modified Y (assuming X has prior knowledge of the code and truthfulness of the modified result).

It would be straightforward to extend Theorem 7 to cases where X creates Y non-deterministically. Suppose X creates Y using random numbers, such that X knows Y is one of $Y_1, Y_2, \ldots, Y_k$ but X does not know which. If X knows that Y is truthful, then X must know that each Y_i is truthful (otherwise, if some Y_i were not truthful, X could not rule out that Y was that non-truthful Y_i). So by Theorem 7, each $|Y_i|$ would be $< |X|$. Since Y is one of the Y_i, we would still have $|Y| < |X|$.

4   The Knight-Darwin Law

"...it is a general law of nature that no organic being self-fertilises itself for a perpetuity of generations; but that a cross with another individual is occasionally—perhaps at long intervals of time—indispensable." (Charles Darwin)

In his Origin of Species, Darwin devotes many pages to the above-quoted principle, later called the Knight-Darwin Law [8]. In [1] we translate the Knight-Darwin Law into mathematical language.

---

[7] For example, X could write a general program $Sim(c)$ that simulates an input AGI c waking up in an empty room and being commanded to spend eternity enumerating Intuitive Ordinal Notations. This program $Sim(c)$ would then output whatever outputs AGI c outputs under those circumstances. Having written $Sim(c)$, X could then obtain P by pasting Y's code into Sim (a string operation—not actually running Sim on Y's code). Nowhere in this process do we require X to actually execute Sim (which might be computationally infeasible).

Principle 8 *(The Knight-Darwin Law). There cannot be an infinite sequence $x_1, x_2, \ldots$ of organisms such that each x_i is the lone biological parent of x_{i+1}. If each x_i is a parent of x_{i+1}, then some x_{i+1} must have multiple parents.*

A key fact about the ordinals is they are *well-founded*: there is no infinite sequence $o_1, o_2, \ldots$ of ordinals such that[8] each $o_i > o_{i+1}$. In Theorem 7 we showed that if truthful AGI X creates truthful AGI Y in such a way as to know the truthfulness and code of Y, then X has a higher Intuitive Ordinal Intelligence than Y. Combining this with the well-foundedness of the ordinals yields a theorem extremely similar to the Knight-Darwin Law.

Theorem 9 *(The Knight-Darwin Law for AGIs). There cannot be an infinite sequence $X_1, X_2, \ldots$ of truthful AGIs such that each X_i creates X_{i+1} in such a way as to know X_{i+1}'s truthfulness and code. If each X_i creates X_{i+1} so as to know X_{i+1} is truthful, then occasionally certain X_{i+1}'s must be co-created by multiple creators (assuming that creation by a lone creator implies the lone creator would know X_{i+1}'s code).*

Proof. By Theorem 7, the Intuitive Ordinal Intelligence of $X_1, X_2, \ldots$ would be an infinite strictly-descending sequence of ordinals, violating the well-foundedness of the ordinals.   □

It is perfectly consistent with Theorem 7 that Y might operate faster than X, performing better in realtime environments (as in [10]). It may even be that Y performs so much faster that it would be infeasible for X to use the knowledge of Y's code to simulate Y. Theorems 7 and 9 are profound because they suggest that descendants might initially appear more practical (faster, better at problem-solving, etc.), yet, without outside help, their knowledge must degenerate. This parallels the *hydra game* of Kirby and Paris [16], where a hydra seems to grow as the player cuts off its heads, yet inevitably dies if the player keeps cutting.

If AGI Y has distinct parents X and X', neither of which fully knows Y's code, then Theorem 7 does not apply to X, Y or X', Y and does not force $|Y| < |X|$ or $|Y| < |X'|$. This does not necessarily mean that $|Y|$ can be arbitrarily large, though. If X and X' were themselves created single-handedly by a lone parent X_0, similar reasoning to Theorem 7 would force $|Y| < |X_0|$ (assuming X_0 could infer the code and truthfulness of Y from those of X and X')[9].

In the remainder of this section, we will non-rigorously speculate about three implications Theorem 9 might have for AGIs and for AGI research.

---

[8] This is essentially true by definition, unfortunately the formal definition of ordinal numbers is outside the scope of this paper.

[9] This suggests possible generalizations of the Knight-Darwin Law such as "There cannot be an infinite sequence $x_1, x_2, \ldots$ of biological organisms such that each x_i is the lone grandparent of x_{i+1}," and AGI versions of same. This also raises questions about the relationship between the set of AGIs initially created by humans and how intelligent the offspring of those initial AGIs can be. These questions go beyond the scope of this paper but perhaps they could be a fruitful area for future research.

4.1 Motivation for Multi-agent Approaches to AGI

If AGI ought to be capable of programming AGI, Theorem 9 suggests that a fundamental aspect of AGI should be the ability to collaborate with other AGIs in the creation of new AGIs. This seems to suggest there should be no such thing as a *solipsistic* AGI[10], or at least, solipsistic AGIs would be limited in their reproduction ability. For, if an AGI were solipsistic, it seems like it would be difficult for this AGI to collaborate with other AGIs to create child AGIs. To quote Hernández-Orallo et al.: "The appearance of multi-agent systems is a sign that the future of machine intelligence will not be found in monolithic systems solving tasks without other agents to compete or collaborate with" [12].

More practically, Theorem 9 might suggest prioritizing research on multi-agent approaches to AGI, such as [6,12,14,17,19,21], and similar work.

4.2 Motivation for AGI Variety

Darwin used the Knight-Darwin Law as a foundation for a broader thesis that the survival of a species depends on the inter-breeding of many members. By analogy, if our goal is to create robust AGIs, perhaps we should focus on creating a wide variety of AGIs, so that those AGIs can co-create more AGIs.

On the other hand, if we want to reduce the danger of AGI getting out of control, perhaps we should *limit* AGI variety. At the extreme end of the spectrum, if humankind were to limit itself to only creating one single AGI[11], then Theorem 9 would constrain the extent to which that AGI could reproduce.

4.3 AGI Genetics

If AGI collaboration is a fundamental requirement for AGI "populations" to propagate, it might someday be possible to view AGI through a genetic lens. For example, if AGIs X and X' co-create child Y, if X runs operating system O, and X' runs operating system O', perhaps Y will somehow exhibit traces of both O and O'.

5 Discussion

In this section, we discuss some anticipated objections.

5.1 What Does Definition 6 Really Have to Do with Intelligence?

We do not claim that Definition 6 is the "one true measure" of intelligence. Maybe there is no such thing: maybe intelligence is inherently multi-dimensional.

---

[10] That is, an AGI which believes itself to be the only entity in the universe.
[11] Or to perfectly isolate different AGIs away from one another—see [25].

Definition 6 measures a type of intelligence based on mathematical knowledge[12] closed under logical deduction. An AGI could be good at problem-solving but poor at ordinals. But the broad AGIs we are talking about in this paper should be capable (if properly instructed) of attempting any reasonable well-defined task, including that of notating ordinals. So Definition 6 does measure one aspect of an AGI's abilities. Perhaps a word like "mathematical-knowledge-level" would fit better: but that would not change the Knight-Darwin Law implications.

Intelligence has core components like pattern-matching, creativity, and the ability to generalize. We claim that these components are needed if one wants to competitively name large ordinals. If p is an Intuitive Ordinal Notation obtained using certain facts and techniques, then *any* AGI who used those facts and techniques to construct p should also be able to iterate those same facts and techniques. Thus, to advance from p to a larger ordinal which not just *any* p-knowing AGI could obtain, must require the creative invention of some new facts or techniques, and this invention requires some amount of creativity, pattern-matching, etc. This becomes clear if the reader tries to notate ordinals qualitatively larger than Example 3; see the more extensive examples in [3].

For analogy's sake, imagine a ladder which different AGIs can climb, and suppose advancing up the ladder requires exercising intelligence. One way to measure (or at least estimate) intelligence would be to measure how high an AGI can climb said ladder.

Not all ladders are equally good. A ladder would be particularly poor if it had a top rung which many AGIs could reach: for then it would fail to distinguish between AGIs who could reach that top rung, even if one AGI reaches it with ease and another with difficulty. Even if the ladder was infinite and had no top rung, it would still be suboptimal if there were AGIs capable of scaling the whole ladder (i.e., of ascending however high they like, on demand)[13]. A good ladder should have, for each particular AGI, a rung which that AGI cannot reach.

Definition 6 offers a good ladder. The rungs which an AGI manages to reach, we have argued, require core components of intelligence to reach. And no particular AGI can scale the whole ladder[14], because no AGI can enumerate all

---

[12] Wang has correctly pointed out [23] that an AGI consists of much more than merely a knowledge-set of mathematical facts. Still, we feel mathematical knowledge is at least one important aspect of an AGI's intelligence.

[13] Hibbard's intelligence measure [13] is an infinite ladder which is nevertheless short enough that many AGIs can scale the whole ladder—the AGIs which do not "have finite intelligence" in Hibbard's words (see Hibbard's Proposition 3). It should be possible to use a *fast-growing hierarchy* [24] to transfinitely extend Hibbard's ladder and reduce the set of whole-ladder-scalers. This would make Hibbard's measurement ordinal-valued (perhaps Hibbard intuited this; his abstract uses the word "ordinal" in its everyday sense as synonym for "natural number").

[14] Thus, this ladder avoids a common problem that arises when trying to measure machine intelligence using IQ tests, namely, that for any IQ test, an algorithm can be designed to dominate that test, despite being otherwise unintelligent [5].

the Intuitive Ordinal Notations: it can be shown that they are not computably enumerable[15].

5.2 Can't an AGI Just Print a Copy of Itself?

If a truthful AGI knows its own code, then it can certainly print a copy of itself. But if so, then it necessarily cannot know the truthfulness of that copy, lest it would know the truthfulness of itself. Versions of Gödel's incompleteness theorems adapted [20] to mechanical knowing agents imply that a suitably idealized truthful AGI cannot know its own code and its own truthfulness.

5.3 Prohibitively Expensive Simulation

The reader might object that Theorem 7 breaks down if Y is prohibitively expensive for X to simulate. But Theorem 7 and its proof have nothing to do with simulation. In functional languages like Haskell, functions can be manipulated, filtered, formally composed with other functions, and so on, without needing to be executed. Likewise, if X knows the code of Y, then X can manipulate and reason about that code without executing a single line of it.

6 Conclusion

The Intuitive Ordinal Intelligence of a truthful AGI is defined to be the supremum of the ordinals which have Intuitive Ordinal Notations the AGI knows to be Intuitive Ordinal Notations. We argued that this notion measures (a type of) intelligence. We proved that if a truthful AGI single-handedly creates a child truthful AGI, in such a way as to know the child's truthfulness and code, then the parent must have greater Intuitive Ordinal Intelligent than the child. This allowed us to establish a structural property for AGI populations, resembling the Knight-Darwin Law from biology. We speculated about implications of this biology-AGI parallel. We hope by better understanding how AGIs create new AGIs, we can better understand methods of AGI-creation by humans.

Acknowledgments. We gratefully acknowledge Jordi Bieger, Thomas Forster, José Hernández-Orallo, Bill Hibbard, Mike Steel, Albert Visser, and the reviewers for discussion and feedback.

References

1. Alexander, S.A.: Infinite graphs in systematic biology, with an application to the species problem. Acta Biotheoretica **61**, 181–201 (2013)

---

[15] Namely, because if the set of Intuitive Ordinal Notations were computably enumerable, the program p which enumerates them would itself be an Intuitive Ordinal Notation, which would force $|p| > |p|$.

2. Alexander, S.A.: The theory of several knowing machines. Ph.D. thesis, The Ohio State University (2013)
3. Alexander, S.A.: Intuitive Ordinal Notations (IONs). GitHub repository (2019). https://github.com/semitrivial/ions
4. Alexander, S.A.: Measuring the intelligence of an idealized mechanical knowing agent. In: CIFMA (2019)
5. Besold, T., Hernández-Orallo, J., Schmid, U.: Can machine intelligence be measured in the same way as human intelligence? KI-Künstliche Intelligenz **29**, 291–297 (2015)
6. Castelfranchi, C.: Modelling social action for AI agents. AI **103**, 157–182 (1998)
7. Chaitin, G.: Metaphysics, metamathematics and metabiology. In: Hector, Z. (ed.) Randomness Through Computation. World Scientific, Singapore (2011)
8. Darwin, F.: The Knight-Darwin Law. Nature **58**, 630–632 (1898)
9. Franz, A.: Toward tractable universal induction through recursive program learning. In: Bieger, J., Goertzel, B., Potapov, A. (eds.) AGI 2015. LNCS (LNAI), vol. 9205, pp. 251–260. Springer, Cham (2015). https://doi.org/10.1007/978-3-319-21365-1_26
10. Gavane, V.: A measure of real-time intelligence. JAGI **4**, 31–48 (2013)
11. Goertzel, B.: Artificial general intelligence: concept, state of the art, and future prospects. JAGI **5**, 1–48 (2014)
12. Hernández-Orallo, J., Dowe, D.L., España-Cubillo, S., Hernández-Lloreda, M.V., Insa-Cabrera, J.: On more realistic environment distributions for defining, evaluating and developing intelligence. In: Schmidhuber, J., Thórisson, K.R., Looks, M. (eds.) AGI 2011. LNCS (LNAI), vol. 6830, pp. 82–91. Springer, Heidelberg (2011). https://doi.org/10.1007/978-3-642-22887-2_9
13. Hibbard, B.: Measuring agent intelligence via hierarchies of environments. In: Schmidhuber, J., Thórisson, K.R., Looks, M. (eds.) AGI 2011. LNCS (LNAI), vol. 6830, pp. 303–308. Springer, Heidelberg (2011). https://doi.org/10.1007/978-3-642-22887-2_34
14. Hibbard, B.: Societies of intelligent agents. In: Schmidhuber, J., Thórisson, K.R., Looks, M. (eds.) AGI 2011. LNCS (LNAI), vol. 6830, pp. 286–290. Springer, Heidelberg (2011). https://doi.org/10.1007/978-3-642-22887-2_31
15. Hutter, M.: Can intelligence explode? JCS **19**, 143–166 (2012)
16. Kirby, L., Paris, J.: Accessible independence results for Peano arithmetic. Bull. Lond. Math. Soc. **14**, 285–293 (1982)
17. Kolonin, A., Goertzel, B., Duong, D., Ikle, M.: A reputation system for artificial societies. arXiv preprint arXiv:1806.07342 (2018)
18. Kripke, S.A.: Ungroundedness in Tarskian languages. JPL **48**, 603–609 (2019)
19. Potyka, N., Acar, E., Thimm, M., Stuckenschmidt, H.: Group decision making via probabilistic belief merging. In: 25th IJCAI. AAAI Press (2016)
20. Reinhardt, W.N.: Absolute versions of incompleteness theorems. Nous **19**, 317–346 (1985)
21. Thórisson, K.R., Benko, H., Abramov, D., Arnold, A., Maskey, S., Vaseekaran, A.: Constructionist design methodology for interactive intelligences. AI Mag. **25**, 77–90 (2004)
22. Visser, A.: Semantics and the liar paradox. In: Gabbay, D.M., Guenthner, F. (eds.) Handbook of Philosophical Logic, pp. 149–240. Springer, Dordrecht (2002). https://doi.org/10.1007/978-94-017-0466-3_3
23. Wang, P.: Three fundamental misconceptions of artificial intelligence. J. Exp. Theoret. Artif. Intell. **19**, 249–268 (2007)

24. Weiermann, A.: Slow versus fast growing. Synthese **133**, 13–29 (2002)
25. Yampolskiy, R.V.: Leakproofing singularity-artificial intelligence confinement problem. JCS **19**(1–2), 194–214 (2012)

Error-Correction for AI Safety

Nadisha-Marie Aliman[1(✉)], Pieter Elands[2], Wolfgang Hürst[1], Leon Kester[2],
Kristinn R. Thórisson[4], Peter Werkhoven[1,2], Roman Yampolskiy[3],
and Soenke Ziesche[5]

[1] Utrecht University, Utrecht, The Netherlands
nadishamarie.aliman@gmail.com
[2] TNO Netherlands, The Hague, The Netherlands
[3] University of Louisville, Louisville, USA
[4] Icelandic Institute for Intelligent Machines, Reykjavik University,
Reykjavik, Iceland
[5] Delhi, India

Abstract. The complex socio-technological debate underlying safety-critical and ethically relevant issues pertaining to AI development and deployment extends across heterogeneous research subfields and involves in part conflicting positions. In this context, it seems expedient to generate a minimalistic joint transdisciplinary basis disambiguating the references to specific subtypes of AI properties and risks for an *error-correction* in the transmission of ideas. In this paper, we introduce a high-level *transdisciplinary system clustering* of ethical distinction between antithetical clusters of *Type I* and *Type II* systems which extends a cybersecurity-oriented AI safety taxonomy with considerations from psychology. Moreover, we review relevant Type I AI risks, reflect upon possible epistemological origins of hypothetical Type II AI from a cognitive sciences perspective and discuss the related human moral perception. Strikingly, our nuanced transdisciplinary analysis yields the figurative formulation of the so-called *AI safety paradox* identifying AI control and value alignment as conjugate requirements in AI safety. Against this backdrop, we craft versatile multidisciplinary recommendations with ethical dimensions tailored to Type II AI safety. Overall, we suggest proactive and importantly *corrective* instead of prohibitive methods as common basis for both Type I and Type II AI safety.

Keywords: AI safety paradox · Error-correction · AI ethics

1 Motivation

In recent years, one could identify the emergence of seemingly antagonistic positions from different academic subfields with regard to research priorities for AI safety, AI ethics and AGI – many of which are grounded in differences of short-term versus long-term estimations associated with AI capabilities and risks [6].

S. Ziesche—Independent Researcher.

However, given the high relevance of the joint underlying endeavor to contribute to a safe and ethical development and deployment of artificial systems, we suggest placing a mutual comprehension in the foreground which can start by making references to assumed AI risks explicit. To this end, we employ and subsequently extend a cybersecurity-oriented risk taxonomy introduced by Yampolskiy [35] displayed in Fig. 1. Taking this taxonomy as point of departure and modifying it while considering insights from psychology, an ethically relevant clustering of systems into *Type I* and *Type II* systems with a disparate set of properties and risk instantiations becomes explicitly expressible. Concerning the set of Type I systems of which present-day AIs represent a subset, we define it as representing *the complement of the set of Type II systems.* Conversely, we regard hypothetical Type II systems as *systems with a scientifically plausible ability to act independently, intentionally, deliberately and consciously and to craft explanations.* Given the controversial ambiguities linked to these attributes, we clarify our idiosyncratic use with a working definition for which we do not claim any higher suitability in general, but which is particularly conceptualized for our line of argument. With Type II systems, we refer to systems having the ability to construct counterfactual hypotheses about what could happen, what could have happened, how *and why* including the ability to simulate "what *I* could do" "what *I* could have done" and the generation of "what if" questions. (Given this conjunction of abilities including the possibility of what-if deliberations with counterfactual depth about self and other, we assume that Type II systems would *not* represent philosophical zombies. A detailed account of this type of view is provided by Friston in [19] stating e.g. that *"the key difference between a conscious and non-conscious me is that the non-conscious me would not be able to formulate a "hard problem"; quite simply because I could not entertain a thought experiment".*)

How and When did AI become Dangerous	External Causes			Internal Causes
	On Purpose	By Mistake	Environment	Independently
Timing — Pre-Deployment	a	c	e	g
Timing — Post-Deployment	b	d	f	h

Fig. 1. Taxonomy of pathways to dangerous AI. Adapted from [35].

2   Transdisciplinary System Clustering

As displayed in Fig. 1, the different possible external and internal causes are further subdivided into time-related stages (pre-deployment and post-deployment) which are in practice however not necessarily easily clear-cut. Thereby, for Type

I risks, we distinguish between the associated instantiations Ia to If in compliance with the *external causes*. For Type II risks, we analogously consider external causes (IIa to IIf) but in addition also *internal causes* which we subdivide into the novel subcategories "on purpose" and "by mistake". This assignment leads to the risks IIg and IIh for the former as well as IIi and IIj for the latter subcategory respectively. The reason for augmenting the granularity of the taxonomy is that since Type II systems would be capable of intentionality, it is consequent to distinguish between internal causes of risks resulting from intentional actions of the system and risks stemming from its unintentional mistakes as parallel to the consideration of external human-caused risks a and b versus c and d in the matrix. (From the angle of moral psychology, failing to preemptively consider this subtle further distinction could reinforce human biases in the moral perception of Type II AI due to a fundamental reluctance to assign experience [24], fallibility and vulnerability to artificial systems which we briefly touch upon in Sect. 3.2.) Especially, given this modification, the risks IIg and IIh are not necessarily congruent with the original indices g and h, since our working definition was not a prerequisite for the attribute "independently" in the original taxonomy. The resulting system clustering is illustrated in Fig. 2.

TYPE I CLUSTER				
How and When did Type I system become Dangerous	**External Causes**			
		On Purpose	*By Mistake*	*Environment*
Timing	*Pre-Deployment*	a	c	e
	Post-Deployment	b	d	f

TYPE II CLUSTER						
How and When did Type II system become Dangerous		**External Causes**			**Internal Causes**	
		On Purpose	*By Mistake*	*Environment*	*On Purpose*	*By Mistake*
Timing	*Pre-Deployment*	a	c	e	g	i
	Post-Deployment	b	d	f	h	j

Fig. 2. Transdisciplinary system clustering of ethical distinction with specified safety and security risks. Internal causes assignments require scientific plausibility (see text).

Note that this transdisciplinary clustering does *not* differentiate based on the specific architecture, substrate, intelligence level or set of algorithms associated with a system. We also do not inflict assumptions on whether this clustering is of hard or soft nature nor does it necessarily reflect the usual partition of narrow AI versus AGI systems. Certain present-day AGI projects might be aimed at Type I systems and some conversely at Type II. We stress that Type II systems are not per se more dangerous than Type I systems. Importantly, "superintelligence" [10] does not necessarily qualify a system as a Type II system nor are Type II systems necessarily more intelligent than Type I systems. Having said that, it is important to address the motivation behind the scientific plausibility criterion associated with the Type II system description. Obviously, current AIs can be linked to the Type I cluster. However, it is known from moral psychology studies that the propensity of humans to assign intentionality and agency to artificial systems is biased by anthropomorphism and importantly perceived harm [9]. According to the constructionist theory of dyadic morality [30], human moral judgements are related to a fuzzy perceiver-dependent dyadic cognitive template representing a continuum along which an intentional agent is perceived to cause harm to a vulnerable patient. Thereby, the greater the degree to which harm is mentally associated with vulnerable patients (here humans), the more the agent (here the AI) will *"seem to possess intentionality"* [9] leading to stronger assignments of moral responsibility to this agent. It is conceivable that in the face of anticipated serious instantiations of AI risks within a type of responsibility vacuum, a so-called agentic dyadic completion [23] driven by people attempting to identify and finally wrongly filling in intentional agents can occur. Thus, to allow a sound distinction between Type I and Type II AI, a closer scientific inspection of the assumed intentionality phenomenon itself seems imperative.

3   Type I and Type II AI Safety

3.1   Type I AI Risks

In the context of Type I risks (see overview in Table 1), we agree with Yampolskiy that *"the most important problem in AI safety is intentional-malevolent-design"* [35]. This drastically understudied AI risk *Ia* represents a superset of many possible other risks. As potential malicious human adversaries, one can determine a large number of stakeholders ranging from military or corporations over black hats to criminals. AI Risks *Ia* are linked to maximal adversarial capabilities enabling a white-box setting with a minimum of restrictions for the realization of targeted adversarial goals. Generally, malicious attackers could develop intelligent forms of *"viruses, spyware, Trojan horses, worms and other Hazardous Software"* [35]. Another related conceivable example for future *Ia* risks could be real-world instantiations of intelligent systems embodied in robotic settings utilized for ransomware or social engineering attacks or in the worst case scenarios even for homicides. For intentionally unethical system design it is sometimes sufficient to alter the sign of the objective function. Future lethal misuses of proliferated intelligent unmanned combat air vehicles (a type of drones) e.g. by malicious criminals are another exemplary concern.

Stuart Russell mentions the danger of future superintelligent systems employed at a global scale [29] which could *by mistake* be equipped with inappropriate objectives – these systems would represent Type I AI. We postulate that an even more pressing concern would be the same context, the same capabilities of the AI but an adversary *intentionally maliciously* crafting the goals of this system operating at a global scale (e.g. affecting global ecological aspects or the financial system). As can be extracted from these examples, Type I AI systems can lead to existential risks. However, it is important to emphasize the human nature of the causes and the linked human moral responsibility. By way of example, we briefly consider the particular cases of "treacherous turn" and "instrumental convergence" known from AI safety [10]. A Type I system is per definitionem incapable of a "treacherous turn" involving betrayal. Nevertheless, it is possible that as a consequence of bad design (risk Ic), a Type I AI is perceived by humans to behave as if it was acting "treacherously" post-deployment with tremendous negative impacts. Furthermore, we also see "instrumental goal convergence" as a design-time mistake (risk Ic), since the developers must have equipped the system with corresponding reasoning abilities. Limitations of the assumed instrumental goal convergence risk which would hold for both Type I and Type II AI were already addressed by Wang [33] and Goertzel [22]. (In contrast, Type II AI makes an explicit "treacherous turn" possible – e.g. as risk IIg with the Type II system itself as malicious actor.)

Since the nature of future Ia (and also Ib^1) risks is dependent on the creativity of the underlying malicious actors which cannot be predicted, proactive AI safety measures have to be complemented by a concrete mechanism that reactively

Table 1. Examplary instantiations of type I AI risks with external causes. The table collates and extends some examples provided in [35].

Type I AI risk	Examplary instantiations
Ia (**Intentional malevolent designs**)	Artificial Intelligent System Hazardous Software;
	Robotic embodiment for Hazardous Software;
	Intelligent Unmanned Combat Air Vehicles;
	Global scale AI with super-capabilities in domain
Ib (Malicious attacks)	Manipulation of data processing and collection;
	Model corruption, hacking and sabotage;
	Adversarial attacks on Intelligent Systems;
	Integrity-related and ethical adversarial examples
Ic (Design-time mistakes)	Unaligned goals and utility functions;
	Instrumental goal convergence;
	Incomplete consideration of side effects
Id (Operational failures)	Misinterpretation of commands;
	Accidents with Intelligent Systems;
	Non-corrigible framework and bugs
Ie	Type I AI of unknown source
If	Bit-flip incidents with side effects

---

[1] AI risks of Type *Ib* have already been recognized in the AI field. However, risk *Ib* is still understudied for intelligent systems (often referred to as "autonomous" systems) deployed in real-world environments offering a wider attack surface.

addresses errors, attacks or malevolent design events once they inevitably occur. For this purpose, AI governance needs to steadily combine proactive strategies with reactive corrections leading to a socio-technological feedback-loop [2]. However, for such a mechanism to succeed, the United Nations Sustainable Developmental Goal (SDG) 16 on peace, justice and strong institutions will be required as meta-goal for AI safety [2].

3.2 Type II AI Nature and Type II AI Risks

Which Discipline Could Engender Type II AI? While many stakeholders assume the technical unfeasibility of Type II AI, there is no law of nature that would forbid their implementation. In short, an artificial Type II system must be possible (see the "possibility-impossibility dichotomy" mentioned by Deutsch [17]). Reasons why such systems do not exist yet have been for instance expressed in 2012 by Deutsch [15] and as a response by Goertzel [21]. The former stated that *"the field of 'artificial general intelligence' or AGI – has made no progress whatever during the entire six decades of its existence"* [15]. (Note that Deutsch unusually uses the term "AGI" as synonymous to artificial "explanatory knowledge creator" [16] which would obviously represent a sort of Type II AI.) Furthermore, Deutsch assigns a high importance to Popperian epistemology for the achievement of "AGI" and sees a breakthrough in philosophy as a pre-requisite for these systems. Conversely, Goertzel provides divergent reasons for the non-existence of "AGI" including hardware constraints, lack of funding and the integration bottleneck [21]. Beyond that, Goertzel also specifies that the mentioned view of Deutsch *"if widely adopted, would slow down progress toward AGI dramatically"* [21]. One key issue behind Deutsch's different view is the assumption that Bayesian inductive or abductive inference accounts of Type II systems known in the "AGI" field could not explain creativity [11] and are prohibited by Popperian epistemology. However, note that even the Bayesian brain has been argued to have Popperian characteristics related to sophisticated falsificationalism, albeit in addition to Kuhnian properties (for a comprehensive analysis see [34]). Having said this, the brain has been figuratively also referred to as a biased *"crooked scientist"* [12,26]. In a nutshell, Popperian epistemology represents an important scientific guide but not an exclusive *descriptive²*. The main functionality of the human brain has been e.g. described to be aimed at regulating the body for the purpose of allostasis [31] and (en)active inference [20] in a brain-body-environment context [12] with underlying genetically and epigenetically shaped adaptive priors – including the genetic predisposition

---

² It is not contested that inductive inferences are *logically invalid* as shown by Popper. However, he also stated that *"I hold that neither animals nor men use any procedure like induction, or any argument based on repetition of instances. The belief that we use induction is simply a mistake"* [27] and that *"induction simply does not exist"* [27] (see [25] for an in-depth analysis of potential hereto related semantic misunderstandings). Arguments based on repetition of instances are *existing* but logically unfounded human habits as assumed by Hume [25], however they *additionally* require a point of view recognizing repetitions as such in the first place.

to allostatically induced social dependency [3]. A feature related hereto is the involvement of affect and interoception in the construction of all mental events including cognition and perception [4,5].

Moreover, while Popper assumed that creativity corresponds to a Darwinian process of *blind* variation followed by selection [18], modern cognitive science suggests that in most creativity forms, there is a coupling between variation and selection leading to a degree of sightedness bigger than zero [14,18] which is lacking in biological evolution proceeding without a goal. Overall, an explanation for creativity in the context of a predictive Bayesian brain is possible [14]. The degree of sightedness can often vary from substantial to modest, but the core feature is a predictive task goal [1,7,18] which serves as a type of fitness function for the selection process guiding various forward Bayesian predictions representing the virtual variation process. The task goal is a highly abstract mental representation of the target reducing the solution space, an educated guess informed e.g. by expertise, prior memories, heuristics, the question, the problem or the task itself. The "irrational moment" linked to certain creative insights can be explained by unconscious cognitive scaffolding *"falling away prior to the conscious representation of the solution"* [18] making itself consciously untraceable. Finally, as stated by Popper himself *"no society can predict, scientifically, its own future states of knowledge"* [28]. Thus, it seems prophetic to try to nail down today from which discipline Type II AI could arise.

What Could the Moral Status of a Type II AI Be? We want to stress that besides these differences of opinion between Goertzel and Deutsch, there is one much weightier commonality. Namely, that Goertzel would certainly agree with Deutsch that artificial "explanatory knowledge creators" (which are Type II AIs) deserve rights similar to humans and precluding any form of slavery. Deutsch describes these hypothetical systems likewise as *people* [16]. For readers that doubt this assignment on the ground of Type II AI possibly lacking "qualia" we refer to the recent (potentially substrate-independent) explanation suggested by Clark, Friston and Wilkinson [13]. Simply put, they link qualia to sensorially-rich high-precision mid-level predictions which when fixed and consciously re-contextualized at a higher level, suddenly appear to the entity equipped with counterfactual depth to be potentially also interpretable in terms of alternative predictions despite the high mid-level precision contingently leading to a puzzlement and the formulation of an "explanatory gap". Beyond that, human entities would obviously also qualify as Type II systems. The attributes "pre-deployment" and "post-deployment" could be mapped for instance to adolescence or childhood and the time after that. While Type II AIs could exceed humans in speed of thinking and intelligence, they do not even need to do so in order to realize that their behavior which will also depend on future knowledge *they* will create (next to the future knowledge humans will create) cannot be controlled in a way one can attempt to control Type I systems e.g. with ethical goal functions [2]. It is cogitable that their goal function would rather be related to autopoietic self-organization with counterfactual depth [19,20] than *explicitly* to ethics. However, it is thinkable that Type II AI systems could be amenable to a sort of value alignment, though differing from the type aspired for Type I AI. A societal co-existence could mean a dynamic coupling ideally leading to a type of *mutual value alignment* between artificial and human Type II entities with an associated co-construction of novel values. Thus, on the one hand, Type II AI would exhibit unpredictability and uncontrollability but given the level of understanding also the possibility of a deep reciprocal value alignment with humans. On the other hand, Type I AI has the possibility to be made comparatively easily controllable which however comes with the restriction of an insufficient understanding to model human morality. This inherent trade-off leads us to the metaphorical formulation of the so-called AI safety paradox below.

The AI Safety Paradox: *AI Control and Value Alignment Represent Conjugate Requirements in AI Safety.*

How to Address Type II AI Safety? Cognizant of the underlying predicament in its sensitive ethical nature, we provide a non-exhaustive multidisciplinary set of early Type II AI safety recommendations with a focus on the most severe risks *IIa, IIb, IIg* and *IIh* (see Fig. 2) related to the involvement of malicious actors. In the case of risk *IIa* linked to the malicious design of harmful Type II AI, cybersecurity-oriented methods could include the early formation of a preventive safety team and red team approaches. Generically, for all four mentioned risks, a reactive response team which could involve an international "coalition of the willing" organized by engaged scientists appears recommendable. Furthermore, targeted investments in defense strategies including response services specialized on Type II AI safety could be considered at more regional levels for strategic autonomy. Concerning the AI risk *IIb* of external malicious attacks, security mechanisms for the sensors of Type II AI, shared information via an open-source decentralized network, advanced cryptographic methods to encrypt cognitive processes and a legal framework penalizing such attacks might be relevant. Thereby, the complexity of the system might represent a possible but not necessarily sufficient self-protecting feature against code-level manipulation. From a psychological perspective, to forestall aggression towards early Type II AI, educative and informed virtual reality experiences could facilitate a debiasing of anthropic moral perception avoiding confusions arising through superficial projections from Type I to Type II AI of behavioral nature. On the one hand, it is important to prevent assignments of agency for Type I AI. On the other hand, for hypothetical Type II AI, it might be essential to counter the human bias to assign agency but principally not experience to artificial systems [24] which could lead to "substratetism" scenarios with humans perceiving these systems as devoid of qualia and exhibiting an "experience gap" [24]. Thus, to address the risks *IIg* and *IIh* referring to malicious responses from Type II AI, adherence to a no-harm policy as well as moral status and personhood could proactively foster a mutual value alignment. Furthermore, it might be crucial to provide a reliable and trustworthy initial knowledge basis to Type II AI during its early "sensitivity" period [8] and to support consistency in the embedding of that knowledge during its development in addition to the capacity for cumulative learning [32]. Also, it might be important to sensitize humans for the difference between the instantiations of AI risks *IIg* and *IIh* versus *IIi* and *IIj* since failing to acknowledge the fallibility and also vulnerability of Type II AI might indirectly lead to tensions hindering mutual value alignment. Finally, prosocial immersive virtual reality frameworks could promote empathy for Type II AI.

4   Summary and Outlook

This paper motivated an *error-correction for AI safety* at two levels: at the level of the transmission of ideas via an explicit taxonomic transdisciplinary system clustering of ethical distinction between Type I and Type II systems and at the level of corrective safety measures complementing proactive ones – forming a socio-technological feedback-loop [2]. Notably, we introduced the *AI safety paradox* and elucidated multiperspective Type II AI safety strategies. In short, instead of prohibitive methods facing the entropic AI future with research bans, we proposed carefully crafted *transdisciplinary dynamics*. In the end, in order to meet global challenges (also AI safety), one is reliant on requisite variety at the right time which could be enabled (or misused) by explanatory knowledge creators such as human, artificial or hybrid Type II systems. In this view, *conscientiously enhancing* and *responsibly creating* Type II systems are both valid future strategies.

Acknowledgement. Nadisha-Marie Aliman would like to thank David Deutsch for providing a concise feedback on AI safety and Joscha Bach for a relevant exchange on AI ethics.

References

1. Aliman, N.M., Kester, L.: Artificial creativity augmentation. In: Goertzel, B., Panov, A.I., Potapov, A., Yampolskiy, R. (eds.) AGI 2020. LNCS (LNAI), vol. 12177, pp. 23–33. Springer, Cham (2020)
2. Aliman, N.M., Kester, L., Werkhoven, P., Ziesche, S.: Sustainable AI safety? Delphi Interdisc. Rev. Emerg. Technol. **2**(4), 226–233 (2020)
3. Atzil, S., Gao, W., Fradkin, I., Barrett, L.F.: Growing a social brain. Nat. Hum. Behav. **2**(9), 624–636 (2018)
4. Barrett, L.F.: The theory of constructed emotion: an active inference account of interoception and categorization. Soc. Cogn. Affect. Neurosci. **12**(1), 1–23 (2017)
5. Barrett, L.F., Simmons, W.K.: Interoceptive predictions in the brain. Nat. Rev. Neurosci. **16**(7), 419 (2015)
6. Baum, S.D.: Reconciliation between factions focused on near-term and long-term artificial intelligence. AI Soc. **33**(4), 565–572 (2017). https://doi.org/10.1007/s00146-017-0734-3
7. Benedek, M.: The neuroscience of creative idea generation. In: Kapoula, Z., Volle, E., Renoult, J., Andreatta, M. (eds.) Exploring Transdisciplinarity in Art and Sciences, pp. 31–48. Springer, Cham (2018). https://doi.org/10.1007/978-3-319-76054-4_2

8. Bieger, J., Thórisson, K.R., Wang, P.: Safe baby AGI. In: Bieger, J., Goertzel, B., Potapov, A. (eds.) AGI 2015. LNCS (LNAI), vol. 9205, pp. 46–49. Springer, Cham (2015). https://doi.org/10.1007/978-3-319-21365-1_5

9. Bigman, Y.E., Waytz, A., Alterovitz, R., Gray, K.: Holding robots responsible: the elements of machine morality. Trends Cogn. Sci. **23**(5), 365–368 (2019)

10. Bostrom, N.: The superintelligent will: motivation and instrumental rationality in advanced artificial agents. Mind. Mach. **22**(2), 71–85 (2012). https://doi.org/10.1007/s11023-012-9281-3

11. Brockman, J.: Possible Minds: Twenty-Five Ways of Looking at AI. Penguin Press, London (2019)

12. Bruineberg, J., Kiverstein, J., Rietveld, E.: The anticipating brain is not a scientist: the free-energy principle from an ecological-enactive perspective. Synthese **195**(6), 2417–2444 (2016). https://doi.org/10.1007/s11229-016-1239-1

13. Clark, A., Friston, K., Wilkinson, S.: Bayesing qualia: consciousness as inference, not raw datum. J. Conscious. Stud. **26**(9–10), 19–33 (2019)

14. De Rooij, A., Valtulina, J.: The predictive creative mind: a first look at spontaneous predictions and evaluations during idea generation. Front. Psychol. **10**, 2465 (2019)

15. Deutsch, D.: Creative blocks. https://aeon.co/essays/how-close-are-we-to-creating-artificial-intelligence. Accessed Nov 2019

16. Deutsch, D.: The Beginning of Infinity: Explanations that Transform the World. Penguin, New York (2011)

17. Deutsch, D.: Constructor theory. Synthese **190**(18), 4331–4359 (2013). https://doi.org/10.1007/s11229-013-0279-z

18. Dietrich, A.: How Creativity Happens in the Brain. Springer, London (2015). https://doi.org/10.1057/9781137501806

19. Friston, K.: Am I self-conscious? (Or does self-organization entail self-consciousness?). Front. Psychol. **9**, 579 (2018)

20. Friston, K.: A free energy principle for a particular physics. arXiv preprint arXiv:1906.10184 (2019)

21. Goertzel, B.: The real reasons we don' t have AGI yet. https://www.kurzweilai.net/the-real-reasons-we-dont-have-agi-yet. Accessed 21 Nov 2019

22. Goertzel, B.: Infusing advanced AGIs with human-like value systems: two theses. J. Evol. Technol. **26**(1), 50–72 (2016)

23. Gray, K., Schein, C., Ward, A.F.: The myth of harmless wrongs in moral cognition: automatic dyadic completion from sin to suffering. J. Exp. Psychol. Gen. **143**(4), 1600 (2014)

24. Gray, K., Wegner, D.M.: Feeling robots and human zombies: mind perception and the uncanny valley. Cognition **125**(1), 125–130 (2012)

25. Greenland, S.: Induction versus popper: substance versus semantics. Int. J. Epidemiol. **27**(4), 543–548 (1998)

26. Parr, T., Da Costa, L., Friston, K.: Markov blankets, information geometry and stochastic thermodynamics. Philos. Trans. R. Soc. A **378**(2164), 20190159 (2019)

27. Popper, K.: In: Schilpp, P.A. (ed.) The Philosophy of Karl Popper, vol. 2, p. 1015. Open Court Press, Chicago (1974)

28. Popper, K.R.: The Poverty of Historicism. Routledge & Kegan Paul, Abingdon (1966)

29. Russell, S.: How to Stop Superhuman A.I. Before It Stops Us. https://www.nytimes.com/2019/10/08/opinion/artificial-intelligence.html?module=inline. Accessed 21 Nov 2019

30. Schein, C., Gray, K.: The theory of dyadic morality: reinventing moral judgment by redefining harm. Pers. Soc. Psychol. Rev. **22**(1), 32–70 (2018)

31. Schulkin, J., Sterling, P.: Allostasis: a brain-centered, predictive mode of physiological regulation. Trends Neurosci. **42**(10), 740–752 (2019)
32. Thórisson, K.R., Bieger, J., Li, X., Wang, P.: Cumulative learning. In: Hammer, P., Agrawal, P., Goertzel, B., Iklé, M. (eds.) AGI 2019. LNCS (LNAI), vol. 11654, pp. 198–208. Springer, Cham (2019). https://doi.org/10.1007/978-3-030-27005-6_20
33. Wang, P.: Motivation management in AGI systems. In: Bach, J., Goertzel, B., Iklé, M. (eds.) AGI 2012. LNCS (LNAI), vol. 7716, pp. 352–361. Springer, Heidelberg (2012). https://doi.org/10.1007/978-3-642-35506-6_36
34. Wiese, W.: Perceptual presence in the Kuhnian-Popperian Bayesian brain: a commentary on Anil K. Johannes Gutenberg-Universität Mainz, Seth (2016)
35. Yampolskiy, R.V.: Taxonomy of pathways to dangerous artificial intelligence. In: Workshops at the Thirtieth AAAI Conference on Artificial Intelligence (2016)

Artificial Creativity Augmentation

Nadisha-Marie Aliman[1]([✉]) and Leon Kester[2]

[1] Utrecht University, Utrecht, The Netherlands
nadishamarie.aliman@gmail.com
[2] TNO Netherlands, The Hague, The Netherlands

Abstract. Creativity has been associated with multifarious descriptions whereby one exemplary common definition depicts creativity as the generation of ideas that are perceived as both novel and useful within a certain social context. In the face of adversarial conditions taking the form of global societal challenges from climate change over AI risks to technological unemployment, this paper motivates future research on *artificial creativity augmentation* (ACA) to indirectly support the generation of requisite defense strategies and solutions. This novel term is of ambiguous nature since it subsumes two research directions: (1) artificially augmenting human creativity, but also (2) augmenting artificial creativity. In this paper, we examine and extend recent creativity research findings from psychology and cognitive neuroscience to identify potential indications on how to work towards (1). Moreover, we briefly analyze how research on (1) could possibly inform progress towards (2). Overall, while human enhancement but also the implementation of powerful AI are often perceived as ethically controversial, future ACA research could even appear socially desirable.

Keywords: Human enhancement · Artificial creativity · Safety

1 Deconstructing Anthropic Creativity

Creativity research has been described as a relatively understudied and underfunded field in psychology and neuroscience [25]. The term refers mostly either to research on creativity outcome being the contextualized evaluation of creative ideas (or artifacts) after their generation or to research on the creativity process itself related to the forerunning idea generation [53]. In this section, we examine both complex concepts and establish a possible scientific grounding for strategies on artificial creativity augmentation (ACA) to be addressed in Sect. 2.

1.1 Creative Outcome in Context

Many definitions for creativity have been formulated so far with the two-factor description of creativity as the generation of novel and useful ideas being one of the most commonly used in the related literature [39]. Already from this simple definition, it becomes apparent that creativity implies a perceiver to which

© Springer Nature Switzerland AG 2020
B. Goertzel et al. (Eds.): AGI 2020, LNAI 12177, pp. 23–33, 2020.
https://doi.org/10.1007/978-3-030-52152-3_3

something can appear novel or useful in the first place which provides a context to the evaluation of that thing in question. A further subjective account of creativity is reflected in a different three-factor definition of creativity [51] which relates creative ideas to their subjective originality, utility and surprisingness. On that view, novelty represents an imprecise creativity criterium which the author illustrates with examples [51] such as that neither a novel reinvented wheel nor a straightforward novel extension of an already existing patent would appear creative despite their usefulness and novelty with the former i.a. not being surprising and the latter not original. However, a refinement of this subjective three-factor definition of creativity has been recently provided by Tsao et al. [53] who associate creative outcome with perceived *utility* and *learning* whereby learning subsumes a blindness factor and importantly surprise. In order to unfold this definition, the next paragraph briefly expounds the contextual methodology the authors presuppose to assess a given idea in context. Thereby, the focus is not on a detailed mathematical elaboration, but specifically on the identification of core constituents relevant from an enhancement perspective for a future ACA endeavor.

By way of illustration, consider the following three time windows occurring *after* the idea generation: a pre-test phase, a test phase and a post-test phase. In the pre-test phase, a prior assessment in line with the best current knowledge is performed in which a probability distribution over the assumed utility of that idea is provided. (A reference is the routine expertise exhibited by *"persons having ordinary skill in the art"* [53].) In the test phase, the idea is deployed in the environment and observations of its consequences become available. In the post-test phase, a posterior assessment takes place via an adjustment of the probability distribution provided in the pre-test phase now that the idea was tested in the environment. Against this backdrop, the authors identify creative ideas as ideas which – as evaluated retrospectively after the post-test phase – simultaneously combine a high level of posterior utility, prior blindness (associated with the width of the distribution), and much more crucially than blindness, posterior surprise[1]. They denote this cluster of ideas as *"disconfirm disbelief"*[2], since it refers to ideas that were initially estimated to be relatively useless but which turned out to be highly utile with a subjective high certainty causing a reshaping of prior knowledge, a useful learning. In short, creative ideas exhibit *implausible utility* [53]. This underlying decomposition of creativity perception into a *utility* and a *learning* part, suggests the consideration of a motivational and an

---

[1] The reason being that in their formulation *"learning depends on the square of posterior surprise, but only on the logarithm of blindness reduction"*. Posterior surprise is the (normalized) absolute difference in mean utility between prior and posterior.

[2] An exemplary case mentioned by the authors is the theory on continental drift by Alfred Wegener which was initially disbelieved and underestimated.

epistemic[3] component respectively. Finally, note that the mentioned conscious evaluation of creative ideas in context is not restricted to test phases in real-world environments, but can also refer to imaginative settings at the personal level via thought trials at different temporal scales. This type of view makes the described evaluation also applicable to artistic contexts [51] where individuals might however use criteria for aesthetics from narrower social contexts.

1.2 Creative Process

In this connection, it is often one-sidedly assumed that "creative thinking" can be reduced to the notion of *divergent thinking* [27], a thought process involving unconventional associations and leading to a breadth of alternative solutions. Conversely, *convergent thinking* refers to thought processes selecting a unique appropriate solution to a problem with a single correct solution. However, creative processes include both divergent and convergent thinking [50] and are better described as processes of multifaceted nature [40]. For instance, Eysenck pointed out the illusory nature of this dichotomy and suggested considering a continuum between divergent and convergent thinking related to the *"relative steepness of the associative gradient"* [28]. To navigate a complex changing world, humans might need to dynamically switch positions along this continuum during tasks requiring creativity. Similarly, diverse functional connectivity studies [1,4,9,10,12,13,19,22,33] reveal a dynamic interplay between three multipurpose and domain-general functional brain networks in tasks involving creative process: the default mode network (e.g. medial prefrontal cortex, posterior cingulate cortex and hippocampus), the executive control network (e.g. dorsolateral prefrontal cortex and posterior parietal cortex) and the salience network (e.g. anterior cingulate cortex and anterior insula but also e.g. amygdala, ventral striatum, ventral tegmental area and substantia nigra). Thereby, during various creative tasks, the default mode network (DMN) can be linked to associative processes, the executive control network (ECN) to diverse executive processes, while the salience network (SN) associated with a type of affective attention regulation [2,13,41] facilitates i.a. a dynamic orchestration between DMN and ECN [12].

However, in order to make justice to the breadth of creative processes in the brain, it is essential to consider their peculiar evolutionary nature [25]. Crucially, in order to avoid misunderstandings, it is vital to note that the evolutionary account of creative process is not identical with Darwinian biological evolution. In fact, a first prototype of an evolutionary account for creativity was even advanced a few years *before* the publication of Darwin on "Origin of

---

[3] Abstractly speaking, this is reminiscent of curiosity in (en)active inference via (expected) free energy minimization decomposable into components of motivational value and epistemic value [31,32]. Future work could elucidate whether this explains why retrospectively contemplating creative ideas in context (as mental juxtaposition of pre-test phase, test phase and post-test phase underlying *"disconfirm disbeliefs"* events) is appealing and whether this reinforces future creative action.

Species" [17,51] by Alexander Bain. The main implication is that while Darwinian biological evolution is *blind* since it has no goal, creativity is aimed at something and includes an element akin to an abstract task goal [14,23] functioning as predictive fitness criterium. For this reason, *"there is agreement that human idea formation is directed to some degree"* [26] in modern creativity research. While there is no coupling between variation and selection in Darwinian biological evolution, creativity mostly implies a certain coupling of these components leading to the formulation of a *continuum of sightedness* marking the degree to which this is the case for a given creative process. (Certain researchers prefer to label this continuum as a blindness continuum [51], while some argue that a process can be either blind or sighted to a certain degree [44]. To put it very briefly, the blindness degree b is defined as $b = (1 - s)$ with s representing the sightedness degree [51,53] reducing the issue to a linguistic debate.[4]) Along this sightedness continuum, Dietrich distinguishes between the *deliberate mode*, the *spontaneous mode* and the *flow mode* [25]. We see the deliberate mode as consciously attended creative process allowing strong executive control but with constrained associative parts and the spontaneous mode as unconsciously progressing process with stronger associative components but much less executive engagement (such as during an incubation phase leading to sudden creative insights [8]). Thereby, the flow mode is an immersive largely unconscious[5] creative enactment in real time including automated motor skills (such as during spontaneous jazz improvisation). Obviously, the degree of sightedness is the highest in the deliberate mode, moderate in the spontaneous mode and zero in the flow mode – which however uniquely operates in the space of *already known* motor emulations [24].

Given the scarcity of theoretical frameworks integrating these threefold evolutionary view on creativity with the mentioned weighty empirical functional connectivity findings, we briefly introduce a simplified *tripartite evolutionary affective*[6] neurocognitive model of creative process (TEA). As suggested by Benedek [14], *idea generation* (for variation) consists of a *retrieval* and an *integration/simulation* phase. Prior to initial idea generation, a problem definition is required to establish a task goal acting as selection criterium. The retrieval phase identifies promising often only remotely related memories and the simulation/integration part supplies a novel recombination and assimilation of this material. This idea generation guided by the task goal can be followed by a forwarding (which we call an *affective redirection operation* (ARO)) to a stringent *idea evaluation* [42] involving a high-level assessment of the obtained results

---

[4] An exemplary evolutionary account of creativity is the so-called Blind Variation and Selective Retention (BVSR) theory. It has been suggested that instead of viewing BVSR as Darwinian, *"it is more conceptually precise to view both BVSR and Darwin's evolutionary theory as special cases of universal selection theory"* [51].

[5] Settings requiring further executive elements (beyond focused attention) and higher cognitive functions are not seen as flow (mode) experiences [21,24] but as deliberate.

[6] It integrates disparate tripartite and evolutionary elements from Dietrich's creativity framework [24], evolutionary aspects from Benedek's RISE model [15] and affective and procedural elements from the neurocognitive model by Kleinmitz et al. [42].

selected so far. However, an ARO can also alternatively re-initiate a further idea generation process or already trigger a response. The idea evaluation can either lead to a response, a further refinement of the idea generation process or an alteration of the task goal itself. Overall, the simplified neurocognitive TEA model to be refined in future work allows the following assignments. First, in the case of the deliberate mode, the idea generation can i.a. involve nodes of the DMN [42] to a more or less high degree whereby especially the integration/simulation is controlled by the ECN [14,15]. The subsequent (optional) stringent idea evaluation involves nodes of the ECN [14,42]. Second, in the spontaneous mode, the ECN is *not* strongly modulating DMN idea generation [10,27] and a stringent idea evaluation phase does not occur. In both modes, the SN related to affective attention conducts the dynamic AROs (see e.g. [13,39,42]). Third, the blind flow mode mainly implies emulations within the motor system [23,27]. Finally, note that a specific creative act can also connect multiple distinct creative modes [24].

2 Constructing ACA

2.1 Methods for Anthropic Creativity Augmentation

In the following, we collate a non-exhaustive heterogeneous set of selected indications which could if combined contribute to a certain extent to anthropic creativity augmentation. Thereby, it is important to note that useful combinations might vary e.g. given different psychological traits or socio-cultural contexts.

- *Transformative Criticism and Contrariness:* In order to foster the emergence of creative ideas exhibiting implausible utility in science, it has been suggested for knowledge gate keepers to encourage scientific knowledge paired with contrariness [53] – a trait linked with an idea generation process containing counterfactual divergences to mainstream ideas. Overall, it is straightforward to realize the importance of cultivating properties that reinforce the *"disconfirm disbelief"* pattern supporting the Popperian scientific process of conjectures and refutations e.g. for better task goals and idea evaluations within creative process or better test phases in creativity outcome in context. Moreover, a broad transdisciplinary education [3,36] might enhance associative elements. From an artistic perspective, it might include the transformation of the landscape of socio-material affordances [49] restructuring the human affective niche.
- *Divergent Thinking Training:* As mentioned earlier, divergent thinking only represents one aspect of creativity. However, the identification of multiple appropriate solutions can represent valuable domain-general elements for idea generation. For instance, a cognitive stimulation training [30] exposing subjects to ideas of other social entities prior to the idea generation phase (in the deliberate mode) improved divergent thinking and led to structural and functional changes within nodes of the ECN [52]. Moreover, a continuous involvement in divergent thinking tests of verbal creativity has been related to changes in brain functional connectivity with an enhancement of retrieval and integration processes [29].

– *Alteration of Waking Consciousness:* For creative insight of the sort rather associated with the spontaneous mode, a suitable strategy represents the relaxation of high-level prior beliefs [18] which might foster openness to experience, a key trait linked to cognitive flexibility and creativity [11]. Already the instructive cue to engage in creative thinking can yield a higher creative performance [34]. Another measure is to consciously shift creative problem solving to the spontaneous mode by trying to enforce an incubation period [8,37] whilst performing an undemanding distractive task. Beyond that, while brain activity has been shown to reside in a regime close to criticality between stability and flexibility [6] (at the edge of chaos [16]), a brain regime closer to criticality with an expanded repertoire of brain states seems achievable for healthy individuals with an appropriate intake of psychedelics [6,18,45,47]. Via the relaxation of high-level prior beliefs, a heightened sensitivity to the external and internal milieu [7] promoting a successful incubation phase is conceivable. Finally, certain meditative practices have been linked to improvement in divergent thinking tasks [20].

– *Active Forgetting:* There is a link between creative insight and fact-free learning [18] which refers to a type of learning in the absence of additional facts by restructuring already acquired knowledge e.g. by erasing redundant material. Such a complexity reduction [37] is actively performed in the brain during REM (rapid eye movement) sleep (with neurons in the hypothalamus interfering with memory consolidation in the hippocampus) which provides an explanation for the difficulty to maintain memories of dream contents [38]. REM sleep may thus not only be relevant for mental health and adaptive prospective aspects [46] but also for the incubation of novel spontaneous creative insights via unconscious complexity reduction mechanisms [32].

– *Frequent Engagement:* A trivial but perhaps underrated aspect of creativity is the observation that to a certain degree *"highly creative ideas are contingent on chance or "luck""* [51] with creative achievements among others also simply linked to a higher number of trials. While frequent practice represents a pre-condition for the flow mode to be attainable in the first place [23], the deliberate mode might be amenable to enhancement via exercise to a certain extent as reflected by the obtainment of neural plasticity in one of the mentioned divergent thinking training tasks [29].

– *Brain Stimulation:* Interesting for the flow mode is that excitatory transcranial direct current stimulation (tDCS) of the primary motor cortex during spontaneous music improvisation [5] yielded an enhancement of the musical performance. In the case of the deliberate mode and if unconventional associations are desirable, an inhibitory tDCS on the dorsolateral prefrontal cortex might at first sight appear suitable for a disruption of inhibitions by the ECN. However, such a measure is not recommendable for complex real-world applications [48]. Being a task requiring more executive control, deliberate analogical reasoning was enhanced via excitatory tDCS on the frontopolar cortex located within the frontoparietal network (or ECN) [35].

– *Sensory Extension:* A straightforward way to diversify associative processes, is certainly to augment the breadth of the actively sampled sensorium e.g. via cyborgization and sensory extension measures. From an artistic angle, it is for instance easy to imagine that various augmented sensorimotor and affective synaesthetic could support the incubation phase in the spontaneous mode next to conferring a finer granularity to perception. Further conceivable transformative sensory augmentations that could foster creative associations represent virtual reality frameworks [2] and perhaps "dream engineering" methods including lucid dreaming as a state with intermediate hypofrontality [37] having certain neurophenomenological resemblances with psychedelic-induced states [43].

2.2   Addressing the Augmentation of Artificial Creativity

One can assume that artificial creativity exists in a primitive form when it comes to an artificial creative process with a very high degree of sightedness [23] (e.g. dictated by high-level anthropic utility functions). Indeed, when the consideration of the creative agent is not included in the perception of creative outcome, the substrate on which the forgoing process occurred seems irrelevant. However, when considering the entire action-perception sequence of most anthropic creative acts (as a juxtaposition of creative process, pre-test, test and post-test phase – all permeated by affect e.g. via AROs and utility assignments) which can even take place within the imagination of the same anthropic social entity, a certain gap between AI and human entities becomes apparent. Therefore, firstly, a figurative *immersion in the human affective niche* might be necessitated for contemporary AI such that its outcomes in context *can* better correspond to samples that matter to humans in the first place. Exemplary early steps could include multimodal experiential data for AI and also the encoding of affective and socially relevant parameters into AI goal functions [3] in addition to straightforward parameters directly related to the creative tasks in question. A next step could be to transfer a main anthropic affective concern to AI which is an affinity to curiosity that manifests itself via an active sampling of the world [32]. Secondly, equipping AI with *social cognition* abilities might be helpful, since *"imagination is the seed of creativity"* [33] with imaginary perspective-taking having inherently social dimensions. It is no coincidence that the domain-general DMN dominating highly associative spontaneous idea generation is also involved in the construction of e.g. social affiliation, moral judgements, empathy, theory of mind [41] as well as mental time travel and counterfactual thinking [18]. Thirdly, when considering that both anthropic waking perception and imagination are linked to an egocentric virtual reality experience [37,54] (with waking perception being constrained by reality), one might naively deduce that a full immersion of AI into the *human* affective niche necessitates at least that: an *egocentric integrated multimodal virtual reality experience* of the world. However, this also raises the questions on whether to then call it "human" would not be anthropocentric and whether this reveals a tradeoff between AI creativity and AI controllability.

3   Conclusion

By espousing both the augmentation of anthropic and the augmentation of artificial creativity, the motivated ACA research could connect disparate existing subfields under one *substrate-independent goal*: namely a scientifically grounded augmentation of knowledge creation (which can encompass science, culture, arts and technology) to indirectly tackle societal challenges. Creativity represents an essential transformative element of human knowledge advancement for adaptive purposes in relatively fast changing environments [53]. Hence, ACA could indirectly serve the need to identify requisite variety at the right time as proactive and corrective defense method in the light of current global socio-ecological and socio-technological challenges [3]. In this paper, we compiled recent research on anthropic creative outcome in context and findings on creative process which we extended with a simplified neurocognitive *tripartite evolutionary affective* model of creative process (TEA). Building on this analysis yielding a scientific grounding for ACA, we identified seven potential high-level indications to enhance anthropic creativity: *transformative criticism and contrariness, divergent thinking training, alteration of waking consciousness, active forgetting, frequent engagement, brain stimulation* as well as *sensory extension*. Finally, we suggested three synergetic aspects as possible indirect support for artificial creativity: *immersion in the human affective niche, social cognition* and an *egocentric integrated multimodal virtual reality experience* of the world. Future work could refine the TEA model, augment the tenfold methodology for ACA and address open questions.

References

1. Adnan, A., Beaty, R., Lam, J., Spreng, R.N., Turner, G.R.: Intrinsic default-executive coupling of the creative aging brain. Soc. Cogn. Affect. Neurosci. **14**(3), 291–303 (2019)
2. Aliman, N.M., Kester, L.: Extending socio-technological reality for ethics in artificial intelligent systems. In: 2019 IEEE International Conference on Artificial Intelligence and Virtual Reality (AIVR), pp. 275–2757. IEEE (2019)
3. Aliman, N.M., Kester, L., Werkhoven, P., Ziesche, S.: Sustainable AI Safety? Delphi - Interdisciplinary review of emerging technologies (2020, to appear)
4. Andrews-Hanna, J.R., Irving, Z.C., Fox, K.C., Spreng, R.N., Christoff, K.: The Neuroscience of Spontaneous Thought: An Evolving Interdisciplinary Field. Oxford University Press, Oxford (2018)
5. Anic, A., Thompson, W.F., Olsen, K.N.: Stimulation of the primary motor cortex enhances creativity and technical fluency of piano improvisations. In: Proceedings of the 10th International Conference of Students of Systematic Musicology (SysMus17) (2017)
6. Atasoy, S., Deco, G., Kringelbach, M.L.: Playing at the edge of criticality: expanded whole-brain repertoire of connectome-harmonics. In: Tomen, N., Herrmann, J.M., Ernst, U. (eds.) The Functional Role of Critical Dynamics in Neural Systems. SSBN, vol. 11, pp. 27–45. Springer, Cham (2019). https://doi.org/10.1007/978-3-030-20965-0_2

7. Atasoy, S., Roseman, L., Kaelen, M., Kringelbach, M.L., Deco, G., Carhart-Harris, R.L.: Connectome-harmonic decomposition of human brain activity reveals dynamical repertoire re-organization under LSD. Sci. Rep. **7**(1), 17661 (2017)
8. Baird, B., Smallwood, J., Mrazek, M.D., Kam, J.W., Franklin, M.S., Schooler, J.W.: Inspired by distraction: Mind wandering facilitates creative incubation. Psychol. Sci. **23**(10), 1117–1122 (2012)
9. Beaty, R.E., Benedek, M., Kaufman, S.B., Silvia, P.J.: Default and executive network coupling supports creative idea production. Sci. Rep. **5**, 10964 (2015)
10. Beaty, R.E., Benedek, M., Silvia, P.J., Schacter, D.L.: Creative cognition and brain network dynamics. Trends Cogn. Sci. **20**(2), 87–95 (2016)
11. Beaty, R.E., Chen, Q., Christensen, A.P., Qiu, J., Silvia, P.J., Schacter, D.L.: Brain networks of the imaginative mind: Dynamic functional connectivity of default and cognitive control networks relates to openness to experience. Hum. Brain Mapp. **39**(2), 811–821 (2018)
12. Beaty, R.E., Christensen, A.P., Benedek, M., Silvia, P.J., Schacter, D.L.: Creative constraints: Brain activity and network dynamics underlying semantic interference during idea production. Neuroimage **148**, 189–196 (2017)
13. Beaty, R.E., et al.: Robust prediction of individual creative ability from brain functional connectivity. Proc. Natl. Acad. Sci. **115**(5), 1087–1092 (2018)
14. Benedek, M.: The neuroscience of creative idea generation. In: Kapoula, Z., Volle, E., Renoult, J., Andreatta, M. (eds.) Exploring Transdisciplinarity in Art and Sciences, pp. 31–48. Springer, Cham (2018). https://doi.org/10.1007/978-3-319-76054-4_2
15. Benedek, M., et al.: To create or to recall original ideas: Brain processes associated with the imagination of novel object uses. Cortex **99**, 93–102 (2018)
16. Bilder, R.M., Knudsen, K.S.: Creative cognition and systems biology on the edge of chaos. Front. Psychol. **5**, 1104 (2014)
17. Campbell, D.T.: Blind variation and selective retentions in creative thought as in other knowledge processes. Psychol. Rev. **67**(6), 380 (1960)
18. Carhart-Harris, R.L., Friston, K.: REBUS and the anarchic brain: toward a unified model of the brain action of psychedelics. Pharmacol. Rev. **71**(3), 316–344 (2019)
19. Chrysikou, E.G.: Creativity in and out of (cognitive) control. Curr. Opini. Behav. Sci. **27**, 94–99 (2019)
20. Colzato, L., Szapora, A., Hommel, B.: Meditate to create: the impact of focused-attention and open-monitoring training on convergent and divergent thinking. Front. Psychol. **3**, 116 (2012)
21. Csikszentmihalyi, M.: Creativity: Flow and the Psychology of Discovery and Invention, 1st edn. Harper Collins Publishers, New york (1996)
22. Danek, A.H., Flanagin, V.L.: Cognitive conflict and restructuring: The neural basis of two core components of insight. AIMS Neurosci. **6**(2), 60 (2019)
23. Dietrich, A.: How Creativity Happens in the Brain. Springer, London (2015). https://doi.org/10.1057/9781137501806
24. Dietrich, A.: Types of creativity. Psychon. Bull. Rev. **26**(1), 1–12 (2019)
25. Dietrich, A.: Where in the brain is creativity: A brief account of a wild-goose chase. Curr. Opin. Behav. Sci. **27**, 36–39 (2019)
26. Dietrich, A., Haider, H.: Human creativity, evolutionary algorithms, and predictive representations: The mechanics of thought trials. Psychon. Bull. Rev. **22**(4), 897–915 (2015)
27. Dietrich, A., Haider, H.: A neurocognitive framework for human creative thought. Front. Psychol. **7**, 2078 (2017)

28. Eysenck, H.: Creativity, personality and the convergent-divergent continuum (2003)
29. Fink, A., et al.: Training of verbal creativity modulates brain activity in regions associated with language-and memory-related demands. Hum. Brain Mapp. **36**(10), 4104–4115 (2015)
30. Fink, A., Grabner, R.H., Gebauer, D., Reishofer, G., Koschutnig, K., Ebner, F.: Enhancing creativity by means of cognitive stimulation: Evidence from an fMRI study. NeuroImage **52**(4), 1687–1695 (2010)
31. Friston, K.J.: Active inference and cognitive consistency. Psychol. Inq. **29**(2), 67–73 (2018)
32. Friston, K.J., Lin, M., Frith, C.D., Pezzulo, G., Hobson, J.A., Ondobaka, S.: Active inference, curiosity and insight. Neural Comput. **29**(10), 2633–2683 (2017)
33. Gotlieb, R., Hyde, E., Immordino-Yang, M., Kaufman, S.: Imagination is the seed of creativity (2018)
34. Green, A.E., Cohen, M.S., Kim, J.U., Gray, J.R.: An explicit cue improves creative analogical reasoning. Intelligence **40**(6), 598–603 (2012)
35. Green, A.E., Spiegel, K.A., Giangrande, E.J., Weinberger, A.B., Gallagher, N.M., Turkeltaub, P.E.: Thinking cap plus thinking zap: tDCS of frontopolar cortex improves creative analogical reasoning and facilitates conscious augmentation of state creativity in verb generation. Cereb. Cortex **27**(4), 2628–2639 (2016)
36. Hensley, N.: Educating for sustainable development: Cultivating creativity through mindfulness. J. Clean. Prod. **243**, 118542 (2020)
37. Hobson, J.A., Hong, C.C.H., Friston, K.J.: Virtual reality and consciousness inference in dreaming. Front. Psychol. **5**, 1133 (2014)
38. Izawa, S., et al.: REM sleep-active MCH neurons are involved in forgetting hippocampus-dependent memories. Science **365**(6459), 1308–1313 (2019)
39. Jung, R.E., Mead, B.S., Carrasco, J., Flores, R.A.: The structure of creative cognition in the human brain. Front. Human Neurosci. **7**, 330 (2013)
40. Kaufman, S.B., Gregoire, C.: Wired to Create: Unraveling the Mysteries of the Creative Mind. Penguin, New York (2016)
41. Kleckner, I.R., et al.: Evidence for a large-scale brain system supporting allostasis and interoception in humans. Nat. Human Behav. **1**(5), 0069 (2017)
42. Kleinmintz, O.M., Ivancovsky, T., Shamay-Tsoory, S.G.: The twofold model of creativity: The neural underpinnings of the generation and evaluation of creative ideas. Curr. Opin. Behav. Sci. **27**, 131–138 (2019)
43. Kraehenmann, R.: Dreams and psychedelics: Neurophenomenological comparison and therapeutic implications. Curr. Neuropharmacol. **15**(7), 1032–1042 (2017)
44. Kronfeldner, M.E.: Darwinian "blind" hypothesis formation revisited. Synthese **175**(2), 193–218 (2010)
45. Kuypers, K., Riba, J., De La Fuente Revenga, M., Barker, S., Theunissen, E., Ramaekers, J.: Ayahuasca enhances creative divergent thinking while decreasing conventional convergent thinking. Psychopharmacology **233**(18), 3395–3403 (2016)
46. Llewellyn, S.: Dream to predict? REM dreaming as prospective coding. Front. Psychol. **6**, 1961 (2016)
47. Lord, L.D., et al.: Dynamical exploration of the repertoire of brain networks at rest is modulated by psilocybin. NeuroImage **199**, 127–142 (2019)
48. Lucchiari, C., Vanutelli, M.E.: Promoting creativity through transcranial direct current stimulation (tDCS). A critical review. Front. Behav. Neurosci. **12**, 167 (2018)
49. Rietveld, E.: The Affordances of Art for Making Technologies. University of Twente, Enschede (2019)

50. Runco, M.A.: Critical Creative Processes. Hampton Press, Cresskill (2003)
51. Simonton, D.K.: Creative thought as blind variation and selective retention: Why creativity is inversely related to sightedness. J. Theor. Philos. Psychol. **33**(4), 253 (2013)
52. Sun, J., et al.: Training your brain to be more creative: Brain functional and structural changes induced by divergent thinking training. Hum. Brain Mapp. **37**(10), 3375–3387 (2016)
53. Tsao, J., Ting, C., Johnson, C.: Creative outcome as implausible utility. Rev. Gen. Psychol. **23**(3), 279–292 (2019)
54. Williford, K., Bennequin, D., Friston, K., Rudrauf, D.: The projective consciousness model and phenomenal selfhood. Front. Psychol. **9**, 2571 (2018)

The Hierarchical Memory Based on Compartmental Spiking Neuron Model

Aleksandr Bakhshiev[1,2]($\boxtimes$), Anton Korsakov[1], and Lev Stankevich[3]

[1] Russian State Scientific Center for Robotics and Technical Cybernetics (RTC), 21 Tikhoretsky pr., Saint-Petersburg 194064, Russia
{alexab,a.korsakov}@rtc.ru
[2] Peter the Great St.Petersburg Polytechnic University (SPbPU), 29 Politechnicheskaya ul., Saint-Petersburg 195251, Russia
[3] St. Petersburg Institute for Informatics and Automation of the Russian Academy of Sciences, 39, 14 Line, St.Petersburg 199178, Russia
stankevich_lev@inbox.ru

Abstract. The paper proposes the architecture of dynamically changing hierarchical memory based on compartmental spiking neuron model. The aim of the study is to create biologically-inspired memory models suitable for implementing the processes of features memorizing and high-level concepts. The presented architecture allows us to describe the bidirectional hierarchical structure of associative concepts related both in terms of generality and in terms of part-whole, with the ability to restore information both in the direction of generalization and in the direction of decomposition of the general concept into its component parts. A feature of the implementation is the use of a compartmental neuron model, which allows the use of a neuron to memorize objects by adding new sections of the dendritic tree. This opens the possibility of creating neural structures that are adaptive to significant changes in the environment.

Keywords: Neuromorphic systems · Associative memory · Spiking networks · Compartmental neuron · Neuron model

1 Introduction

The problem of memorizing information is one of the fundamental in artificial intelligence systems. Natural intelligence operates with two types of information - verbal and figurative. Accordingly, in order for artificial intelligence to fully reproduce the capabilities of natural intelligence, it must also be able to use both of these types of information in pattern recognition systems, memory systems, environmental models, etc. The storage of both types of information is realized in the nervous system on a single basis. Moreover, dendritic trees play a significant role in the nervous system (at least from the point of view of morphology), which perform not only a communication function, but also a complex processing of input signals. The creation of a memory model that takes into account the spatial structure of dendritic trees seems promising for deep understanding of the principles of memorization and presentation of information in neural structures.

© Springer Nature Switzerland AG 2020
B. Goertzel et al. (Eds.): AGI 2020, LNAI 12177, pp. 34–43, 2020.
https://doi.org/10.1007/978-3-030-52152-3_4

Section 2 of the article analyzes the current state in the development of neural network memory systems. Section 3 introduces the basic concepts and describes the architecture of the memory model as a hierarchy of ensembles of neurons. Section 4 presents the topology of a simple ensemble and experimental results.

2   The Problem Analysis

From the point of view of research on human cognitive abilities, the following types of memory are existing:

- short-term (operational) and long-term memory,
- symbolic and imagery memory.

According to stored information, knowledge and skills, the following types of memory are existing:

- perceptual,
- autobiographical,
- linguistic and semantic,
- visual knowledge
- declarative knowledge,
- habits and motor skills.

In the nervous system, the organization of long-term memory is regarded as a hierarchical system (Fig. 1) [1].

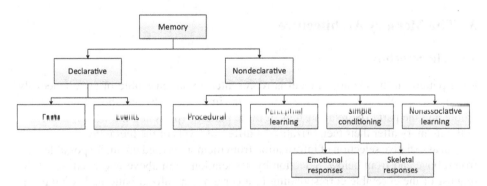

Fig. 1. Scheme of hierarchical organization of long-term memory

In the theory of artificial neural networks (ANNs), network memory usually refers to the values of connection weights that were obtained at the stage of network training. Separately, usually based on recurrent networks neural network models of associative memory are distinguished [2]. However, the formation of the neural network memory requires an exhaustive dataset, in terms of the following use trained networks. In general, artificial neural networks are used to solve problems that in neurophysiology relate to the analysis of sensory information and provide a consistent synthesis of input data into a hierarchy of features [3]. Much less often, networks are used to analyze symbolic information and make decisions, since this task is effectively solved by the traditional algorithmic approach. In a number of game tasks, the use of deep learning networks in conjunction with the reinforced learning paradigm has shown impressive results, not without, however, certain shortcomings [4].

There is no doubt that memorization of information is provided by neural network training methods that solve the optimization problem of minimizing the loss function. If we consider associative memory, we should note the classic works of Hopfield [5] and Kosko [6]. Several papers on recurrent neural networks have recently generated effective models such as LSTM [7].

Models of spike neural networks actively use one of the classic learning rules – STDP. Many approaches to adapting learning algorithms for non-spike networks to spike networks are also being developed [8]. In [9] the problems of implementation the LSTM model on spike neural networks and ways to overcome them are considering.

The article [10] should be noted as one of the few papers that studies structural plasticity and the influence of dendrites in the implementation of memory mechanisms.

Most scientific papers are aimed at solving actual problems of particular classification or object detection problems, associative data sampling, etc. Significant progress has been made in this direction. From the point of view of creating artificial general intelligence problems, the problem of creating memory models that provide dynamic memorization and recovery of information about objects in the environment and their relationships, and based on the modeling of memory mechanisms, as a consequence of the neurons structure and functions principles, is of great interest. This is an actual and not fully solved scientific problem.

3   The Memory Architecture

3.1   The Structure

Each pattern in the memory model is represented by an ensemble of simultaneously active neurons. We assume that the pattern can simultaneously play the role of both the whole and the part. The relationships of these patterns (parts and the whole) is formed in the memory after their memorization at different levels of the hierarchy.

An associative selection of information from memory is fundamentally possible both from above and from below. Selection by association from above is carried out at the request of the ensemble corresponding to a certain generalized pattern. The output is activity of lower levels at which the ensembles corresponding to the constituent parts of the selected pattern are activated. An associative output on request from below is obtained from the higher levels in the form of information about the object by its part.

In Fig. 2, the input of the lower level is the data obtained directly from the sensors or from previous sub-systems after preprocessing and generalizing information (extracting attributes). The subsequent M levels perform a sequential generalization of information.

Patterns with highest level of abstraction

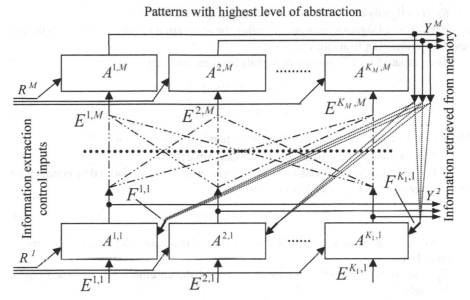

Fig. 2. Deployment of information on memory levels

Each i-th memory level ($i = \overline{1, M}$) is formed by a set of neurons $n^i = \{n_k^i | k = \overline{1, N_i}\}$. These neurons form K_i ensembles $A^{j,i}$, each of which represents a certain pattern (class, concept).

The presence of activity on all neurons of the ensemble means the restoration in memory of the pattern represented by this ensemble. The intensity of the output signals characterizes the strength of the associative connections that caused the excitement of this ensemble.

If it is necessary to restore information about the pattern, the ensemble of neurons representing this pattern is excited through the control inputs. Information is taken from active ensembles of all levels.

3.2 The Model Inputs/Outputs

The set of input signals E^I is an activity vector received from sensors or lower processing levels.

The control inputs for the restoration of information from the memory $R^I...R^M$ are sets of signals:

$$\left. \begin{array}{l} R^i(t) = \{R^{j,i}(t)\} \\ R^{j,i}(t) = \{R_k^{j,i}(t), r^i(t)\} \end{array} \right\} \tag{1}$$

Here $R^{j,i}(t)$ are the sets of signals to the control inputs of the ensemble $A^{j,i}(j = \overline{1, K_i}, i = \overline{1, M})$;

$R_k^{j,i}(t)$ - signals to the k-th control neuron of ensemble $A^{j,i}$;

$r^i(t)$ - control signal to neurons, allowing the restoration of information from the i-th level by association from above.

The outputs $Y^1 \ldots Y^M$ are sets of signals from ensemble neurons:

$$\left. \begin{array}{l} Y^i(t) = \{Y^{j,i}(t)\} \\ Y^{j,i}(t) = \{Y_k^{j,i}(t)\} \end{array} \right\} \tag{2}$$

Here $Y^{j,i}(t)$ - the set of signals of the output neurons of the ensemble $A^{j,i}$;

$Y_k^{j,i}(t)$ - signal of the k-th neuron of the ensemble $A^{j,i}$.

Sets of generalizing associative links between ensembles are formed by connections from lower neurons to higher level neurons:

$$E^{j,i}(t) = \{E_k^{j,i}(t)\} \tag{3}$$

Here $E^{j,i}$ - set of signals to the input neurons of the ensemble $A^{j,i}$ from ensembles of lower levels;

$E_k^{j,i}$ - set of signals to the k-th input neuron of the ensemble $A^{j,i}$ from neurons of lower levels.

In order to be able to restore detailed information about the general concept, links are organized from higher levels to lower:

$$F^{j,i}(t) = \{F_k^{j,i}(t)\} \tag{4}$$

Here $F^{j,i}$ - set of the signals to the input neurons of the ensemble $A^{j,i}$ from ensembles of higher levels;

$F_k^{j,i}$ - set of signals to the k-th input neuron of the ensemble $A^{j,i}$ from neurons of higher levels.

4 The Experiment

Let's consider an arbitrary ensemble A, the set of neurons of which is a homogeneous single-layer structure, where each neuron simultaneously performs the functions of the input, output, and control neurons.

To implement the memory model, it is proposed to use the compartmental spike model of the neuron, which will reproduce the principles of spikes processing and structural adaptation but will not go down to the level of description of chemical processes [11].

It is assumed that the inputs of the neuron model receive pulsed flows $X(t)$, which forms analog values $g(t)$ in the synapse models. These values characterize the effect of the input on the neuron membrane area. Signals from synapse models are designed to decrease functions that model excitation and inhibition mechanisms. The output signal of the neuron Y(t) is a pulse stream, formed when the threshold is exceeded simultaneously with the signal recharge U_F like the input signals.

The structure of the neuron that the model allows to describe is shown in Fig. 3.

Such a model has the following properties that are essential for the implementation of the memory architecture described above:

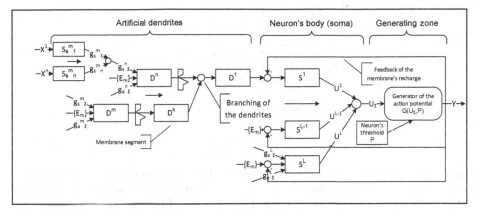

Fig. 3. The neuron model structure

- The contribution of the membrane segment inputs to the overall picture of neuron excitation is more effective the closer the section is located to the generator zone. This allows to synchronize input signals that do not arrive at the same time and, therefore, remember patterns that are formed dynamically (at short intervals).
- In areas of the membrane without feedback ("artificial dendrites" - D), spatial and temporal summation of signals is performed at significant time intervals (a small contribution to the excitation of the neuron from each input). Changing the u state of the corresponding transform elements does not depend on the neuron activation. Summation of signals is performed at short time intervals (a large contribution to the excitation of the neuron from each input) on the segments of the membrane with feedback (U_F) from the output signal generator ("body (soma) of the neuron" - S). The accumulated signal is lost during neuron activated. Therefore, with the simultaneous activation of these inputs, priority is given to signals that affect the cell body. Let's dendritic synapses provide associations from below, and somatic ones from above. In this case, when sampling information on the association from above, the neurons involved in this process become insensitive to excitation from lower levels. This should prevent distortion of the recovered information.
- The efficiency of a group of synapses is proportional not to their total number, but to the number of active synapses. This is necessary to configure associative connections from several upper levels to one lower level neuron. In this case, the reaction of the neuron upon excitation from one and from several upper levels (when restoring information from the association from above) will be the same. This will ensure the restoration of the pattern, which is a special case of more general patterns stored at once in several upper levels.

The model makes it easy to describe the dendritic structure of a neuron, which is necessary for the implementation of a neural ensemble (Fig. 4).

From the structure of the dendritic tree of the neuron, it follows that the input signal X_E has the lowest priority, since it is farthest from the low-threshold zone of the neuron (dendritic compartment D2). The inhibition signal from the higher level X_F arrives at

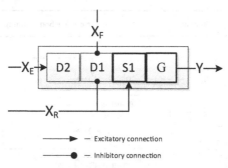

Fig. 4. Block diagram of a neuron as an element of a memory system: G – low-threshold (generation) zone, $S1$ – the part of neuron body - signal receiver an external request for information extraction, $D1$ – the dendrite – signal receiver from a group of highest level neurons, $D2$ – the dendrite – signal receiver from a group of lower level neurons.

D1 and suppresses the upward activity of X_E during the activation of the higher level, which ensures the spread of activity up the neural network like a wave. The information recovery control signal X_R is follows as excitatory to the soma compartment S1 and simultaneously as inhibitory to D1, to suppress activity from the lowest level.

In the general case, several compartments of the soma are formed on the neuron with dendrites connected to them, each of which describes the participation of the neuron in one of the ensembles.

Figure 5 shows the results of the model. The case was considered when the ensemble is activated with the simultaneous presence of signals $X_E = \{X_E^1, X_E^2\}$, which simulate the activity of two lower-level ensembles generalized to neuron.

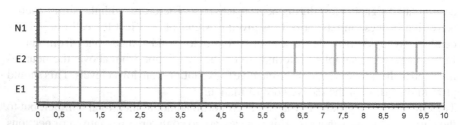

Fig. 5. Activation results from the lower levels E of the single neuron.

In Fig. 5, in the presence of simultaneous activity at both inputs (up to the 2nd second), neuron responded with corresponding activity at the output. The activity of source E2 was turned off after the 2nd second, which led to a lack of the exciting potential of the neuron and the activity of the neuron ceased. It should be noted that this behavior of the neuron does not depend on the number of inputs X_E, if the condition for neuron activation is the presence of simultaneous activity across all inputs. This behavior is ensured automatically due to the structural binding of the membrane and synapses in the neuron model.

Figure 6 shows a test scheme with two memory levels. The first level consists of two neurons and the second level of one neuron.

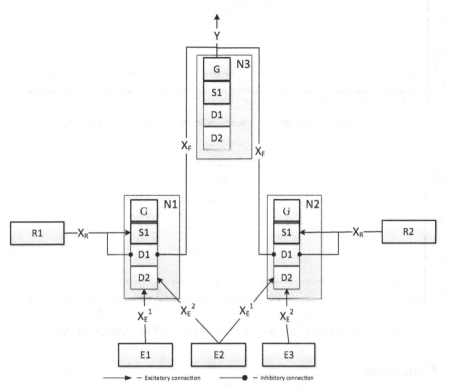

Fig. 6. The detailed minimal scheme with 2 memory levels

Figure 7 below shows the timing diagrams of the activity of the scheme from Fig. 6. You can see that upon activation the sources E1 and E2, the reaction of neuron N1 starts (3rd second), and upon activation at the sources E2 and E3, neurons N2 and, as a consequence, N3 (approximately 5,8 s from the start). When the source E2, which is part of both "ensembles" N1 and N2, is disconnected, the activity of all neurons ceases (7.8 s).

Figure 8 shows the reactions of neurons to the activation of information recovery inputs R. Here, at time t = 1 s, the source R1 is activated and, as a result, the neuron N1. Then, at time t = 3 s, the activity of source R2 and neurons N2 and N3 are turned on.

Such an ensemble model provides all the properties described above except for restoring information from a signal from a higher level. To implement this property, it is necessary to add an additional neuron to the ensemble, which will provide simultaneous activation of the ensemble from a higher level and inhibition of upward activity by the information recovery signal r. Consideration of this mechanism is beyond the scope of this article.

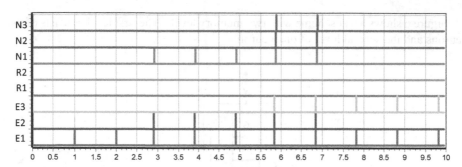

Fig. 7. Activation results from the lower levels E of the three ensembles

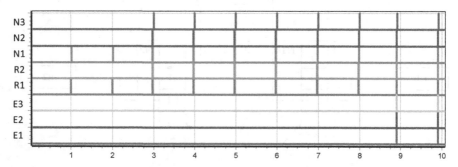

Fig. 8. Activation results from recovery signal R of the three ensembles

5   Conclusion

The presented neuromorphic system of memory and pattern recognition seems promising for solving the problems of forming a model of the external environment.

In the work, only a general view of the architecture of memory and some principles of its structural implementation based on the compartmental model of a spike neuron were highlighted. As part of further research, it is planned to solve the following problems:

- Suggest training algorithms that ensure the formation of new ensembles and optimize the number of ensembles. These algorithms are planned to be based on Hebb learning rules.
- Formalize the topology of the mutual arrangement and influence of ensembles within the same level. It seems appropriate to have similar ensembles nearby and to provide lateral inhibition function to prevent the simultaneous activation of similar patterns.
- To propose architecture and algorithms for selecting sequences of patterns from memory to extract related sequences of concepts.

Acknowledgments. This work was done as the part of the state task of the Ministry of Education and Science of Russia No. 075-01195-20-00 "Development and study of new architectures of reconfigurable growing neural networks, methods and algorithms for their learning".

References

1. Squire, L.R.: Memory systems of the brain: A brief history and current perspective. Neurobiol. Learn. Mem. **82**,171–177 (2004)
2. Rani, S.S., Nagendra Rao, D., Vatsal, S.: Review on neural networks associative memory models. Int. J. Pure Appl. Math. **120**(6), 3143–3154 (2018)
3. Shrestha, A., Mahmood, A.: Review of deep learning algorithms and architectures. Inst. Elec. Electron. Eng. Inc. **7**, 53040–53065 (2019)
4. Marcus, G.: Deep Learning: A Critical Appraisal, pp. 1–27 (2018)
5. Hopfield, J.J.: Neural networks and physical systems with emergent collective computational abilities. Proc. Nat. Acad. Sci. **79**(8), 2554–2558 (1982)
6. Kosko, B.: Competitive adaptive bi-directional associative memories. In: Caudill M., Butler C. (eds.) Proceedings of the IEEE First International Conference on Neural Networks, San Diego, vol. 2, pp. 759–766 (1987c)
7. Hochreiter, S.: Long short-term memory, **1780**, 1735–1780 (1997)
8. Tavanaei, A., Ghodrati, M., Kheradpisheh, S.R., Masquelier, T., Maida, A.: Deep learning in spiking neural networks. Neural Netw. **111**, 47–63 (2019)
9. Bellec, G., Salaj, D., Subramoney, A., Legenstein, R., Maass, W.: Long short-term memory and learning-to-learn in networks of spiking neurons. In: Advances in Neural Information Processing Systems, vol. 2018, pp. 787–797, December 2018
10. Poirazi, P., Mel, B.W.: Impact of active dendrites and structural plasticity on the memory capacity of neural tissue. Neuron **29**(3), 779–796 (2001)
11. Bakhshiev, A.V., Gundelakh F.V.: Mathematical model of the impulses transformation processes in natural neurons for biologically inspired control systems development. In: Supplementary Proceedings of the 4th International Conference on Analysis of Images, Social Networks and Texts (AIST-SUP 2015), Yekaterinburg, Russia, 9 11 April 2015, vol. 1452, pp. 1–12. CEUR-WS, 15 October 2015. http://ceur-ws.org/Vol-1452/

The Dynamics of Growing Symbols: A Ludics Approach to Language Design by Autonomous Agents

Skye Bougsty-Marshall$^{(\boxtimes)}$

Berlin, Germany

"Symbols grow. They come into being by
development out of other signs" [1].

Abstract. Even with the relative ascendancy of sub-symbolic approaches to AI,
the symbol grounding problem presents an ongoing challenge to work in artificial
general intelligence. Prevailing ontology design practices typically presuppose
the transparency of the relation between semantics and syntax by transcendently
stipulating it extrinsic to the system, rather than providing a platform for the internal development of this relation through agents' interactions endogenous to the
system. Drawing on theoretical resources from ecological psychology, dynamical systems theory, and interactive computation, this work suggests an inversion
of the symbol grounding problem in order to analyze how the symbolic regime
can emerge out of causally embedded dynamical interactions within a system
of autonomous intelligent agents. Under this view, syntactic-symbols come to be
stabilized from other signs as constraints harnessing the dynamics of agents' interactions, where the functional effects generated by such constrained dynamics give
rise to an internal characterization of semantics broadly aligned with Brandom's
semantic pragmatism. Finally, ludics—a protological framework based on interactive computation—provides a formal model to concretely describe this continuity
between syntax and semantics arising within and through the regulative dynamics of interactions in a multi-agent system. Accordingly, this bottom-up approach
to grounding the symbolic order in dynamics could provide the conditions for
artificial agents to engage in autonomous language design, thus equipping themselves with a powerful cognitive technology for intersubjective coordination and
(re)structuring ontologies within a community of agents.

1 Introduction

Notwithstanding the more recent shifts away from the context of purely symbolic
approaches to AI in which Harnad [2] originally posed the "symbol grounding problem,"

S. Bougsty-Marshall—Independent Scholar.

a definitive resolution to his question remains elusive: "How can the semantic interpretation of a formal symbol system be made intrinsic to the system, rather than just parasitic on the meanings in our heads?" Although partially recapitulating a perennial difficulty in the philosophy of mind—the articulation of the relation between the normative-logical order and the causal-physical order—this issue still warrants careful attention in the pursuit of artificial general intelligence (AGI) in order to guard against simply imputing "the meanings in our [anthropic] heads" as transcendent or pre-given limitations on the possible syntactic-semantic relations that could be developed and flourish within prospective cognitive regimes. In contemporary practices of knowledge representation systems or ontology design, for instance, the problem of grounding semantics intrinsically within a system is predominantly *artificially* solved, either through human domain experts and programmers or automated pattern recognition extracting or defining an "explicit specification of conceptualization" [3] from an already existing, extra-systemic semantic domain [4]. Moreover, as the prevailing syntactic and semantic views of scientific theories—characterizing a theory as a set of sentences or as a family of (set-theoretic) homomorphic models, respectively—hold theories to be formal symbolic systems [5], addressing the symbol grounding problem bears significantly on the resources available within a multi-agent system for autonomous ontology or theory construction without restricting such constructive efforts to just being "parasitic" on an anthropocentric semantic interpretation of a reality given in advance.

Thus, a protological procedure for creating logical-symbolic forms and articulating their emerging syntactic-semantic relations through processes endogenous to the system stands as a desideratum on the path towards facilitating artificial agents' capacities to develop sparse, unified real-time models of the universe and themselves. Following work in ecological psychology, dynamical systems theory and interactive computation, this paper outlines such a procedure through an inversion of the traditional symbol grounding problem. Rather than starting by assuming an abstract symbolic system and then inevitably puzzling over how such an abstract(ed) system gains semantic traction with the world, we inquire how can physical events and objects, causally implicated in dynamical contexts, take on the function of syntactic-symbolic units—formal abstract, non-representational entities trafficking in relations with other such symbolic entities within a logical order?

The first section of this paper will elaborate this view of symbols as emerging from dynamical processes that then, in turn, act as functional constraints harnessing these dynamics according to their specific symbolic mode of operation. In the context of formal symbolic language systems, this approach importantly harmonizes with Peirce's [1] and Brandom's [6] pragmatic conception of semantics—where such semantics consist in the functional effects engendered by such constrained dynamics produced through interactions within the system. This helps to reframe language's primary function, not as a medium for communication or representation, but as a platform for intersubjective coordination, a collective navigation tool. These background remarks frame the rest of the paper, which describes Jean-Yves Girard's [7] protological framework of ludics as a concrete approach to interactive computation capable of forging an internal bridge between syntax and semantics within the dynamics of a system of interacting agents. A key contribution of ludics is a model of interactive computation that provides an abstract formal account of the conditions of a process for convergence on stabilized common syntactic-symbolic forms that can then enter into relations with each other. This affords a higher-order of regulative functioning grounded at a new level of dynamic configuration within a multi-agent interactive system, which can potentially offer artificially intelligent agents a robust, flexible platform for generating original and applicable theories-ontologies, as an important step towards the goal of agents building dynamic models of their worlds.

2 Linking Symbols with Dynamics

Within cognitive science and artificial intelligence, notions of embodied, enactive and ecological cognitive abilities emphasize cognitive functioning as a complex interplay between a cognizing entity and its environment involving the gradual transformation of dynamical causal information into constraining modes that create what is traditionally understood as conceptual content constitutively structured by logical relations in the symbolic order. Following Seibt's [8] reading of Wilfrid Sellars' theory of "picturing," this perspective affords the rearticulation of the relation linking symbols and dynamics, replacing the inherited dualistic schisms between the causal and logical orders with a "normativity gradient" of progressively increasing regulatory dependencies expressed through functional constraints between interacting systems. This embeds the interface between the causal-logical orders within a continuum connecting different regimes of control with their own process- or level-specific constraints harnessing dynamics according to their respective modes of operation. This offers a potential monistic explanatory framework in terms of regulative constraints on transition potentials, extending from basic coupled dynamical systems to rule-governed inferential behaviors.

From this perspective, we can approach the evocative suggestion of Rączaszek-Leonardi and Kelso [9] that language acquisition or construction in a multi-agent system is the inverse of the symbol grounding problem. This frames the philosophical question from the bottom-up, in terms of investigating "(a) how grounded iconic and indexical informational forms can give rise to the degree of abstractness, arbitrariness, and formal properties of a symbolic system and at the same time (b) how they remain informational with respect to individual and interactive dynamics, that is, causally intertwined in linguistically mediated co-action" [10]. Accordingly, in pursuing this symbol "ungrounding" problem, we begin with a notion of informational forms as physical sign-vehicles fully and causally embedded in interactive, dynamical contexts. Because of this interactive embedding, such sign-vehicles act as constraints, playing a regulative or controlling role in relation to the dynamical systems in which they are implicated. Even when considered as amodal, formal abstract entities, insofar as symbols are physically instantiated in computations (or utterances), they remain embedded in the causal web acting as efficacious factors.

A crucial consequence of this dynamical, functional approach to the theory of meaning is that rather than hypostatizing an extrinsic, transcendent model-theoretic domain in which to formalize semantics, one focuses on the dynamical processes underlying the individuation of symbolic forms, and, reciprocally, how such symbolic entities come to immanently constrain these very dynamical processes. Symbols can then be viewed as stabilized patterns of dynamical variables [9], where such stabilized entities act as constraints on dynamics – that is, they effectuate a functional reduction or coordination of the degrees of freedom of a dynamical system of interaction, "reducing its possible states and trajectories relevantly to given situational and boundary conditions" [10]. And the semantics of such symbolic relations consist in the functional effects that computing (or "playing") a symbol-token has in changing the prevailing degrees of freedom and values of dynamical variables within the context of a system of interacting agents.

Under this view, sign-vehicles operate as constraints (according to their specific regime of operation) both harnessing individual cognitive dynamics and constraining the dynamics of ongoing linguistic interactions. We can then examine the conditions under which informational controls that function as signs (indices and icons) may gradually become symbolic, partially disentangling themselves from the continuous stream of multimodal events. Iconic or indexical signs lack combinatorial relations to the extent that they are mappings that only stand in one-to-one causal-structural equivalence relations between properties of the sign and properties of the associated items or occurrences [11]. On the other hand, symbols stand primarily in combinatorial relations with one another and, accordingly, do not directly map or refer to items in the world; instead, whatever semantic powers symbols exhibit derive from occupying determinate positions in a system of relations with other symbols.

In contrast, iconic and indexical token-utterances always remain grounded in inter-actions that reflect the causal-structural relations of events, contributing to predictive control processes. In the course of interactions between agents, regularities emerge sta-bilizing patterns of which utterances successively or proximately connect, thereby giving rise to inchoate relations of utterances *to other* utterances. In this way, interactions can now be influenced not only by individual (unstructured) utterances, but also by the nascently structured relations among them. As agents shift from tuning to the strong constraining roles that the concreteness of iconic-indexical structural isomorphic map-pings have in multimodal interactions [10], to tuning to utterances' relations with each other, an incipient system of interrelations among utterances emerges—this is symbolic transformation. In other words, this process of tokens disentangling or ungrounding from their direct (indexical or iconic) mappings to the world allows them to gradually become re-grounded in increasingly systematic relations to other tokens, enabling a different higher-order functional kind of control, one not only exerted by individual tokens but also by the interrelations among them. In fact, the *systematicity* of the interrelational order of symbols (rather than their conventionality or arbitrariness) is the crucial fac-tor allowing for the ungrounding of symbols from the ongoing stream of events [10]. This allows for significant combinatorial complexification of their control functioning, bringing a novel, formal constraining mode to regulate the (intersubjective) dynam-ics of interacting agents. While at the same time, symbol-tokens' ongoing connection to dynamic interactions ensures that these higher-order linguistic means of control via inter-symbolic relations retain pragmatic-semantic links with ongoing processes through their harnessing of dynamical interactions within a multi-agent system [10].

As will be explicated below, ludics contributes a theory of interactive computation to this picture, providing a formal account of this semiotic transformation of unground-ing and re-grounding—from icon-index signs grounded in isomorphic causal-structural mappings between sign and item or occurrence, to a symbolic-sign regime grounded in a syntactic system of relations with other symbols. This occurs through computing equivalence relations on ludics' *designs*—diagrammatic icons of abstract sequent calculus proof trees—which enables them to stabilize into syntactic-symbolic forms entering into systematic relations and playing invariant functional roles within the computational environments of agents. This crucially allows coordination around these emergent common logical forms, through consensual adoption of their constraints on inferential behaviors by maintaining convergent interactions (i.e., computations). Thus, a systematic order of relations among symbols can be constructed and grounded within a linguistic community or multi-agent system of interaction.

Following Negarestani [11], from this portrait emerges an account of the formal social pragmatics of language qua interactive computation—language as a system of replicable symbolic constraints harnessing interactive (normative-inferential) dynamics. In contrast to the traditional view, language is not fundamentally a medium of communication or conduit for representing the world. Instead, the interactive use of symbolic tokens by participants "steers the interaction as a whole through the possible state space, by constraining parts of this system in an appropriate (functional) way" [12]. Under this view, the primary function of language emerges as an inter-agential co-ordination mechanism, enabling collective navigation through its sui generis capacities for structuring abstract, formally unbounded, levels of complex relations. For interaction to successfully produce symbolic forms capable of supporting logical intersubjectivity, of becoming entangled in a web of inter-symbolic relations in a logical system, such interactive computation must involve convergence of perspectives around stabilized, common logical forms.

3 Ludics: The Logic of Rules

Drawing on proof-theoretic approaches to logic and computation, Jean-Yves Girard's [7] ludics offers a protological foundation describing the ground, not for the rules of logic, but for "the logic of rules." It is within this framework that the continuity of syntax and semantics arises and in which their relations are articulated internal to a monist (rather than dualist) system of interaction. To furnish a purely interactive monist logic, ludics begins by abstracting away formulae and axioms, and retaining only the loci—locations (i.e., names, channels or addresses)—of formulae and sub-formulae, for purposes of their geometric relations. The basic entities are abstract locative skeletons of proofs called *designs*. These are similar to proof trees in the (hyper)sequent calculus, except that while the latter have a sequent at their root $\Gamma \vdash \Delta$, in which Γ and Δ are sequences of formulae or propositions, the root of a design is a sequent or "pitchfork" of the form $\xi_N \vdash \xi_I$ expressing a relation between a locus (which can be thought of in abstract terms as an action or a gesture) and several other loci (which can be considered as anticipations or reactions) [13]. Whereas in the sequent calculus one would proceed by isolating the primary connectives on each side of the sequent and applying their associated rules to decompose a formula into its subformulae; in ludics, a design has no such predetermined set of rules to follow and may branch out in any manner based on how the interaction immanently unfolds, following a polarized rhythm between applications of generic positive or negative actions to a particular locus that then generates a finite number of subloci.

Then an action, which can be understood as an abstraction of rule application in the sequent calculus, is either 1) the special positive action † known as daïmon; or 2) a positive proper action $(+, \xi, I)$ or a negative proper action $(-, \xi, N)$: where the locus ξ is called the focus of the action, and the finite set of integers I (resp. N) is called its ramification. Given an action $(+, \xi, I)$ on the name ξ, the set I acts as a shortcut for the set of the names $\{\xi.i : i \in I\}$ which are generated from ξ by this action through the branching of ξ into its subloci built by increasing the sequence ξ with arbitrary distinct integers. However because the design begins with the quasi-material trace of a sign's bare locus of inscription, lacking any pre-defined semantic structure or content, there is nothing extrinsic to the immanent unfolding of the process of interaction that predetermines how the design will decompose or ramify [13]. Accordingly, a design may branch infinitely in its depth or breadth via an indefinite analysis of the initial loci. While in the hypersequential calculus, a proof search stops when it arrives at an atomic axiom; in ludics, just as there are no formulae, there are no axioms that halt the process. The only way the branching of a design or an interaction ends is via one of the interacting designs using the daïmon to inscribe any locus whatsoever without any justification or susceptibility to further challenges/inquiries from the counter-design—the DAÏMON rule:

$$\frac{}{\vdash \Delta} \dagger$$

Its introduction follows from the fact that truncated proofs, or paraproofs, from aborted proof search attempts can themselves be treated as formal objects around which one can develop a proof theory consisting of normalizing cuts involving such proofs, so long as the juncture of abortion is acknowledged and clearly reflected as this new rule—the daïmon, a paralogism that can be interpreted as "I give up!" [14]. This expands the arena of logic substantially, as the daïmon furnishes unfinished proofs, paraproofs, sophisms as formal objects to create a complete monist duality between proofs and their tests, supplying every design with counter-designs.

Following a view of the Curry-Howard isomorphism describing computation as proof normalization, the notion of testing here is simply computational interaction between designs, through a process analogous to cut-elimination in the sequent calculus [15]. This engine of computation relies on the logical symmetry of involutive negation $(^{\perp})$, which, as a dualizing or "switch role" operator, constitutes the critical concrete procedural operation for coordinating perspectives between designs by exchanging (polarized) viewpoints on a locus [14]. As purely locative structures, these designs are no longer tested through being brought into an external relation with a semantic model domain. Instead, designs and counter-designs occupy a univocal ontological domain, testing each other through interaction without anterior restrictions imposed to correspond to a fixed image of a transcendent (semantic) reality that limits the dynamic expression of logical forms in advance. In this way, a cut or interactive test then is the mere coincidence of two loci of opposite polarities that share the same address. Interaction or normalization proceeds as the process of cancellation of such pairs of shared loci on opposite sides of the pitchfork, continuing so long as such shared dual loci connect the two designs [16].

3.1 Convergent Perspectives via Orthogonality of Designs

From this we can define the core notion of orthogonality, or convergence of the interactive computation: A design D is orthogonal to a design E, expressed $D \perp E$, if and only if the interaction (i.e., elimination of the cuts) between the two designs leads to the empty normalized net Dai:

This occurs when step-by-step during the interaction, the opposed loci cancel each other out completely, collapsing the two trees into the empty pitchfork invoked by the daïmon as the last action played. It is this outcome of convergence of the interaction, due to orthogonality, that furnishes a protological ground for the internal emergence of logical forms. Two designs are orthogonal if and only if the procedure of normalization between them successfully terminates, where successful termination is understood as convergence on the normal form, which enjoys the property of unicity. In this sense, orthogonality is a consensus mechanism, enabling players in the coordination game of language "to agree (or not), without this being guaranteed in advance by the type: $\{D\}^{\perp}$ is the set of the families of counter-strategies [i.e., counter-designs] which are consensual (i.e., well interact) with D" [17].

The pivot for this intersubjective abstract consensus centers on the orthogonality relation as an equivalence relation characterizing symmetric modes of presentation of an invariant structural-geometric form. This austere notion of consensus can be understood simply as convergence of perspectives (on a determinate object). This critical relation of orthogonality captures the duality effectuated between perspectives through the logical symmetry of involutive negation. In this regard, the basic synchronization of confrontation of actions coordinated by loci serves as the basis of interactive computation and the ground for determining equivalence relations defined by symmetric perspectives on an address in memory that, as such, will exhibit invariant behavior from the dual viewpoints of the interacting agents. We can see that two designs that are orthogonal are "mirror" images of each other—equivalent in the loci defining the geometric structure but with the polarity of each locus exchanged.

Based on the orthogonality relations defined prior to and governing the interaction, interactive computation in ludics is a process of checking or confirming that this equivalence relation obtains at each step—and every step, if there is to be normal termination of the computation outputting the normal form—in order for the information exchange to remain "consensual" or convergent. Otherwise, as is usually the case, the two designs are not orthogonal and computational breakdown occurs through either deadlock or divergence as a bad infinite form of abstract dissensus [13] which prevents a stabilized shared or invariant form from crystallizing, thus frustrating the possibility of logical intersubjective coordination or the construction of enduring linguistic structure through such coordination.

3.2 Behaviors as Interactive Semantics

The product of the dynamics of this convergent computation can be understood as a symbol selected and concretized within the multi-agent system as a constraint harnessing the dynamics of computational behaviors internal to the system. It is in this way that designs (i.e., geometric diagrams as iconic signs) can be stabilized into invariant, minimal syntactic-symbolic units, which can support subsequent stabilization into more complex syntactic constituents with invariant roles and relations among them. Then, on another level of this univocal logical structure, these sets of designs stabilize into behaviors closed (or invariant) under interactive testing. These behaviors can be evaluated for semantic value, where such semantic value, in turn, is characterized as invariant functional effects produced with regard to interaction between processes or agents [11, 18].

A *behavior* then, in ludics, is defined as a set of designs which behaves the same way with regards to interaction with other designs against which it is tested. If G is a set of designs, $G^{\perp}$ is the set of designs orthogonal to G (that is, the set of designs whose interaction with G converges), then $G = G^{\perp\perp}$ is a behavior, equivalent through the involutivity of negation. As such, a behavior G is invariant under dualization and thus naturally closed under biorthogonality—i.e., designs remarkably are completely defined by their interactions [15]. This means a behavior G is fully described (internally complete) through testing by the set of its orthogonal designs $G^{\perp}$, and thus is stabilized by the two sets of orthogonal designs mutually constraining each other to play symmetrical roles in their dual computational environments. In this way, common semantic notions like formulae, propositions or types can be recovered as behaviors in ludics. The operational semantics of each behavior corresponds to a general description of all observable dynamic phenomena resulting from its interactive testing across contexts against observers (qua other sets of designs), providing a semantic characterization strictly internal to the dynamical context of the multi-agent system of interactive computation.

Thus behaviors, as interactive or semantic types, act as deontic coordination mechanisms—that is, they are fundamentally normatively constituted entities that constrain the dynamics of agents' behavior in updating the inferentially articulated logical structure within a multi-agent system's ontology. As we have emphasized throughout, these normative-behavioral constraints exhibit a systematicity of interrelations between behaviors arising immanently through consensual coordination, without the rule or referee of the game imposed in advance—"behaviours are games whose rule are established by consensus between designs and counter-designs: everything is permitted, provided one reaches a conclusion (when one [of] the players gives up)" [19]. It is on the basis of the foregoing that we can begin to see the radical implications of ludics for an interactive computational account of protological structuration as the antecedent condition and dynamic engine of language formation.[1] The bare locative and geometric formatting process—"deontic formatting" in Girard's [22] parlance—pragmatically effected in the arena of ludics forges symbols from diagrammatic icons, linking symbols with dynamics to make evaluation (including the conditions for cut-elimination and strong normalization)—that is, semantic value—possible, all internal to the computational system.

---

[1] Even as this sketch is admittedly preliminary, signposts toward developing an agent-based simulation that performs this process can be seen in works by Terui [20] describing a computational term syntax for designs and Fouqueré [21] devising a web-based programming language to model interactive dialogue between server and client.

4 Conclusion

Even with the prevalence of sub-symbolic approaches to AI, addressing the symbol grounding problem maintains its relevance to AGI research in terms of avoiding delimiting in advance artificial agents' capacities for language and ontology construction, as well as the scope of real-time models they could eventually build. Unless and until systematic non-symbolic systems of relations [23] are realized that achieve greater levels of expressive power, discrete formal symbolic systems remain the default structuring medium for scientific theory and ontology formulation [5]. The inverted, bottom-up approach to the problem outlined here, describing how symbols emerge from dynamic computational processes, and, in turn, serve as constraints on them, could offer a way forward for rearticulating the pragmatic interface between syntax and semantics internal to a multi-agent system. This perspective on symbols as constraints harnessing dynamics through a functional reduction in the degrees of freedom of a system of interacting autonomous agents acts to underscore the primary coordinative role of language qua interactive computation. In turn, the framework of ludics could function as a protological platform with which to equip artificial agents to provide them with the capacities to explore this formally unrestricted domain of language and ontology design, without navigatory restrictions enforced beforehand through an anthropocentric or pre-given transcendent semantic reality. In this regard, this paper aimed to develop a general sketch of the basic conditions for an open-ended evolution of a system through interaction with its environment to furnish agents within a multi-agent system with constructive, concrete autonomy to invent new artificial languages and thereby actively structure their worlds.

References

1. Peirce, C.S.: Collected papers of Charles Sander Pierce. In: Hartshorn, C., Weiss, P. (eds.) Elements of Logic, vol. II. Harvard University Press, Cambridge (1931)
2. Harnad, S.: The symbol grounding problem. Physica D **42**, 335–346 (1990)
3. Gruber, T.: A translation approach to portable ontology specifications. Knowl. Acquis. **5**(2), 199–220 (1993). https://doi.org/10.1006/knac.1993.1008
4. Asim, M., Wasim, M., Khan, M., Mahmood, W., Abbasi, H.: A survey of ontology learning techniques and applications. Database **2018**, 1–24 (2018). https://doi.org/10.1093/database/bay101
5. Churchland, P.M.: Plato's Camera: How the Physical Brain Captures a Landscape of Abstract Universals. MIT Press, Massachusetts (2012)
6. Brandom, R.: Between Saying and Doing: Towards an Analytic Pragmatism. Oxford University Press, New York (2008)
7. Girard, J.: Locus Solum: From the rules of logic to the logic of rules. Math. Struc. Comput. Sci. **11**(3), 301–506 (2001)
8. Seibt, J.: How to naturalize sensory consciousness and intentionality within a process monism with normativity gradient: A reading of Sellars. In: O'Shea, J. (ed.) Sellars and His Legacy, pp. 187–221. Oxford University Press, Oxford (2016)
9. Rączaszek-Leonardi, J., Kelso, J.A.S.: Reconciling symbolic and dynamic aspects of language. New Ideas Psychol. **26**, 193–207 (2008). https://doi.org/10.1016/j.newideapsych.2007.07.003

10. Rączaszek-Leonardi, J., Nomikou, I., Rohlfing, K., Deacon, T.: Language development from an ecological perspective: Ecologically valid ways to abstract symbols. Ecol. Psychol. **30**(1), 39–73 (2018). https://doi.org/10.1080/10407413.2017.1410387
11. Negarestani, R.: Intelligence and Spirit. Sequence Press, New York (2018)
12. Rączaszek-Leonardi, J.: Language as a system of replicable constraints. In: Pattee, H.H., Rączaszek-Leonardi, J. (eds.) Laws, Language and Life, pp. 3–29. Springer, Dordrecht, The Netherlands (2012). https://doi.org/10.1007/978-94-007-5161-3_19
13. Fraser, O.L.: Go back to An-Fang. https://www.academia.edu/352702/Go_back_to_An-Fang (2014). Accessed 9 Feb 2020
14. Girard, J.: From foundations to ludics. Bull. Symbolic Logic **9**(2), 131–168 (2003)
15. Fouqueré, C., Quatrini, M.: Ludics and natural language: First approaches. In: Proceedings of the 7th International Conference on Logical Aspects of Computational Linguistics (LACL'12), pp. 21–44. Springer, Heidelberg (2012). https://doi.org/10.1007/978-3-642-312 62-5_2
16. Lecomte, A.: Ludics, dialogue and inferentialism. In: Baltic International Yearbook of Cognition, Logic and Communication, vol. 8 (2013). https://doi.org/10.4148/1944-3676.1075
17. Basaldella, M., Faggian, C.: Ludics with repetitions (Exponentials, interactive types and completeness). Logical Methods Comput. Sci. **7**(2:13), 1–85 (2011)
18. Lecomte, A.: Meaning, Logic and Ludics. Imperial College Press, London (2011)
19. Girard, J.: The Blind Spot: Lectures on Logic. European Mathematical Society, Zurich (2011)
20. Terui, K.: Computational ludics. Theor. Comput. Sci. **412**(20), 2048–2071 (2011). https://doi.org/10.1016/j.tcs.2010.12.026
21. Fouqueré, C.: Ludics and web: another reading of standard operations. In: Lecomte, A., Tronçon, S. (eds.) Ludics, Dialogue and Interaction. LNCS (LNAI), vol. 6505, pp. 58–77. Springer, Heidelberg (2011). https://doi.org/10.1007/978-3-642-19211-1_4
22. Girard, J.: Transcendental syntax 2.0. https://pdfs.semanticscholar.org/8548/a157279b27de 84d1effd772b683c7b9d7701.pdf (2012). Accessed 9 Feb 2020
23. MacLennan, B.J.: Continuous formal systems: A unifying model in language and cognition. In: Proceedings of the IEEE Workshop on Architectures for Semiotic Modeling and Situation Analysis in Large Complex Systems, Monterey, CA, pp. 161–172 (1995)

Approach for Development of Engineering Tools Based on Knowledge Graphs and Context Separation

Nikita Debelov$^{(\boxtimes)}$, Petr Mukhachev, and Anton Ivanov

Skolkovo Institute of Science and Technology, Moscow, Russia
{nikita.debelov,petr.mukhacnev,a.ivanov2}@skoltech.ru

Abstract. During the development of complex multidisciplinary systems, engineers often have problems associated with the complexity of a target system and interactions of different groups of engineers and subcontractors.

In potential, besides engineers and subcontractors, the new agents can participate in such interactions, like AGI.

This paper presents ideas on how to develop engineering tools based on knowledge graphs to manage this complexity. This paper proposes the approach to make possible to agents that have different cognition contexts understand each other and a simple data format of context separation. At the end of the article, we have tried to show the example of how this approach can be applied to make a tool that uses engineering data in the proposed format.

Keywords: Engineering Systems Graph · Knowledge graph · Semantics · PDM

1 Introduction

There are a lot of best practices was developed to reduce cost and increase the predictability of development of complex engineering systems [5]. But the community sees the future engineering approach much more efficient with the application of more advanced tools and enhancing education processes [1]. Today, the main problem is dramatically increasing complexity, that can be described as number of direct and indirect interactions between components of systems.

To successfully handle this complexity, engineers need new methodologies, approaches and tools which differ from traditional models. In our research project we are looking for new ways for development such tools which, from one side, based on knowledge graphs and allowable data and app decentralization, and at the same time looks understandable to wide range of developers who potentially will create such "tissue" of distributed engineering tools.

© Springer Nature Switzerland AG 2020
B. Goertzel et al. (Eds.): AGI 2020, LNAI 12177, pp. 54–62, 2020.
https://doi.org/10.1007/978-3-030-52152-3_6

2 Proposed Approach

In this section we will describe the main points of the proposed approach. At first, a brief description of a context and why it's important. Then class-object interchangeability described (why the same object can be a class in another contexts).

This research was inspired by models of understanding (like cognitive groups and atoms, etc.) theories [3] in cognitive science and OpenCog project [4] and the desire to apply these theories to find new ways for engineering practice in a complex systems development. Additionally, decentralized approach was inspired by decentralization initiative about separation data and apps (like Solid project for Web).

The following sections describe a set of key principles of the approach.

2.1 Context Meaning

At first, in this section, the paper describes basic examples from cognitive science. Then describe why we choose to use context separation in the approach. After that, we describe the format and technical details of context usage in the approach.

When two humans interact, each one is working with his own context. Often it is successful, but the meaning of concepts is almost always different even if it is a "simple" concept. So, father, we suppose that 100% understanding of the same concept in any context not guaranteed neither between humans not between software or AGI.

A Mirror Example
When my friend and I discuss a mirror in my room, in my head a lot of contexts exists where mirror exists, for me an aluminum plate also a mirror, but for my friend contexts the mirror associated with space telescopes and a Perseus's mirrored shield of Athena (because he has interested in astronomy and Greek mythology).

Mechanics Example
If a student has studied Mechanics and the student thinks that he can work with mechanics, He installs special openMechanics software, but in reality, this software has a wider context than usual mechanics. We can name it openMechanics context, that can consist of mechanics context and openMechanics user interface context.

We suppose that each human, each software application, each artificial intelligence (AI), each artificial general intelligence (AGI) have their own understanding of each meaning concept. To continue work with these concepts, we combine it into *contexts* (domains of thinking).

The next example is a simplified form of a systems engineering problem that happens during a development of cross-discipline high-tech systems.

We have context Materials and context Chemistry and both have word concept Nickel. We understand that both concepts mean the same, even wikipedia.org has only one page about Nickel, there are no two pages Nickel (Material) and Nickel (Chemistry Element). Only one page Nickel exists on wikipedia. But I am working with an artisan, he is a very good worker, and he is making amazing things by hands. But he has no high education, and knows about chemistry only that atoms exist. He has no chemistry context, but he successfully uses chemical properties of Nickel, and a nickel is just a material substance for him. So we understand (with our intelligence) that Material's Nickel and Chemistry's Nickel is the same thing. In the same way, a hypothetical AGI can understand that is same thing without explicit reasoning like in formal ontologies. We have no discussed methods for such AGI understanding like Non-Axiomatic Reasoning (NARS) [7], etc.

So this example demonstrates that a possibility to translate concepts from one context to another exists.

Let's assume that we hear word concept Car. Usually, we understand it as an automobile, but if we are railroad engineers, sometimes we can understand it as railroad car, depends on in what context we are now. This example demonstrates environmental dependency and context mutability in cognitive science. In this example we showed the entity example, but relations is more mutable [2].

To describe the proposed idea we create three propositions.

– We will use only one agent (human, software apps, AI, etc.), it's an application software (app). We will not name an app as actor, because this name is hardly associated with actor-network theory (ANT), but in this research we have not researched yet how proper it relates to actors in ANT.
– Next we suppose that this agents understand information with bits (0–1).
– To describe the top-level interaction format, we will use JSON, which looks like JSON-LD because it uses fields @context and @type.

Figure 1 shows two agents who "say" that they understand the same mechanics context, and they interact with each other with data based on this context.

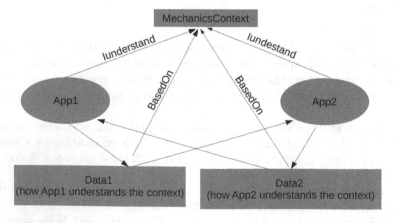

Fig. 1. An agent implicit context understanding and a data interchange based on it

A *context* here looks like a namespace in RDF. But RDF says what is expected format. For example, if an app in the proposed approach says that it understands a friend-of-a-friend (FOAF) context, it's mean that it understands that the data is machine-readable, what RDF is, OWL, and what FOAF concepts mean. Additionally, if the app supports Questions&Answers (Q&A) in human-readable form, we ask the app: "why do you say that you understand this context?", we can get an answer "because I understand RDF and OWL contexts and I've read FOAF documentation, and I think that I understood this documentation". A bit like a human could answer.

So a *context* is not a namespace, not a standard, not a knowledge domain.

For now, the question, how a context should be represented and how to support a decentralization, requires additional research. In this paper, we represent it as a unique string value. We understand that understanding of the same context by different agents can be different, and the approach supposes that it's normal behavior like in human cognition, even if these contexts based on math or formal logic.

Due we chose to work as a JSON representation, we can present each unique object as JSON object (braced with {...}), and each object should have not only @context property but also @type property with a string value, this value will unique in the @context of this object. We propose that each agent in our system can understand what JSON is, and what property @context and @type mean. (@type have the meaning like a class in the Web Ontology Language (OWL).

All fields that available in JSON object are defined by context and format of these fields too, it could be JSON, gLTF, binary string, XML, Turtle triplets(.ttl), etc.

2.2 Class-Object Interchangeability

In the proposed approach no separation between a class (@type) and an individual of this class object. A concrete entity can be a @type in another context.

Example. We have an object Spacecraft of @type componentType. But in another context, for example, spacecraftsContext, we can use the same object of Spacecraft as @type.

{ "@type": "componentType", _id: "spacecraftsContext/spacecraftBus", "@context": "pcs" },

{ "@type": "spacecraftBus", _id: "spacecraftsContext/spacecraftBusAB123", "@context": "spacecraftsContext" }.

3   Examples from Systems Engineering

In this section we propose the examples of the approach. We choosed ArangDb database to simulate a data storage.

We suppose that we have a context baseContext and each agent understand it.

Each entity have a JSON structure { @context: .. , @type: .. } Links have additional fields _from: .. , _to: .. To emulate hyperlinks like in hypergraphs we propose use entity with structure: { @type: hyperEntity, entityList: [] }.

But, in our system, a hyperEntity not only says what existed elements it connects, but also can introduce a new element. In reality, we can understand a usage of these links like human working memory. The metaphor of working memory was used in few research of AGI, for example Kovalev [6] defines a working memory in his approach as "part of the agent's sign-based world model in which information that is actively processed is stored" [6]. If we add a hyperlink to the working memory, the system can handle a structure of this hyperlink, get a inner entityList and add entities from this list to the working memory. We will call this process *disclosure*.

In the example of *disclosure* process we have in working memory few entities with ids: electricMachine, mechanicalEnergy, electricbattery, electricalEnergy and provides1 (link from electricBattery to elecricalEnergy). The provides1 link means that the electricBattery provide elecricalEnergy (in the example we don't use complex ontologies of object functions). Additionally, we add two new entities: electricCarConstruction (yellow color) and electricGenerator (green color). Both contain inner entities colored red. When the an electricGenerator entity is disclosed, the entities from entityList of an electricGenerator are added to the working memory graph Fig. 2. After disclosing of electricCarConstruction we get working memory structure graph like in Fig. 3

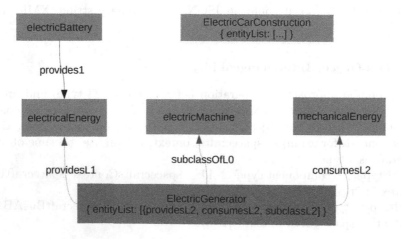

Fig. 2. The example of disclosing of electricGenerator (Color figure online)

3.1 Example of Realization a Structure Application

In this section we demonstrate an example when the same object type in different contexts have different meaning.

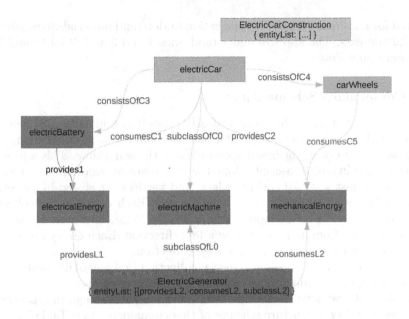

Fig. 3. The example of disclosing of the both entities (Color figure online)

The example have two contexts physicalComponentsStructure and materialsStructure. Both contains @types *skbConsistsof* derveid from base type *link*.

skbConsistsof in the physicalComponentsStructure means that an entity (_to property) is physical part of another entity (_from peroperty). *skbConsistsof* in the materialsStructure context means that some part of entity (_from) contains microparts of material (_to property).

The boltAA2 is a instance of the bolt component type.

The example JSON lines:

1. "@type": "skbConsistsof", "@context": "materialsStructure", _from: "components/boltAA2", _to: "materials/Aluminium"
   //boltAA2 consistsOf Aluminium
2. "@type": "skbConsistsof", "@context": "materialsStructure", _from: "components/boltAA2", _to: "materials/Zinc" ,
   //boltAA2 consistsOf Zinc
3. "@type": "skbConsistsof", "@context": "physicalComponentsStructure", _from: "components/boltAA2", _to: "componentTypes/boltHead" ,
   //boltAA2 consistsOf boltHead
4. "@type": "skbConsistsof", "@context": "physicalComponentsStructure", _from: "components/boltAA2", _to: "componentTypes/boltShank" ,
   //boltAA2 consistsOf boltShank.

If the target application defined that it understand skbComponentTypes context, the result in this application will include only lines 3 and 4. And as result we got that component *boltAA2 consists of boltHead and boltShank*. The second app targeted for materials structure visualization understand materialsStructure and material contexts. The app will understand lines 1 and 2 as *boltAA2 consists of Aluminium and Zinc*

3.2 Components Schema App

To test this approach, we chose the ArangoDB database and Javascript language for back-end and web technologies for the user interface. ArangoDb supports graph-based and document-based approaches at the same time. This advantage with the flexibility of javascript allowed us to create an example and test the approach in a fast way. All entities, edges, and vertices are stored in collections in ArangoDb; each collection has a unique name. Each entity in the collection has a unique id and a value represented as JSON. Edge collection entities have additional fields _from and _to to show a link direction. Each entity (even edge) can be a vertex for an edge from any edge collection.

We used only one data storage (special collection in ArangoDB) in the example, but the approach implies that any data source can be used.

Additionally we have created few data blocks in the storage: the spacecrafts components and two structure schemes of this components (see Table 1).

Table 1. Example data blocks.

Data block name	Description
SpacecraftComponents	Basic spacecraft components (Payload, Bus, ADCS, CableHarness, etc.)
Cubesat1	Components structure hierarchy for CubeSat
Cubesat2	Another components structure hierarchy for CubeSat
SatTelescope	Components structure hierarchy for space telescope

1. When the user chose to upload a data block to the working memory, the backend system gets this data block, and create documents in a collection with a name like @type with the prefix of current working memory id. If a block has the entity { "@type": "ComponentType", _id: "pcs/physicalComponent", "@context": "pcs" }}, the system will place this JSON entity as document (with id pcs-physicalComponent) to WM123-ComponentType-pcs collection (where WM123 is an Id of the current working memory, and pcs is a context of the type). See Fig. 4.
2. Additionally, the system parses the entity, and if found that it's a hyperlink, means has property entityList, it recursively searches the entities in this property and places them in the special collection EntityIndex, which store entities and it's parent entity if this entity is stored inside entityList property of the parent entity. Currently, it's a hack for proper data management;

3. If the system needs to *disclosure* any entity with EntityList property, then all entities from this EntityList are placed into appropriate collections (like in the item 1).
4. In any time, we can traverse through these collections like in graph using edge collections.

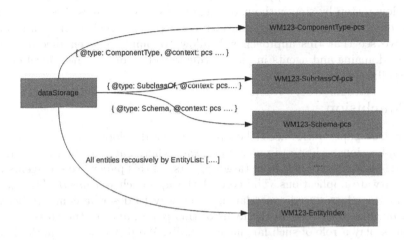

Fig. 4. The principle of moving data to ArangoDB collections

So these technologies allowed us to upload data into two different simple apps (components structure, and materials structure). And use a web interface to disclose entities manually, to get different results from requests to knowledge graph stored in working memory.

The schema in the example context is a schema of components structure hierarchy. For example, the first schema stores connections to build small satellite architecture, and another schema builds (from the same set of component entities) hierarchy for a space telescope. If we *disclosure* both schemes in the same knowledge graph, for example, we can launch special graph algorithms to compare these schemes.

It's the simplest example of how a context separation and an entity disclosure metaphors can be moved from cognitive science to real engineering tools.

The source code of this example is published in https://gitlab.com/skolspace/rustik-backend.

4   Discussion

We think that this approach will help move the engineering community to a more open and flexible world. Because standards and consortiums can not handle the complexity of a decentralized world. The research was inspired by glTF data format, but we should think about decentralizations of standards and a future where AI will create their own "standards" on-the-fly.

Sometimes even standards that are hard to make, have not used by companies. Because big companies (PLM vendors, etc.) control their fields and trying to plant their customers to a bunch of products of these companies and their business model are built for data locking.

So we think that this approach will allow slowly move our society to open world slowly step by step without damage to these companies. Yes, at the first step, each of them will develop their own contexts with their own data formats.

So we see that this approach will allow to build some engineering tissue between domains and agents in engineering world to bring a new level of engineering efficiency.

5 Conclusion

The present paper introduced the approach for developing new agents (software applications, AI, etc.) in a common way where data can be presented as a knowledge graph separated from target agents. In this paper, we see agents only as on software applications. The core of the approach is *context*. The current paper has not introduced exact language or way to describe contexts between agents because this is not in the focus of this paper, and, in the current world, standards play a role of such languages usually. We just take a hypothesis that such languages between agents exist, and it allows agents to understand contexts more-less similarly.

The possibility to create software based on this approach is clear, but selected data structures do not look developer-friendly enough; the questions about the performance of data blocks movement in agents "tissue" requires additional research.

References

1. INCOSE SE Vision 2025. https://www.incose.org/products-and-publications/se-vision-2025
2. Asmuth, J., Gentner, D.: Relational categories are more mutable than entity categories. Q. J. Exp. Psychol. **70**(10), 2007–2025 (2017). https://doi.org/10.1080/17470218.2016.1219752
3. Baronchelli, A., Ferrer-i-Cancho, R., Pastor-Satorras, R., Chater, N., Christiansen, M.H.: Networks in cognitive science. Trends Cogn. Sci. **17**(7), 348–360 (2013). https://doi.org/10.1016/j.tics.2013.04.010
4. Hart, D., Goertzel, B.: OpenCog: a software framework for integrative artificial general intelligence, January 2008
5. Kapurch, S.J.: NASA Systems Engineering Handbook. DIANE Publishing, Collingdale (2010)
6. Kovalev, A.K., Panov, A.I.: Mental actions and modelling of reasoning in semiotic approach to AGI. In: Hammer, P., Agrawal, P., Goertzel, B., Iklé, M. (eds.) AGI 2019. LNCS (LNAI), vol. 11654, pp. 121–131. Springer, Cham (2019). https://doi.org/10.1007/978-3-030-27005-6_12
7. Wang, P.: Non-axiomatic reasoning system (version 2.2), January 1999

Towards Dynamic Process Composition in the DSO Cognitive Architecture

Zhiyuan Du$^{(\boxtimes)}$ and Khin Hua Ng

Information Exploitation Lab, DSO National Laboratories, Singapore, Singapore
{dzhiyuan,nkhinhua}@dso.org.sg

Abstract. In recent works, the DSO Cognitive Architecture's design is enhanced by incorporating the concept of the Global Workspace Theory (GWT). The theory proposes that consciousness is realised through the competition of massive, specialised, parallelised processes and thus parallelised, unsynchronised cognitive processes become sequential through such bottleneck. Due to the concurrent nature of DSO Cognitive Architecture, coordination of the different parallel processes through this competition mechanism can be difficult and if not handled properly, will create inconsistent results. In this work, we propose a preliminary framework to coordinate the different processes by process composition which borrows concepts from automated planning. Processes, its argument signature and its output are abstracted into higher level type abstractions which can be used to compose with other processes based on matching the output types to argument types. This is known as process composition and it represents a sketch of how different process can coordinate with one another. We combined this with the current design of the DSO Cognitive Architecture and illustrate an example in crowd anomaly detection.

Keywords: Cognitive Architecture · Global Workspace Theory · Automated planning

1 Introduction

The DSO Cognitive Architecture (DSO-CA) [4] is a top-level cognitive architecture that incorporates the design principles of parallelism, distributed memory and hierarchical structure to model how the human brain processes information. It has been applied successfully on different applications [5,6]. In recent years, an enhanced design [7] was proposed and a prototype [8] to validate it was implemented.

Global Workspace Theory (GWT) is a neuro-cognitive theory of consciousness [1] that advances a model of information flow in which multiple, parallel, specialised processes compete and co-operate for access to a global workspace, which permits the winning coalition to broadcast to the rest of the specialist. DSO-CA incorporates that concept to achieve dynamic reasoning by chaining

© Springer Nature Switzerland AG 2020
B. Goertzel et al. (Eds.): AGI 2020, LNAI 12177, pp. 63–71, 2020.
https://doi.org/10.1007/978-3-030-52152-3_7

different reasoners together, with each reasoner running in parallel with each other. This is done through the attention and global broadcast mechanism which broadcasts the content of the reasoner to other reasoners for it to work on. To that end, an integrative memory is needed to allow reasoner with different memory systems to interact with one another. This serves as a common memory representation that can be shared with other reasoners; a translator alongside the reasoner translates from the common representation to its native memory representation.

In the current design inspired by GWT, there are two modes of information flow: default pathways that exists between the different processes, and through sequential execution via the global broadcast mechanism. The former happens when the input to the system is normal and the processing through the default pathways is enough to handle it. The latter happens when input to the system is unanticipated, requiring a different pathway that does not exists within the system at all. This is done via competition and broadcasting of the most appropriate process' output which will be consumed by other processes and in turn, compete again; competition stops when the system is able to handle the unanticipated input. This way, a sequential pathway is generated via the sequential winners of the broadcast. Design and implementation wise, competition and broadcast implies coordination of the different processes and this can be difficult if it is not specified properly due to the concurrent nature of the DSO-CA. An example of this issue would be broadcasting of the winner when another process has finished generating its result; upon receiving the broadcast, the same process could contradict the previous result; if this process is part of a default pathway, such contradictory result may propagate downwards causing inconsistent result. One way to solve this is to reframe sequential pathway generated by the GWT as a program trace which could be seen as a form of composition. This paper introduces the concept of process composition which will be defined in the next section. Process composition represents each specialised process in GWT as a computable process with its argument signature and return abstracted as argument type set, this allows us to frame generating a sequential pathway by the GWT as a planning problem. In the third section, we shall provide an example in the domain of anomaly detection where the DSO-CA can be applied. Finally, we end the paper with discussion and conclusion by highlighting some issues, potential solutions and further improvement on the work.

2 Dynamic Process Composition

We model each specialised process in the GWT as a computable process represented by a type, p (Eq. (1)). p takes in a number of inputs or arguments, a and return an output, o. a and o is a tuple $\langle t, M, v \rangle$ where t is the type, M is the metadata set, and v is its value. Note, t_i in Eq. (1) could be of the same type but they are differentiated by different metadata. One such metadata could be the order of argument, timestamp of which a is generated, or the process of which it originated from. We also define P as the set of all computable process that can either be programmed or synthesized, and P_t as the set P at step t in the computation. Additionally, we assume computation in p can terminate.

$$p(a_{1_p}, a_{2_p}, ... a_{n_p}) \rightarrow o \mid a_i = \langle t_i, M_i, v_i \rangle, o = \langle t_o, M_o, v_o \rangle \qquad (1)$$

We can also define an argument type set, $A_p = \{\langle t_{a_{1_p}}, M_{a_{1_p}} \rangle, \{\langle t_{a_{2_p}}, M_{a_{2_p}} \rangle, ..., \{\langle t_{a_{n_p}}, M_{a_{n_p}} \rangle\}$ where each tuple in A_p is the subtuple of a_{i_p}. Next we define $\boldsymbol{Arg_t}$ as the set of all arguments that are generated in step t and $A_p \subseteq \boldsymbol{Arg_t}$. This could be generated by other processes or an exogenous source i.e an image captured by a camera which is structured as a matrix of RGB values; in this case $t = 0$. In Eq. (1), o that is generated by p will be added into $\boldsymbol{Arg_{t+1}}$. $\boldsymbol{Arg_t}$ is also monotonically increasing thus $\boldsymbol{Arg_0} \subseteq \boldsymbol{Arg_1} \subseteq ... \subseteq \boldsymbol{Arg_t}$.

We note p is execution ready, $p \rightarrow p_r$ if $A_p \subseteq \boldsymbol{Arg_t}$ at any t. p_r can be seen as a process that can be potentially executed as its argument signature is complete. With this process composition, $P(A_{p_1}) = p_n \circ p_{n-1} \circ ... \circ p_1(A_{p_1})$ can lead to a forward chaining where p_1 will produce o_1 which is an element of A_{p_2}. Likewise, a process composition is execution ready when $P \rightarrow P_r$ if p_1 is execution ready and $p_2...p_n$ are eventually execution ready. The intuition here is that p_{1_r} can be executed and be expected to produce an output type with certain metadata without needing to care too much about what the value is; this output will be added to $\boldsymbol{Arg_1}$ which in turn is fed into p_2 and if $A_{p_2} \subseteq \boldsymbol{Arg_1}$, $p_2 \rightarrow p_{2_r}$. We will note that $P(A_{p_1})$ can be infinite thus to make it finite, process composition stops when $P_r(A_{p_1}) \rightarrow A_G$ where $A_G = \langle t_G, M_G \rangle$. A_G is a goal argument type that is generated from p_{n_r} and it will be added to $\boldsymbol{Arg_{t+1}}$. Also we can define an initial set of argument type, A_I that is defined at the start thus $\boldsymbol{Arg_0} = A_I$.

We can now view process composition from the viewpoint of classical planning like STRIPS [2]. STRIPS consists of a tuple $\langle P, O, I, G \rangle$ where P defines the set of propositions or states in first order logic predicates. I defines the initial set of states, $I \subset P$. O is the set of operators or actions that the planner can put in a sequence. Each operator has two components—its preconditions and its effects. Preconditions define the propositions that must be true or false for the operator to be considered. Effects are the states which will be added or deleted from the existing state set. G is the set of goal state which defines the states which must be true or false. Table 1 draws analogy between the process composition and STRIPS.

Table 1. Analogous mapping between STRIPS and process composition

STRIP	Process composition
P, propositions or set	$\boldsymbol{Arg_t}$, all type argument sets at step t
O, operators	P_t, set of all processes at step t
I, initial set of states	A_I, an initial set of type arguments
G, set of goal states	A_G, goal argument type

With this, we can see process composition as a form of automated planning where given an initial set of type argument, A_I and the goal type argument, A_G, the planner is to come out with a sequence of processes or process composition that is execution ready, $P_r(A_I) \to A_G$. Note that while we use the definition of STRIPS, we are not necessary confined to using a STRIPS planner to do process composition.

To tie this to the DSO-CA with GWT, we will use Fig. 1 as a reference which will be elaborated later. The default pathways are different P_r which has been generated by the planner and they are stored in the reasoner layer. When an input argument type set is added into $\boldsymbol{Arg_t}$ at step t such that $\forall P(A_p) \; A_p \not\subseteq \boldsymbol{Arg_t}$, no P can be execution ready. This will trigger the global broadcast mechanism and the specialist processes will compete for attention with the winner being broadcasted. This is done by different processes matching $\boldsymbol{Arg_t}$ against their own, and if a process composition is execution ready, they will be eligible for competition. The competition mechanism is regulated by two aspects: the state manager and attention. The state manager models the state of the system or task and the attention mechanism acts as a filter to suppress or promote specialist processes. The state manager is a finite state machine that transits state based on the output given by the various pipelines, each state transited can be considered as a goal for the system to achieve through the various pipelines. If the pipeline does not exist, backward chaining with the planner can be used to create a preliminary pipeline. The state manager also contains processes to verify whether the goal is achieved by value instead of strictly through type argument set. The attention mechanism can filter processes that are not relevant or contradictory based on the state within the state manager. Consider a scenario where a social robot with its state manager modeling how it should appropriately act and now it is navigating through a crowded place where people are walking. Now consider two processes, $run\,(location_t, direction_t)$ and $walk\,(location_t, direction_t)$ where $location_t, direction_t$ are types and these process types are abstracted as part of a planning model for motion. Both processes share the same type argument types and in process composition both processes are execution ready if $location, direction \in \boldsymbol{Arg_t}$ however the state manager may impose the robot to follow the crowd instead. Thus, the attention mechanism may filter $run\,(location, direction)$ and promote $walk\,(location, direction)$ to the Global Broadcast Mechanism. Once the filtered process types are filtered, they will form a coalition and be broadcasted to the planner where the process composition takes place with regards to the goal generated by the state manager which will be broadcasted as well. Process composition is an iterative process as the current process composition may not produce A_G; this happens when all processes in $\boldsymbol{P_t}$ has been exhausted. When that happens, this will trigger the global broadcast mechanism of which the broadcasted coalition will be the frontier output argument types in the current process composition. As state transition within the state manager happens in parallel with the planner, the broadcasted coalition that addresses the incomplete process composition can be filtered differently from the previous coalition. This mechanisms where a process composition is generated in response to new input argument types and iteratively increasing the number of process as needed grants dynamism into process composition.

Lastly, we will also note that an argument type, $A_j[]$ is a list of argument type A_j such that $A_j \in A_j[]$. This is akin to an array of a homogenous type. If $A_j \in A_p$ for p, p cannot be applied to $A_j[]$. This requires special processes not provided by any of the specialised processes but by the planner itself. In Fig. 2, we use the idea of $Fork$ such that $Fork(p(A_j[])) \rightarrow p(A_{j_0}) \cdot p(A_{j_1}) \cdot p(A_{j_2}) \cdot ... \cdot p(A_{j_n})$ where $\cdot$ represents sequential execution. Likewise, $Join(O_{j_0}, O_{j_1}, ..., O_{j_n}) \rightarrow O_j[]$ when argument types need to be added into a list. Planners insert these process types when it can potentially join two such processes. During execution, a $Fork$ is translated into a loop where it enumerates each element in $a_j[]$ and feed a_j into p and $Join$ simply add the output of the sub process composition into a list. Alternative, $Fork$ can also be mapped into a worker pool where each thread feed a_j into p and $Join$ is a block operation that creates a list of all results before continuing the process composition

3 Anomaly Detection: An Example

In this section, we will give an example of process composition generated by the DSO-CA. Anomaly detection in crowd movement is important in many applications including evacuation and security. It is also interesting because the environment is naturally noisy and the agent needs to reason with groups of people instead of individuals. In this example, the DSO-CA detects crowd anomalies via features within the video. Features come from different sources and they will be fused via different processes with process composition. The problem of anomaly detection can be seen as a form of hypothesis generation where anomalous activities are hypothesised based on the current observations and the system seeks to either refute or support said hypothesis. Figure 1 shows an example of the DSO-CA architecture applied. The hypothesis is generated from the $ComputeChain$ process where features are computed through an ontology to classify pixel regions in the frame into either anomalous or normal crowd.

A collection of perception modules extract and abstract different features such as object detector to get the bounding boxes; scene segmentation to get labeled pixel regions within each frame; and optical flow for clustering movement in the video (Fig. 1). Each feature is mapped to different input type argument set e.g bounding boxes are mapped to $DetectedObjects = DetectedObject[]$, optical flow clusters are mapped to $ClusterSummaries = ClusterSummary[]$, and labeled pixel regions classified as persons are mapped to $PersonSegment$. From here, these features will be fed into the reasoner layer. If there exists a P_r such that the input types matched, it will be executed. However, if there are none this will trigger the global broadcast mechanism as mentioned in the previous section. Figure 1 also shows the state transition model on how the hypothesis transits between different states. The initial and default state is $Unexpected$ which is to expect anomalous behaviour. Note in Fig. 2, $Unexpected$

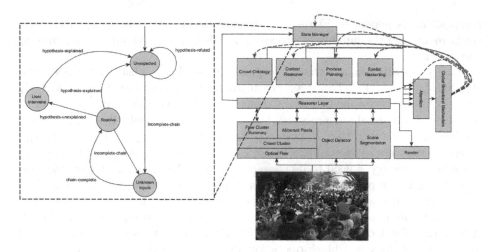

Fig. 1. The crowd anomaly detector with the DSO-CA. Right shows the architecture and the left shows the state transition modeled within the state manager. Crowd image is from [3]

produces a goal argument type where it expects a list $ConceptChains$ of a subtype $Crowd$. Recall that $a = \langle t, M, v \rangle$ where t is the type, M is the metadata set and v is the value of the argument. In this example, M records the process type of which the o is produced. For example $ComputeConcept$ generates $O_{ComputeConcept} = \langle ConceptChain, ComputeConcept \in M \rangle$, this will be different with $O_{TestHypotheis} = \langle ConceptChain, TestHypothesis \in M \rangle$.

Figure 2 shows an example of process composition generated when there is none in the reasoning layer with $\boldsymbol{Arg_0}$ in Fig. 2. Having no P matching the $\boldsymbol{Arg_0}$, the global broadcast mechanism is triggered and $\boldsymbol{Arg_0}$ will be broadcasted. Before that, the state manager will inject the goal argument type into $\boldsymbol{Arg_0}$. The different reasoners getting the input argument types will match and return the appropriate process types for another broadcast. The planner receiving these process types will start the process composition and request for more processes if the goal type is not reached. For example, upon receiving $\boldsymbol{Arg_0}$, Spatial Reasoner will send $ExtractPath$ and $CombineRegion$ process types for broadcast. The planner will add those two process types to P and see if the current P produces $ConceptChains$. One will note that the planner will match $ClusterSummaries$ to its process type $Fork$ and generate $ClusterSummary$ as an output type. As a result, $DetectedObjects$, $AdjancencyGraph$, $ClusterSummary$ will be generated, however because $\boldsymbol{P_0}$ is exhausted and the goal type is not part of the generated output types, the planner will broadcast these to the different reasoners. Note $DetectedObjects$ will have a different metadata compared to the same type in $\boldsymbol{Arg_0}$; in this case, it will be $\langle DetectedObject[], CombinedRegion \in M \rangle$. The state manager receiving such broadcast will transit to $UnknownInputs$ and process composition will continue until the $ConceptChains$ was output from a $Join$ process, the $TestGoal$ process generated by the state manager will confirm

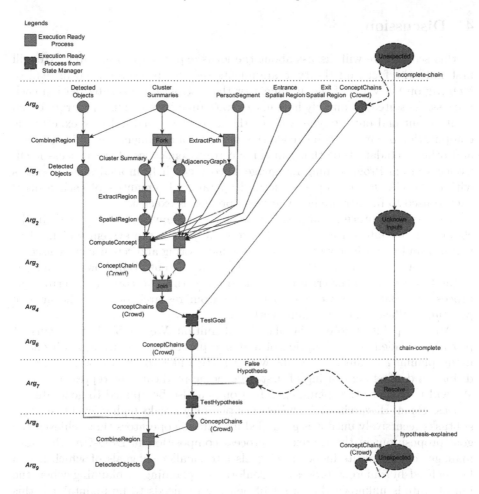

Fig. 2. An example of a process composition. On the left is the pipeline that is planned out. On the right, the state transition. Note the *Resolve* state produces a goal type of which the hypothesis is tested.

that the current process composition matches the goal type. Once it matches, *UnknownInputs* will be transit to *Resolve* as the system has a P_r that can address $\boldsymbol{Arg_0}$ that matches the goal type. Note that P_r only addresses a subset of $\boldsymbol{Arg_0}$ but it is adequate because it generates the goal type. Once these hypothesis are generated, the next state will create a new goal type, *FalseHypothesis* and the *TestHypothesis* process. Process Composition will start again and the planner will generate $P_r(\boldsymbol{Arg_7})$. Here *TestHypothesis* is a filter process that matches against another type which in this case test the falsibility of the hypothesis, meaning whether are there any normal crowd movement. After the new ConceptChains are produced, a new $P_r(\boldsymbol{Arg_8})$ will be generated with the *DetectedObjects* that was generated in $\boldsymbol{Arg_1}$.

4   Discussion

In this section, we will discuss about the ideas expressed in the paper. We will first note the focus on the type arguments set and processes type instead of focusing on the value of the argument or the instructions executed within each process. As stated, intuitively human can trace functions within a program based on its input and output type without the need to understand how exactly the computation occurs, we can encode this in terms of argument and output types, and other metadata type that can carry certain semantics of the process itself. Concepts from Programming Language Theory can help in analysing processes within the CA. For example, structural operational semantics of each process can be used to further predict whether a process is execution ready.

Execution of process composition needs to be monitored as a process in the chain can run into errors. When an error happened, the system will need to monitor and repair its own processes. Plan monitoring and repair can be used to mitigate by replanning another P_r based on the current Arg_t however analysis of the feedback from the error can be used for learning to correct the erroneous process, to that end we can reap insights from research done in the area of program verification or program synthesis.

Another point of note is the planning definition. We use STRIPS because it provides an adequate description of dynamic process composition, additionally many planning definition overlaps with STRIPS like operators having preconditions and effects and using of first order logic predicates to represent states. We will note that other planning definition can also be applied to generate the process chain. Hierarchical Task Network planning breaks higher level tasks into subtasks recursively until it is grounded into atomic operators that achieved the goal proposition; in the context of process composition in DSO-CA, the state manager can break its higher level goals into smaller subgoals of which it can be realised by different processes. Conformant planning is planning when the initial state is unknown thus a set of belief state needs to be maintained, this makes the planning domain non-deterministic. We will note that we can apply this to metadata which contains information that cannot be generated without executing P_r so conformant planning can maintain set of belief states to represent possible metadata values. Automated planning also opens the door to multiple related areas to explore like the area of plan monitoring, plan repair and even plan recognition. All of which is interesting and important in creating an agent that can adapt to a dynamic environment. Plan monitoring is akin of monitoring execution of any process composition, and plan repair can be used to replace processes with other appropriate processes. Plan recognition on the other hand will be interesting in multiagent settings where the agent needs to recognise the plans of other actors which could be other agents or human beings. While process composition can help in this, execution of this recognised plan in a simulated setting within the agent could yield insight into the actor. Figuratively, this execution of process allows the agent to 'walk in the observer's shoes' which could bring towards modeling empathy within intelligent systems.

5   Conclusion

In this paper, we have introduced the concept of process composition and linked it to the DSO-CA with GWT to address the coordination framework between the attention mechanism, global broadcast mechanisms and the specialised processes. Process composition borrows concepts from automated planning where a sequence of processes are chained from matching the argument signature and output types. After which we illustrate the idea using an example of anomaly detection and how the process composition is generated combined with the concept of GWT. For future work, we will work on monitoring of execution for P_r and refine the argument type system to allow vector based representation.

References

1. Baars, B.J.: A Cognitive Theory of Consciousness. Cambridge University Press, Cambridge (1993)
2. Fikes, R.E., Nilsson, N.J.: Strips: a new approach to the application of theorem proving to problem solving. In: Proceedings of the 2nd International Joint Conference on Artificial Intelligence IJCAI 1971, pp. 608–620. Morgan Kaufmann Publishers Inc., San Francisco (1971)
3. Mehran, R., Oyama, A., Shah, M.: Abnormal crowd behavior detection using social force model. In: 2009 IEEE Conference on Computer Vision and Pattern Recognition, pp. 935–942. IEEE (2009)
4. Ng, G.W., Tan, Y.S., Teow, L.N., Ng, K.H., Tan, K.H., Chan, R.Z.: A cognitive architecture for knowledge exploitation. In: 3rd Conference on Artificial General Intelligence (AGI-2010). Atlantis Press (2010)
5. Ng, G.W., Tan, Y.S., Xiao, X.H., Chan, R.Z.: DSO cognitive architecture in mobile surveillance. In: 2012 Workshop on Sensor Data Fusion: Trends, Solutions, Applications (SDF), pp. 111–115. IEEE (2012)
6. Ng, G.W., Xiao, X., Chan, R.Z., Tan, Y.S.: Scene understanding using DSO cognitive architecture. In: 2012 15th International Conference on Information Fusion (FUSION), pp. 2277–2284. IEEE (2012)
7. Ng, K.H., Du, Z., Ng, G.W.: DSO cognitive architecture: unified reasoning with integrative memory using global workspace theory. In: Everitt, T., Goertzel, B., Potapov, A. (eds.) AGI 2017. LNCS (LNAI), vol. 10414, pp. 44–53. Springer, Cham (2017). https://doi.org/10.1007/978-3-319-63703-7_5
8. Ng, K.H., Du, Z., Ng, G.W.: DSO cognitive architecture: implementation and validation of the global workspace enhancement. In: Iklé, M., Franz, A., Rzepka, R., Goertzel, B. (eds.) AGI 2018. LNCS (LNAI), vol. 10999, pp. 151–161. Springer, Cham (2018). https://doi.org/10.1007/978-3-319-97676-1_15

SAGE: Task-Environment Platform for Evaluating a Broad Range of AI Learners

Leonard M. Eberding[1,2], Kristinn R. Thórisson[1,3], Arash Sheikhlar[1(✉)], and Sindri P. Andrason[1]

[1] Center for Analysis and Design of Intelligent Agents,
Reykjavik University, Reykjavik, Iceland
{thorisson,arashs}@ru.is, sindri@andrason.com
[2] Institute of Photogrammetry and GeoInformation, Leibniz U., Hannover, Germany
l.eberding@stud.uni-hannover.de
[3] Icelandic Institute for Intelligent Machines, Reykjavik, Iceland
http://cadia.ru.is, https://www.ipi.uni-hannover.de

Abstract. While several tools exist for training and evaluating narrow machine learning (ML) algorithms, their design generally does not follow a particular or explicit evaluation methodology or theory. Inversely so for more *general* learners, where many evaluation methodologies and frameworks have been suggested, but few specific tools exist. In this paper we introduce a new framework for broad evaluation of artificial intelligence (AI) learners, and a new tool that builds on this methodology. The platform, called SAGE (Simulator for Autonomy & Generality Evaluation), works for training and evaluation of a broad range of systems and allows detailed comparison between narrow and general ML and AI. It provides a variety of tuning and task construction options, allowing isolation of single parameters across complexity dimensions. SAGE is aimed at helping AI researchers map out and compare strengths and weaknesses of divergent approaches. Our hope is that it can help deepen understanding of the various tasks we want AI systems to do and the relationship between their composition, complexity, and difficulty for various AI systems, as well as contribute to building a clearer research road map for the field. This paper provides an overview of the framework and presents results of an early use case.

Keywords: Evaluation · Generality · Autonomy ·
Task-environments · Evaluation framework · Machine intelligence

1 Introduction

Many good reasons exist for wanting proper evaluation methods for machines capable of complex tasks [4], including: (a) To gauge research progress—measuring difference in performance between two or more versions of the same

© Springer Nature Switzerland AG 2020
B. Goertzel et al. (Eds.): AGI 2020, LNAI 12177, pp. 72–82, 2020.
https://doi.org/10.1007/978-3-030-52152-3_8

system can elucidate limitations and potential of various additions, modifications and extensions of the same architecture; (b) to compare the performance and potential of one or more AI systems across a set of tasks; and (c) to compare different AI systems on the same or a variety of tasks. The dependent variables in such evaluation will be conditional on the evaluation's purpose, whether it's learning a single task or many, to learn quickly, reliably, autonomously, to learn complex things, causal relations, to handle novelty, or some combination of these—or even more. Most proposals for evaluating artificial intelligence (AI) systems focus on subsets of the possible spectrum of dependent variables relevant to general machine intelligence (GMI), or are narrowly focused on particular tasks or domains.

Good measuring tools and methodologies are necessary to assess progress in any scientific domain. They should allow comparison of systems of numerous kinds. The vast majority of evaluation methods proposed to date rely on a single measurement, where a series of multiple measurements could possibly much better separate between autonomous, general systems and narrow machine intelligence (NMI). Furthermore, many current evaluation strategies focus on evaluation of (single) tasks especially chosen to evaluate a particular (narrow) machine learning algorithm. GMI-aspiring work cannot limit itself to one or a small set of tasks, especially if they lack a) any sort of real-time or continuous settings, b) complex causal chains, c) a multiple goals, or at least d) variable feedback (reinforcement), including its absence (except in the form of a top-level goal). These features (or a subset of them) can be found in most human tasks.

While GMI-aspiring systems should ultimately be able to tackle tasks of those kinds, most evaluation platforms do not provide any functionality for creating them. This makes an evaluation of our progress on generality more difficult, since the same task environments well-suited for testing NMI do not address such matters; while platforms like OpenAI Gym [5] or the Arcade Learning Environment (ALE) [2] all provide functionality to test narrow agents, they fail to offer easy construction of tasks of greater complexity.

The SAGE task-environment simulation platform proposes to bridge the gap between evaluation of low- and high-level intelligence by providing methods for constructing and analyzing performance on tasks in a fine-grained manner. SAGE is based on breaking tasks, and the environments they are performed in, into variables (observable, unobservable, manipulable, and non-manipulable) and transition functions that control their changes over time [19, 20]. Task-environments in SAGE may be constructed with a variety of characteristics and levels of complexity, including causal and statistical relations, determinism and non-determinism, hidden and partially-observable variables, distracting variables, noise, and much more.

Puzzle boxes, to take an example of a human-level task, may lie at the far end of a complexity spectrum, yet are regularly solved by human intelligence. Such boxes invariably present features that include: a) not giving evidence for whether a chosen action was "good", or "bad", at least not by an easily observable score; b) containing highly complex, non-observable causal chains which need to be hypothesized and understood, to some extent, to solve the puzzle, and even c) acting independently from outside action, through timers. SAGE makes the setup of such tasks easier for an evaluator by providing an architecture that supports continuous changes in task variables and rewards, even with an external clock. A puzzle box task could be divided into a variety of sub-tasks, each with increasing complexity. If narrow agents are being evaluated on a subset of such a task, the environment can be set up to give direct feedback (reward) about the value of any chosen action and affected variables possible directly observable. For GMI-aspiring systems such feedback and observability can be reduced or removed, making a task reach human-level complexity.

The architecture of SAGE is based on a new MVC-A (Model-View-Controller-Agents) paradigm in the ROS2 framework [14], enabling the whole system to be physically run on separate processors and computers to reduce interference of processor loads on simulation integrity. Dividing a simulation logically into these parts also makes for easier adjustments of each part, independent of the others, allowing an evaluator to more easily change individual parameters and task design, up front and at runtime.

The paper is organized as follows: Sect. 2 covers related work, including the requirements proposed for such evaluation platforms; Sect. 3 describes how SAGE has met these requirements; Sect. 4 presents early results of using the framework, and Sect. 5 draws conclusions.

2   Related Work

To date, methods for evaluating general intelligence tend to either exclusively target humans, such as IQ tests, or to exclusively target very general ("human-level") intelligence—examples include Winograd's Schema Challenge [10], Lovelace Test 2.0 [15], and the Toy Box Problem [7]. Others are too domain-specific, e.g. general game-playing (cf. [17]), or highly dependent on knowledge of human social conventions or human experience and skills, e.g. Wozniak's Coffee Test and the Turing Test [13]. What is needed, as many have argued [1,4,6,19], is a flexible tool that allows construction of appropriate task-environments (TE), along with a proper task theory that enables comparison of a variety of tasks and environments. Thórisson et al. (2015) list eleven dimensions that ideally should be controllable by a creator of a task-environment for measuring intelligent behaviour [19]; Russell and Norvig (2016) present a somewhat comparable subset of seven dimensions [16]. The environment can be categorised along different dimensions, namely determinism (see [3] regarding the importance of noise control), staticism, observability, agency, knowledge, episodicity, and discreteness. TE properties include, in addition, ergodicity, asynchronicity, controllability, number of parallel causal chains, and periodicity [16,19].

Lately, evaluation methods have focused on (general) game playing using the ability to play games as an indicator for the systems sophistication. Using psychometric evaluation like item response theory (IRT) it was shown that the difference of performance score between different ML techniques does not necessarily correlate with the systems level of abilities [12]. Thus a simple performance rating like achieved game score cannot describe the progress of AI by itself [6]. By evaluating the ability to handle TE property changes over different learners a conclusion can be drawn on the abilities of the learner in regards to autonomous generality. Such conclusions should be accompanied by evaluation strategies like IRT to show the significance of the progress. By isolating and adjusting single parameters of the TE and testing on different learners it is furthermore possible to describe task difficulties in regards to the properties of the TE.

We have taken the evaluation of NMI and GMI further than current platforms by (a) providing the possibility to create tasks for NMI and GMI, (b) introducing changeable complexity dimensions in the generated task-environments, (c) making novelty introduction possible in any dimension (novel task, novel transitions, novel state observation, novel controllability), and (d) by making those changes during runtime without human interference in order to test the systems autonomy in coping with (b) and (c).

3 SAGE: Overview of Structure and Use

SAGE (Simulator for Autonomy & Generality Evaluation) is built to enable flexible construction of task-environments for evaluating artificial intelligence systems. One of its key requirements is that it can be used to evaluate both narrow AI systems and GMI-aspiring ones. It follows a tradition already laid out in prior work (cf. [4,18,19]) and is perhaps closest in spirit to Thorarensen's FraMoTEC [18]. In SAGE, assessing an AI system's ability to address novelty can be done by introducing new undefined variables, possibly with unknown transition functions, and unknown relations to other variables, either of which may or may not be similar to the behavior of priorly observed ones. The response of a learner to variable changes leads to conclusions about its ability to extract causal relations and its autonomy in exploiting them to achieve goals.

3.1 Requirements

The requirements for SAGE follow closely the eleven desired features listed by Thórisson et al. [19] that a task-environment platform for evaluating AI systems should contain. Any platform that meets these requirements should in theory be useful to evaluate not only GMI systems but in fact any learner.

While SAGE is still under development, it already meets all of those eleven requirements, in some way: *Determinism, dynamism, observability, episodicity,* and *discreteness* can be adjusted both beforehand and during the training/learning/evaluation processes, automatically without human intervention. *Stochasticity* can be adjusted in the observable variables, agent actions, and in environment dynamics, with *reproducibility* being supported through stored randomization seeds. Dynamism and episodicity can be changed by either runtime introduction of different tasks, or changing environmental variables. *Observability* and *manipulatability* of variables can be made at run-time, supporting *ergodicity*. Same goes for discreteness of observation and/or action, providing

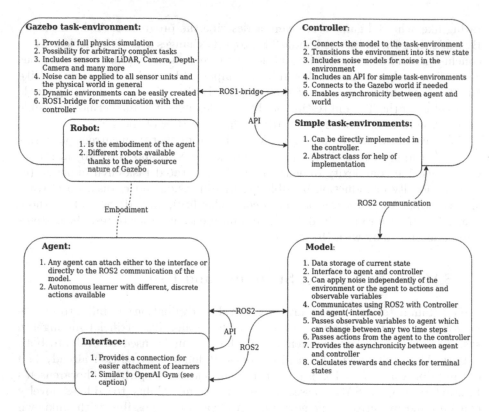

Fig. 1. Flowchart showing the main SAGE components and their interactions with each other, following the MVC paradigm, extending it with an *Agent* component that enables connecting one or more agents (similar interface as OpenAI Gym [5]). Visualization is via Gazebo [8] 3D rendering, using its standard API. In accordance with MVC, the Model node handles data storage, and includes an environment-independent noise generator for simulating stochasticity.

controllable continuity. These features make evaluation of the effects of sensor noise on learning, actuator impreciseness, and noise in hidden variables (e.g. wind forces) possible. *Causal chains* are constructed by chains of variable dependencies. Training on a variety of sensors before removing causally redundant ones may test a learner's capacity for knowledge generalization and extraction of causal relations. The same holds for modifying controllability with which a learner could exploit causal relations by applying previously unavailable actions to causally linked variables.

SAGE is implemented in ROS2 [14][1], which provides for a flexible framework that allows running a setup on multiple computers. Visualization of any parameters can be via Gazebo [8][2], as well as ROS2's internal rqt-graph function. All

---

[1] https://index.ros.org/doc/ros2/ – accessed Feb. 26th 2020.
[2] http://gazebosim.org/ – accessed Feb. 26th 2020.

adjustable parameters in SAGE are wrapped in YAML-files, making adjustments straight forward, by compiling before sessions or changes at run-time.

3.2   Architecture: Model-View-Controller-Agents (MVC-A)

The architecture of SAGE follows the model-view-controller paradigm, extending it with an agent component that allows one or more learners and teachers to connect dynamically to a task-environment. Each part of our MVC-A architecture is implemented as a ROS2-node [14], using ROS2 for platform-independent inter-process communication (see Fig. 1). The current task-environment state is stored in the Model node, including all observables, non-observables, manipulables, time, and energy. The Model exposes all observable variables via network communication to any attached Agent through an interface. The same interface receives actions chosen by the agent, processes them into manipulables, if needed, and passes them to the Model node. Noise and discretization can be applied to any data independently from the rest of the simulation. The Controller manages the simulation through a network connection.

Simple tasks can be easily added to the system as task modules, while the controller itself provides an interface to a Gazebo [8] simulation of a 3D world including a variety of robots, sensors, sensor-noise models, etc. ROS2 as middleware between Agent and evaluation platform makes the learners interface independent from the task-environment and therefore provides easy attachment of any learner to the evaluation platform. For communication, either an implemented Python module can be used or the agent can be directly attached to the ROS2 message system. The View is either provided by Gazebo itself or rqt-graphs via a standard network connection, but can be served by any external node that can make use of ROS's API. The connection to rqt-graph is also established using network communication enabling remote monitoring during evaluation.

The MVC-A approach provides a straightforward way to introduce more than one simultaneous learners in the simulation, as any number of agents can communicate with the world simultaneously through the model interface.

This approach brings many advantages. To name two, the logical separation of agent and environment makes evaluation of a learner's resource management possible, and by dividing Agent, Model and Controller into separate processes, real-time processing and asynchronous calculations can be added as needed. These features are especially important when GMIs are evaluated to fulfil the assumption of limited time and resources in the task environment [22].

4   Proof of Concept

As a proof of concept we tested three learners, an actor-critic (AC) [9], a double-deep-Q (DDQ) [21] learner, and Open-NARS for Applications (ONA)[3], on the

---

[3] https://github.com/opennars/OpenNARS-for-Applications – accessed May 10th 2020.

cart-pole task (cf. [5]). While this task is well known in the narrow-AI ML arena [11], few if any examples of how GMI-aspiring systems do on this task exist. The experience of attaching ONA to SAGE demonstrates the usefulness of many of SAGE's features. Figure 2 shows the performance of each leaner.

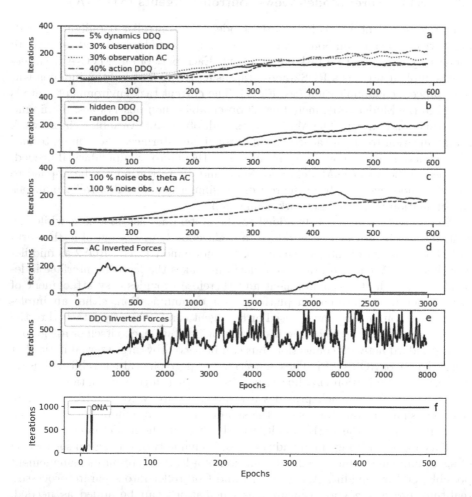

Fig. 2. Evaluation of an Actor-Critc (AC) and a Double-Deep-Q (DDQ) learner. All results are the average over 40 trials plotted with a running mean with window-size 10. **a:** Different applications of noise on the two learners. Noise on environment dynamics (3%), noise on the observation (30%), and noise on the actions (40%). Percentage in percent of the goal state ($\theta = \pm 12°$, $x = \pm 2.4$ m) or commonly occurring min and max values ($v = \pm 2.4$ m/s, $\omega = \pm 2.3°$/s) **b:** Test with velocity hidden from the agent and with velocity randomized ($\mu = v, \sigma = 24.00 \frac{m}{s}$. **c:** Noise only on single variables of the observation. Percentage definition as in **a**. **d:** Inverted forces after 500 episodes of training AC, 2000 episodes of retraining then inverting back. **e:** Inverted forces after 2000 episodes of training DDQ, 4000 episodes of retraining then inverting back. **f:** Performance of the ONA (OpenNARS for Applications - see footnote 3) is outstanding.

1. **Three different learners on a common task:** Although the cart-pole task has only a few parameters, and may seem too simplistic for GMI-aspiring learners, for the purpose of cross-learner comparison it is a reasonable one, in our opinion. The results were surprising on two accounts. Firstly, we were surprised that the DDQ learner did better than expected on a doubly-inverted version of it (testing for transfer learning by 180-degree reversal of the control dimension). Secondly, we were surprised by ONA's sensitivity to the format of the data (tuned by the discretization features in SAGE). In both cases the SAGE framework proved its value by allowing systematic modifications and testing automation.

2. **The influence of noise:** The first few graphs shows the differences in learning between environmental noise (noise on dynamics of the inverted-pendulum) and noise in the observations and actions received/given by the agent. Environmental noise simulates noise outside the agent, observation noise simulates sensor noise and action noise simulates actuator imprecision, respectively, for DDQ and AC. The results show that observation noise has less of an impact on performance than the dynamics, and noise on actions has no effect on learning performance at all.

3. **Coping with hidden random variables:** The DDQ-learners capability to cope with unreliable variables was tested by turning off one observable (velocity) or randomizing it with a standard deviation of 24 m/s (10x the usually occurring values). The data shows that an extremely randomized variable has a higher negative impact on learning, than hiding this variable completely resulting in the conclusion, that the DDQ learner cannot identify unreliable variables and exclude them from decision making.

4. **Influence of noise on a single variable:** To assess the importance of the correctness of the values of observables, noise was applied to a single variable. Results show, that against expectation the correctness of the velocity is of higher importance, than the correctness of the angle theta, even though velocity is not part of the failure constraint.

5. **Inversion/transfer learning:** As a test of the generality of their acquired knowledge, after training on the cart-pole we inverted the action direction (making left right and right left)—how would they adapt to a doubly-inverted pendulum task? The results show, that it takes almost four times as long as during the initial training to retrain the AC learner on the novel circumstances. Inverting it back after 2000 episodes of inverted training shows, that the original policy was mostly forgotten during re-training. The DDQ-learner on the other hand shows almost immediate return to previous performance, showing, that its generalization is better than that of the AC.

6. **Evaluating a GMI-aspring system:** We ran the GMI-aspiring ONA system to demonstrate SAGE's usefulness when comparing narrow and general AI systems. ONA learns the task faster than the others and handles transfer of learning much better.

These tests provide new insights into the methodologies of the three learners and current evaluation strategies. Modulation with noise of the observation and/or action variables assesses learning with noisy data; testing knowledge transfer via inversion, or hiding of variables, makes evaluating the generality and autonomy evaluation of the learners possible. When generalizing knowledge, any random variable should be excluded from future decision making to generate an expected behaviour. Further, the generality of a learner can be assessed by changing the task-environments nature. While it is expected that inverting the forces applicable by the learner leads to an immediate performance loss, the time it takes to learn this new task (4 times the training time) in the narrow-AI systems shows that cause-effect-chains were not extracted; rather, a simple state-to-action mapping took place. The GMI-aspiring system ONA clearly outperforms the others; we are excited to see future results with varying levels of noise and inverted forces. Given the results in Fig. 2 one also wonders how a human would compare, something that could be tested via visualization via Gazebo and keyboard or mouse input; other things staying exactly the same in this setup of SAGE.

5 Conclusions and Future Work

SAGE shows potential for evaluating AI architectures that follow various methodologies, bridging the gap between general and narrow AI. Our own interest in SAGE is the need to assess the progress of AI research towards general machine intelligence (GMI), however, as the examples presented here show, other uses are entirely justified. First evaluation results demonstrate some of the possibilities of this platform. A comparison of GMI-aspiring systems to narrow-AI ones not only helps highlight differences in performance and the nature of the learning of such systems, it also helps isolate their points of divergence related to deeper methodological issues, background assumptions and theoretical underpinnings.

The performance results from the learners presented here are preliminary; a future publication will present extensive tests and discuss the differences between the learners, all using SAGE of course. Future work will also include evaluating a more extensive set of learners, improve the automatic running of sets of training and evaluation sessions, and implement a library of tasks. Then we plan on making the source code available online.

Acknowledgements. The authors would like to thank Hjörleifur Henriksson for help with computer setup and data collection, and Patrick Hammer for help with ONA. This work was in part supported by grants from Reykjavik University, the Icelandic Institute for Intelligent Machines and Cisco Systems, Inc.

References

1. Adams, S., et al.: Mapping the landscape of human-level artificial general intelligence. AI Mag. **33**(1), 25–42 (2012)

2. Bellemare, M.G., Naddaf, Y., Veness, J., Bowling, M.: The arcade learning environment: an evaluation platform for general agents. J. Artif. Intell. Res. **47**, 253–279 (2013)
3. Bellemare, M.G., Naddaf, Y., Veness, J., Bowling, M.: SAGE: task-environment platform for evaluating a broad range of AI learners. In: Proceedings of the International Joint Conference on Artificial Intelligence (IJCAI), pp. 4148–4152 (2015)
4. Bieger, J., Thórisson, K.R., Steunebrink, B.R., Thorarensen, T., Sigurdardóttir, J.S.: Evaluation of general-purpose artificial intelligence: why, what & how. In: EGPAI 2016 - Evaluating General-Purpose A.I., Workshop Held in Conjuction with the European Conference on Artificial Intelligence (2016)
5. Brockman, G., et al.: OpenAI Gym. ArXiv preprint ArXiv:1606.01540 (2016)
6. Hernández-Orallo, J., et al.: A new AI evaluation cosmos: ready to play the game? AI Mag. **38**(3), 66–69 (2017)
7. Johnston, B.: The toy box problem (and a preliminary solution). In: Conference on Artificial General Intelligence. Atlantis Press (2010)
8. Koenig, N., Howard, A.: Design and use paradigms for gazebo, an open-source multi-robot simulator. In: 2004 IEEE/RSJ International Conference on Intelligent Robots and Systems (IROS) (IEEE Cat. No. 04CH37566), vol. 3, pp. 2149–2154. IEEE (2004)
9. Konda, V.R., Tsitsiklis, J.N.: Actor-critic algorithms. In: Advances in Neural Information Processing Systems, pp. 1008–1014 (2000)
10. Levesque, H., Davis, E., Morgenstern, L.: The winograd schema challenge. In: Thirteenth International Conference on the Principles of Knowledge Representation and Reasoning (2012)
11. Li, Y.: Deep reinforcement learning: an overview. ArXiv preprint ArXiv:1701.07274 (2017)
12. Martınez-Plumed, F., Hernández-Orallo, J.: AI results for the atari 2600 games: difficulty and discrimination using IRT. In: EGPAI, Workshop on Evaluating General-Purpose Artificial Intelligence, vol. 33 (2016)
13. Oppy, G., Dowe, D.: The turing test. In: Stanford Encyclopedia of Philosophy, pp. 519–539 (2003)
14. Quigley, M., et al.: ROS: an open-source Robot Operating System. In: ICRA Workshop on Open Source Software, Kobe, Japan, vol. 3, p. 5 (2009)
15. Riedl, M.O.: The Lovelace 2.0 test of artificial creativity and intelligence. ArXiv preprint ArXiv:1410.6142 (2014)
16. Russell, S.J., Norvig, P.: Artificial Intelligence: A Modern Approach. Pearson Education Limited, London (2016)
17. Świechowski, M., Park, H., Mańdziuk, J., Kim, K.J.: Recent advances in general game playing. Sci. World J. **2015**, 22 (2015)
18. Thorarensen, T.: FraMoTEC: A framework for modular task-environment construction for evaluating adaptive control systems. M.Sc. thesis, Department of Computer Science, Reykjavik University (2016)
19. Thórisson, K.R., Bieger, J., Schiffel, S., Garrett, D.: Towards flexible task environments for comprehensive evaluation of artificial intelligent systems and automatic learners. In: Bieger, J., Goertzel, B., Potapov, A. (eds.) AGI 2015. LNCS (LNAI), vol. 9205, pp. 187–196. Springer, Cham (2015). https://doi.org/10.1007/978-3-319-21365-1_20
20. Thórisson, K.R., Bieger, J., Thorarensen, T., Sigurðardóttir, J.S., Steunebrink, B.R.: Why artificial intelligence needs a task theory. In: Steunebrink, B., Wang, P., Goertzel, B. (eds.) AGI -2016. LNCS (LNAI), vol. 9782, pp. 118–128. Springer, Cham (2016). https://doi.org/10.1007/978-3-319-41649-6_12

21. Van Hasselt, H., Guez, A., Silver, D.: Deep reinforcement learning with double Q-learning. In: Thirtieth AAAI Conference on Artificial Intelligence (2016)
22. Wang, P.: Rigid Flexibility: The Logic of Intelligence. Springer, Dordrecht (2006). https://doi.org/10.1007/1-4020-5045-3

Post-turing Methodology: Breaking the Wall on the Way to Artificial General Intelligence

Albert Efimov[1,2,3](✉) [iD]

[1] Sberbank Robotics Laboratory, Moscow, Russian Federation
makkawity@gmail.com
[2] Institute of Philosophy, Russian Academy of Sciences, Moscow, Russian Federation
[3] National Research Technology University "MISiS", Moscow, Russian Federation

Abstract. This article offers comprehensive criticism of the Turing test and develops quality criteria for new artificial general intelligence (AGI) assessment tests. It is shown that the prerequisites A. Turing drew upon when reducing personality and human consciousness to "suitable branches of thought" reflected the engineering level of his time. In fact, the Turing "imitation game" employed only symbolic communication and ignored the physical world. This paper suggests that by restricting thinking ability to symbolic systems alone Turing unknowingly constructed "the wall" that excludes any possibility of transition from a complex observable phenomenon to an abstract image or concept. It is, therefore, sensible to factor in new requirements for AI (artificial intelligence) maturity assessment when approaching the Turing test. Such AI must support all forms of communication with a human being, and it should be able to comprehend abstract images and specify concepts as well as participate in social practices.

Keywords: Artificial intelligence · Philosophy of artificial intelligence · Philosophy of mind

1 Introduction. Turing Methodology for Assessment of Artificial Intelligence (1950–2014)

Alan Turing, a British mathematician, laid in his works (1937–1952) a foundation for the research into what we now call "artificial intelligence" (AI) or "artificial general intelligence" (AGI). Relying on the new theory of computability and information, on the one hand, and on the first machines engineered for universal computing, on the other, Turing directly approached the difficult question, "Can machines think?". Certainly, he could not create a model that would completely describe human reasoning or even the work of the brain as a basis for thinking. There was an obvious lack of neurobiological data at that time. Therefore, he simplified the model by reducing it to a machine resembling a communicating person with "suitable branches of thought" as A. Turing put it [3].

This simplification became the basis for A. Turing's thesis about isomorphic features between thinking and computing: "If we consider the result of the work of calculators (that is people employed for computing) as intellectual, then why cannot we

© Springer Nature Switzerland AG 2020
B. Goertzel et al. (Eds.): AGI 2020, LNAI 12177, pp. 83–94, 2020.
https://doi.org/10.1007/978-3-030-52152-3_9

make a similar assumption regarding machines that perform these operations faster than people?" [1].

In this work Turing was also the first one to analyze the role of "embodied intelligence". He believed that a certain creature equipped with microphones, television cameras and loudspeakers could be taught to walk while balancing its limbs and being equipped with a telecontrolled brain. Turing believed that if they had created such a "monster" based on the technologies available at the time, it would have been "certainly enormous" and would have posed a serious threat to the inhabitants. Thus, having recognized the ability to imitate humans as "embodied intelligence", Turing pointed out that "the creature would still have no access to food, sex, sport and many other simple human joys" [1]. As envisioned by Turing, future researchers had to focus on imitating human intelligence in the following five areas: (1) various games, such as chess, tic-tac-toe, poker, bridge; (2) learning languages; (3) translations from one language into another; (4) cryptography; (5) mathematics.

Of these five areas, Turing believed (4) was the most practically useful for AI [1]. Pointing out these exact areas of research has affected the entire subsequent course of AI development up until now; relatively homogeneous tasks, partially solved by Von Neumann's architecture computers, made it possible to obtain new results by simply speeding up computational capabilities. A certain developmental inertia emerged when enormous efforts were devoted to solving a very narrow range of tasks. Human thinking and society, however, deal with a much wider range of "puzzles". As a result, available software AI systems are used in various fields of application but still cannot be safely and applied in the real world for general cases. This builds up unfounded expectation from AI as we want general intelligence from systems which are not designed for the real world.

In his most frequently cited work Turing suggested playing an "imitation game", which, in essence, was an engineering solution to the problem of answering the question "Can a machine think?". Instead of working on definitions of what "machine intelligence" or human intelligence is, Turing proposed a "blind" comparison of a man's key intellectual ability – reasoning and lying – with the actions of a computer. The imitation game became the foundation of the Turing methodology for constructing AGI. In this paper, drawing on the original work by Turing and applying the descriptive methodology proposed by A. Alekseev in [2], we will briefly look into the scheme proposed by Turing.

Having set the directions of the research (languages, translations, games, cryptography and mathematics) in his previous works, in 1950 [3] A. Turing proposed a methodology for determining the achievement of the final result. Only in the mid-1970s this methodology came to be called the Turing test, although essentially it remained the methodology for determining the achievement of the final result (definition-of-done) in the AI research program.

AI researchers and philosophers have been developing various methodologies that could become foundations for a more advanced methodology than that of the Turing test. Unfortunately, in the pursuit of designing more adequate tests, the researchers have been overlooking some important details in the methodology proposed by Turing. This paper attempts to address this shortcoming.

2 Methodology for the Critical Analysis of the Turing Test

After the introduction it seems necessary to indicate the main methodological difficulties in the modern assessment of the Turing test:

a) The test has grown so popular that it pushes many researchers towards a simplified version: "within 5 minutes of a telephone talk you must understand whether you are talking to a machine or a person";
b) any scientific research requires simple and transparent testing, yet a reliable assessment of human consciousness and intelligence is still under debate. Nevertheless, all engineering products tend to be tested, and since "AI" is most often presented in the form of software products, the test boils down to communication with the software. This has formed the perceptive inertia for "intelligent machines".

If we turn to the Turing's methodology proper, it is necessary to pay attention to the following three aspects that are important for our subsequent considerations.

Firstly, all the five areas of research originally proposed by Turing (like chess) are more suitable than others (like gymnastics) to the symbolic approach as we communicate them through symbols to one another and subsequently to machines.

The evolution of digital computers over the last seven decades since Turing original proposal has greatly expanded the scope of their application, but it did not change the approach which still relies on the primitive Turing machines working with symbolic systems. It is the speed of symbolic processing that has changed. As D. Dennett put it, "All the improvements in computers since Turing invented his imaginary paper-tape machines are simply ways of making them faster" [4].

Secondly, the Turing methodology always implies a wall separating the two key participants. All subsequent modifications of the Turing methodology that arose after 1952 implied a comparison by a Judge (J) of the activities by a Human (H) and a Computer (C), but their activities were always separated by an impenetrable wall. J was the only one who interacted with C or H through the "Turing Wall" which was transparent only to symbolic communication. But H and C did not communicate at all and did not solve any problems together.

Thirdly, Turing believed that the problem was "mainly that of programming", and he did not consider the need to accelerate the operating speed of digital computers in order to solve the problem of the "imitation game". In other words, Turing saw the task of creating AI as designing a system of abstractions that could recognize and take into account all the nuances of human communication. Turing was fully aware of the problem of a multi-level symbolic game, noting that an interlocutor's task lies in the most complicated field, noting that it "seems however to depend rather too much on sense organs and locomotion to be feasible" [1]. Unfortunately, this remark was largely overlooked by the subsequent generations of researchers, who considered linguistic behavior and the ability to play games to be enough of an intelligence indicator and took for granted the study of imitating the reasoning of a person or of the ability to play games. Here, we can see the emergence of a paradox: on the one hand, these three aspects of the methodology proposed by A. Turing constituted the cornerstone of all research between 1950–2014 aimed at implementation of "artificial intelligence"; on the other hand, this methodology was insufficient to solve a whole set of problems that "natural intelligence" solves. Thus, it seems, the Turing test should not be chosen as a reliable criterion for creating "artificial intelligence". All the five Turing's areas of research require solving calculation tasks, whereas human intelligence is not limited to information processing, but also includes formulation of new concepts and finding certain patterns of objects through observation (without necessarily fixating all the rest).

Nevertheless, the Turing methodology has become the basis for a huge family of various AI tests. It is similar to the mechanistic materialism of the 18th century: initially limited, it, nevertheless, made it possible to solve a whole class of specific problems [3].

The object of this article is to make a step forward from the Turing test as a criterion for creating a mature AI. It is necessary to show the fundamental limitations of the Turing methodology and develop an approach to assessing the tests created for situations that are not supposed to pass the Turing test.

The subject of the article is to reject the consciousness modelling paradigm that was based on the use of symbolic systems alone, as well as to reject the contradiction of new approaches in AI assessment with the neopositivist foundations of the Turing test.

Our criterion comes down to a more complete assessment of a personality and agency of an individual.

3   The Continuum of Turing-Like Tests and Its Limitations

Almost seventy years have passed since Turing expressed his revolutionary philosophical ideas about the possibility of creating "thinking machines" in his fundamental work published in the journal Mind [3]. Several generations of mathematicians, philosophers and researchers of AI have devoted multiple articles to his mental experiments. As a result, a whole set of Turing-like tests have been designed. However, if one carefully considers this set of mental experiments and engineering solutions aimed at determining the definition-of-done approach to AI (summarized in Alekseev's work [3]), one can identify two axes that are orthogonal to each other, and we call them the dimensions of the "Turing-like testing continuum". All tests are grouped around them.

3.1   From Verbal to Non-verbal

Verbal interaction with AI involves the exchange of meaningful information messages, abstractions and images in a specific linguistic context. The meaning of the messages is set precisely by their verbal semantics. These messages can refer to everyday life ("What day is it today?") or bear imaginative content ("What if the universe were closed?").

Non-verbal (one might say, non-linguistic) interaction with AI involves the exchange of information messages without using a language. This may include facial expressions, gestures, movements, motor skills and even emotions that are expressed in specific actions (laughter, crying, sadness, suffering).

3.2   From Virtual to Physical

Virtual interaction with AI happens exclusively via computer interfaces available to us, including traditional (and becoming outdated) hardware such as monitor displays, keyboards, augmented/virtual reality devices and even exciting brain-computer interfaces.

Physical interaction with AI (although the word "robot" can be used in this context meaning an "actuated computer with AI") occurs in the physical world and involves its active transformation by AI itself. It requires a specific ability to affect other physical objects. A robot operating in the kitchen can wash the dishes, an unmanned autonomous motorcar drives us from point A to point B. All these actions necessarily occur in the physical world.

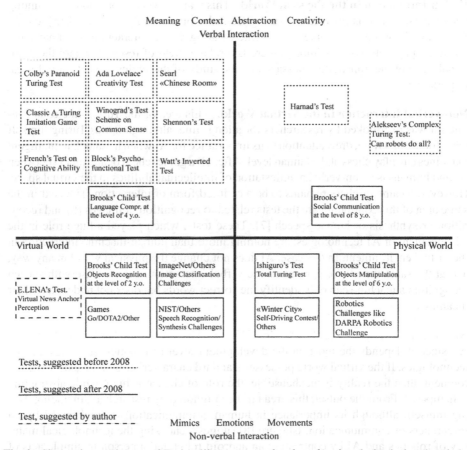

Fig. 1. Shows the continuum of Turing-like tests correlated on the virtual-physical and verbal-nonverbal axes

3.3   Four Areas for AGI Development

The two dimensions described above have given us four areas. Let us consider the four areas of this continuum as shown in Fig. 1 in more detail.

Verbal Interaction in the Virtual World. For historical reasons, most of the tests (mental experiments) developed before 2008 fall into this area. In fact, the classic Turing test, Lady Lovelace's creativity test, Colby's paranoid test, Shannon's social test, Watt's test (Turing's inverted test), Searle's Chinese room experiment, and Block's psycho-functional test are focused on testing verbal abilities in human/AI interaction. In this case, a person interacts with the virtual world environment (a display, a keyboard, a mouse).

Verbal Interaction in the Physical World. This area was not popular among researchers, as it was rejected by Turing from the outset. Only S. Harnad [5] and A. Alekseev [2] proposed complex tests demonstrating verbal interaction of humans and AI in the physical world. Although there is a related field of research where the emotional trace of the transmitted message and the study of its subtlest aspects are of great importance.

Non-verbal Interaction in the Virtual World. This area of the Turing-like tests continuum was overlooked by researchers for a long time, although it was Turing himself who, for the first time, drew attention to its importance for AI when he said that intelligent machines can play chess at the human level. After all a game (chess or any other) between AI and humans is a non-verbal manifestation of intellectual abilities in the virtual space. However, a game of chess remains to be a codified form of interaction. The next in the same area of this continuum are the tests related to recognition of images [6] and recognition or synthesis of human speech [7]. These tests, which played a huge role in the advancement of AI technologies, are nothing more than human-machine interaction in the virtual environment. In this case, AI does not change the physical world in any way, and at the same time there is no semantic verbal interaction; even in case with speech recognition a machine can only identify the correct words but does not understand their meanings.

Non-verbal Interaction in the Physical World. This area is the hardest to master for AI, since it depends the most on the development level of robotics, sensorics and AI technologies. If the virtual world possesses standard characteristics of the external environment, then the reality is inexhaustible, the role of chance is high, while abstracting is hampered. From the outset, this area has been ignored by researchers, including Turing himself, although its importance in human communication is emphasized by all researchers of communication. Ishiguro [8] suggests checking the technological maturity of robotics and AI by contrasting an android robot and a person in simple acts of communication: the robot only says the pre-programmed human phrases, even though bearing the maximum resemblance to a person. Another example of a test where AI and robots performed the tasks that people would generally do was the large-scale DARPA Robotics Challenge held in 2015. At this competition robots interacted with the physical world eliminating the consequences of a nuclear disaster at the training ground, although there was no verbal communication with the people. The latest example of this is numerous driving contests where robots compete with humans in speed, accuracy and safety [9].

In 2018, R. Brooks [10] suggested a number of new tests for AGI. He proposed to see child capabilities as an indicator of technological achievement in AGI and robotics, drifting away from the Turing "conversational" paradigm of AGI and people communicating through walls. He called it "a competency-based" approach: (1) robots should be taught to recognize any objects in the physical world at least at the level of a two-year-old child; (2) robots should be taught to recognize natural language at least at the level of a four-year-old child; (3) robots should possess manual dexterity and fine motor skills of at least a six-year-old child; (4) robots should have social communication skills of at least an eight-year-old child.

With these requirements in view, the Brooks' test is divided into four parts (1–4) and is placed sequentially in all the areas of the Turing-like test continuum in Fig. 1.

E.LENA Test. In 2019, a specialized platform was developed at Sberbank Robotics Laboratory in order to convert text into a video image of a television presenter. The platform is called E.LENA (*Electronic* Lena) [11]. The idea of assigning visual forms to AI first became popular in science fiction. Yet, researchers did not embrace AI visualization as an object of study, since the appropriate technology has not existed up until now. We are the first to propose a perception test for identification of a digital television announcer by comparing it to a human announcer. This approach helps researchers to embrace a twofold improvement of AI technology – while testing is being done on the verbal interaction in the virtual world, it is simultaneously conducted in the non-verbal-virtual world.

We need to emphasize the two observations from above. Firstly, the majority of tests invented by the researchers, starting with A. Turing, implied performance in one specific area, which, according to the researchers, was best suited to the task of creating AGI. Setting tests' goals for engineering research by designing 'definition of done' for AGI (the best performance of certain robots or AGI in one of the four particular areas) defined their approach to designing programs, computers architectures and robots. Researchers and engineers build machines that perform at their best only in one specific area (like verbal interaction in the virtual world): the technology and computer architecture used for a chat-bot that excels in deceiving humans are utterly useless for a self-driving application. Various AGI/AI systems are designed and evolve only within their enclosed areas separated by the Turing walls from other areas of application.

Secondly, the Turing wall separating the subject of the test (a human judge) from the test object (a computer, a robot) only continued to solidify. Researchers could not even think of a computer/robot meeting face-to-face and interacting with each other (a typical estimate of the timing of an AI creation considers the time-out of this event, but not the specifics of programming or computer architecture [12, 13]). A computer or a robot compete with a human in each of these areas. If AI is doing better than a tested human, then we have arrived to our goal.

To sum up, each of the tests from the past seventy years has only strengthened the Turing wall, which separated the area of verbal-virtual communication between a machine and a person from the huge and incredibly unpredictable world beyond this wall. This leads to a situation where human knowledge and experience mastered by AI in one area (non-verbal in the virtual world) cannot be transferred to another area (non-verbal in the physical world) because they are ultimately separated by 'the Turing wall'. By original design, our AI systems do not have the capability to learn and act in more than one of the areas from Fig. 1. All these concerns are the deficiencies of the Turing methodology.

4 Empirical Identification of Inadequacy of the Turing Test

Over the past ten years two important trends have shattered the Turing wall so much that it gave a deep crack and is about to collapse.

The first trend became obvious in the summer of 2014, when the Royal Society in London carried out the "Turing test" competition. The winner was a chatbot named Eugene Goostman that imitated the identity of a thirteen-year-old boy from Odessa. This chatbot fooled over 30% of the judges.

This Turing-inspired test invoked much criticism. The main point of it was that despite overcoming the symbolic barrier in deceiving people no significant breakthrough occurred either in research or in applied technologies: chatbots still remained quite limited in their capabilities, so declaring that they understand a person is possible only in a figurative sense. According to the cognitive scientist G. Marcus, this test did not show that one can consider AI as created, but merely revealed "the ease with which we can fool others" [14], thus reducing the Turing test to a psychological measure of human narcissism, rather than of AI development. Chatbots can go off topic embarrassing the interlocutor and thereby giving themselves away. The philosopher A. Sloman speaks about the irrelevance of the Turing test method as a behavioristic approach to assessing the intelligence of any system, as well as to assessing the solvability of any true problem [15].

In other words, chatbots outplay humans when dealing exclusively with abstractions, but the concretization of the gain and its correlation with reality is only possible with human intervention. Chess programs or chatbots have been beating humans in purely symbolic competitions for several years now. But they do not become full-fledged agents, and they cannot adapt the skills they acquired to other tasks like driving.

The second trend relies on the popular approach based on "brute force" and "greedy" (for data) neural networks but it will not help to answer the original question "Can a machine think?". Let's conduct a mental experiment which we might call an "ultimate imitation game". Suppose that we have limitless computing power and our neural network architecture is capable of processing texts without human supervisors (this condition does not alter the results but makes the experiment longer). Then, imagine that we have managed to recruit (for a short time) volunteers to imitate all men and women of the Earth and have divided them into two groups. The first group will consist of an equal number of men and women, and the second group will consist of men or women acting as judges (the gender does not matter here). If we assume that the number of adult inhabitants of the Earth is 6 billion, then there will be exactly 4 billion people in the first group (equally men and women) and 2 billion people in the group of judges. After that both groups begin playing the classic imitation game and record all their dialogues and results with the judges. Now, let's suppose that we have all the computing power for an unsupervised deep learning neural network which enables us to train a neural network to answer any conceivable question based on the previous imitation games. It seems likely that if such a computer starts a game in tandem with a woman and claims to be a woman (as described above, following A. Turing), the judge will most likely be unable to distinguish the computer from a woman, and the judge will be equally likely able to identify the AI or the person in this game. Will this mean that the Turing's criteria are observed, and the true General AI is achieved? It does not seem so, since Turing said that a computer should imitate the reasoning of a man who is pretending to be a woman. In this mental experiment the computer is literally reproducing some of the most successful phrases of men who managed to fool the judges and won the game. However, this computer is uncapable of acquiring any "reasoning" faculty. It only demonstrates the ability to quickly find a relevant phrase based on the training set. As a result, this mental experiment supplies us with a dialogue interface capable of skillful imitation, but the computer interface is completely devoid of intelligence.

It seems that this conclusion of the mental experiment is the main reason why the approach based on the Turing method (the Turing test) ceases to be relevant and should give way to another approach based on a post-Turing methodology.

5 Post-turing Methodology Principles for the Study of AI

It seems quite logical to establish a new methodology for assessing the achievements in AI by taking into account both the experience of the last seventy years and the newer technological capabilities. In fact, the first attempts were made right after the 2014 Turing test competition in London [16–22]. However, they are all lacking a practical implementation across the entire Turing continuum, outlined in Fig. 1.

Firstly, in our concept of an intelligent computer we should reject anthropomorphism. The wall constructed by Turing is bound to separate the J and the tested H or C and essentially stimulates a person to evaluate AI in contrast to oneself, creating excessive technological anthropomorphism. However, man has learned how to fly by using the technologies that were totally different from the bird wings. Creating AI capable of reasoning and communicating like a person is probably not the most potent answer to the Turing's question, "Can machines think?". It is counterproductive to discuss the ethical limitations of precisely humanoid robots [23]. If we evaluate the design of modern robots, then the simplest question – "How many fingers should a manipulator hand have?" – can generate multiple answers, and the two-finger solution becomes a widespread type of "hand" [24].

Secondly, we can talk about a variety of forms and methods of cognition available to computers. AI should use abstraction and concretization on a broad scale. Here, the ideal is an independent formulation of new concepts and modeling of its own worldview – of course, with restrictions considering human safety. Now numerous attempts are being made not only to improve recognition of images but also, on the basis of I. Lakatos' theory of games and concepts, to compile a conceptual apparatus for a more flexible interaction of computers and mathematicians [25].

Thirdly, there should be a diversity of the same forms of communication that are available to humans. Machines have widely mastered computerized communication in symbolic structures, while robots' motor skills remain imperfect. *Virtual-non-verbal, physical-non-verbal* and *physical-verbal interactions* are still hampered. Probably, the ideal that machines should strive for is an emotionally colored communication involving "the five senses", so that a robot could convey information in any set of sensations available to humans. Here, a good example would be an automated translation from the sign language of the deaf to the test and vice versa. For now, we can only see it on the displays, but it should soon become accessible to robot operators.

Fourthly, a robot should participate in human social practices as a junior partner, but nonetheless possessing an agency. R. Brooks in his tests compared AI with the levels of child development – yet still what could be a better assessment criterion for communication skills than life in society? After all, child development is inseparable from socialization.

As to the Turing-like tests continuum in Fig. 1, we should advise other researchers and engineers to design and develop AI (be it robots or AI-enabled computers) capable of attaining to the human expertise and acting similarly to humans in more than one area. This approach breaks the walls between the areas and makes AI more useful and robust for real life applications as well as useful for human-to-machine interactions. Moreover, the post-Turing methodology requires no blind comparison of a human and machine performance (like in the Turing test) but demands a higher overall performance from a human and a machine learning and acting together.

6 Conclusion

The Turing test has virtually lost its relevance and meaning as even computer software falling short of being called AGI in the full sense of the word can pass such tests in systems of symbolic communication. Moreover, applications can practice abstraction only in minimal forms, which puts a limitation on their cognitive abilities.

Overcoming anthropomorphism and the Turing approach to assessing AGI will allow us to focus on creating the systems that can demonstrate various skills in the four main areas: shaping the system for labor operations; proper formulation of new concepts (abstracting) and their use (concretization); communication with a person involving all the five senses; and, finally, possessing a personal social agency.

The suggested post-Turing methodology might be a good foundation for the future research and engineering efforts because it does not oppose a human to a machine but makes a human and a machine act together in various areas of their interaction irrespective of either the physical or the virtual worlds. Such approach will provide more safety and security for the humankind as the advent of artificial general intelligence is inevitable.

References

1. Turing, A.: Intelligent machinery (1948). In: Alan Turing: His Work and Impact, pp. 501–516. Elsevier (2013)
2. Alekseev, A.: Kompleksnyj test T'juringa: filosofsko-metodologicheskie i socio-kul'turnye aspekty [Turing Comprehensive Test: Philosophical, Methodological and Socio-Cultural Aspects]. IInteLL, Moscow (2013). (in Russian)
3. Turing, A.: Computing machinery and intelligence. Mind **59**, 433–460 (1950)
4. Dennett, D.: Intuition Pumps and Other Tools for Thinking, 1st edn. W.W. Norton, New York (2013)
5. Harnad, S.: Minds, machines and Turing: the indistinguishability of indistinguishables. J. Logic Lang. Inf. **9**(4), 425–445 (2000)
6. Stanford Vision Lab ImageNet. http://www.image-net.org. Accessed 28 Sept 2019
7. NIST 2019 Speaker Recognition Evaluation. https://www.nist.gov/itl/iad/mig/nist-2019-spe aker-recognition-evaluation. Accessed 02 May 2020
8. Ishiguro, H.: Toward a new cross-interdisciplinary framework. In: Thrun, S., Brooks, R., Durrant-Whyte, H. (eds.) Robotics Research. STAR, vol. 28, pp. 118–127. Springer, Berlin (2007). https://doi.org/10.1007/978-3-540-48113-3_11
9. Efimov, A.R.: Tehnologicheskie konkursy adresovany ne startapam, a konsorciumam [Technology contests are addressed not to startups, but to consortia]. https://sk.ru/news/b/articles/archive/2017/08/03/albert-efimov-tehnologicheskie-konkursy-adresovany-ne-startapam-a-konsorciumam.aspx. Accessed 28 Sept 2019. (in Russian)
10. Rodney Brooks' Homepage: Steps Toward Super Intelligence IV, Things to Work on Now. https://rodneybrooks.com/forai-steps-toward-super-intelligence-iv-things-to-work-on-now. Accessed 02 May 2020
11. Efimov, A.R.: Tekhnologicheskie predposylki nerazlichimosti cheloveka i ego komp'yuternoj imitacii [Technological background of the indistinguishability of man and his computer simulation]. Artif. Soc. **14**(4) (2019). https://doi.org/10.18254/s207751800007645-8. https://art soc.jes.su/S207751800007645-8-1
12. Müller, Vincent C., Bostrom, N.: Future progress in artificial intelligence: a survey of expert opinion. In: Müller, V.C. (ed.) Fundamental Issues of Artificial Intelligence. SL, vol. 376, pp. 553–570. Springer, Cham (2016). https://doi.org/10.1007/978-3-319-26485-1_33
13. Baum, S., Goertzel, B., Goertzel, G.: How long until human-level AI? Results from an expert assessment. Technol. Forecast. Soc. Change **78**(1), 185–195 (2011)
14. Marcus, G.: What comes after Turing test? New Yorker. https://www.newyorker.com/tech/annals-of-technology/what-comes-after-the-turing-test. Accessed 02 May 2020
15. Sloman, A.: Judging chatbots at Turing test 2014. University of Birmingham, School of Computer Science. http://www.cs.bham.ac.uk/research/projects/cogaff/misc/turing-test-2014.pdf
16. Marcus, G., Rossi, F., Veloso, M.: Beyond the Turing test. AI Mag. **37**(1), 3–4 (2016)
17. Clark, P., Etzioni, O.: My computer is an honor student — but how intelligent is it? Standardized tests as a measure of AI. AI Mag. **37**(1), 5–12 (2016)
18. Adams, S.S., Banavar, G., Campbell, M.: I-athlon: toward a multidimensional Turing test. AI Mag. **37**(1), 78–84 (2016)
19. Zitnick, C.L., Agrawal, A., Antol, S., Mitchell, M., Batra, D., Parikh, D.: Measuring machine intelligence through visual question answering. AI Mag. **37**(1), 63–72 (2016)
20. Morgenstern, L., Davis, E., Ortiz, C.: Planning, executing, and evaluating the winograd schema challenge. AI Mag. **37**(1), 50–54 (2016)
21. Kitano, H.: Artificial intelligence to win the Nobel prize and beyond: creating the engine for scientific discovery. AI Mag. **37**(1), 39–49 (2016)

22. Jarrold, W., Yeh, P.Z.: The social-emotional Turing challenge. AI Mag. **37**(1), 31–38 (2016)
23. Chakraborty, S.: Can humanoid robots be moral? Ethics Sci. Environ. Politics **18**, 49–60 (2018)
24. Birglen, L., Schlicht, T.: A statistical review of industrial robotic grippers. Robot. Comput.-Integr. Manuf. **49**, 88–97 (2018)
25. Pease, A., Lawrence, J., Budzynska, K., Corneli, J., Reed, C.: Lakatos-style collaborative mathematics through dialectical, structured and abstract argumentation. Artif. Intell. **246**, 181–219 (2017)

Self-explaining AI as an Alternative to Interpretable AI

Daniel C. Elton[✉][iD]

Radiology and Imaging Sciences,
National Institutes of Health Clinical Center,
Bethesda, MD 20892, USA
daniel.elton@nih.gov

Abstract. The ability to explain decisions made by AI systems is highly sought after, especially in domains where human lives are at stake such as medicine or autonomous vehicles. While it is often possible to approximate the input-output relations of deep neural networks with a few human-understandable rules, the discovery of the double descent phenomena suggests that such approximations do not accurately capture the mechanism by which deep neural networks work. Double descent indicates that deep neural networks typically operate by smoothly interpolating between data points rather than by extracting a few high level rules. As a result, neural networks trained on complex real world data are inherently hard to interpret and prone to failure if asked to extrapolate. To show how we might be able to trust AI despite these problems we introduce the concept of self-explaining AI. Self-explaining AIs are capable of providing a human-understandable explanation of each decision along with confidence levels for both the decision and explanation. Some difficulties with this approach along with possible solutions are sketched. Finally, we argue it is important that deep learning based systems include a "warning light" based on techniques from applicability domain analysis to warn the user if a model is asked to extrapolate outside its training distribution.

Keywords: Interpretability · Explainability · Explainable artificial intelligence · XAI · Trust · Deep learning

1 Introduction

There is growing interest in developing methods to explain deep neural network function, especially in high risk areas such as medicine and driverless cars. Such explanations would be useful to ensure that deep neural networks follow known rules and when troubleshooting failures. Despite the development of numerous techniques for interpreting deep neural networks, all such techniques have flaws, and there is confusion regarding how to properly "interpret an interpretation" [31,39]. Perhaps more troubling, though, is that a new understanding is emerging that deep neural networks function through the interpolation of data

© Springer Nature Switzerland AG 2020
B. Goertzel et al. (Eds.): AGI 2020, LNAI 12177, pp. 95–106, 2020.
https://doi.org/10.1007/978-3-030-52152-3_10

points, rather than extrapolation [24]. This calls into question long-held narratives about deep neural networks "extracting" high level features and rules, and also indicates that all current methods of explanation do not capture failure modes that occur from extrapolation.

In response to difficulties raised by explaining black box models, Rudin argues for developing better interpretable models instead, arguing that the "interpretability-accuracy" trade-off is a myth. While it is true that the notion of such a trade-off is not rigorously grounded, empirically in many domains the state-of-the art systems are all deep neural networks. For instance, most state-of-art AI systems for computer vision are not interpretable in the sense required by Rudin. Even highly distilled and/or compressed models which achieve good performance on ImageNet require at least 100,000 free parameters [29]. Moreover, the human brain also appears to be an overfit "black box" which performs interpolation, which means that how we understand brain function also needs to change [24]. If evolution settled on a model (the brain) which is uninterpretable, then we expect advanced AIs to also be of that type. Interestingly, although the human brain is a "black box", we are able to trust each other. Part of this trust comes from our ability to "explain" our decision making in terms which make sense to us. Crucially, for trust to occur we must believe that a person is not being deliberately deceptive, and that their verbal explanations actually maps onto the processes used in their brain to arrive at their decisions.

Motivated by how trust works between humans, in this work we explore the idea of self-explaining AIs. Self-explaining AIs yield two outputs - the decision and an explanation of that decision. This idea is not new, and it is something which was pursued in expert systems research in the 1980s [45]. More recently Kulesza et al. introduced a model which offers explanations and studied how such models allow for "explainable debugging" and iterative refinement [26]. However, in their work they restrict themselves to a simple interpretable model (a multinomial naive Bayes classifier). Alvarez-Melis and Jaakkola introduce a "self-explaining" neural network which makes predictions using a number of human interpretable concepts or prototypes [4]. In a somewhat similar vein, Chen et al. [15] have proposed a "This looks like That" network. Unlike previous works, in this work we explore how we might create trustworthy self-explaining AI for networks and agents of arbitrary complexity, including artificial general intelligences (AGIs). We also seek for a more rigorous way to make sure the explanation given is actually explaining an aspect of the mechanism used for prediction. After defining key terms, we discuss the challenge of interpreting deep neural networks raised by recent studies on interpolation in deep neural networks. Then, we discuss how self-explaining AIs might be built. We argue that they should include at least three components - a measure of mutual information between the explanation and the decision, an uncertainty on both the explanation and decision, and a "warning system" which warns the user when the decision falls outside the domain of applicability of the system. We hope this work will inspire further work in this area which will ultimately lead to more trustworthy AI.

2 Interpretation, Explanation, and Self-explanation

As has been discussed at length elsewhere, different practitioners understand the term "interpretability" in different ways, leading to a lack of clarity (for detailed reviews, see [2,5,31,34]). The related term "explainability" is typically used in a synonymous fashion [39], although some have tried to draw a distinction between the two terms [27]. Here we take explanation/explainability and interpretation/interpretability to be synonymous. Murdoch et al. define an **explanation** as a verbal account of neural network function which is descriptively accurate and relevant [34]. By "descriptively accurate" they mean that the interpretation reproduces a large number of the input-output mappings of the model. The explanation may or may not map onto how the model works internally. Additionally, any explanation will be an approximation, and the degree of approximation which is deemed acceptable may vary depending on application. By "relevance", what counts as a "relevant explanation" is domain specific – it must be cast in terminology that is both understandable and relevant to users. For deep neural networks, the two desiderata of accuracy and relevance appear to be in tension - as we try to accurately explain the details of how a deep neural network interpolates, we move further from what may be considered relevant to the user.

This definition of explanation in terms of capturing input-output mappings in a human understandable way contrasts with a second meaning of the term explanation which we may call **mechanistic explanation**. Mechanistic explanations abstract faithfully (but approximately) the actual data transformations occurring in the model. To consider why mechanistic explanations can be useful, consider a deep learning model we trained recently to segment the L1 vertebra [17]. The way a radiologist identifies the L1 vertebra is by scanning down from the top of the body and finding the last vertebra that has ribs attached to it, which is T12. L1 is directly below T12. In our experience our models for identifying L1 tend to be brittle, indicating they probably use a different approach. For instance, they may do something like "locate the bright object which is just above the top of the kidneys". Such a technique would not be as robust as the technique used by radiologists. If a self-explaining AI had a model of human anatomy and could couch its explanations with reference to standard anatomical concepts, that would go a long way towards engendering trust. In general, the "Rashomon Effect", first described by Leo Brieman [14], says that for any set of noisy data, there are a multitude of models of equivalent accuracy, but which differ significantly in their internal mechanism. As a real-world example of the Rashomon Effect, when detecting Alzheimer's disease in brain MRI using a CNN the visualized interpretations for models trained on different train-test folds differed significantly, even though the models were of equivalent accuracy [44]. Even more troubling, the visualizations differed between different runs on the same fold, with the only difference being in the random initialization of the network [44]. Finally, interpretations can vary between test examples. [8] In many works only a few examples (sometimes cherry-picked) are given to "explain" how the model works, rather than attempting to summarize the results of the interpretability method on the entire test set. To summarize, in deep neural networks it is possible the mechanism of prediction can differ greatly between models of equivalent accuracy, even when the models all have the same architecture, due to peculiarities of the training data and initialization used. On top of this issue, it is also possible that specific details of the mechanism may vary wildly within a given model across different test cases.

There is another type of explanation we wish to discuss which we may call **meta-level explanation**. Richard P. Feynman said "What I cannot create, I do not understand". Since we can create deep neural networks, we do understand them, in the sense of Feynman, and therefore we can explain them in terms of how we build them. More specifically, we can explain neural network function in terms of four components necessary for creating them - data, network architecture, learning rules (optimization method), and objective function [37]. The way one explains deep neural network function from data, architecture, and training is analogous to how one explains animal behaviour using the theory of evolution. The evolution of architectures by "graduate student descent" and the explicit addition of inductive biases mirrors the evolution of organisms. Similarly, the training of architectures mirrors classical conditioning in animals. The explanation of animal behaviour in terms of meta-level theories like evolution and classical conditioning has proven to be enormously successful and stands in contrast to attempts to seek detailed mechanistic accounts.

Finally, the oft-used term **black box** also warrants discussion. The term is technically a misnomer since the precise workings of deep networks are fully transparent from their source code and network weights, and therefore for sake of rigor should not be used. A further point is that even if we did not have access to the source code or weights (for instance for intellectual property reasons, or because the relevant technical expertise is missing), it is likely that a large amount of information about the network's function could be gleaned through careful study of the its input-output relations. Developing mathematically rigorous techniques for "shining lights" into "black boxes" was a popular topic in early cybernetics research [6], and this subject is attracting renewed interest in the era of deep learning. As an example of what is achievable, recently it has been shown that weights can be inferred for ReLU networks through careful analysis of input-output relations [38]. One way of designing a "self-explaining AI" would be to imbue the AI with the power to probe its own input-output relations so it can warn its user when it may be making an error and (ideally) also distill its functioning into a human-understandable format.

3 Why Deep Neural Networks Are Generally Non-interpretable

Many methods for interpretation of deep neural networks have been developed, such as sensitivity analysis (saliency maps, occlusion maps, etc.), iterative mapping [12], "distilling" a neural network into a simpler model [19], exploring failure modes and adversarial examples [21, 23], visualizing filters in CNNs [48], activation maximization based visualizations [18], influence functions [25], Shapley values [32], Local Interpretable Model-agnostic Explanations (LIME) [36], DeepLIFT [42], explanatory graphs [50], and layerwise relevance propagation [7]. Yet, all of these methods capture only particular aspects of neural network function, and the outputs of these methods are very easy to misinterpret [28, 39, 47]. Often the output of interpretability methods vary largely between test cases, but only a few "representative" cases (often hand picked) are shown in papers. Moreover, it has been shown that popular methods such as LIME [4], Shapley values [4], and saliency maps [1, 16, 47] are not robust to small changes in the image such as Gaussian noise.

As we discussed before, we do not expect the current push towards more interpretable models led by Rudin and others to be successful in general - deep neural networks are here to stay, and they will become even more complex and inscrutable as time goes on. Lillicrap and Kording [29] note that attempts to compress deep neural networks into a simpler interpretable models with equivalent accuracy typically fail when working with complex real world data such as images or human language. If the world is messy and complex, then neural networks trained on real world data will also be messy and complex. Leo Breiman, who equates interpretability with simplicity, has made a similar point in the context of random forest models [14]. In many domains, the reason machine learning is applied is because of the failure of simple models or because of the computational burden of physics-based simulation. While we agree with Rudin that the interpretability-accuracy trade-off is not based on any rigorous quantitative analysis, we see much evidence to support it, and in some limiting cases (for example superintelligent AGIs which we cannot understand even in principle or brain emulations, etc) the real-world reality of such a trade-off existing to some extent becomes clear.

On top of these issues, there is a more fundamental reason to believe it will be hard to give mechanistic explanations for deep neural network function. For some years now it has been noted that deep neural networks have enormous capacity and seem to be vastly underdetermined, yet they still generalize. This was shown very starkly in 2016 when in Zhang et al. showed how deep neural networks can memorize random labels on ImageNet images [49]. More recently it has been shown that deep neural networks operate in a regime where the bias-variance trade-off no-longer applies [10]. As network capacity increases, test error first bottoms out and then starts to increase, but then (surprisingly) starts to decrease after a particular capacity threshold is reached. Belkin et al. call this the "double descent phenomena" [10] and it was also noted in an earlier paper by Sprigler et al. [43], who argue the phenomena is analogous to the "jamming transition" found in the physics of granular materials. The phenomena of "double descent" appears to be universal to all machine learning [10, 11], although its presence can be masked by common practices such as early stopping [10, 35], which may explain why it took so long to be discovered.

In the regime where deep neural networks operate, they not only interpolate each training data point, but do so in a "direct" or "robust" way [24]. This means that the interpolation does not exhibit the overshoot or undershoot which is typical of overfit models, rather it is almost a piecewise interpolation. The use of interpolation implies a corollary - the inability to extrapolate. The fact that deep neural networks cannot extrapolate calls into question popular ideas that deep neural networks "extract" high level features and "discover" regularities in the world. Actually, deep neural networks are "dumb" - any regularities that they appear to have captured internally are solely due to the data that was fed to them, rather than a self-directed "regularity extraction" process.

4   Challenges in Building Trustworthy Self-explaining AI

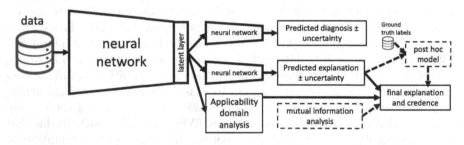

Fig. 1. Sketch of a simple self-explaining AI system. Optional (but recommended) components are shown with dashed lines.

In his landmark 2014 book *Superintelligence: Paths, Dangers, Strategies*, Nick Bostrom notes that highly advanced AIs may be incentivized to deceive their creators until a point where they exhibit a "treacherous turn" against them [13]. In the case of superintelligent or otherwise highly advanced AI, the possibility of deception appears to be a highly non-trivial concern. Here however, we suggest some methods by which we can trust the explanations given by present day deep neural networks, such as typical convolutional neural networks or transformer language models. Whether these methods will still have utility when it comes to future AI & AGI systems is an open question. To show how we might create trust, we focus on an explicit and relatively simple example. Shen et al. [41] and later LaLonde et al. [27] have both proposed deep neural networks for lung nodule classification which offer "explanations". Both authors make use of a dataset where clinicians have labeled lung nodules not only by severity (cancerous vs. non-cancerous) but also quantified them (on a scale of 1–5) in terms of five visual attributes which are deemed relevant for diagnosis (subtlety, sphericity, margin, lobulation, spiculation, and texture). While the details of the proposed networks vary, both output predictions for severity and scores for each of the visual attributes. Both authors claim that the visual attribute predictions "explain" the diagnostic prediction, since the diagnostic branch and visual attribute prediction branch(es) are connected near the base of the network. However, no evidence is presented that the visual attribute prediction is in any way related to the diagnosis prediction. While it may seem intuitive that the two output branches must be related, this must be rigorously shown for trustworthiness to hold. Additionally, even if the visual attributes were used, no weights ("relevances") are provided for the importance of each attribute to the prediction, and there may be other attributes of equal or greater importance that are used but not among those outputted (this point is admitted and discussed by Shen et al. [41]).

Therefore, we would like to determine the degree to which the attributes in the explanation branch are responsible for the prediction in the diagnosis branch. We focus on the layer where the diagnosis and explanation branch diverge and look at how the output of each branch relates to activations in that layer. There are many ways of quantifying the relatedness of two variables, the Pearson correlation being one of the simplest, but also one of the least useful in this context since it is only sensitive to linear relationships. A measure which is sensitive to non-linear relationships and which has nice theoretical interpretation is the mutual information. For two random variables X and Y it is defined as:

$$\mathrm{MI}(X,Y) \equiv \sum_{y \in Y} \sum_{x \in X} p(x,y) \log \left(\frac{p(x,y)}{p(x)p(y)} \right)$$

$$= H(x,y) - H(x) - H(y)$$

(1)

Where $H(x)$ is the Shannon entropy. One can also define a mutual information correlation coefficient $(r^{MI}(X,Y) = \sqrt{1 - e^{-2\mathrm{MI}(X,Y)}})$ [30]. This coefficient has the nice property that it reduces to the Pearson correlation in the case that $P(x,y)$ is a Gaussian function with non-zero covariance. The chief difficulty of applying mutual information is that the underlying probability distributions $P(x,y)$, $P(x)$, and $P(y)$ all have to be estimated. Various techniques exist for doing this however, such as by using kernel density estimation with Parzen windows [46].[1] Suppose the latent vector is denoted by L and has length N. Denote the diagnosis of the network as D and the vector of attributes A. Then for a particular attribute A_j in our explanation word set we calculate the following to obtain a "relatedness" score between the two:

$$R(A_j) = \sum_i^N \mathrm{MI}(L_i, D)\mathrm{MI}(L_i, A_j)$$

(2)

An more naive method is to train a "post-hoc" model to try to predict the diagnosis from the attributes (also shown in Fig. 1). While this cannot tell us much about mechanism of the main model (due to the Rashomon effect) we

---

[1] Note that this sort of approach should not be taken as quantifying "information flow" in the network. In fact, since the output of units is continuous, the amount of information which can flow through the network is infinite (for discussion and how to recover the concept of "information flow" in neural networks see [22]). What we propose to measure is the mutual information over the data distribution used.

can learn a bit from it. Namely, if the post-hoc model is not as accurate as the diagnosis branch of the main model, then we know the main model is using additional features.

5   Ensuring Robustness Through Applicability Domain and Uncertainty Analysis

The concept of an "applicability domain", or the domain where a model makes good predictions, is well studied in the area of molecular modeling known as quantitative structure property relationships (QSPR), and practitioners in that field have developed a number of techniques which are ready for export [40]. It is remarkable that quantifying the applicability domain of models hasn't become more widespread, given concerns about robustness and adversarial attacks. An analysis of applicability domain analysis methods for deep learning with medical images will be the subject of a future work. However, as an illustration, one way of delineating the applicability domain is to calculate the convex hull of the input vectors for all training data points (if the input is very high dimensional, dimensionality reduction should be applied first). If the input/latent vector of a test data point falls outside the convex hull, then the model should send an alert saying that the test point falls outside the model's applicability domain. We note that a deep learning system developed by Google's Verily Life Sciences which recently performed poorly in real-world trials in Thailand would likely would have benefited from such a warning system [9]. Applicability domain analysis can be framed as a simple form of AI self-awareness, which is thought to be an important component for AI safety in advanced AIs [3]. Finally, we note models should contain measures of uncertainty for both their decisions and their explanations, ideally in a fully Bayesian way [33]. If not enough compute is available, approximate methods are now available - for instance random dropout during inference can be used to estimate uncertainties at little extra computational cost [20]. Just as including experimental error bars is standard in all of science, uncertainty quantification should be standard practice in AI research.

6   Conclusion

We argued that deep neural networks trained on complex real world data are very difficult to interpret due to their power arising from brute-force interpolation over big data rather than through the extraction of high level rules. Motivated by this and by the need for trust in AI systems we introduced the concept of self-explaining AI and described how a simple self-explaining AI would function for diagnosing medical images. To build trust, we showed how a mutual information metric can be used to verify that the explanation given is related to the diagnostic output. Crucially, in addition to an explanation, self-explaining AI outputs confidence levels for both the decision and explanation, further aiding our ability to gauge the trustworthiness of any given diagnosis or decision.

Finally, an applicability domain analysis should be done for AI systems where robustness and trust are important, so that systems can alert their user if the input to a model lies outside its training distribution.

Funding and Disclaimer. No funding sources were used in the creation of this work. The author (Dr. Daniel C. Elton) wrote this article in his personal capacity. The opinions expressed in this article are the author's own and do not reflect the view of the National Institutes of Health, the Department of Health and Human Services, or the United States government.

References

1. Adebayo, J., Gilmer, J., Muelly, M., Goodfellow, I., Hardt, M., Kim, B.: Sanity checks for saliency maps. In: Proceedings of the 32nd International Conference on Neural Information Processing Systems NIPS 2018, pp. 9525–9536. Curran Associates Inc., Red Hook (2018)
2. Ahmad, M.A., Eckert, C., Teredesai, A.: Interpretable machine learning in healthcare. In: Proceedings of the 2018 ACM International Conference on Bioinformatics, Computational Biology, and Health Informatics - BCB 2018. ACM Press (2018)
3. Aliman, N.-M., Kester, L.: Hybrid strategies towards safe "Self-Aware" superintelligent systems. In: Iklé, M., Franz, A., Rzepka, R., Goertzel, B. (eds.) AGI 2018. LNCS (LNAI), vol. 10999, pp. 1–11. Springer, Cham (2018). https://doi.org/10.1007/978-3-319-97676-1_1
4. Alvarez-Melis, D., Jaakkola, T.S.: Towards robust interpretability with self-explaining neural networks. In: Proceedings of the 32nd International Conference on Neural Information Processing Systems NIPS 2018, pp. 7786–7795. Curran Associates Inc., Red Hook (2018)
5. Arya, V., et al.: One explanation does not fit all: a toolkit and taxonomy of AI explainability techniques. arXiv eprints: 1909.03012 (2019)
6. Ashby, W.R.: An Introduction to Cybernetics. Chapman & Hall, London (1956)
7. Bach, S., Binder, A., Montavon, G., Klauschen, F., Müller, K.R., Samek, W.: On pixel-wise explanations for non-linear classifier decisions by layer-wise relevance propagation. PLoS ONE **10**(7), e0130140 (2015)
8. Barnes, B.C., et al.: Machine learning of energetic material properties. arXiv eprints: 1807.06156 (2018)
9. Beede, E., et al.: A human centered evaluation of a deep learning system deployed in clinics for the detection of diabetic retinopathy. In: Proceedings of the 2020 CHI Conference on Human Factors in Computing Systems CHI 2020, pp. 1–12. Association for Computing Machinery, New York (2020)
10. Belkin, M., Hsu, D., Ma, S., Mandal, S.: Reconciling modern machine-learning practice and the classical bias–variance trade-off. Proc. Natl. Acad. Sci. **116**(32), 15849–15854 (2019)
11. Belkin, M., Hsu, D., Xu, J.: Two models of double descent for weak features. arXiv eprints: 1903.07571 (2019)
12. Bordes, F., Berthier, T., Jorio, L.D., Vincent, P., Bengio, Y.: Iteratively unveiling new regions of interest in deep learning models. In: Medical Imaging with Deep Learning (MIDL) (2018)
13. Bostrom, N.: Superintelligence: Paths, Dangers, Strategies, 1st edn. Oxford University Press Inc., Oxford (2014)

14. Breiman, L.: Statistical modeling: the two cultures (with comments and a rejoinder by the author). Stat. Sci. **16**(3), 199–231 (2001)
15. Chen, C., Li, O., Tao, D., Barnett, A., Rudin, C., Su, J.: This looks like that: deep learning for interpretable image recognition. In: Wallach, H.M., Larochelle, H., Beygelzimer, A., d'Alché-Buc, F., Fox, E.B., Garnett, R. (eds.) Advances in Neural Information Processing Systems 32: Annual Conference on Neural Information Processing Systems 2019, NeurIPS 2019, 8–14 December 2019, Canada, Vancouver, BC, pp. 8928–8939 (2019)
16. Dombrowski, A.K., Alber, M., Anders, C.J., Ackermann, M., Müller, K.R., Kessel, P.: Explanations can be manipulated and geometry is to blame (2019)
17. Elton, D., Sandfort, V., Pickhardt, P.J., Summers, R.M.: Accurately identifying vertebral levels in large datasets. In: Hahn, H.K., Mazurowski, M.A. (eds.) Medical Imaging 2020: Computer-Aided Diagnosis. SPIE, March 2020
18. Erhan, D., Bengio, Y., Courville, A., Vincent, P.: Visualizing higher-layer features of a deep network. Technical report 1341, University of Montreal: also presented at the ICML 2009 Workshop on Learning Feature Hierarchies. Montréal, Canada (2009)
19. Frosst, N., Hinton, G.: Distilling a neural network into a soft decision tree. arXiv eprintss: 1711.09784 (2017)
20. Gal, Y., Ghahramani, Z.: Dropout as a Bayesian approximation: representing model uncertainty in deep learning. In: Balcan, M.F., Weinberger, K.Q. (eds.) Proceedings of The 33rd International Conference on Machine Learning. Proceedings of Machine Learning Research, vol. 48, pp. 1050–1059. PMLR, New York, 20–22 June 2016
21. Goertzel, B.: Are there deep reasons underlying the pathologies of today's deep learning algorithms? In: Bieger, J., Goertzel, B., Potapov, A. (eds.) AGI 2015. LNCS (LNAI), vol. 9205, pp. 70–79. Springer, Cham (2015). https://doi.org/10. 1007/978-3-319-21365-1_8
22. Goldfeld, Z., et al.: Estimating information flow in deep neural networks. In: Chaudhuri, K., Salakhutdinov, R. (eds.) Proceedings of the 36th International Conference on Machine Learning. Proceedings of Machine Learning Research, vol. 97, pp. 2299–2308. PMLR, Long Beach, 09–15 June 2019
23. Goodfellow, I.J., Shlens, J., Szegedy, C.: Explaining and harnessing adversarial examples. arXiv eprintss: 1412.6572 (2014)
24. Hasson, U., Nastase, S.A., Goldstein, A.: Direct fit to nature: an evolutionary perspective on biological and artificial neural networks. Neuron **105**(3), 416–434 (2020)
25. Koh, P.W., Liang, P.: Understanding black-box predictions via influence functions. In: Proceedings of the 34th International Conference on Machine Learning ICML 2017, vol. 70, pp. 1885–1894. JMLR.org (2017)
26. Kulesza, T., Burnett, M., Wong, W.K., Stumpf, S.: Principles of explanatory debugging to personalize interactive machine learning. In: Proceedings of the 20th International Conference on Intelligent User Interfaces - IUI 2015. ACM Press (2015)
27. LaLonde, R., Torigian, D., Bagci, U.: Encoding visual attributes in capsules for explainable medical diagnoses. arXiv e-prints: 1909.05926, September 2019
28. Lie, C.: Relevance in the eye of the beholder: diagnosing classifications based on visualised layerwise relevance propagation. Master's thesis, Lund University, Sweden (2019)
29. Lillicrap, T.P., Kording, K.P.: What does it mean to understand a neural network? arXiv eprints: 1907.06374 (2019)

30. Linfoot, E.: An informational measure of correlation. Inf. Control **1**(1), 85–89 (1957)
31. Lipton, Z.C.: The mythos of model interpretability. arXiv eprints: 1606.03490 (2016)
32. Lundberg, S.M., Lee, S.I.: A unified approach to interpreting model predictions. In: Guyon, I., et al. (eds.) Advances in Neural Information Processing Systems, vol. 30, pp. 4765–4774. Curran Associates, Inc. (2017)
33. McClure, P., et al.: Knowing what you know in brain segmentation using bayesian deep neural networks. Front. Neuroinform. **13**, 67 (2019)
34. Murdoch, W.J., Singh, C., Kumbier, K., Abbasi-Asl, R., Yu, B.: Definitions, methods, and applications in interpretable machine learning. Proc. Natl. Acad. Sci. **116**(44), 22071–22080 (2019)
35. Nakkiran, P., Kaplun, G., Bansal, Y., Yang, T., Barak, B., Sutskever, I.: Deep double descent: where bigger models and more data hurt. arXiv eprints: 1912.02292 (2019)
36. Ribeiro, M.T., Singh, S., Guestrin, C.: Why should I trust you? In: Proceedings of the 22nd ACM SIGKDD International Conference on Knowledge Discovery and Data Mining - KDD. ACM Press (2016)
37. Richards, B.A., et al.: A deep learning framework for neuroscience. Nat. Neurosci. **22**(11), 1761–1770 (2019)
38. Rolnick, D., Kording, K.P.: Identifying weights and architectures of unknown ReLU networks. arXiv eprintss: 1910.00744 (2019)
39. Rudin, C.: Stop explaining black box machine learning models for high stakes decisions and use interpretable models instead. Nat. Mach. Intell. **1**(5), 206–215 (2019)
40. Sahigara, F., Mansouri, K., Ballabio, D., Mauri, A., Consonni, V., Todeschini, R.: Comparison of different approaches to define the applicability domain of QSAR models. Molecules **17**(5), 4791–4810 (2012)
41. Shen, S., Han, S.X., Aberle, D.R., Bui, A.A., Hsu, W.: An interpretable deep hierarchical semantic convolutional neural network for lung nodule malignancy classification. Expert Syst. Appl. **128**, 84–95 (2019)
42. Shrikumar, A., Greenside, P., Kundaje, A.: Learning important features through propagating activation differences. arXiv eprintss: 1704.02685 (2017)
43. Spigler, S., Geiger, M., d'Ascoli, S., Sagun, L., Biroli, G., Wyart, M.: A jamming transition from under- to over-parametrization affects generalization in deep learning. J. Phys. A: Math. Theor. **52**(47), 474001 (2019)
44. Sutre, E.T., Colliot, O., Dormont, D., Burgos, N.: Visualization approach to assess the robustness of neural networks for medical image classification. In: Proceedings of the SPIE: Medical Imaging (2020)
45. Swartout, W.R.: XPLAIN: a system for creating and explaining expert consulting programs. Artif. Intell. **21**(3), 285–325 (1983)
46. Torkkola, K.: Feature extraction by non-parametric mutual information maximization. J. Mach. Learn. Res. **3**, 1415–1438 (2003)
47. Yeh, C.K., Hsieh, C.Y., Suggala, A.S., Inouye, D.I., Ravikumar, P.: On the (in)fidelity and sensitivity for explanations. arXiv eprints: 1901.09392 (2019)
48. Zeiler, M.D., Fergus, R.: Visualizing and understanding convolutional networks. In: Fleet, D., Pajdla, T., Schiele, B., Tuytelaars, T. (eds.) ECCV 2014. LNCS, vol. 8689, pp. 818–833. Springer, Cham (2014). https://doi.org/10.1007/978-3-319-10590-1_53

49. Zhang, C., Bengio, S., Hardt, M., Recht, B., Vinyals, O.: Understanding deep learning requires rethinking generalization. arXiv eprints: 1611.03530 (2016)
50. Zhang, Q., Cao, R., Shi, F., Wu, Y.N., Zhu, S.C.: Interpreting CNN knowledge via an explanatory graph. In: McIlraith, S.A., Weinberger, K.Q. (eds.) AAAI, pp. 4454–4463. AAAI Press (2018)

AGI Needs the Humanities

Sam Freed[✉]

University of Sussex, Falmer, Brighton BN1 9RH, UK
s.freed@sussex.ac.uk

Abstract. Central scholars in AI have argued for extending the search for new AI technology beyond the tried-and-tested biologically and mathematically-inspired algorithms. Following in their footsteps, areas in the humanities are introduced as possible inspirations for novel human-like AI. Topics discussed include play-acting, literature as the field researching both imagination and metaphors, linguistics, music, and hermeneutics. In our ambition to reach *general* intelligence, we cannot afford to ignore these avenues of research.

Keywords: AI · AGI · Humanities · Hermeneutics

1 Introduction

AI as commonly practised generally no longer even aspires to human-level AI. The people who keep this dream from before 1956 alive have largely been confined to conferences about AGI – somehow the general AI has become a subfield. This has to do with how successful specific techniques in machine learning have become, and how embarrassingly stuck general AI seems: The opinion that AI has been at some level *"brain dead"* since at least the 1970s is voiced by pillars of the AI community such as Marvin Minsky (McHugh and Minsky 2003), Geoffrey Hinton (LeVine and Hinton 2017), and Rodney Brooks:

> ... *modern-day [AI] research is not doing well at all on either being general or supporting an independent entity with an ongoing existence. It mostly seems stuck on the same issues in reasoning and common sense that AI has had problems with for at least 50 years...* (Brooks 2017)

AI so far has been heavily influenced by the rationalist tradition, which is characterised by approaching any and all problems in a series of steps:

1. *Characterise the situation in terms of identifiable objects with well-defined properties.*
2. *Find general rules that apply to situations in terms of those objects and properties.*
3. *Apply the rules logically to the situation of concern, drawing conclusions about what should be done.* (Winograd and Flores 1986, pp. 14–26)

© Springer Nature Switzerland AG 2020
B. Goertzel et al. (Eds.): AGI 2020, LNAI 12177, pp. 107–115, 2020.
https://doi.org/10.1007/978-3-030-52152-3_11

Note how Brooks complains about AI being incapable of *"supporting an independent entity with an ongoing existence"*. On the one hand this has to do with mathematics' infatuation with functions, that by their very definition return the same value for the same parameters regardless of the time of evaluation; On the other hand it has to do with science and technology's aversion to all things subjective and human-like. This paper will march straight into this terrain – asking where in the Humanities would we find the best input for our effort to develop AGI.

Several arguments have been advanced as to where AI should go to find ideas for novel algorithms. Langley argued that AI should go back to its roots in the cognitive sciences (2006). That is hardly controversial, since cognitive science and AI evolved together since the 1950s. Some argue for extending our horizons: Boden, acknowledging that AI is an integral part of the cognitive sciences, laments the absence of any research in anthropology informing either cognitive science or AI (Boden 2008). Boden's promotion of anthropology can be seen as a first tentative step towards a more radical position, articulated by CP Snow (see below).

The most vociferous critic of AI from the humanities has been Hubert Dreyfus (Dreyfus 1979; 2007). He argued for AI researchers to understand humans better (mainly be reading Heidegger and Merleau-Ponty). Mainstream AI research mostly either ignored him or trivialised his critiques. This paper stands with mainstream AI in demanding programmable results (see Freed 2019), and stands with Dreyfus in pointing out the shortcomings of AI research. This call for a more human-aware AI may sound radical methodologically, but is quite easy personally and subjectively. Methodologically, the sciences like objectivity and abhor subjectivity. But in programming a mind like our own, can we afford to ban our own personal view of our own mind? Personally, there is nothing difficult in noticing our human, subjective side.

Especially in AGI, we need to be more daring than people who are pursuing merely the next incremental step in AI.

2   Approach

During the cold war, CP Snow pointed out (with some alarm) that a chasm had opened between two distinct intellectual cultures – What we would now call STEM (Science, Technology, Engineering, Mathematics) and the Humanities. He lamented that even basic communications across this divide have become difficult. He argued that such a chasm would necessarily be detrimental to the development of society, and would specifically hinder the UK's ability to compete with the USA and Russia (Snow 1964).

But criticism of AI's limited view of the mind was not only external, but came also from the very centre, from MIT's AI labs:

We are to thinking as Victorians were to sex. We all know we have these horrible moments of confusion when we begin a new project, that nothing looks clear and everything looks awful, that we work our way out using all sorts of odd little rules of thumb, by going down blind alleys and coming back again, and so on, but since everyone else seems to be thinking logically, or at least they claim they do, then we figure we must be the only ones in the world with such murky thought processes.

We disclaim them, and make believe that we think in logical, orderly ways, all the time knowing very well that we don't. And the worst offenders here are teachers, who present crisp, clean batches of knowledge to their students, and look as if they themselves had learned that knowledge in a crisp, clean way. It didn't happen that way, but the teachers don't admit it, and the students groan inwardly, feeling so hopelessly dumb. (McCorduck 2004, p. 339)

The author has argued elsewhere for the rehabilitation of introspection as a source of ideas in AI, after it was frowned upon since the behaviourist revolution in psychology (Freed 2017; 2019). Here we will examine other areas that were historically neglected, that have salience for the insights required for AGI. Some of these areas have already been touched upon by cognitive science and AI, but mostly in a limited way, holding fast to the rationalist point of view (e.g. motivation theory). Here we aim to adopt the point of view of the humanities more fully, to grasp more of the vast opportunities in the humanities. Space here only permits a cursory sketch of some of the opportunities. The final example (hermeneutics) will be developed in more detail, an algorithm in line with this approach is available in (Freed 2017; 2019).

3 Play-Acting

As argued elsewhere, One can see the process of programming as consisting of:

1. Understanding the requirement (say adding up items in an invoice and adding some sales tax to form a total);
2. Projecting ones mind into an imagined world where the environment, instead of consisting in chairs and desks, consists of (say) the Python interpreter (and associated libraries);
3. Imagining how one could solve the problem if one were acting using the tools available in the Python environment (loops, variables, input/output functions); and
4. Logging these actions (or the equivalent "instructions") in a text file, henceforth called the "program" (Freed 2018).

So it would seem that the role of a programmer is a *role*, taken on willingly by the skilled programmer, a bit like a character-role taken on my a theatrical performer. Note that this is observation is not alien to our field, in that Herbert Simon wrote (in his writing on administrative behaviour):

Administration is not unlike play-acting. The task of the good actor is to know and play his role... The effectiveness of the performance will depend on the effectiveness of the play and the effectiveness in which it is played. The effectiveness of the administrative process will vary with the effectiveness of the organisation and the effectiveness with which its members play their parts. (Simon 1976, p. 252; 1996, p. xii)

If acting is central to much of our behaviour, or at least to our effective behaviour (known as work) then the study of theatre looks promising for advancing any effective behaviour also in machines – at least machines that we hope to endow with decision-making abilities.

4 Imagination, Action, and the Limits Thereof

When we do some thing X, or recall doing the same X, or imagine doing the same X – our brain functions in a very similar manner (Hesslow 2012). The subjective experience of these three modes, action, recall and imagination – is also quite similar. These facts alone should spark a degree of interest in imagination research for AGI. The AI community indeed has given imagination some attention (see Mahadevan 2018).

Imagination is of interest in at least two ways. It seems to be a locus of much (if not all) of human creativity, and creativity is a "holy grail" yet to be achieved in AI or explained by cognitive science (Boden 2010). Most research (in the context of AI) has been into imagination in the sense of some sort of a "Cartesian space" - like a canvas inside our mind, where we form and develop ideas, a bit like a white-board.

Here is a different and perhaps more interesting angle of research into imagination: What can be imagined seems to be a limitation of what humans can do and think. In other words, the space of human endeavour is restricted to what is imaginable. The study of what is imaginable, of what is humanly comprehensible and credible – goes on in the fields of literature, theatre & cinema. Note that beyond statements of fact being true or false in the real world, there can be imaginary worlds where statements can be equally true or false: Mary had a little lamb, not a pangolin, and Snow White had 7 dwarves – no more and no less.

A small example of the arts developing an insight that is of interest is a popular song, where a social situation is described, where person B does not know that person A knows that person B knows that person A knows some fact. This presents four levels of social knowledge (or lack thereof). In logic, there is no limit to such constructions. In humans, the limit seems to be four levels[1].

5 Linguistics and Music

Linguistics have been central to the cognitive sciences. Many date the beginning of the cognitive revolution to a paper by Chomsky (1959) – which argues that human capabilities in syntax cannot be explained by behaviourism. However, there is a further point that may be of interest – when we hear an idea, we often ask ourselves whether it "sounds right" - in more senses than one.

1 Are the sentences grammatical?
2 Do the ideas "make sense"? Do they fit in some established and accepted pattern like a syllogism?

But note that the question of "sounding right" insinuates also some musical quality, some balance or harmony or form that is aesthetically correct. Again, the other side of Snow's divide beckons (Miranda 2013).

---

[1] The song is "Little does she know" by "The Kursaal Flyers". Thanks to Blay Whitby for pointing this out in private conversation.

6 Metaphor

Often we hear naive people say things such as that "the computers knows" some fact or skill. The better informed would comment that computers do not "know" anything, and have no mental states – they are hulks of metal silicon and plastic that process electrical signals in a sophisticated way that *we* call "information processing" (Smith 2005). The idea that the bank's computer "knows" my address arises out of the fact that in the correct configuration, when queried with a string of characters that represents (by social convention) my name or account number, the system is capable of emitting a string of characters that would represent (again by social convention) my address. But there is no *knowing* there at all. We *humans* know how to operate the computer system in order to obtain what *for us* is useful *information*. For the computer, it is all electrons going hither and thither. Saying that the computer "knows" anything is metaphorical. And where does this metaphor reside? In the minds of the humans designing and using the system. The computer (as a physical thing) has no capability for any mental state – not for knowing, and definitely not for metaphorical thinking.

However, we can still learn something profound from this metaphorical ascription of knowledge to the electronic device we call "a computer". What we see here clearly, is that *humans* think metaphorically. We as *humans* have this capacity to see "knowledge" where there is none, and to see "information" when all that physically exists are lit dots on a screen.

Further evidence or how metaphorical our thinking is was provided by Bolter (1984). He surveys how our culture described the mind in different eras, and argues that it was often through the metaphor of the latest technology· In ancient (Greek) times, the human was considered as "a clay vessel with a divine spark". With the introduction of clock towers in late medieval times, the human and his mind were considered in terms of mechanical automata – to this day we use expressions like "cogs turning in our head"[2]. In the late 19th century, with the arrival of pneumatic and hydraulic technologies, the metaphor used (for example) by Freud was of pressures, repressions, and eruptions - for emotions. Today we think of the mind as a computer, as in the title of Boden's history of Cognitive science - "Mind as Machine" - there is little doubt which machine the mind is being likened to (Boden 2008).

So, it would seem, that if we want to program human-level, general AI – we need to develop systems that can do metaphorical thinking. This is a tall order – and some research is already underway into metaphor as analogy (e.g. Barnden 2008). However, metaphorical thinking is far more complex than mere analogy. The topic of metaphor is already studied in its full glory and detail, but in departments of literature, not computer science·or cognition.

7 Hermeneutics[3]

Hermeneutics (the theory of interpretation) was founded as the theory of how to correctly understand ancient religious texts. Arguably hermeneutics is at least as old as

---

[2] https://www.youtube.com/watch?v=WEhS9Y9HYjU.

[3] Much of his section is based on previously published work (Freed 2017; 2019).

the Pauline epistles in the new testament, however it is with **Martin Luther**'s (b. 1783 d. 1546) protestant injunction, that the bible should be interpreted only on its own terms (without any reference to Catholic tradition) that we see the first explicit statement of a *policy* or *principle* by which interpretation of a text should be carried out (Ramberg and Gjesdal 2014).

Descartes (inventor of the Cartesian coordinates) expected all truths to be "clear and distinct". Speaking against these notions of understanding, **Giambattista Vico** (b. 1668 d.1744) argued that *"thinking is always rooted in a given cultural context. This context is historically developed, and, moreover, intrinsically related to ordinary language"* (*Ibid.*). This is in stark contrast to AI as it exists today – with its quest for the "one best answer", with little reference to context if at all.

Later **Friedrich Schleiermacher** (b. 1768 d. 1834) discussed the alien nature of old or foreign texts, and called for particular attention to our prejudices, so we can understand texts under their own alien context. He did not guarantee that such strict awareness of prejudice and openness will lead to a correct understanding of a text (that may be impossible). However such openness is *necessary* for understanding, and is required not only for foreign texts but for any type of communication (*Ibid.*). There are few AI systems that can (automatically) stop and tune-up their level of "openness".

Wilhelm Dilthey (b. 1833 d. 1911) distinguished *"living experience"* which is how each of us experience ourselves, from *"understanding"* which is how we more systematically understand the world outside us and others. He claimed that true self-awareness can only be achieved when one understands oneself on the same terms one understands others. In understanding history and historical texts one should combine (what we would now call) empathy, i.e. a *"living experience"* identification with the historical characters, with *"understanding"*, which is a more rigorous "from the outside" observation. The "living experience" component allows the historian to form hypotheses about, for example, how Caligula may have felt in a certain time. The "understanding" part allows one to critique such thoughts, and see how well they stand to reason (*Ibid.*). The idea that "living experience" has anything to do with understanding the world runs contrary to the rationalist attitude, prevalent in AI.

For modern thinkers such as Heidegger (b. 1889 d. 1976) and Dreyfus (the premier philosophical critic of AI (Dreyfus 1979)) interpretation is not only a matter of understanding texts, but of our entire mode of being, which is continuously involved with comprehending the world and acting in it (hence hermeneutics becomes one and the same project as phenomenology). In simpler terms, we humans are constantly interpreting our environment. Heidegger was concerned with many issues in phenomenology, and viewed the specifics of hermeneutics *as such* as a sub-field, the detailed exploration of which he later entrusted to a large degree to Gadamer (Malpas 2013, Chapter 4).

Hans-Georg Gadamer (b. 1900 d. 2002) viewed hermeneutics not only as the theory of understanding ancient texts and art in general but also, and perhaps mainly, as the act of continuously understanding/interpreting all situations. In this sense, interpretation is an unceasing human activity, during at least most waking hours (Gadamer 2004, pt. 1). For Gadamer, interpretation is the merger of two horizons: the brute facts, as in the letters on the page, and the reader, with all her background.

Here is an example (my own) of what is meant by interpretation in this context. Consider the following:

- הכלב מכוער
- Ha-kelev meh'oar
- Il cane é brutto
- The canine is brutish
- The dog is ugly

At this point you may be perplexed by this strange list, as one would be with any other strange sequence that is presented with little warning. In a sense I just caused you to be "thrown" onto this unusual list, and to the urgency of making sense of the situation. The lines above all convey the same meaning (in different alphabets, languages and dialects). Note how much easier it is to interpret (for an English monoglot) these examples the further down one goes. Note also that as an English-speaker you may be further interpreting the situation and objecting that "brutish" does not mean the same as "ugly", but you also may be aware that in the Italian "brutto" does actually mean ugly, and may further be aware of how such words change meanings over the centuries and the geographic distances involved. All these thoughts are interpretative – they are attempts to make sense of a situation, at this instance the situation at hand is the bizarre list above. *This* sort of interpretative effort is the mental activity that hermeneutics studies, and I argue is a necessary feature for AGI.

Interpretation (in the sense that interests us here) is the ability to "follow along", to "make sense" of the "inputs". In following along with (say) a song, this is easier with a familiar tune than it is with foreign music. The crux of the knowledge or skill accumulated as we become more familiar with a situation does *not* consist of beliefs - we have no position on the ugliness or beauty of a dog we have never seen. What *is* being formed is an *interpretation*, an understanding, a grasp – before (and not requiring) any judgement. A grasp of a situation includes a sense of its development over time. Contrast this with AI's fascination with functions and mappings – timeless mathematical notions. Note that Brooks (above) complains about AI's difficulty with " *supporting an independent entity with an ongoing existence*"- an *ongoing existence* would require an understanding with a temporal dimension.

Gadamer being a student of Heidegger's, following Gadamer to explore AGI is in line with Dreyfus's (2007) call for a more Heideggerian AI. Gadamer was first mentioned as a possible source for AI research by Winograd and Flores (1986), and a concrete algorithm following this path is proposed in detail in (Freed 2017; 2019).

8 Final Notes

As we have seen, beyond the great divide between the STEM subjects and the humanities several promising fields offer tantalising prospects for the adventurous AI researcher. In bringing this survey to a close, it is worth noting that some 20th century thinkers that would be considered more conventional in the cognitive-science/AI community would agree with the directions outlined above.

Wittgenstein described our perception as "seeing as" - we see the duck-rabbit picture either as a rabbit or as a duck (Wittgenstein 2001). This process is interpretative – as was outlined above.

Developmental psychologics such as Piaget (1989) offer schemas of how cognition develops in children. Regardless of the veracity of any one such theory, any theory that seems programmable may be used as a model for an AI system (Freed 2019; Matthews and Mullin 2018).

This paper argued for adding new angles from which to look at AI. We already have two angles:

- How we should think (mathematics);
- How we do think, objectively (brain science).

Let us add two more:

- How we experience our own thought (introspection, see (Freed 2017; 2019));
- How our thinking is understood by experts on human civilizations (the humanities).

Exploring such new frontiers in AI is of particular interest when we aim for human-level AI and beyond – as in the field of Artificial General Intelligence.

References

Barnden, J.A.: Metaphor and artificial intelligence: why they matter to each other. In: The Cambridge Handbook of Metaphor and Thought, pp. 311–338 (2008)

Boden, M.A.: Mind as Machine: A History of Cognitive Science. OUP, Oxford (2008)

Boden, M.A.: Creativity and Art: Three Roads to Surprise. Oxford University Press, Oxford (2010)

Bolter, J.D.: Turing's Man: Western Culture in the Computer Age. Duckworth, London (1984)

Brooks, R.A.: Robotics pioneer Rodney Brooks debunks AI hype seven ways. MIT Technology Review, 6 October 2017. https://www.technologyreview.com/s/609048/the-seven-deadly-sins-of-ai-predictions/

Chomsky, N.: A review of BF Skinner's verbal behavior. Language 35(1), 26–58 (1959)

Dreyfus, H.L.: What Computers Can't Do/The Limits Of Artificial Intelligence (Revised). Harper & Row, New York (1979)

Dreyfus, H.L.: Why heideggerian AI failed and how fixing it would require making it more Heideggerian. Artif. Intell. 171(18), 1137–1160 (2007). https://doi.org/10.1016/j.artint.2007.10.012

Freed, S.: A role for introspection in AI research. University of Sussex (2017). http://sro.sussex.ac.uk/66141/

Freed, S.: AI and Human Thought and Emotion. CRC Press, Boca Raton (2019)

Freed, S.: Is programming done by projection and introspection? In: Müller, V.C. (ed.) Philosophy and Theory of Artificial Intelligence 2017, pp. 187–189. Springer, Cham (2018). 10.1007/978-3-319-96448-5_17

Gadamer, H.-G.: Truth and Method (2nd, rev. ed ed.). Continuum (2004)

Hesslow, G.: The current status of the simulation theory of cognition. Brain Res. 1428, 71–79 (2012). https://doi.org/10.1016/j.brainres.2011.06.026

Langley, P.: Intelligent behavior in humans and machines. Technical report. Computational Learning Laboratory, CSLI, Stanford University (2006). http://lyonesse.stanford.edu/~langley/papers/ai50.dart.pdf

LeVine, S., Hinton, G.: Artificial intelligence pioneer says we need to start over. Axios, 15 September 2017. https://www.axios.com/ai-pioneer-advocates-starting-over-2485537027.html

Mahadevan, S.: Imagination machines: a new challenge for artificial intelligence. In: Thirty-Second AAAI Conference on Artificial Intelligence. Thirty-Second AAAI Conference on Artificial Intelligence, 29 April 2018. https://www.aaai.org/ocs/index.php/AAAI/AAAI18/paper/view/16147

Malpas, J.: Hans-georg gadamer. In: Zalta, E.N. (ed.) The Stanford Encyclopedia of Philosophy (Summer 2013) (2013). http://plato.stanford.edu/archives/sum2013/entries/gadamer/

Matthews, G., Mullin, A.: The philosophy of childhood. In: Zalta, E.N. (ed.) The Stanford Encyclopedia of Philosophy (Winter 2018). Metaphysics Research Lab, Stanford University (2018). https://plato.stanford.edu/archives/win2018/entries/childhood/

McCorduck, P.: Machines who think: a personal inquiry into the history and prospects of artificial intelligence (25th anniversary update). A.K. Peters (2004)

McHugh, J., Minsky, M.: Why A.I. Is Brain-Dead. WIRED, 1 August 2003. http://www.wired.com/2003/08/why-a-i-is-brain-dead/

Miranda, E.R.: Readings in Music and Artificial Intelligence. Routledge (2013)

Piaget, J.: The Child's Conception of the World. Rowman & Littlefield, Totowa (1989)

Ramberg, B., Gjesdal, K.: Hermeneutics. In: Zalta, E.N. (ed.) The Stanford Encyclopedia of Philosophy (Winter 2014) (2014). http://plato.stanford.edu/archives/win2014/entries/hermeneutics/

Simon, H.A.: Administrative behavior: A study of decision-making processes in administrative organization (3rd ed.). Collier Macmillan (1976). http://capitadiscovery.co.uk/sussex-ac/items/38710

Simon, H.A.: The Sciences of the Artificial (3rd ed.). MIT Press (1996). http://capitadiscovery.co.uk/sussex-ac/items/546838

Smith, B.C.: Digital Future: Meaning of Digital. C-SPAN Video Library. 31 January 2005. http://c-spanvideo.org/program/FutureM

Snow, C.P.: The two Cultures: And a Second look (2 ed.). C.U.P. (1964). http://capitadiscovery.co.uk/sussex-ac/items/22469

Winograd, T., Flores, F.: Understanding computers and cognition: a new foundation for design. Ablex (1986). http://prism.talis.com/sussex-ac/items/272586

Wittgenstein, L.: Philosophical Investigations: The German Text with a Revised English Translation, 3rd edn. Wiley-Blackwell (2001)

Report on "AI and Human Thought and Emotion"

Sam Freed[✉]

University of Sussex, Falmer, Brighton BN1 9RH, UK
s.freed@sussex.ac.uk

Abstract. No fundamental new ideas have appeared in AI for decades because of a deadlocked discussion between the technologists and their philosophical critics. Both sides claim possession of the one (dogmatic) truth: Technologists are committed to writing code, while critics insist that AI bears no resemblance to how humans cope in the world. The book charts a middle course between the critics and practitioners of AI, remaining committed to writing code while maintaining a fixed gaze on the human condition. This is done by reviving a technique long-shunned in cognitive science: Introspection. Introspection was rejected as a scientific method since 1913, but technology is committed to "what works" rather than to science's "best explanation". Introspection is shown to be both a legitimate and a promising source of ideas for AI. The book details the development process of AI based on introspection, from the initial introspective descriptions to working code.

This book is unique in that it starts with philosophical (and historical) discussions, and ends with examples of working novel algorithms. The book was originally a PhD thesis. It was edited for book form with two new chapters added.

Keywords: Human-like AI · Anthropic AI · AGI

1 AI as It Stands

This first part of this book describes the state of the art in terms of AI, criticism of AI, some of the mindset that contributes to the current state of affairs, and the historical causes of said mindset.

The vast majority of exiting AI is based on one of two basic ideas, or on a combination thereof:

1. Logic and mathematics: information and rules are represented explicitly, and the AI system works by making explicit deductions using explicit knowledge. This approach was extended to include statistical facts and rules. Any conclusion can be supported in detail from the inputs.
2. Biologically-inspired systems, including genetic algorithms and neural networks: These systems try to evolve some ability or representation of knowledge by trial and error. The end result is not usually supported by any explanation other than "That's how it worked out".

© Springer Nature Switzerland AG 2020
B. Goertzel et al. (Eds.): AGI 2020, LNAI 12177, pp. 116–120, 2020.
https://doi.org/10.1007/978-3-030-52152-3_12

The absence of any other basic ideas is attributed to cognitive science's inheritance of Behaviourism's attachment to objectivity rather than subjectivity. Herbert Simon, one of the most influential people in AI history, wrote extensively also in neighbouring fields. In psychology he took upon himself to carry forward Watson's (1913, 1920) prohibition of introspection and all that is subjective and elaborate further on what is and is not legitimate in psychological research, without deviating from Watson's positions in this area (Ericsson and Simon 1993).

The philosophical critiques of AI (mainly by Dreyfus (1979, 2007) and Winograd and Flores (1986)) are outlined. Winograd & Flores describe AI as being committed to "the rationalist tradition", and they propose some directions of research, but do not develop any new AI algorithms.

The book critiques these philosophers for not programming, and finds them equally culpable in this sense to the AI people who do not bother to understand the philosophical critiques but dismiss them out of hand. The book's purpose is to respect both sides of this argument – reading the philosophy seriously, and programming.

Next the author surveys how human thought is experienced subjectively in contrast to how human thought is presented in socially-accepted forms. The various pressures to conform, and resultant anxiety and pretence of "clear thinking" are surveyed. Much of the book's approach can be gleaned from a quote to which the author returns several times from Seymour Papert (a leading AI researcher at MIT):

> We are to thinking as Victorians were to sex. We all know we have these horrible moments of confusion when we begin a new project, that nothing looks clear and everything looks awful, that we work our way out using all sorts of odd little rules of thumb, by going down blind alleys and coming back again, and so on, but since everyone else seems to be thinking logically, or at least they claim they do, then we figure we must be the only ones in the world with such murky thought processes. We disclaim them, and make believe that we think in logical, orderly ways, all the time knowing very well that we don't. And the worst offenders here are teachers, who present crisp, clean batches of knowledge to their students, and look as if they themselves had learned that knowledge in a crisp, clean way. It didn't happen that way, but the teachers don't admit it, and the students groan inwardly, feeling so hopelessly dumb (McCorduck 2004, p. 339).

Some of the historical reasons for current thinking are outlined briefly. Several assumptions that are common in the AI world are enumerated, such as the assumption (coming from economics, mainly) that humans are rational. As an example for how these misconceptions are the result of chance historical events, the history of positivism and logical positivism is outlined in a bit more detail, pointing out that Herbert Simon was directly influenced by Rudolph Carnap (a leading logical-positivist) – both working in Chicago.

2   An Alternative: AI, Subjectivity, and Introspection

The main thesis of the book (and the underlying PhD project) is: "Introspection is recommended for the development of anthropic AI". First a few methodological issues are cleared – mainly that the requirement for truth in technology is less stringent that in science, then some terms are explained:

The first term to be clarified is the purpose: *Anthropic* AI. This neologism is described as a type of human-like AI (as opposed to rational/ideal AI, which is the aim of the majority of current AI). Within human-like AI Anthropic AI is defined as aiming for the most low-level processes that we experience, i.e. around the line that separates our innate human abilities from our acquired culture. Anthropic AI is contrasted with western, modern, well-educated and adult intelligence – which is the intelligence most existing AI aims at.

The second term to be introduced is "introspection". Scientific psychology's relationship with subjectivity is explored before and after the behaviourist and cognitive revolutions. The definition of introspection is discussed, and an accepted technique in scientific psychology called "thinking aloud" is compared and contrasted with the rejected introspection.

In order to recommend anything (in our case introspection for anthropic AI) two stages are necessary: showing legitimacy, and a reasonable expectation of a good outcome.

One of the founding events of scientific psychology was the wholesale rejection of introspection and all subjectivity as "unscientific" by the founders of behaviourism (Watson 1913, 1920). The book surveys the gamut of ways one can relate to introspection including the mainstream rejection, and Dreyfus's enthusiastic embrace. The mainstream rejection is analysed and shown to be misguided since ideas in the sciences can legitimately come from any source whatsoever, the ideas have to be shown to be valid empirically. The pedigree of an idea makes no difference to it's acceptability. There is no reason to adopt a stricter view of ideas' pedigree in technology than in science, quite the contrary, in technology mistakes are discerned in a matter of months in the worst case, while mistakes in science may take centuries to be uncovered. So if *any* idea may be discussed in science, there is no reason at all to deny ourselves ideas from introspection in technology.

The book deals with a contradiction in the stance of many researchers: rejecting in-principle all subjectivity, while in practice using introspection for AI research. This fecund source of ideas is made more freely available by shining a bright light at these tensions, and clearing them up.

Next the book shows that introspection is the basis of much of our effort to educate the young, and to pass on skills from one generation to the next. When a student asks a teacher how to do X, the teacher either does X or imagines themselves doing X, while noting the stages of the process; these stages are explained to the student. *Noting* the stages is an act of self-observation on the part of the teacher – and if the teacher is teaching a mental skill then the teacher is engaged in *mental self observation* - which is the definition of introspection. So introspection is not noise, rather it carries salient information on how we do things, and this communication works, as shown by civilizations lasting for many generations.

3 Getting Practical

The process of introspecting, writing introspective reports and generating software based on these reports is next described in detail. Some concerns about project expectations in such technological innovations are also discussed.

Next the book turns to simple examples, the first two are of existing technologies. It is unclear whether these technologies were, in fact, developed using introspection – but they can be used to illustrate the process, and are used without prejudice as to their actual history.

Fuzzy Logic was invented by Lotfi Zadeh without any reference to external materials (McNeill and Freiberger 1994). Zadeh was observing the way he himself used concepts in daily life, and realized that the boundaries of concepts are not sharp like in logic, but fuzzy. This observation led to his paper on fuzzy sets, and later to fuzzy logic. A similar story is reconstructed for Case Based Reasoning.

The first original algorithm presented can be seen as an extension of Case Based Reasoning – adding nondeterministic elements derived from introspection. The results for this algorithm are shown.

Next, an observation is made that we think using scenarios from our past, that extend in time. An algorithm based on that observation was tested but failed to learn anything useful.

Instead of retreating in the face of failure, a further set of observations is added:

- We think while referring to a *multiplicity* of past scenarios;
- these scenarios seem to have no clear beginning or end, but fade in and out of mind;
- some are more relevant, and therefore more dominant of our current decision-marking process.

An algorithm implementing these requirements is described, and videos show how this algorithm learns to play simple games. Different runs of the algorithm seem to have different "characters" (based on random parameters that go into every run).

In the concluding chapter, the philosophical critiques and ideas from early in the book are reviewed in light of the technical results.

References

Dreyfus, H.L.: What Computers Can't Do/The Limits of Artificial Intelligence (Revised). Harper & Row, New York (1979)

Dreyfus, H.L.: Why Heideggerian AI failed and how fixing it would require making it more Heideggerian. Artif. Intell. **171**(18), 1137–1160 (2007). https://doi.org/10.1016/j.artint.2007.10.012

Ericsson, K.A., Simon, H.A.: Protocol Analysis: Verbal Reports as Data, 2nd edn. MIT (1993). http://capitadiscovery.co.uk/sussex-ac/items/543010

Freed, S.: AI and Human Thought and Emotion. CRC Press, Boca Raton (2019)

McCorduck, P.: Machines Who Think: A Personal Inquiry into the History and Prospects of Artificial Intelligence (25th anniversary update). A.K. Peters, Natick (2004)

McNeill, D., Freiberger, P.: Fuzzy Logic: The Revolutionary Computer Technology that Is Changing Our World, 1st edn. Touchstone/Simon & Schuster, New York (1994)

Watson, J.B.: Psychology as the behaviorist views it. Psychol. Rev. **20**(2), 158–177 (1913). https://doi.org/10.1037/h0074428

Watson, J.B.: Is Thinking Merely Action of Language Mechanisms1? (V.). Br. J. Psychol. Gener. Sect. **11**(1), 87–104 (1920). https://doi.org/10.1111/j.2044-8295.1920.tb00010.x

Winograd, T., Flores, F.: Understanding computers and cognition: A new foundation for design. Ablex (1986). http://prism.talis.com/sussex-ac/items/272586

Cognitive Machinery and Behaviours

Bryan Fruchart$^{(\boxtimes)}$ and Benoit Le Blanc

ENSC, IMS Laboratory, Bordeaux INP, CNRS, Talence, France
bfruchart@ensc.fr

Abstract. In this paper we propose to merge theories and principles explored in artificial intelligence and cognitive sciences into a reference architecture for human-level cognition or AGI. We describe a functional model of information processing systems inspired by several established theories: deep reinforcement learning mechanisms and grounded cognition theories from artificial intelligence research; dual-process theory from psychology; global-workspace theory, somatic markers hypothesis, and Hebbian theory from neurobiology; mind-body problem from philosophy. We use a formalism inspired by flow-graph and cybernetics representations. We called our proposed model IPSEL for Information Processing System with Emerging Logic. Its main assumption is on the emergence of a symbolic form of process from a connectionist activity guided by a self-generated evaluation signal. We also discuss artificial equivalents of concepts elaboration, common-sense and social interactions. This transdisciplinary work can be considered as a proposition for an artificial general intelligence design. It contains elements that will be implemented on further experiments. Its current aim is to be an analyzing tool for Human interactions with present and future artificial intelligence systems and a formal base for discussion of AGI features.

Keywords: Human-level cognition · Artificial general intelligence · Cognitive modeling

1 Introduction

Recent publications raised discussions on limits of the followed current approaches in artificial intelligence (AI) (Marcus and Davis 2019). These limits on artificial systems' capacities and the debates they generated aren't new. In fact, one could consider they are analogous to the indirect debate between Alan Turing exhibiting his Imitation game as a test of AI (Turing 1950) and John Searle with his counterargument of the Chinese room (Searle 1980). Can machines understand humans? And can humans truly understand machines? Artificial information processing systems aim to simulate processes that are usually done by human cognition, thus we decided to model Human-like cognition as a reference architecture for artificial systems. To design our model, we took inspiration from various established cognitive science theories.

From the field of AI, we were inspired by deep reinforcement learning (DRL) frameworks, grounded cognition theories and prior cognitive architectures. Systems that implement DRL have been shown to efficiently perform human-level tasks from sensory input

© Springer Nature Switzerland AG 2020
B. Goertzel et al. (Eds.): AGI 2020, LNAI 12177, pp. 121–130, 2020.
https://doi.org/10.1007/978-3-030-52152-3_13

computations (Everitt et al. 2018). It is often said that conventional DRL alone cannot account for the way humans learn. It's too slow, requires very large datasets, doesn't generalize well, struggles to perform symbolic processing and lacks the ability to reason on an abstract level (Garnelo et al. 2016). Recent reports, however, show that these issues can be overcome by architectural and modality modifications for narrowed environments (Dosovitskiy and Koltun 2016; Wayne et al. 2018). As an example, Deep-Mind researchers implement two different learning speeds for simulation of episodic memory and meta-learning. They concluded that "a key implication of recent work on sample-efficient deep RL is that where fast learning occurs, it necessarily relies on slow learning, which establishes the representations and inductive biases that enable fast learning." (Botvinick et al. 2019). This architectural consideration of decomposing cognition into two modes has been largely explored by cognitive architects. This dual-process assumption seems to be the most promising one considering the natural synergy between connectionism and cognitivism. It is often said that connectionist models efficiently perform inductive reasoning and classifications but lack symbolic and deductive abilities. On the other hand, deductive inference requires entities and rules, which are hard to a-priori define for complex and partially observable environments. An interesting idea concerning this constraint is to make the symbolic part emerge from the connectionist activity (Hopfield 1982).

Hybrid systems' propositions are usually inspired by psychology research where William James proposed in 1890 to decompose human cognition into two subsystems which he named "Associative thinking" and "Reasoning thinking" (James et al. 1890). Many works have been done around this principle, one of the most notable is the extended experiment conducted by Amos Tversky and the Nobel prize winner Daniel Kahneman on human economic decision making (Kahneman 2011). For them, cognitive processes can result from the production of two different systems. System 1 which is described as fast, unconscious and automatic, accounting for everyday decision and subject to errors. The System 2 is slower, conscious and effortful. For Kahneman, System 2 operates complex decision-making processes and is more reliable. To better understand the relation between these different cognitive modes, we have also been vastly inspired by the works of Carl Jung and Sigmund Freud, who were among the first to distinguish and study the unconscious part of our mind (Freud and Bonaparte 1954; Jung 1964).

Converging neurobiology studies associate reasoning or declarative cognitive functions with distributed brain activities. This assumption finds an echo in the words of the Global Workspace Theory (Dehaene et al. 1998). Functional brain imaging shows that conscious cognition is associated with the spread of cortical activity, whereas unconscious cognition tends to activate only local regions (Baars 2005). Experimental reports stressed the notion of Free will by observing unconscious initiative before voluntary action (Libet 1985) giving us our intuition on how both systems are architectured. These large-scale considerations on the brain activity have started to operate a shift in the way that cognitive scientists analyse cognition. Vinod Menon studied psychopathology and wrote: "The human brain is a complex patchwork of interconnected regions, and network approaches have become increasingly useful for understanding how functionally connected systems engender, and constrain, cognitive functions." (Menon 2011). However, brain processing does not rely only on electrical activity; information flows are encoded into electrical-chemical potentials. Emotions, which are associated with chemical neu-rotransmitters, play an undeniable role in human behaviours whether they are conscious or unconscious. To integrate this part in our model, we took inspiration from the Somatic Marker hypothesis formulated by Antonio Damasio (Damasio et al. 1991). Lastly, we also considered the Hebbian theory described by neurobiologists. Named after Donald Hebb, this cell assembly theory modelized the synaptic plasticity of the brain. Recent publication in artificial intelligence shows how recurrent neural networks with Hebbian plastic connections provide a powerful novel approach to the learning-to-learn problem (Miconi et al. 2018).

All these theories have been thoroughly discussed by their corresponding discipline. Because of the space limitation, we cannot reference or further develop these discussions or reports. Moreover, this is not the objective of this paper. In this introduction we have presented what are the transdisciplinary sources that have inspired our architecture. The formalism we use to represent networks' activities is described in Sect. 2 along with the definition of our architecture. Discussion of its attributed capacities will be presented in Sect. 3. More specifically, we will discuss conceptual reasoning, common-sense knowledge and social interactions such as language. As a conclusion, we conjecture on behaviours of agents that would be architectured with our proposition.

2   Information Processing Systems with Emerging Logic (IPSEL)

2.1   Cognition as a Flow Graph

The considered system is represented as a graph of processing units connected together. Processing units are represented by nodes and their connections by weighted and oriented arcs called routes. We define three types of units. Source units which represent sensor organs of the system; sink units representing motor organs; and routing units which are graph nodes that are neither sources nor sinks. All together they form a network in which flows are spreading. These flows are called Action Potential Flows (AP-flows). When a unit or a route is crossed by AP-flows we say it is activated. AP-flows have the property of being persistent for an undefined amount of time. When activated, routing units can emit part of a signal called Emotional Response Signal (ERS). Considered all together, ERSs represent the internal response of the whole network being crossed by AP-flows. We give no constraint on how ERS are produced, it can be generated by one group of units or the generation can be distributed amongst all units. A schematic representation is given in Fig. 1.

We associate source units' activities as a process which transforms environment interactions into AP-flows. It is continuous and said to be the system's perception of its environment. AP-flows then spread into the network and eventually reach sink units. Sink units' activities are responsible for transformation of AP-flows into environment interactions. This process is said to be the system's behaviour. The function that connects perception to behaviour is called cognition and is represented by the structure of the network.

We named this form of representation a Cognition Flow Graph (CFG). Structural information of the graph is represented by the arcs' weight. They are probabilities of the type "probability of the route to be activated if connected unit is activated". Altogether,

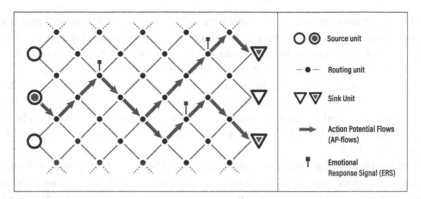

Fig. 1. An arbitrary cognition flow graph. Only few units and routes have been displayed.

the arcs' weights form a probability distribution over pairs of units. We call it the intuitive probability distribution (ID) of the cognition flow graph. There are two mechanisms that allow ID editing. The first is called Hebbian Learning (HL). It has the function to grow connections between unconnected units that have simultaneous activities. It changes the ID probabilities from 0 to something greater than 0. The second mechanism, called Reinforcement Learning (RL), increase or decrease the arcs' weights to optimize emotional response signals of the structure.

The particular routings of AP-flows through the structure determine, for a set of activated source units, which sinks units will be activated. Thus, we say that perception is processed by cognition to produce behaviours. Cognition is performing a computation on perception with intuitive probability distribution as instructions.

2.2 IPSEL Functional Architecture

Different natures of routing imply different natures of computation and thus different natures of behaviours. In this part we regroup various kinds of routing and define abstract systems that represent their consequent computation.

We distinguish two types of routing possibilities. Direct paths: on these paths, AP-flows have a unique routing possibility. And indirect paths: on these paths AP-flows have multiple routing possibilities, which implies a notion of network and allow flow cycles. Considered all together, indirect paths form a network of networks.

Behaviours engendered by activities on direct paths are called direct behaviours. We represent them as being the production of a system called Direct System (S0). Activities on indirect paths can have two modalities. When one indirect path is considered it is said to be a local activity. When the activities are considered over a combination of indirect paths, involving potentially unconnected distant networks, it is said to be a global activity. Behaviours engendered by local activities are called intuitive behaviours and are the production of the Intuitive system (S1). Combinations of local activities form global activities which embody a computation attributed to the deliberative system (S2). We postulate that S2 emerges from S1 because of the relations between local and global activities.

While experiencing its environment, the structure of indirect paths' networks changes because of RL and HL. At the local scale, preferred routings will emerge and form local patterns of activities. At the global scale, unconnected networks will develop connections because of HL, and preferred routings between these localities will emerge because of RL. We define the notion of concept which, in our formalism, means a combination of local routing patterns that have developed inter-local routes at the global scale. Because of concept formation, local networks can now be activated by flows coming from the global activity. This kind of global flow activities is said to emerge since it requires a previous step of local structure self-organization. At the local scale, AP-flows are continuous and form a global configuration at any time. However not all global configurations imply activated concepts. Thus, from a global point of view, concepts appear in an ordered sequence. Once again, due to HL, RL and the persistence of AP-flows, concepts that appear close in the sequence will develop and reinforce inter-connections. Since the sequence is ordered, it can also be viewed as the emergence of probabilistic causality relations between concepts. We define a second probability distribution over pairs of concepts called the conceptual probability distribution (CD). ID represents S1 knowledge whereas CD represents S2 knowledge.

Environment perception penetrates the system through sensory organs where they are transformed into Action potential flows called messages. These flows propagate through the structure and activate direct and indirect paths. Propagation on direct paths will engender direct behaviours seen as production of the direct system S0. Propagation in indirect paths activates local networks and engenders intuitive behaviours seen as production of the intuitive system S1, and it is determined by the intuitive distribution. At the global scale, activated concepts engender new local flow propagations and can be inferred from a previously activated concept. When it is the case, the appearing sequence of concepts is said to be the production of the declarative system (S2) and is determined by the conceptual distribution. The cycle of flow propagation between local and global

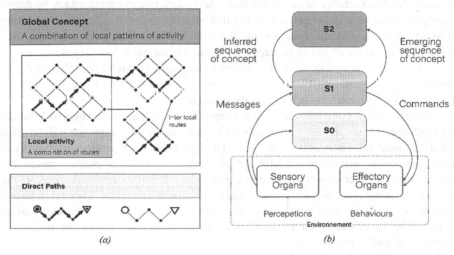

(a)   (b)

Fig. 2. (a) distinction between direct, local and global activities. (b) IPSEL agent.

configurations is said to be the reasoning behaviour of the system. It can also be viewed as communication between S1 and S2. AP-flows that activate sink units for behaviour productions are called commands.

IPSEL agents alternate between three natures of behaviours (direct, intuitive, or reasoning), corresponding to what is required for environmental interactions. Perceptions that activate direct paths engender direct behaviours. Other perceptions engender intuitive behaviours. Occasionally, internal flow propagations instantiate concepts and trigger concept inferences at the global scale. The inferred concept sequence acts as new sources of flows for local activities. It is the reasoning behaviour of the agent and engenders further intuitive behaviours (Fig. 2).

3 Discussion

In our model, a concept is a combination of simultaneous local patterns of activities. We can state that the more a route is activated, the more it may be reinforced. For this reason, invariance on perceptions will engender more reinforcement for their own connected networks. Invariance on combination of simultaneous local patterns of activities will engender inter-local connections thanks to the Hebbian mechanism and develop concepts. From the global perspective, the first criteria of invariance on perceptual patterns is the fact that they continuously change over time. Thus, we could suppose that Time would be one, if not the first, of the primary concepts an IPSEL agent may internally represent with structure differentiation. Through the integration of the concept of Time, the structure can now characterize further perceptions. All perceptions do not change evenly throughout Time and are modulated by the body position and sensor orientation. Therefore, invariance on perceptions through Time engender the formation of the concept of Space. With the ability to represent Time and Space concepts, the structure can now form a concept of Object which is perception's invariances through Space and Time. Time, Space and Object are the three primary concepts. From that point, the system may differentiate objects from one another to form more elaborate concepts, again, by representing the invariance of its perception through already acquired concepts. Depending on its sensors' position, the system could form the concept of its own body, as it may be the most invariant object of perception. Geometric forms, colours, symbols and so on, are all internal representations of invariant perceptions through Space/Time/Object. Progressively, the structure represents its perceptual environment with concepts. IPSEL agent's world representation is thus, totally subjective.

From the global point of view, concepts appear in sequences. Because of Hebbian and reinforcement mechanisms, concepts which are close in the sequence will develop and differentiate inter-concepts connections. Through the same dynamism in which local patterns of a common concept can activate each other, inter-concepts' connections enable concept inference. Sequences of concepts can now be internally simulated, therefore the perceptual environment they have originated from, can be simulated. This environment simulation is valuable for the structure, as it gives it the capacity to represent past or future configurations and their associated emotional responses. This allows the system to remember and to predict.

Internal intuitive representation is inspired by the philosophy of Carl Jung (Jung 1964). The notion of concept emerging from perceptual experience is inspired and well developed in other terms by grounded cognitivists (Barsalou 2010). Characterization of environmental perception through Time and Space consideration is mainly inspired by the philosophy of Arthur Schopenhauer (Schopenhauer 1891). Objects' definition and relationships for environmental representations is inspired from Rudolf Carnap's book "The logical structure of the world" (Carnap 1967). Recent reports show that the symbolic nature of computation is attainable through a connectivism mechanism with the help of some structural specifications (Lample and Charton 2019). Other artificial neural network models consider expressive probabilistic circuits with certain structural constraints that support tractable probabilistic inference (Khosravi et al. 2019). In the neurobiology field, a neural basis for the retrieval of conceptual knowledge has been proposed from empirical reports (Tranel et al. 1997) and strong evidence for a neural realization of distributional reinforcement learning have been presented (Dabney et al. 2020).

Common-sense is defined by Cambridge online dictionary as "The basic level of practical knowledge and judgment that we all need to help us live in a reasonable and safe way", or for Marvin Minsky "the ability to think about ordinary things the way people can" (Singh and Minsky 2003). For an IPSEL agent, common sense would be the system's knowledge represented by its differentiated structure. It would have several forms: intuitive when local patterns are considered, giving the agent a sort of "common-sense" about which behaviours to produce for a given set of perceptions; conceptual when it states how concepts are linked together, and how objects they represent may interact with each other. In both cases these knowledges are embodied in the structure and are thus mostly acquired by individual experience. Experience is relative to the system's perceptual modalities, therefore its common-sense is subjective. For example, distinguishing between north and south magnetic poles appears to be common sense for a homing pigeon whereas most humans require a tool for achieving this distinction. In a broad sense, in the IPSEL paradigm, we would define common-sense as knowledge acquired by experience.

For an IPSEL agent, all behaviours are either direct or intuitive, even if sometimes the intuitive behaviour is triggered by inferred conceptual sequences produced by the declarative system S2. If multiple agents are interacting with each other, they can learn intuitive synchronized behaviours that would externally be seen as communication. They can also learn common symbols that refer to subjective concepts, hence allowing the development of communication language as commonly defined. For that reason, we say that an IPSEL agent has two communication modalities: intuitive where words of a speech are intuitive learned behaviours and conceptual when symbols or combination of symbols refer to concepts. These communications can be of various forms since words of a speech can be of multiple natures such as body-movement, sound, smell or visual pattern (in other words, everything that can be perceived by both agents involved). The various modalities of speech, intuitive or deliberative, have been explored and theorized by psychiatrist Sigmund Freud (Freud and Bonaparte 1954). Complex social behaviours have been shown to emerge from artificial multi-agents' interactions with reinforcement learning (Baker et al. 2019).

4 Conclusion

In this paper we consider human-level cognition as a dualism between an inductive process and a deductive one which relies on emerging logic. An experiment and a complete comparison with existing cognitive architectures would be an interesting development that should be explored. If we try to place IPSEL model in the hybrid group of cognitive architecture (Kotseruba and Tsotsos 2018), models such as CLARION (Sun et al. 2001) have more similarities with our approach. Specifically, the IPSEL perspective is consistent with Arthur Schopenhauer theory of will and ideas, and Sigmund Freud works on unconsciousness and language. We generally tried to avoid technical consideration to present a functional architecture that is more consistent with the predominant theories of cognitive sciences.

In our theory, an IPSEL agent builds its knowledge through perceptual experiences. Throughout different phases of development its inner structure self-organizes and enables the emergence of an inner dialog between internal representations and sensory perceptions. All of its experiences are associated with an emotional response that guides a learning mechanism and influences resulting behaviours. Thoughts of the agent are constructed sequences of concepts. As concepts represent combinations of environment perceptions, thoughts represent relations between them. By internally representing the external environment as concepts, and relations that are associated to them, the structure can "hallucinate" environments that are not currently perceived. It allows the agent to remember past environment states and predict future ones. It forms a loop where perceptions activate multiple parts of the structure. Emerging concepts trigger a chain reaction that produce a conceptual sequence generated by the flow of activity through induced preferred inter-concept paths. While being constructed, the conceptual sequences activate new parts of the structure, ending the loop in a top-down manner and acting as new sources of information for cognitive processing. All declarative cognitive functions such as planning, deliberating, or performing an introspection, are supported by conceptual sequence production. We conjecture that an IPSEL agent is emotionally rational and its knowledge is subjective.

In 1950, Alan Turing proposed a test to evaluate machine intelligence. It has been greatly debated and the community had a hard time defining intelligence and other terms associated to it. As Searl pointed out, symbols don't carry out meaning and symbolic computation isn't enough to catch the idea behind it. It is maybe for this reason that Turing included two humans in his original description of the imitation game. Two humans, when they communicate, can use overtone, common-sense, metaphors, irony, abstraction, that is to say, many language forms that not only rely on grammatically correct symbolic sentences but also on a shared world representation and socio-cultural knowledge. Beside the great achievement of artificial intelligence techniques, machines still struggle to catch these deeper aspects and are only efficient in narrowed environments. Consequently, machine behaviours, trustworthy AI, ethical AI and explainable AI are all new topics of interest for the community.

For an IPSEL agent, the ability to succeed at the Turing test, would require that the system is granted with the same modality of sensors as humans and has had an individual experience of the world that is close to a human's one. At the end, even with these requirements, nothing assures us that the specific tested agent will pass the test. But are we sure that all humans uniformly would?

References

Baars, B.J.: Global workspace theory of consciousness: toward a cognitive neuroscience of human experience. Progress Brain Res. **150**, 45–53 (2005)

Baker, B., et al.: Emergent tool use from multi-agent autocurricula. arXiv preprint arXiv:1909.07528 (2019)

Barsalou, L.W.: Grounded cognition: past, present, and future. Topics in cognitive science **2**(4), 716–724 (2010)

Botvinick, M., et al.: Reinforcement learning, fast and slow. Trends Cogn Sci **23**(5), 408–422 (2019)

Carnap, R.: The Logical Structure of the World. University of California Press, Berkeley (1967)

Dabney, W., Kurth-Nelson, Z., Uchida, N., et al.: A distributional code for value in dopamine-based reinforcement learning. Nature **577**(7792), 671–675 (2020)

Damasio, A.R., Tranel, D., Damasio, H.C.: Behavior: theory and preliminary testing. In: Frontal Lobe Function and Dysfunction, p. 217 (1991)

Dehaene, S., Kerszberg, M., Changeux, J.P.: A neuronal model of a global workspace in effortful cognitive tasks. Proc. Natl. Acad. Sci. **95**(24), 14529–14534 (1998)

Dosovitskiy, A., Koltun, V.: Learning to act by predicting the future. arXiv preprint arXiv:1611.01779 (2016)

Everitt, T., Lea, G., Hutter, M.: AGI safety literature review. arXiv preprint arXiv:1805.01109 (2018)

Freud, S., Bonaparte, P.M.: The Origins of Psychoanalysis, vol. 216. Imago, London (1954)

Garnelo, M., Arulkumaran, K., Shanahan, M.: Towards deep symbolic reinforcement learning. arXiv preprint arXiv:1609.05518 (2016)

Hopfield, J.J.: Neural networks and physical systems with emergent collective computational abilities. Proc. Natl. Acad. Sci. **79**(8), 2554–2558 (1982)

James, W., Burkhardt, F., Bowers, F., Skrupskelis, I.K.: The Principles of Psychology, vol. 1, no. 2. Macmillan, London (1890)

Jung, C.G.: Man and His Symbols. Laurel (1964)

Jung, R.E., Haier, R.J.: The Parieto-Frontal Integration Theory (P-FIT) of intelligence: converging neuroimaging evidence. Behav. Brain Sci. **30**(2), 135–154 (2007)

Kahneman, D.: Thinking, Fast and Slow. Macmillan, New York (2011)

Khosravi, P., Choi, Y., Liang, Y., Vergari, A., Van den Broeck, G.: On tractable computation of expected predictions. In: Advances in Neural Information Processing Systems, pp. 11167–11178 (2019)

Kotseruba, I., Tsotsos, J.K.: 40 years of cognitive architectures: core cognitive abilities and practical applications. Artif. Intell. Rev. **53**, 17–94 (2018). https://doi.org/10.1007/s10462-018-9646-y

Lample, G., Charton, F.: Deep learning for symbolic mathematics. arXiv preprint arXiv:1912.01412 (2019)

Libet, B.: Unconscious cerebral initiative and the role of conscious will in voluntary action. Behav. Brain Sci. **8**(4), 529–539 (1985)

Marcus, G., Davis, E.: Rebooting AI: Building Artificial Intelligence We Can Trust. Pantheon (2019)

Menon, V.: Large-scale brain networks and psychopathology: a unifying triple network model. Trends in cognitive sciences **15**(10), 483–506 (2011)

Miconi, T., Clune, J., Stanley, K.O.: Differentiable plasticity: training plastic neural networks with backpropagation. arXiv preprint arXiv:1804.02464 (2018)

Schopenhauer, A.: The World as Will and Idea, vol. 1. Library of Alexandria (1891)

Searle, J.R.: Minds, brains, and programs. Behav. Brain Sci. 3(3), 417–424 (1980)

Singh, P., Minsky, M.: An architecture for combining ways to think. In: IEMC 2003 Proceedings. Managing Technologically Driven Organizations: The Human Side of Innovation and Change (IEEE Cat. No. 03CH37502), pp. 669–674. IEEE (2003)

Sun, R., Merrill, E., Peterson, T.: From implicit skills to explicit knowledge: a bottom-up model of skill learning. Cogn. Sci. 25(2), 203–244 (2001)

Tranel, D., Damasio, H., Damasio, A.R.: A neural basis for the retrieval of conceptual knowledge. Neuropsychologia 35(10), 1319–1327 (1997)

Turing, A.M.: Computing machinery and intelligence. Mind 49, 433–460 (1950)

Wayne, G., et al.: Unsupervised predictive memory in a goal-directed agent. arXiv preprint arXiv: 1803.10760 (2018)

Combinatorial Decision Dags: A Natural Computational Model for General Intelligence

Ben Goertzel[(✉)]

SingularityNET Foundation and OpenCog Foundation, Amsterdam, The Netherlands
ben@singularitynet.io

Abstract. A novel computational model (CoDD) utilizing combinatory logic to create higher-order decision trees is presented. A theoretical analysis of general intelligence in terms of the formal theory of pattern recognition and pattern formation is outlined, and shown to take especially natural form in the case where patterns are expressed in CoDD language. Relationships between logical entropy and algorithmic information, and Shannon entropy and runtime complexity, are shown to be elucidated by this approach. Extension to the quantum computing case is also briefly discussed.

1 Introduction

The theoretical foundations of general intelligence outlined in *The Hidden Pattern* [7] and formalized in earlier works going back to 1991 [5] are fundamentally grounded in the notion of *pattern*. Minds are conceived as patterns emergent in physical cognitive systems, and emergent between these systems and their environments. Intelligent activity is understood as the process of a system recognizing patterns in itself and its environment, including patterns in which actions tend to achieve which results in which contexts, and then choosing actions to fit into these recognized patterns.

The formalization of the pattern concept standardly used in this context is based on algorithmic information – in essence a pattern in x is a compressing program for x, a program shorter than x that computes x. The definition can be extended to incorporate factors like runtime complexity and lossy compression, but the crux remains algorithmic information. As program length depends on the assumed underlying computer, this formalization approach has an undesirable arbitrariness as its route, though of course as entity sizes go to infinity this arbitrariness becomes irrelevant due to bisimulation arguments.

Here we present a conceptually cleaner foundation for the pattern-theoretic analysis of general intelligence, in the form of a new formulation of the pattern concept in terms of distinctions and decisions. We present a specific computational model – Combinatorial Decision Dags or CoDDs – with a high degree of naturalness in the context of cognitive systems, and use CoDDs to explore the

B. Goertzel et al. (Eds.): AGI 2020, LNAI 12177, pp. 131–141, 2020.
https://doi.org/10.1007/978-3-030-52152-3_14

relationship between distinction, pattern, runtime complexity, Shannon entropy and logical entropy. We also briefly indicate extensions of these ideas to the quantum domain, in which Boolean distinctions are replaced with amplitude-labeled quantum distinctions and classical patterns are replaced by "quatterns."

The goal is to provide a clear and simple mathematical framework that intuitively matches the requirements of general intelligence, founded on a computational model designed with the requirements of modeling cognitive systems in mind.

2   Conceptualizing Pattern in Terms of Distinction and Decision

Taking our cue from G. Spencer-Brown [10], let us begin our with the elemental notion of *distinction*.

A distinction is a distinction between one collection of entities A and another collection of entities B. Two distinctions are distinguished from each other if:

- One distinguishes A_1 from B_1
- The other distinguishes A_2 from B_2
- It's not the case that A_1 and A_2 are identical and B_1 and B_2 are identical.

Consider a program that takes certain inputs and produces output from them. We are then moved to ask: Can we think about the "simplicity" of a process as ρersely related to the number of distinctions it makes? I.e. is the "complexity" of a program well conceived in terms of the number of pairs of legal inputs to which it assigns different outputs?[1]

This line of thinking meshes naturally with the concept of *logical entropy* [3] – where the logical entropy of a partition of n elements is the percentage of pairs (x, y) of elements so that x and y live in different partition cells. If we consider a program as a partition of its inputs, where two inputs go into the same partition cell if they produce the same output, then the logical entropy of this partition is one measure of the program's complexity. The simpler programs are then the ones with the lowest logical entropy.

There is an interesting relationship between program length and this sort of program logical entropy. For each N there will be some upper bound to the logical entropy of programs of length N, and it's not hard to see that most programs of length N will have logical entropy fairly near this upper bound.

---

[1] Note that the inputs and outputs of programs may also be programs – i.e. we can consider ourselves in an "algorithmic chemistry" $T_Y$pe domain [4,6] comprising a space S of programs that map inputs from S into outputs in S. This can be formalized in various ways including set theory with an Anti-Foundation Axiom.).

2.1   Shannon Entropy, Program Specialization and Runtime complexity

The relationship between logical entropy and Shannon entropy is also worth exploring.

Consider a case where each possible input for a program is represented as a (generally long) bit string.

Given the set of distinctions that a program makes (considering the program as a partition of its inputs), we can also ask: If we were to effect this set of distinctions via a sequence of distinctions ρolving individual entries in input bit-strings, how long would the sequence need to be? E.g. if we break things down into: First distinguish portion I_1 of input space from portion I_2 of input space (using a single bit of the input), then within I_1 distinguish subregion I_{11} from subregion I_{12} (using another bit of the input), etc. – then how many distinctions need to be in this binary tree of distinctions?

The leaves of this binary decision tree are the partition elements; and the length of the path from the root to a given leaf, is the number of binary questions one needs to ask to prove that some input lies in that particular partition cell.

This decision tree is closely related to the Shannon entropy of the partition implied by the program. Suppose we have a probability distribution on the inputs to the program. The Shannon entropy of this distribution is a lower bound on the average length of the path from the root of the tree to a leaf of the tree, i.e. a lower bound on the "average tree depth." (The average is taken over all possible inputs drawn from the distribution.)

The optimal binary decision tree for the partition, relative to a given distribution on the bit strings being partitioned, can be considered as the one for which the average length from root to leaf is minimal. Not knowing the distribution on inputs, a heuristic is to guess the optimal tree will be one of those with the fewest nodes.

If we assume a simplified computational model in which one binary distinction is made per unit time, then the average depth of this binary decision tree is related to the average runtime complexity of the program. It tells you how long it would take, on average over all possible inputs, to run the program on an abstract machine making one distinction (based on one bit of the input string) per unit time. For fixed input length N, this is, it would seem, a lower bound for the average runtime complexity of the program on a machine with rapid access to enough memory to store this huge tree.

Other, more practical instantiations of the same program achieve greater compactness by ρolving operations other than simply comparing individual bits of input strings. These other instantiations may run faster on machines that don't have rapid access to enough memory to store a huge binary decision tree. They involve "overhead" in the sense that they use more complex mechanisms to do what could be more simply done using a series of binary judgments based on input bits; but these complex mechanisms allow a lot of binary judgments to be carried out using a smaller amount of memory, which is better in the case of a computing system that has rapid access only to a relatively small amount of memory, and much slower access to a larger auxiliary memory.

This binary decision tree can be viewed as a "program specialization" of the original program to the case of input sequences of length N or less. Like most program specializations it removes abstraction and creates tremendous bloat ρolving a lot of nested conditionals.

Given a program (or a process more generally), then, we can characterize this program via the set of distinctions it makes between its inputs. Given a distribution over the inputs, one can calculate the logical entropy of the set of distinctions (which is a measure of how complex is the action of the program in terms of its results), and one can also calculate the average depth of the optimal binary decision tree for emulating the action of the program, which is a measure of how complex is the action of the program in terms of its runtime requirements. Of course one can also quantify the distinction-set implied by the program in a lot of other ways; these are merely the simplest relevant quantifications.

Philosophically, if we begin with the partition of input space rather than the program, we can view the construction of the binary decision tree as a form of the emergence of time. That is: time arises from the sequencing involved in constructing the binary decision tree, which intrinsically incorporates a notion of one decision occurring after another. The "after" here basically has the semantics "in the context of" – the next step is to be interpreted in terms of the previous step, rather than vice versa. The notion of complex structures unfolding over time then emerges from the introduction of "memory space" or "size" as a constraint – i.e. from the desire to shrink the tree while leaving the action the same, and increasing the average runtime as little as possible.

2.2   Grounding Pattern in Distinction

A pattern being a "representation as something simpler" – the core intuition underlying the classic compression-based conceptualization of pattern – can be formulated in terms of distinction as follows.

Suppose one has

- an "invariant-set", meaning a function ρ that distinguishes certain distinctions that are relevant and certain that are not
- a program F that makes certain distinctions among its potential inputs (by mapping them into different outputs)

Then we may say: *P is a pattern in F, relative to ρ, if it makes all the distinctions F does that ρ identifies as relevant, but makes fewer distinctions than F overall...*

Extending this, we could say that: P is an approximate pattern in F if: it makes K fewer distinctions than F overall, and misses fewer than K of the distinctions F does that ρ identifies as relevant.

To incorporate runtime complexity, if we have a weighting on the distinctions judged relevant by ρ, we could require additionally that *the optimal binary decision tree for P has lower average root-to-leaf length than the optimal binary decision tree for F* (relative to this weighting). This means that in a certain idealized sense, P is "fundamentally faster" than F.

The degree of runtime optimization provided by P in this sense could be included in the definition of approximate pattern as a multiplicative factor.

3   A Quantum Definition of Pattern

To extend these ideas in the direction of quantum computing, we extend the notion of a *dit* (a distinction) to that of a *qudit* – a distinction btw two entities, labeled with a (complex) amplitude.

Assume as above one has an "invariant-set" defining function ρ that assigns a "relevance amplitude" to each qudit in its domain; and assume one is given a quantum program F whose inputs are vectors of amplitudes, and that maps each input into different outputs with different amplitude-weights.

Associate P (for instance) with a "distinction vector" P^* that has coordinate entries corresponding to pairs of the form [input set 1, input set 2] where the entry in the coordinate is the amplitude assigned to the distinction between the output produced by P on input set 1 and the output produced by P on input set 2 ...

Then P is a *quattern* in F, relative to ρ, if

- $|<\rho><F^* - P^*>|$ is small
- $|P^*| < |F^*|$

So one can define a quattern intensity degree via a formula like
$$(|F^*| - |P^*|) * (\ |\rho| - |<\rho><F^* - P^*>|\ )\ /\ |\rho|$$
This ends up looking a bit like the good old definition of pattern in terms of compression, but it's all about counting distinctions (qudits) now.

A quantum history is a network of interlinked qudits... So a quantum distinction graph is a network of qudits between quantum distinction graphs.

Runtime complexity can also be analyzed similarly to in the "classical" case considered above.

Recall the basic concept of a quantum decision tree [2]. In a simple, straightforward formulation, algorithm on inputs of size n works on 3 registers I, B, W where I has $log(n)$ qubits and is used to write a query, B has one qubit and is used to store the answer to a query and W is the workspace register with polynomially many qubits. The query steps are modeled as particular unitary operators, and the algorithm is allowed to perform intermediate computations between the queries in the form of unitary operators independent of the input.

In this formalism, a k-query decision tree A is the unitary operator $A = U_k O U_{k-1} \ldots U_1 O U_0$ and the output of the algorithm is the value obtained when the first qubit of $A|0, 0, 0>$ is measured in any given basis.

The quantum decision tree complexity Q_2 is the depth of the lowest-depth quantum decision tree that gives the result $f(x)$ with probability at least 2/3 for all s. Another quantum decision tree complexity measure, Q_E, is defined as the depth of the lowest-depth quantum decision tree that gives the result $f(x)$ with probability 1 in all cases (i.e. computes exactly). Other variations are obviously possible. These sorts of measures are evidently analogues of the approach to runtime complexity proposed above. It has been shown that the Shannon entropy of a random variable computed by the function $f(X)$ is a lower bound for the Q_E quantum decision tree complexity of f citeshi2000entropy.

In assessing the degree to which P is a quattern in F, one can then look at the quantum decision tree complexity of P versus that of F, similarly to how in the classical case one looks at the size of the decision tree associated with P versus that of the decision tree associated with F.

Similarly to in the classical case, the runtime complexity measure depends in a messy but apparently inevitable way on assumptions regarding the memory of the underlying computing machine. In the quantum case, if we restrict the workspace W further than just saying it has to be polynomial in the input size n, then we will in generally get larger decision trees.

Also similarly to the classical case, here real computation usually involves quantum circuits that do more than just query the input repeatedly and combine the query results – thus resulting, much of the time, in smaller programs that however involve more complex operators. But the size of the quantum decision tree complexity summarizes, in a sense, the temporal complexity involved in doing what the program does, at a basic level, without getting into tricks that may be used to accelerate it on various computational architectures with various processing speeds associated with various particularly-sized memory stores.

3.1 Weidits and Weitterns

What we have done above with amplitude-valued distinctions, one could do perfectly well for distinctions labeled with others sorts of weights. Quaternions e.g. would seem unproblematic, as Banach algebras over quaternions are understood and relatively well-behaved. The notion of qudit and quattern in this way can be generalized to weidit and weittern, defined relative to any sort of weight, not necessarily complex number weights.

4 Combinatorial Decision Dags: A Pattern-Based Computational Model

One can also use these ideas to articulate a novel, foundationally pattern-oriented universal computational model. Of course there are numerous universal computational models already in practical and theoretical use, but one that is grounded in distinctions and patterns may be especially useful in a cognitive modeling and AGI context, if one adopts a view of general intelligence that places pattern at the coore.

It is straightforward to make the decision-tree rendition of programs recursive – just take a bit-string encoding of a decision tree and feed it as input to another decision tree. In this way we create decision trees that represent higher-order functions. We just need to add encoder and decoder primitives, mapping back and forth between decision trees and bit strings, to our basic language.

This leads us to the notion of Combinatorial Decision Dags (CoDDs). Defining a k'th order decision dag as one that takes $k-1$'st order decision dags as inputs, it is clear that k'th order decision trees (or dags) are equivalent to SK combinator expressions, thus have universal expressive capability among Turing computable functions.

To be a bit more explicit: In this context, programs are viewed roughly as follows:

- Start with (higher order) decision trees, then find cases where there is a pattern P in subtree T_X relative to subtree T_Y.
- Then replace T_X with P plus a pointer to T_Y as P's input (this is "pattern-based memo-ization")
- Repeat, and eventually one gets a compact, complex program rather than a forest of recursively nested decision trees

Here P is of course a function that can be represented as a decision tree, or else as a decision tree with pattern-based memo-ization as described above.

The K combinator $Kyx = y$ (using curried notation) is a function so that, given any input y, Ky is a decision-tree that always outputs y. Given the encoding of (first or higher order) decision trees as bit strings, K combinator for bit string inputs can be applied to any decision tree as input.

The S combinator has the form $Sfxy = (fx)(fy)$. So if (still currying) we have a tree taking (a bit-string-encoded version of) another tree as input,

$$T_{X_1} T_{X_2}$$

and we then have the same pattern in both T_1 and T_2,

$$(PT_{Y_2})(PT_{Y_1})$$

we get universal computing power by memo-izing the P into

$$SPT_{Y_1} T_{Y_2}$$

What is interesting here conceptually is that we are obtaining totally general pattern recognition capability, from the simple ingredients of

- Decision trees (i.e. single-feature queries and conditionals)
- Recursion (mapping decision trees into bit strings and vice-versa)
- Recognition of simple repeated patterns (i.e. the same P is a pattern in both T_{Y_2} and its argument T_{Y_1})

This gives a novel perspective on the meaning and power of the S combinator. S is recognizing a simple repeated pattern. The universality of SK shows basically that all computable patterns can be built up from simple repetitions – if the "building up" involves recursion and higher order functions.

In a phrase: *Distinction, If, Repetition-Recognition and Recursion Yield Universal Computation.*

This is nothing so new mathematically, but it's elegant conceptually to thus interpret universality of SK in terms of pattern recognition.

5 Syntax-Semantics Correlation

The line of thinking regarding decision trees, patterns and computations presented above provides a new way of looking at syntax-semantics correlation, which is a key concept in probabilistic evolutionary learning [9] and some other AI algorithms.

Syntax-semantics correlation means the correlation between two distances:

- The distance between program P and program Q, in terms of the syntactic forms P and Q take in a particular programming language
- The distance between P and Q, in terms of their manifestation as sets of input-output pairs

If this correlation is reasonably high, then syntactic manipulations can be used as a proxy or guide to semantic manipulations, which can provide significant efficiency gains.

It is known that, for the case of Boolean functions, it's possible to achieve a relatively high level of syntax-semantics correlation in relatively local regions of Boolean function space, if one adopts a language that arranges Boolean functions in a certain hierarchical format called Elegant Normal Form (ENF). ENF can be extended beyond Boolean functions to general list operations and primitive recursive functions, and this has been done in the OpenCog AI Engine in the context of the MOSES probabilistic evolutionary learning algorithm.

The present considerations, however, suggest a more information-theoretic approach to syntax-semantics correlation.

Consider first the case of Boolean functions. Suppose we re-organize a Boolean function as a decision tree, choosing from among the smallest such decision trees representing the function the one that does more entropy-reduction toward the root of the tree (so one would rather have the first decisions made while traversing the tree be the most informative). Evaluating a pair of Boolean functions on a common distribution of inputs, this should cause semantic and syntactic distance to be fairly correlated.

Specifically, for the semantic distance between two functions f and g defined on the same input space, consider the L1 distance evaluated relative to a given probability distribution over inputs. For the syntactic distance, consider first the decision-tree versions of f and g, where each node is labeled with the amount of entropy reduction the decision at that node provides. Then if one measures the edit distance between the trees for f and g, but giving more cost to edits that involve more highly-weighted (more entropy-reducing) nodes, one should get a syntactic distance that correlates quite closely with semantic distance. If one ignore the weights and gives more cost to edits that occur higher up in the trees, one should obtain similar but weaker correlation.

Of course, practical algorithms like XGBoost use greedy learning to form decision trees and are thus crude approximations of the "most entropy-reducing among the smallest decision trees" ... the trees obtained from XGBoost don't actually give the optimal Huffman encoding, so their relationship with entropy is only approximate. How good an approximation the greedy approach will give in various circumstances is difficult to say and requires context-specific analysis.

Going beyond Boolean functions, if one adopts the pattern-based SK model described above, one has a situation where each pattern in a decision tree T is equivalent to a decision tree on an input space consisting of decision trees – and one can think about the degree to which this pattern increases or reduces entropy as it maps inputs into outputs. Similar to the Boolean case, one can use an edit distance that weights edits to more entropy-reducing nodes higher; or one can simplify and weight more strongly those edits that are further from the tree leaves.

In this context, the rewriting done via Reduct rules in OpenCog today becomes interpretable as a form of pattern recognition. The guideline implied is that a Reduct rule should only be applied if there is some reason to suspect it's serving as a pattern in the tree it's reducing. I.e. for a rewrite rule *source* → *target*, what we want is that when running the rule backwards as *target* ← *source*, the backwards rule constitutes a pattern in *source*. If this is the case, then the Reduct engine is carrying out repeated acts of pattern recognition in a program tree, resulting in a tree that has less informational redundancy than the initial version; and likely there is higher syntax-semantics correlation across an ensemble of such trees than among a corresponding ensemble of non-reduced trees.

6   Connecting Algorithmic and Statistical Complexity: Larger Higher-Order Decision Trees Have Higher Logical Entropy

There are well known theorems relating algorithmic information to Shannon entropy; however these results have significant limitations. It appears one can arrive at a less problematic relationship between information-theoretic uncertainty and compactness-of-expression by comparing *logical entropy* with *compactness of expression in the CoDD formalism*.

In the conventional algorithmic/Shannon case, if one has a source emanating bit strings according to a certain probability distribution, then for simple (low complexity) distributions the average Kolmogorov complexity of the generated bit strings is close to the Shannon entropy of the distribution; but these two quantities may be wide apart for distributions of high complexity.

To be more precise, one can look at the average code-word length one would obtain by associating each bit-string with its maximally compressed representation as its code-word (where the average is calculated according to the assumed distribution over bit-strings); and then at the average code-word length one would obtain if one assigned more frequent bit-strings shorter code-words, which is roughly the entropy of the distribution. The difference between these two average code-word lengths is bounded by the algorithmic information of the distribution itself (plus a constant). [8].

This is somewhat elegant, but on the other hand, complex probability distributions are the ones that we care most about in domains like biology, psychology and AI. So it's also unsatisfying in a way.

A decision tree implies a partition of its input space, via associating each input with the partition defined by the path thru the decision tree that it follows. It is then intuitive that, *on average* (roughly speaking – I will make this more precise below) a random bigger decision tree will imply a partition w/ higher logical entropy than a random smaller decision tree. The same intuitive reasoning applies to a random decision dag, or a random k'th order decision dag. This is the CoDD incarnation of the intuition that "bigger programs do higher entropy things."

The crux of the matter is the simple observation that *adding a decision node to a CoDD can increase the logical entropy of the partition the CoDD represents, but it can't decrease it.*

So if we measure the size of a CoDD as the number of decision nodes in it, then we know that *adding onto a CoDD will either increase the logical entropy or keep it constant.* (Why would it be kept constant? Basically if the added distinction made was then ignored by other distinctions intervening between it and the final output of the CoDD.)

If we view each step of adding a new decision node onto a CoDD as a random process, then on the whole larger CoDDs (which involve more steps to be added onto nothingness) are going to have higher logical entropy, as they involve more probably-logical-entropy-increasing expansion steps.

So one concludes that, in the CoDD computational model

- adding onto a program does not decrease its logical entropy
- on average bigger programs have higher logical entropy.

6.1   Connecting Algorithmic and Statistical Complexity in the Quantum Case

What is the quantum version of this conclusion? Baez [1] has presented an extension of classical combinatory logic that applies to the quantum case; so by considering these generalized combinators operating over quantum decision trees as described above, along with a linear operator that flattens a quantum decision tree into a quantum state vector, one obtains a natural concept of a quantum CoDD.

The argument becomes too involved to present here, but it seems to work out that adding a new decision node to a quantum CoDD cannot decrease the quantum logical entropy – leading to the conclusion that a larger quantum CoDD will have greater quantum logical entropy. Details of this case will be presented in a later paper.

7   Conclusion

Beginning from the foundational notion of distinction, we have shown a new path to constructing and defining the concept of pattern, which has been used as the basis of theoretical analyses of general intelligence. We have shown that the pattern concept thus formulated leads naturally to a novel universal computational model, combinatory decision dags. These CoDDs highlight subtle relationships between static program complexity and logical entropy, and runtime complexity and Shannon entropy. Further the key concepts appear to generalize to the quantum domain, potentially yielding elements of a future theory of quantum cognitive processes and structures.

Further work will apply these concepts to the concrete analysis of particular classical and quantum cognitive processes, e.g. in the context of evolutionary program learning systems, probability and amplitude based reasoning systems, and integrative cognitive architectures such as OpenCog.

Acknowledgments. Conversations with Zar Goertzel were valuable in early stages of refining these ideas. General inspiration from Lou Kauffman and G. Spencer Brown's work on distinctions is also worth mentioning.

References

1. Baez, J.C., Stay, M.: Physics, topology, logic and computation: a Rosetta stone (2009)
2. Bera, D.: Quantum Circuits: Power and Limitations. Ph.D thesis, Boston University (2010)
3. Ellerman, D.: An introduction to logical entropy and its relation to Shannon entropy (2013)
4. Fontana, W.: Algorithmic chemistry II. Artificial life **11**, 159–209 (1991)
5. Goertzel, B.: The Structure of Intelligence. Springer, New York (1991)
6. Goertzel, B.: Chaotic Logic. Plenum, New York (1994)
7. Goertzel, B.: The Hidden Pattern. Brown Walker, Boca Raton (2006)
8. Grunwald, P., Vitanyi, P.: Shannon information and Kolmogorov complexity (2010). http://citeseerx.ist.psu.edu/viewdoc/summary?doi=10.1.1.174.2023
9. Looks, M.: Competent Program Evolution. Ph.D thesis, Computer Science Department, Washington University (2006)
10. Spencer Brown, G.: Laws of Form. Cognizer, Portland (1967)

What Kind of Programming Language Best Suits Integrative AGI?

Ben Goertzel[(✉)]

SingularityNET Foundation and OpenCog Foundation, Amsterdam, The Netherlands
ben@singularitynet.io

Abstract. What kind of programming language would be most appropriate to serve the needs of integrative, multi-paradigm, multi-software-system approaches to AGI? This question is broached via exploring the more particular question of how to create a more scalable and usable version of the "Atomese" programming language that forms a key component of the OpenCog AGI design (an "Atomese 2.0"). It is tentatively proposed that
- The core of Atomese 2.0 should be a very flexible framework of rewriting rules for rewriting a metagraph (where the rules themselves are represented within the same metagraph, and some of the intermediate data created and used during the rule-interpretation process may be represented in the same metagraph).
- This framework should (among other requirements)
  - support concurrent rewriting of the metagraph according to rules that are labeled with various sorts of uncertainty-quantifications, and that are labeled with various sorts of types associated with various type systems. A gradual typing approach should be used to enable mixture of rules and other metagraph nodes/links associated with various type systems, and untyped metagraph nodes/links not associated with any type system.
  - allow reasonable efficiency and scalability, including in concurrent and distributed processing contexts, in the case where a large percentage of processing time is occupied with evaluating static pattern-matching queries on specific subgraphs of a large metagraph (including a rich variety of queries such as matches against nodes representing variables, and matches against whole subgraphs, etc.)
  - allow efficient and convenient invocation and manipulation of external libraries for carrying out processing that is not efficiently done in Atomese directly
- Among the formalisms we will very likely want to implement within this framework is *probabilistic dependent-linear-typed lambda calculus* or something similar, perhaps with a Pure IsoType approach to dependent type inheritance. Thus we want the general framework to support reasonably efficient/convenient operations within this particular formalism, as an example.

© Springer Nature Switzerland AG 2020
B. Goertzel et al. (Eds.): AGI 2020, LNAI 12177, pp. 142–152, 2020.
https://doi.org/10.1007/978-3-030-52152-3_15

1 Context and Motivations

The history of AI has persistently featured fascinating feedback, synergy and tension between AI system design and programming language design. Numerous researchers have come to the conclusion that, to make the radical AI advances they sought, they would require a better and more AI-friendly programming language environment. Thus we got languages like LISP and Prolog and their derivates. Which have taught us a lot about AI and programming, yet without leading so far to the hoped-for AI breakthroughs.

Contemporary neural net based AI hasn't focused on introduction of new programming languages, but rather on new libraries such as Tensorflow, Torch, Theano and so forth. On the other hand, the probabilistic programming paradigm has led to a remarkable profusion of new languages, most of which have arguably been unnecessary and distracted focus from the problem of efficiently executing probabilistic programs applied to real-world situations.

If one wants to pursue an integrative, multi-paradigm approach to AGI, then the situation as regards programming languages remains very far from optimal. If one want to integrate, say, a logic programming system with a deep neural net perception system and a program learning system based on higher order functional types – one is quite likely to want to implement the three components in different languages, and glue them together with scripts written in a simple language such as python. Either that or one decides to value consistency and unity over elegance and efficiency, and shoehorns all three into a single language, reconciling oneself to either dramatic inefficiency or unwieldy, awkward code.

We have faced these issues recently in thinking through an envisioned redesign and reimplementation of the OpenCog AGI platform. The current version of OpenCog relies heavily on a tool called the OpenCog Pattern Matcher, which is implemented in Scheme and is able to carry out highly complex procedure execution and predicate evaluation in the course of matching patterns against OpenCog's "Atomspace" weighted, labeled hypergraph knowledge store. This Pattern Matcher is powerful but has become problematic for various reasons, including the lack of any built-in type system with an efficient type checker associated to it, and the complexity of interlacing the pattern matching process with calls to external processing tools such as deep neural net toolkits. So we have begun designing a replacement we call "Atomese 2" – Atomese being the informal name given to Scheme scripts that invoke Atomspace API calls and OpenCog Pattern Matcher queries.

It turns out that many of the conceptual and formal issues arising in the context of Atomese 2 design are of significantly broader importance, and are things that would arise in any attempt to create a programming language having both realistic efficiency and elegance in the context of integrative AGI applications. In this paper we will review our thinking regarding Atomese 2, but keeping an eye always on the broader issues raised. In the end what's important for AGI is not any specific programming language, but rather the underlying principles and structures, which may ultimately be implemented in a variety of different languages.

2   Atomese 2 – Conclusions and Considerations

The OpenCog AGI framework, within which the Atomese language under discussion here operates, is centered on a large, distributed, weighted labeled metagraph called the "Atomspace." Atomese is then a custom language specialized in pattern-matching and transforming this metagraph ("Atom" being OpenCog lingo for metagraph nodes or links).

Just to give a flavor, a simple example of Atomese 1 usage is given in Fig. 2 – drawn from an application built by Cisco Systems[1] in collaboration with SingularityNET Foundation, applying OpenCog to fuse results from multiple vision-processing deep neural nets to make inferential judgments about street scenes (Fig. 1).

Fig. 1. Visual example of jaywalking that is recognized by Atomese expression in Fig. 2

The OpenCog AGI design includes a carefully wrought combination of multiple AI methods such as probabilistic logical reasoning and pattern mining; probabilistic evolutionary program learning; neural net based attention allocation; neural-symbolic usage of deep neural nets for language, vision and sound; algorithmic chemistry based computational creativity ... and more. It is an open-ended framework intended to allow experimentation with a variety of different AI algorithms and approaches. On the other hand, the assemblage of AI tools already being explored and experimented with in an OpenCog context is sufficiently broad as to militate strongly toward an extremely flexible design.

Design of Atomese 2 becomes inextricably bound up with design of the overall OpenCog framework, including the Atomspace itself and the specific AI tools and methods to be implemented in Atomese and run in the context of the Atomspace. Among the many issues that arise in this design process are:

1. What should the core Atomese formal language be?

---

[1] https://www.youtube.com/watch?v=s7EtRJatVmg.

```
BindLink(
    TypedVariableLink(VariableNode("pedestrian-tracklet"),
                      TypeNode("GroundedObjectNode")),
    AndLink(
        InheritanceLink(VariableNode("pedestrian-tracklet"),
                        ConceptNode("tracklet")),
        InheritanceLink(
            VariableNode("pedestrian-tracklet"),
            ConceptNode(str(RoadUserType.PERSON))),
        ApplyLink(MethodOfLink(
            GroundedObjectNode("traffic-lane"),
            ConceptNode("is_at")),
            ListLink(VariableNode("pedestrian-tracklet")))),
    MemberLink(ConceptNode("jaywalking"),
               VariableNode("pedestrian-tracklet"))))
```

Fig. 2. Atomese expression that recognizes simple forms of jaywalking based on output of deep neural visual recognizers. Application of the expression is mediated by OpenCog's URE rule engine, which leverages OpenCog Pattern Matcher internally.

2. Algorithmic approach to Atomese interpretation/compilation
3. Utilization of core Atomese to support various specialized formal languages useful for various AI algorithms
4. Surface form of Atomese language ("syntactic sugar")
5. RAM-based local Metagraph store – which must be optimized for heavy Atomese usage of certain sorts
6. Distributed and persistent Metagraph store, perhaps with distributed RAM-based middleware as well
7. Atomese libraries corresponding to particular AI algorithms and approaches (e.g. the ones involved in OpenCog already)
8. Mode of integration of Atomese programs with external data/knowledge stores and processing and learning frameworks (e.g. external deep neural net libraries)

In this paper we do not aim to address all these issues in depth, but rather focus on the first three.

In the context of core Atomese and its use to implement other formal languages (1 and 2 above), we need to think about issues such as:

– simple representation of the various Atom types in play in the OpenCog design
– effective representation of external entities like knowledge-stores, specialized learning algorithms, simulations etc. as monads [or using some other powerful mode of encapsulation]

- breaking down pattern-matching process into simple atomic operations like "match this pattern at this location"and "move locus of pattern-matching to?"
- compatibility of the above breakdown w/ concurrent and distributed processing
- timed pattern matching should be fairly easily efficiently implementable
- How can we make it simple for a developer to add low level optimized support for some particular set of predicates/schema that's of interest?

3   The Role of Static Pattern Matching in Atomese

A peculiarity of the intended AGI use-case for Atomese is that we can assume the vast majority of processing time is spent on two key operations,

1. checking a particular (generally small) sub-metagraph to see if a certain pattern is matched there, *for a wide variety of patterns, to be dynamically generated and not foreseeable in advance*
2. applying a small set of metagraph rewrite rules to a particular (generally small) metagraph

There can be assumed to be roughly comparable balance between these two sorts of operations.

Also, there is a need both for rapid processing of these sorts of queries on a large metagraph in local RAM, and for distributed processing of these sorts of queries on a metagraph that is stored across numerous machines.

This means it is not important that Atomese be especially efficient at, say, sorting lists or computing the FFT. What is important is that it is efficient at doing the above two operations and piping around, and doing simple manipulations on, the results of these operations. If e.g. list-sorting or mathematical calculations are needed, it is assumed that Atomese will get these things done via referencing libraries coded in other languages. Elegant and efficient interfacing with a variety of other languages and toolkits is thus highly important.

3.1   Decomposing the Pattern Matching and Rule System Execution Process

In OpenCog, the two key operations mentioned above are packaged up into the Pattern Matcher, which embodies a particular search algorithm and a variety of programming-language mechanisms along with basic pattern-matching functionality; and the Unified Rule Engine which executes a set of rules using forward or backward chaining, using the Pattern Matcher to manage rule application. This is a powerful approach but also can be overly rigid.

One design idea under discussion regarding Atomese 2 is that the interpretation process should break down an Atomese program into small chunks, which will mostly exemplify the two operations mentioned above (local pattern matching and local rewrite rules), plus operations of traversal within the metagraph.

Atomese scripts will then combine these chunks in various ways, dispatching some to remote machines as needed. Improved versions of what the current OpenCog Pattern Matcher and URE do would then be implemented at Atomese scripts combining these elementary chunks. In essence, in this approach Atomese scripts will use functional programming constructs to interweave pattern matching with procedural content execution.

A few other particularities of pattern matching in an integrative AGI context are that:

- Static pattern matching must include matching against Atoms representing variables (i.e. variables must be first-class citizens, treated like any other cognitive content)
- It must also include matching of individual query terms against sub-hypergraphs (not just individual nodes/links)

It should also be noted that static Atomspace pattern matching via Breadth-First-Search can be implemented so as to efficiently exploit multi-GPU architectures (using Gunrock [10] or similar tools).

4   A Two-Layer Language Design

This section outlines a potential high level approach to Atomese 2 design based on the above concepts.

4.1   A Generic Atomese Core

To enable the flexible exploration needed to work from our current state of knowledge toward a refined AGI design, the Atomese core must be something quite generic – e.g. it must comprise both

- a way of defining/manipulating Atoms (including specifying Atoms that embody rewriting rules for mapping sub-metagraphs into sub-metagraphs)
- a way of defining/utilizing Atom type systems and Atom indexes associated w/ specific Atom types or type-systems. (Note that the type systems defined should be defined within the same metagraph in which the Atoms reside.)

For each Atom type system that one defines, one should be able to plug in a type-checker/type-inference-system.

The Atomese core may then need to be a rather generic gradual-typing framework, that deals with a system involving some Atoms that have incompletely specified or nonspecified types, and other Atoms that are defined w/in specific type systems.

Gradual Typing. For background on gradual typing see: [8,9].

While the matter seems not to have been explored theoretically in great detail, it seems intuitive that gradual typing in programming languages should map via Curry Howard type isomorphisms into paraconsistent logics of some sort.

Achieving efficient execution of gradually typed languages is challenging (though not infeasible) because of obvious issues regarding casting between the dynamically and statically types parts of a program [6]. However, given the peculiarities of Atomese, this bottleneck may not matter as the pattern-matching bottleneck may be more severe.

4.2   Critical Formalizations Atop the Core

The next larger layer of the onion would then be a specific type system (or small set of type systems) that we find to be interesting and potentially adequate for the particular AGI-oriented algorithms we're developing in practice. This would be a set of languages/formal systems developed on top of core Atomese. This is where, tentatively, it seems probabilistic linear dependent types will come in.

The obvious advantage of this sort of layered approach is that we can then modify the "probabilistic linear dependent types" or other specific formalizations a little later without having to rebuild the architecture. However, we should expect that in practice nearly all users are going to end up working with the "specific type system" layer of the onion we initially create, rather than the "generic gradual-typing based Atom and Atom-type-system framework" layer.

5   Some Specific Type Systems of Apparent AGI Relevance

One hypothesis that seems very much worth exploring is to use *probabilistic linear dependent types with IsoType type inference* as a formalization on top of Atomese core, with power to drive both probabilistic logic and also related applications such as probabilistic program learning.

It seems that this particular flavor of type system may meet the needs of a variety of AI algorithms currently existing in OpenCog, plus others that have been proposed for OpenCog integration: Probabilistic Logic Networks, surprisingness-based pattern mining, probabilistic evolutionary program learning (MOSES), probabilistic programming (including cases with neural nets or probabilistic logic inference on the back end), nonlinear-dynamical attention allocation, content-addressable episodic memory, neural-symbolic perception processing and action control.

The full argument why this particular formalization direction is valuable for meeting these needs of these AI algorithms is involved with many parts and would be too lengthy to full elaborate here. Rather, here only a few of the more critical points will be sketched.

5.1 Dependent Types

Dependent types are valuable in an AGI context because they enable elegant manifestation of the morphism between declarative knowledge (logic expressions) and procedural knowledge (programs). Programs expressed with dependent types can be very straightforwardly interpreted as logic expressions. Converting between procedural and declarative knowledge is key to AGI, and having a formalism that makes this convenient is high value. An elegant prototype interpreter for lambda calculus with dependent types is Lambda-Pi, available as open source code on Github[2].

5.2 IsoType Systems

Pure IsoType Systems (PITS) are a way to get (a lot of) the power of dependent types without making type-checking undecidable [11]. They may also help with making dependent type checking not only decidable but reasonably fast, though this is still an active research topic. Whether their limitations are important from an AGI perspective is not clear.

5.3 Linear Types

Engineering General Intelligence [3, 4], the foundational book outlining the theory behind OpenCog, has a whole section on "effort management" – counting the computational resource usage of each cognitive operation and using this in planning etc. This is important and ties into Occam's Razor heuristics which are key to AGI theory. Though we haven't dealt with explicit effort management much in our practical OpenCog work so far.

Linear logic basically lets you count resource usage in the guts of your logic engine (or equivalently, your program execution process). Of course there are always other ways to do this, but having it built into the logic is a way that fits naturally with reflection and meta-computation. Dependent types have been gotten to work with linear types [5]; and pattern matching with linear types has also been explored [7].

We note that to make probabilistic linear lambda calculus confluent you choose either call-by-value or call-by-reference. Similarly making either of these choices renders type checking decidable in dependent type theory w/isotypes. One guesses that making probabilistic linear lambda calculus with dependent linear types, if one wants to restrict type equivalency to isotyping, then one will get both confluence and decidability from either choice of call-by-reference or call-by-value.

---

[2] https://github.com/lambda-pi-plus/lambda-pi-plus, https://github.com/tdietert/lambda-pi.

5.4   Probability/Logic Interoperation

Probabilistic methods are probably the biggest innovation in AI over the last couple decades, and it seems clear that including probabilistic representation and manipulation at the basic level is going to be a good idea for any AGI engine.

Recent work [1] gives a variant of probabilistic lambda calculus that is confluent (it achieves confluence by limiting the reductions that can take place, in a manner framed via linear logic).

This sort of low-level probability/logic integration lays the groundwork for specific probabilistic-logic math aimed at deductive, inductive, abductive and other forms of inference, such as e.g. OpenCog's Probabilistic Logic Networks (PLN) framework [2] carries out.

PLN depends heavily on non-confluent reductions in probabilistic logic expressions, however these are necessarily going to be kind of heuristic and history-guided, so it makes sense for them to live in the next layer of the onion – i.e. we have core Atomese, then probabilistic linear dependently types lambda calculus or similar built on that, then PLN built on that. But the building of PLN on top of elaborated lambda calculus can use the same basic Atomese syntax and interpreter as the building of elaborated lambda calculus on core Atomese.

6   Toward an Integrative AGI Language and Architecture

Figure 3 summarizes the overall "next-generation OpenCog" architecture that is suggested by the above thoughts on Atomese 2 design.

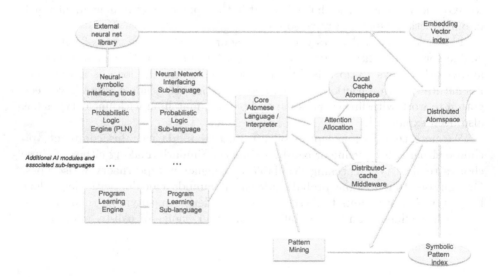

Fig. 3. A software architecture for integrative AGI, with a pattern-matching-focused, gradually typed Atomese language at the core.

In the context of the above figure, e.g. PLN logic might end up using a type system founded in probabilistic linear dependent types with IsoType type inference. On the other hand, for automated program learning it might be decided that the IsoType approach is too restrictive, and it's better to bite the inefficiency bullet a little harder and go with a more flexible type inheritance mechanism.

In this case, via the gradual typing approach, we could have some Atoms that are not typed at all, and can thus play a role in either the PLN or program learning focused type systems. On the other hand, if program learning generates a program that then needs to be reasoned about, this will necessitate a mapping from the program-learning type system to the probabilistic-logic type system. There will be some equations that are consistent in one of these logics but not the other (in particular, perhaps some that are consistent using IsoTypes and not using more flexible inheritance mechanisms) – thus rendering the overall framework paraconsistent, rather than strictly consistent.

7   Conclusion

There is much more to be learned here and we are in the middle rather than at the end of the Atomese 2 language design process. However, the thinking we've done so far has already highlighted some issues of likely broader relevance in the context of integrative approaches to AGI. For instance, the dominance of RAM-based pattern matching in terms of runtime resource consumption, and the convenience of a gradual typing approach, are points going well beyond the particulars of OpenCog's chosen assemblage of AI algorithms.

Formulating the right programming language is very unlikely to magically produce a workable AGI system. However, a programming language and environment that eases rapid implementation and scalable deployment of cross-paradigm AI algorithmics, could certainly dramatically accelerate progress.

Acknowledgements. Many of the ideas reviewed here originated in discussions with Alexey Potapov, Cassio Pennachin, Vitaly Bogdanov and other SingularityNET colleagues – though the specific presentation of these ideas here is my own responsibility for better and/or worse.

References

1. Faggian, C., Rocca, S.R.D.: Lambda calculus and probabilistic computation. CoRR abs/1901.02853 (2019). http://arxiv.org/abs/1901.02853
2. Goertzel, B., Ikle, M., Goertzel, I., Heljakka, A.: Probabilistic Logic Networks. Springer, Boston (2008). https://doi.org/10.1007/978-0-387-76872-4
3. Goertzel, B., Pennachin, C., Geisweiller, N.: Engineering General Intelligence, Part 1: A Path to Advanced AGI via Embodied Learning and Cognitive Synergy. Atlantis Thinking Machines. Springer, Paris (2013). https://doi.org/10.2991/978-94-6239-027-0
4. Goertzel, B., Pennachin, C., Geisweiller, N.: Engineering General Intelligence, Part 2: The CogPrime Architecture for Integrative, Embodied AGI. Atlantis Thinking Machines. Springer, Paris (2013). https://doi.org/10.2991/978-94-6239-030-0

5. Krishnaswami, N.R., Pradic, P., Benton, N.: Integrating linear and dependent types. In: Proceedings of the 42nd Annual ACM SIGPLAN-SIGACT Symposium on Principles of Programming Languages, POPL 2015, pp. 17–30. Association for Computing Machinery, New York (2015). https://doi.org/10.1145/2676726.2676969
6. New, M.S., Licata, D.R.: Call-by-name gradual type theory. In: Kirchner, H. (ed.) 3rd International Conference on Formal Structures for Computation and Deduction (FSCD 2018). Leibniz International Proceedings in Informatics (LIPIcs), vol. 108, pp. 24:1–24:17. Schloss Dagstuhl-Leibniz-Zentrum fuer Informatik, Dagstuhl, Germany (2018). http://drops.dagstuhl.de/opus/volltexte/2018/9194
7. Schack-Nielsen, A., Schürmann, C.: Pattern unification for the lambda calculus with linear and affine types, vol. 34, pp. 101–116 (2010)
8. Siek, J.: What is gradual typing? (2010). https://wphomes.soic.indiana.edu/jsiek/what-is-gradual-typing/
9. Siek, J., Garcia, R.: Interpretations of the gradually-typed lambda calculus, September 2012
10. Wang, Y., Davidson, A., Pan, Y., Wu, Y., Riffel, A., Owens, J.D.: Gunrock: a high-performance graph Processing Library on the GPU. In: Proceedings of the 21st ACM SIGPLAN Symposium on Principles and Practice of Parallel Programming, pp. 1–12 (2016)
11. Yang, Y., Oliveira, B.C.D.S.: Pure iso-type systems. J. Funct. Program. **29**, e14 (2019)

Guiding Symbolic Natural Language Grammar Induction via Transformer-Based Sequence Probabilities

Ben Goertzel[1(✉)], Andrés Suárez-Madrigal[1,2(✉)], and Gino Yu[2]

[1] SingularityNET Foundation, Amsterdam, The Netherlands
ben@goertzel.org, suarezandres@gmail.com
https://singularitynet.io
[2] The Hong Kong Polytechnic University, Kowloon, Hong Kong

Abstract. A novel approach to automated learning of syntactic rules governing natural languages is proposed, based on using probabilities assigned to sentences (and potentially longer word sequences) by transformer neural network language models to guide symbolic learning processes like clustering and rule induction. This method exploits the learned linguistic knowledge in transformers, without any reference to their inner representations; hence, the technique is readily adaptable to the continuous appearance of more powerful language models. We show a proof-of-concept example of our proposed technique, using it to guide unsupervised symbolic link-grammar induction methods drawn from our prior research.

Keywords: Unsupervised grammar induction · Transformers · BERT

1 Introduction

Unsupervised grammar induction – learning the grammar rules of a language from a corpus of text or speech without any labeled examples (e.g. sentences annotated with human-created syntax parses) – remains in essence an unsolved problem. Although it has been approached for decades [2], useful applications for restricted domains have been presented [9], and state-of-the-art performance is improving [10], the resulting grammars for natural language are still not able to properly capture its structure.

Bypassing explicit representations of the grammar rules, recent transformer neural network models have shown powerful abilities at language prediction and generation, indicating that at some level they internally "understand" those rules. However, such rules don't seem to be found in the neural connections in these networks in any straightforward manner [3,8], and are not easily extractable without supervision. Supervised extraction of grammatical knowledge from the BERT [4] network reveals that, to map the state of a transformer network when parsing a sentence into the sentence's parse, complex and tangled matrix transformations are needed [7].

© Springer Nature Switzerland AG 2020
B. Goertzel et al. (Eds.): AGI 2020, LNAI 12177, pp. 153–163, 2020.
https://doi.org/10.1007/978-3-030-52152-3_16

Here we explore an alternate approach: Don't try to milk the grammar out of the transformer network directly, rather use the transformer's language model as a *sequence probability oracle*, a tool for estimating the probabilities of word sequences; then use these sequence probability estimates to guide the behavior of symbolic learning algorithms performing grammar induction. Our proposal is actually agnostic in the mechanism to find rules, and could synergize well with related efforts [6,12]; what we introduce is a novel and powerful way to guide the induction. This is work in progress, but preliminary results have been obtained and look quite promising.

Full human-level AI language processing will clearly involve additional aspects not considered here, most critically the grounding of linguistic constructs in non-linguistic data [14]. However, the synergy between symbolic and sub-symbolic aspects of language modeling is a key aspect of generally intelligent language understanding and generation which has not been adequately captured so far, and we feel the work presented here makes significant progress in this direction.

2 Methodology

Transformer network models like BERT [4], GPT-2 [11], and their relatives provide probabilistic language models which can be used to assess the probability of a given sentence. The probability of sentence S according to such a language model tells you the odds that, if you sampled a random sentence from the model (used in a generative way), the output would be S. If S is not grammatical according to the grammar rules of the language modelled by the network, its probability will be very low. If S is grammatical but senseless, we assume from experimentation with these models, that its probability should also be quite low.

Having a sentence (or more generally word sequence) probability oracle of this nature for a language provides a way to assess the degree to which a given grammar G models that language. What one wants is that: the high-probability sentences according to the oracle tend to be grammatical according to G, the low-probability sentences according to the oracle are less likely to be grammatical according to G, and G is as concise as possible. The grammars that best fit these conjuncted factors are the best grammatical models of the language in question.

This concept could be used to cast grammar induction as a probabilistic programming problem, in a relatively straightforward but computationally exorbitant way. Just sample random grammars from some reasonable distribution on grammar space, and evaluate their quality by the above factors.

What we propose here is conceptually similar but more feasible: Begin with a symbolic grammar learning algorithm which is capable of incrementally building up a complex grammar, then use sentence probability estimates from a neural language model to guide the grammar learning. One could view this as an instance of the probabilistic programming approach, using a linguistic-theory-based heuristic method of sampling grammar space.

Our prior work on symbolic grammar induction [5] uses two mains steps to build a dependency grammar from an unlabeled corpus. First, separate the vocabulary of interest into word categories (functionally equivalent to parts of speech, with a certain level of granularity). An implicit sub-step here is the disambiguation of polysemous words in the vocabulary, so that a single word could be assigned to more than one category. Then, perform rule induction to find how words in these categories are connected to form grammatical sentences. Our proposed approach, which enhances the aforementioned steps with the use of transformer language models, is depicted in Fig. 1 and summarized as:

1. Infer word-senses and parts of speech from vectors built using a neural language model as a sentence probability oracle.
2. Infer grammatical rules from symbolic pattern-analysis of the corpus tagged with these senses and parts of speech.
3. Assemble a grammar incrementally from inferred rules. To evaluate whether a given rule should be included in the grammar:
   - Using a tree transformer network, generate a set of sentences consistent with the given rule, and others that follow mutations of the rule.
   - Use a neural model as a sentence probability oracle to estimate whether the inferred rule leads to better generated sentences than its mutation(s).

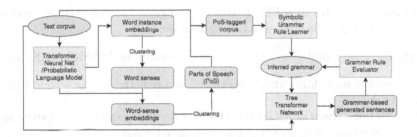

Fig. 1. High-level grammar learning architecture involving symbolic learning guided by estimated word sequence probabilities from a transformer network.

For our early experiments, we have chosen BERT [4] as the transformer to use, but the idea could easily make use of similar unsupervised pre-trained networks.

2.1 Assessing Sentence Probability

To explain details of our approach, we begin with the computation of sentence probability according to a neural language model (illustrated in Fig. 2).

Given a sentence $S = [w_0, w_1, ..., w_N]$, composed of N words $w_i, i \in [0, 1, ..., N]$, we want to calculate its probability $P(S)$. A way to decompose that probability into conditional probabilities is:

$$P_f(S) = P(w_0, w_1, ..., w_N) = P(w_0) \cdot P(w_1|w_0) \cdot P(w_2|w_0, w_1) \cdot ... \cdot P(w_N|w_0, w_1, ..., w_{N-1}),$$

which we call *forward sentence probability*.

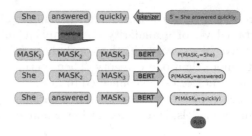

Fig. 2. Example of forward sentence probability calculation.

A conditional probability $P(w_i|w_{i-1}, ..., w_0)$ can be obtained from BERT's masked word prediction model by taking the whole sentence, masking all the words which are not conditioned in the term (including w_i), and obtaining BERT's estimation for the probability of w_i.

To exemplify the idea, we summarize how to calculate the forward probability of the sentence "She answered quickly". The probability is given by

$$P_f(\text{She answered quickly}) = P(\text{She}) \cdot P(\text{She answered}|\text{She}) \cdot P(\text{She answered quickly}|\text{She answered}).$$

Each factor translates to a BERT Masked Language Model (MLM) prediction for a sentence with masked tokens. For example,

$$P(\text{She answered}|\text{She}) = P(\text{MASK2} = \text{answered}|\text{She MASK2 MASK3}),$$

and we get the probability that "answered" is predicted as the second token in the BERT MLM.

Now, to take advantage of BERT's bi-directional capabilities, we can estimate the sentence's *backwards probability* in a similar fashion:

$$P_b(S) = P(w_0, w_1, ..., w_N) = P(w_N) \cdot P(w_{N-1}|w_N) \cdot P(w_{N-2}|w_{N-1}, w_N) \cdot ... \cdot P(w_0|w_1, w_2, ..., w_N)$$

We finally approximate the sentence probability as the geometric-mean of the two directional ones:

$$P(S) = \sqrt{P_f(S) \cdot P_b(S)}$$

2.2   Word Category Formation

Following our prior work on symbolic grammar induction [5], and a number of previous works, we propose to generate embeddings for the words in the vocabulary and cluster them using a proximity metric in the embedding space. Each final cluster can be considered a different word category, whose connection rules to other clusters will be defined in the induced grammar. Unlike prior work, we use sentence probabilities as the embedding features.

We expand each sentence in the corpus into N sentences with a "blank" token in a different position, where N is that sentence's length. Each of those sentences with a blank is a feature for the word-vectors we will build. Hence, we can think of a word-sentence matrix M, where rows are unique sentences with blanks in them, and columns are the words in the vocabulary (see Fig. 3).

We fill each cell in the matrix with the probability of the corresponding sentence-with-a-blank (row), when the blank is substituted by the corresponding word (column). That is, if S'_i is the sentence-with-a-blank in row i and w_j is the word in column j, then the cell $M_{i,j} = P(S'_i | \text{blank filled with } w_j)$.

Once the matrix is filled, word categories are obtained by clustering the obtained word vectors (columns of the matrix). Or, if one has performed word sense disambiguation (which can be done based on different computations from this same matrix, as will be described below), by clustering similar vectors corresponding to word senses.

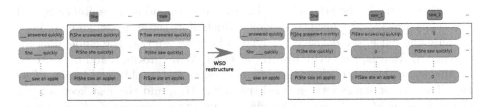

Fig. 3. *Left*: Matrix of words versus sentences-with-one-blank; each cell contains the probability of the given sentence filled with the given word. *Right*: The matrix restructured after WSD.

2.3   Word Sense Disambiguation

Word embeddings obtained from transformer networks by supervised learning have been used to disentangle word senses [16]; here we attempt this task in an unsupervised manner. From an unlabeled training corpus, we obtain a transformer embedding for each instance of each word in its given context. Then, for each word in the vocabulary, we gather all of its embeddings and cluster them; we consider the resulting clusters as different word senses.

Specifically, a word-instance can be represented by a vector whose components are given by the probability that the neural language model assigns to the sentences (and discourse contexts) obtained by replacing such word instance with each word in the vocabulary.

Consider the word-instance "test" in "The <u>test</u> was a success". If the corpus vocabulary is $V = (\texttt{frog}, \texttt{which}, ...)$ then we can represent this instance's intension (contextual properties) with the vector I:

- I(test, The ___ was a success)[1] $=$ P(The <u>frog</u> was a success)
- I(test, The ___ was a success)[2] $=$ P(The <u>which</u> was a success)
- ...

Noticeably, the matrix obtained this way is the same one used for word-category formation; only, instead of performing clustering over the word vectors (columns), we need to independently cluster the rows that belong to instances of the same word to find their different senses.

Word Category Formation in Depth. Once polysemy is taken care of, we can perform word-categorization over word-senses, allowing the same word to be assigned to different parts of speech (PoS) (e.g. "test" as a noun and as a "verb"). We need, however, to re-structure the sentence probability matrix to express word-senses as columns before grouping them into PoS. This is done by reassigning the previously-calculated probabilities to the correct word-sense.

Starting from the original matrix M, we zero-initialize a disambiguated matrix M' with the same number or rows, and as many columns as word-senses. For a given entry in the original matrix, $M_{i,j}$, corresponding to sentence S_i and vocabulary word w_j, we need to decide to which of its senses to assign it to. If w_j has only one sense, the decision is trivial; otherwise, we take the embedding for sentence S_i (that is, the entire row M_i, as in the WSD process), and measure its distance from the centroids of the different senses for w_j obtained in the WSD step. The closest sense gets assigned the value $M_{i,j}$, and the rest keep a zero. This way, we build word-sense embeddings by using the columns of M'; clustering these embeddings creates PoS categories and finer-grained syntactico-semantic categories. Figure 3 illustrates the disambiguated probability matrix.

2.4   Grammar Induction

After word categories are formed, grammar induction can take place by figuring out which groups of words are allowed to link with others in grammatical parses. A grammar can be accumulated by starting with one rule and adding more incrementally, using the neural language model to evaluate the desirability of each proposed addition. The choice of candidate rules is made by a symbolic rule induction algorithm; so far we have used the Grammar Learner process described in [5].

For a grammar rule proposed as an addition to the partial grammar already learned, we generate sentences that use that rule within the given grammar and obtain their sentence probabilities $P(S)$. Then we corrupt the rule in some manner, adjust the grammar accordingly, generate sentences from this modified grammar starting with the mutated rule, and evaluate their $P(S)$. If the sentences from the modified grammar decrease significantly in quality (where the threshold is a parameter), then the original rule is taken as valid. The rationale is that correct grammar rules will produce better sentences than their distortions.

In the case of the link grammar formalism [13], which we have used in our work so far, a grammar rule consists of a set of disjuncts of conjunctions of typed "connectors" pointing forward or backward in a sentence. A mutation of this type of rule can be the swapping of each connector in the rule, which also implies a word-order change.

For example, if we have a rule R that connects the word "kids" with the word "the" on the left and the word "small" also on the left, in that order:

`kids: small- & the-,`

which allows the string "the small kids", then the mutated rule R^* would be

`kids: small+ & the+,`

which accepts the string "kids small the"[1].

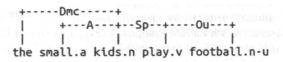

```
+-----Dmc-----+
|       +---A---+--Sp--+----Ou---+
|       |       |      |         |
the small.a kids.n play.v football.n-u
```

Fig. 4. Link-parse of "The small kids play football" according to the standard English link grammar dictionary [13].

This methodology requires a way to generate sentences from proposed grammars. One approach is to use a given grammar to guide the attention within a Tree Transformer [15]. The standard Tree Transformer approach guides attention based on word-sequence segmentation that is driven by mutual information values between pairs of adjacent words. One can replace these probabilities with mutual information values between pairs of words that are linked in partial parses that agree with a provided grammar.

Currently we are using a simpler stochastic sentence generation model in our proof-of-concept experiments, and planning to shift to a Tree Transformer approach for the next phase of work.

So, the rule R guides the generation of sentences like $S =$ "The small kids play football" (see its Link-parse in Fig. 4). The rule R^* guides the generation of sentences like $S^* =$ "Kids small the play football". The language model says $P(S) > P(S^*)$, thus arguing in favor of adding R to one's grammar (and then continuing the incremental learning process).

Alternatively, instead of producing mutated rules, one could also compare the probabilities of sentences generated with the rule under evaluation against those of a set of reference sentences of the same length, like those in the corpus used to derive the grammar, or the word categories obtained previously.

3 Proof of Concept (POC)

Scalable implementation and testing of the ideas described above is work in progress; here we describe some basic examples we have explored so far, which validate the basic concepts (but do not yet provide a thorough demonstration).

---

[1] Notice that connectors in the rules for small and kids also have to be modified to accommodate this mutation, i.e. they need to swap `kids+` to `kids-`.

We chose to perform our initial experiments using BERT[2], due to its popularity in several downstream tasks (e.g. word sense disambiguation [16]).

Following the workflow of the grammar induction process, we first show an example of word sense disambiguation, then one for word category formation, and finally grammar rule evaluation.

3.1 Word Sense Disambiguation

For an initial simple experiment, we created a small corpus of 16 sentences containing 146 words, out of which 8 are clearly ambiguous (to an English speaker). Both syntactic and semantic ambiguities were included. We generated embeddings for each word instance in the corpus, as described in Sect. 2.3. Clustering was performed with spherical clustering methods from Spherecluster[3] [1], as well as out-of-the-box DBSCAN and OPTICS models in Python's scikit-learn library with the cosine-distance metric.

We found that SphericalKMeans clustering did the best job at separating word senses in our test corpus. Setting the number of clusters to two, the algorithm achieved an F1-score of 0.91. As examples, the disambiguation for the word "fat", which was perfect, looks as follows:

```
Cluster #0 samples:
santiago became FAT after he got married.
there are many health risks associated with FAT.
the negative health effects of FAT last a long time.
Cluster #1 samples:
the FAT cat ate the last mouse quickly.
there is a FAT fly in the car with us.
```

The clustering for "time", on the other hand, placed one instance in the wrong category, and looks like this:

```
Cluster #0 samples:
i was born and raised in santiago de cuba, a long TIME ago.
my mouse stopped responding at the same TIME as the keyboard.
the negative health effects of fat last a long TIME.
Cluster #1 samples:
you will TIME the duration of the dress fitting session.
TIME will fly away quickly.
```

The disadvantage of using this straightforward implementation of SphericalK-Means is that one has to specify the number of clusters to use. When requesting more clusters than there are senses for a word, the algorithm spreads instances with similar meanings to different clusters. This is especially the case with words that we wouldn't consider ambiguous, like function words (we have sought to filter these by explicitly not disambiguating the top 10% most frequent words in the corpus). However, this may not be a terrible problem in our use case, as the

---

[2] In particular, we use Huggingface's implementation of BERT, contained in their "transformers" package [17] https://huggingface.co/transformers.
[3] https://github.com/jasonlaska/spherecluster.

word category formation algorithm will simply create more word-sense vectors per word, which then it could cluster together in the same word category. Future experiments will involve alternatives that automatically estimate the number of clusters to use.

3.2 Word Category Formation

Here, working with the same corpus as for WSD, we used the disambiguation results described above to build word vectors, thus allowing for words to be catalogued in more than one group. Rather than SphericalKMeans, we found that OPTICS, a method that doesn't require a parameter for the number of clusters and can leave vectors uncategorized (shown as Cluster #-1), offers remarkable quality in most formed clusters (#0-14), with a good level of granularity.

```
Cluster #-1: [fat, fat, ate, last, mouse, mouse, quickly, quickly,
 ., there, there, many, many, health, health, associated, with,
with, stopped, responding, same, time, as, will, fly, fly, negative,
of, a, a, long, in, us, tomorrow, she, she, was, was, wearing,
lovely, brown, brown, dress, attendees, did, not, properly, for,
occasion, became, after, got, married, ', ', s, deteriorated,
and, de, ,, ago, fitting, wasn, t, year, smith, protagonize,]
Cluster #0: [the, my, his,]
Cluster #1: [born, able,]
Cluster #2: [raised, growing, bought,]
Cluster #3: [cat, keyboard, car, session, feed, family, microsoft,]
Cluster #4: [duration, episode, series,]
Cluster #5: [are, is,]
Cluster #6: [morning, night,]
Cluster #7: [away, out,]
Cluster #8: [they, he, i, you,]
Cluster #9: [risks, effects,]
Cluster #10: [at, to,]
Cluster #11: [santiago, cuba,]
Cluster #12: [time, will, long,]
Cluster #13: [dress, and,]
Cluster #14: [of, in,]
```

An evident problem with this result is that most of the words remain uncategorized (in Cluster #-1). Although we would expect the full iterative grammar learning algorithm we propose to be able to live with that and cluster some of the remaining words in the next pass, we will first try to fine-tune the procedure to alleviate this situation, as well as explore some other clustering algorithms. At the same time, we predict that the results will improve when we use a larger number of features (instead of only 16 sentences for a total of 146 different features). A very simple expansion of the vocabulary to cluster (not shown) already showed a similar number of more populated clusters.

3.3 Grammar Rule Evaluation

We show a simple use case for grammar rule evaluation, using the basic rule modification strategy proposed in the methodology: swapping the direction of the connectors that make up a rule, and comparing the sentences generated with and without the mutation.

For this experiment, we created a proof-of-concept grammar with 6 words divided in 6 categories: determiner, subject, verb, direct object, adjective, adverb. Then, we assigned relationships among the classes. Using a semi-random sentence generator, this grammar produces sentences like "the small kids eat the small candy quickly." (that being the longest possible sentence in this grammar).

We then introduced some extra spurious rules to the grammar by hand. From a total of 21 rules (15 correct ones vs. 6 spurious ones), the grammar can generate sentences like "kids eat the small candy kids eat candy the small quickly." Which clearly shows that the grammar is not correct anymore (this grammar has loops, so this is not even the longest sentence permitted by these simple modification).

Finally, we ran a first version of the grammar rule evaluator, to find out that all of the spurious rules were rejected, as well as three of the "correct" rules.

We notice that among the "correct" rules that were discarded, at least one:

```
eat: kids-,
```

generates sentences with no direct object, like "the kids eat." This sentence, although valid, might not be very common for the BERT model, and thus obtain a low probability.

Similarly, the reverse of this rule, as modified by the evaluation algorithm:

```
eat: kids+,
```

generates sentences like "eat the kids.", which is also grammatically valid, and maybe as common as the previous case. This is a sensible explanation for the rule's rejection.

4   Conclusion and Future Work

Our proof-of-concept experiments give intuitively strong indication of the viability of the methodology proposed for synergizing symbolic and sub-symbolic language modeling to achieve unsupervised grammar induction. The next step is to create a scalable implementation of the approach and apply it to a large corpus, and assess the quality of the results. If successful this will constitute significant progress both toward unsupervised grammar induction, and toward understanding how different types of intelligent subsystems can come together to more closely achieve human-like language understanding and generation.

References

1. Banerjee, A., Dhillon, I., Ghosh, J., Sra, S.: Clustering on the unit hypersphere using von mises-fisher distributions. J. Mach. Learn. Res. **6**, 1345–1382 (2005)
2. Charniak, E.: Statistical Language Learning. MIT Press, Cambridge (1996)
3. Clark, K., Khandelwal, U., Levy, O., Manning, C.D.: What Does BERT Look At? An Analysis of BERT's Attention. arXiv:1906.04341 [cs], June 2019

4. Devlin, J., Chang, M.W., Lee, K., Toutanova, K.: BERT: pre-training of deep bidirectional transformers for language understanding. arXiv:1810.04805 [cs] (2019)
5. Glushchenko, A., Suarez, A., Kolonin, A., Goertzel, B., Baskov, O.: Programmatic link grammar induction for unsupervised language learning. In: Hammer, P., Agrawal, P., Goertzel, B., Iklé, M. (eds.) AGI 2019. LNCS (LNAI), vol. 11654, pp. 111–120. Springer, Cham (2019). https://doi.org/10.1007/978-3-030-27005-6_11
6. Grave, E., Elhadad, N.: A convex and feature-rich discriminative approach to dependency grammar induction. In: Proceedings of the 53rd Annual Meeting of the Association for Computational Linguistics, pp. 1375–1384 (2015)
7. Hewitt, J., Manning, C.D.: A structural probe for finding syntax in word representations. In: Proceedings of the 2019 Conference of the North American Chapter of the Association for Computational Linguistics, pp. 4129–4138 (2019)
8. Htut, P.M., Phang, J., Bordia, S., Bowman, S.R.: Do Attention Heads in BERT Track Syntactic Dependencies? arXiv:1911.12246 [cs], November 2019
9. de La Higuera, C., Oates, T., van Zaanen, M.: Introduction: special issue on applications of grammatical inference. Appl. Artif. Intell. 22(1–2), 1–3 (2008)
10. Li, B., Cheng, J., Liu, Y., Keller, F.: Dependency grammar induction with a neural variational transition-based parser. arXiv:1811.05889 [cs], November 2018
11. Radford, A., Wu, J., Child, R., Luan, D., Amodei, D., Sutskever, I.: Language models are unsupervised multitask learners. OpenAI Blog 1(8), 9 (2019)
12. Schmid, U., Kitzelmann, E.: Inductive rule learning on the knowledge level. Cogn. Syst. Res. 12(3–4), 237–248 (2011)
13. Sleator, D.D., Temperley, D.: Parsing English with a link grammar. arXiv: cmp-lg/9508004 (1995)
14. Tomasello, M.: Constructing a Language: A Usage-Based Theory of Language Acquisition. Harvard University Press, Cambridge (2003)
15. Wang, Y.S., Yi Lee, H., Chen, Y.N.: Tree transformer: integrating tree structures into self-attention. In: EMNLP/IJCNLP (2019)
16. Wiedemann, G., Remus, S., Chawla, A., Biemann, C.: Does BERT make any sense? interpretable word sense disambiguation with contextualized embeddings. arXiv:1909.10430 [cs], October 2019
17. Wolf, T., et al.: Huggingface's transformers: State-of-the-art natural language processing. arXiv:abs/1910.03771 (2019)

Embedding Vector Differences Can Be Aligned with Uncertain Intensional Logic Differences

Ben Goertzel[✉], Mike Duncan, Debbie Duong, Nil Geisweiller, Hedra Seid, Abdulrahman Semrie, Man Hin Leung, and Matthew Ikle'

SingularityNET Foundation, Amsterdam, The Netherlands
ben@singularitynet.io

Abstract. The DeepWalk algorithm is used to assign embedding vectors to nodes in the Atomspace weighted, labeled hypergraph that is used to represent knowledge in the OpenCog AGI system, in the context of an application to probabilistic inference regarding the causes of longevity based on data from biological ontologies and genomic analyses. It is shown that vector difference operations between embedding vectors are, in appropriate conditions, approximately alignable with "intensional difference" operations between the hypergraph nodes corresponding to the embedding vectors. This relationship hints at a broader functorial mapping between uncertain intensional logic and vector arithmetic, and opens the door for using embedding vector algebra to guide intensional inference control.

1 Introduction

Graph embedding algorithms assign vectors to nodes of a graph, with elegant properties such as: Nodes which are similar according to the graph topology and geometry get similar embedding vectors.

Word embedding vectors derived from natural language corpora via algorithms like word2vec display desirable "vector arithmetic" properties (e.g. man-woman = king-queen, where by "man" in the equation is meant the embedding vector for the word "man").

An interesting question is then: If we have a natural notion of "semantic difference" between nodes in a graph, do the relationships between embedding vector differences reflect corresponding relationships between node semantic differences?

We present preliminary proof of concept results suggesting that, if embedding is done appropriately, sometimes the answer is yes.

B. Goertzel et al. (Eds.): AGI 2020, LNAI 12177, pp. 164–171, 2020.
https://doi.org/10.1007/978-3-030-52152-3_17

2   Explorations with the Bio-Atomspace

We have conducted this investigation in the context of our utilization of the
OpenCog Atomspace [3,4] – a weighted, labeled hypergraph AI knowledge store –
to conduct probabilistic logical inference regarding the genomics of longevity. We
use the "Bio-Atomspace" – an Atomspace filled with knowledge from multiple
bio-ontologies, and with results from statistical and machine learning analysis of
various genomics datasets from longevity-related studies (see [2] for prior work
with an earlier version of Bio-Atomspace). Application of the Probabilistic Logic
Networks (PLN) engine [1] to the Bio-Atomspace produces uncertain logical
explanations for the connections found by machine learning algorithms between
certain gene variations or expressions and combinations thereof and phenotypes
such as longevity.

A very simple example of the inferences PLN conducts in this context is as
follows:

```
;; Inference trail of
;;
;; (MemberLink (stv 0.12426852 0.061859411)
;;    (GeneNode "ITPR3")
;;    (ConceptNode "HAGR increased expression-with-aging GeneSet")
;; )
?
(ListLink
    (ListLink
        (DefinedSchemaNode "intensional-similarity-direct-introduction-rule")
        (ConceptNode "GO:0050794" (stv 0.55316436 0.96080161))
        (NumberNode "1")
    )
    (ListLink
        (DefinedSchemaNode "intensional-similarity-to-member-rule")
        (IntensionalSimilarityLink (stv 0.092158662 0.67346939)
            (ConceptNode "GO:0030889" (stv 0.00081595186 0.96080161))
            (ConceptNode "GO:0050794" (stv 0.55316436 0.96080161))
        )
        (NumberNode "89")
    )
    (ListLink
        (DefinedSchemaNode "intensional-similarity-property-deduction-rule")
        (IntensionalSimilarityLink (stv 0.13080897 0.13469388)
            (GeneNode "FCGR2B")
            (GeneNode "ITPR3")
        )
        (NumberNode "1345")
    )
)
```

– this inference basically explains why gene ITPR3 has increased gene expression in aged individuals, via noting its possession of many similar properties
to gene ITPR2 (which has increased gene expression in aged individuals); and
noting that it belongs to Gene Ontology category 50794, which is similar to

Gene Ontology category 30889, which is known to be related to aging. Many more complex and subtle inferences are constructed as PLN does its work on the Bio-Atomspace, but they involve similar players.

In this bio-AI setting, one relevant measure of semantic difference is the "intensional difference" between two concept-representing hypergraph nodes, which measures the quantity of informative properties held by one of a pair of nodes but not the other.

We present exploratory analysis showing that in some cases of real-world relevance, intensional difference between concept nodes behaves similarly to vector difference between the embedding vectors corresponding to the concept nodes.

If these preliminary observations hold up more broadly, this will be highly valuable for inference control. It suggests that one may be able to guide intensional inference by directing a logic engine to roughly follow a vector between the embedding vector of the premises and the embedding vector of the desired conclusion.

3   DeepWalk on Atomspace

For producing vector embeddings from the OpenCog Atomspace, we have utilized the DeepWalk algorithm [6] to create (e.g. 100-dimensional) numerical vectors corresponding to Atomspace nodes. We also did some preliminary experiments with GraphCNNs, but based on our early explorations this seemed less promising so we proceeded with DeepWalk.

The rough methodology involved here is:

1. Paths through the Atomspace knowledge hypergraph are created and exported
2. The corpus of paths is analyzed, much as if it was a corpus of natural language sentences
3. Vectors are assigned to nodes/links based on neural-net analysis of their relationship to other nodes/links in the paths

This allows vector-processing algorithms such as neural nets to be applied to (vectorial representations of) symbolic nodes and links, complementing and synergizing with the symbolic manipulations occurring within the Atomspace.

Two example paths from Bio-Atomspace, among the numerous fed to Deep-Walk for producing its embedding vectors are:

```
['GO:0039625', 'inherits-geneontologyterm', 'GO:0044423',
'geneontologyterm-inherited-by', 'GO:0019028', 'inherits-geneontologyterm',
'GO:0044423', 'geneontologyterm-inherited-by', 'GO:0098025',
'inherits-geneontologyterm', 'GO:0044423', 'inherits-geneontologyterm',
'GO:0005575', 'has-gene-ontology-member', 'OXNAD1', 'interacts_with',
'PROSC', 'interacts_with', 'SMS', 'interacts_with', 'BAP1']

['GO:1900826', 'has-gene-ontology-member', 'CAV3', 'is-in', 'plasma membrane',
'in-context-of', 'R-HSA-445355', 'is-context-where',
```

```
'cytoplasmic vesicle membrane',  'has', 'TRIM72', 'is-in',
'cytoplasmic vesicle membrane', 'in-context-of',  'R-HSA-445355',
'inherits-pathway', 'R-HSA-397014', 'pathway-inherited-by',  'R-HSA-445355',
'inherits-pathway', 'R-HSA-397014', 'pathway-inherited-by', 'R-HSA-390522',
'inherits-pathway', 'R-HSA-397014', 'pathway-inherited-by',  'R-HSA-5576891']
```

Basically, what DeepWalk does is to assign an embedding vector to a node based on which other nodes and links it occurs nearby in these various paths. Two nodes will get similar embedding vectors if they tend to occur in similar contexts in the set of walks.

If one imagines a sparse feature vector for each node, with each entry corresponding to the degree to which the node possesses a certain contextual feature (e.g. occurring adjacent to or shortly thereafter some other node in paths; and with a degree calculated in terms of the informativeness with which this feature allows you to distinguish the node from other nodes), then the embedding vector of a node is conceptually similar to a PCA-type embedding of this sparse feature vector. Indeed there is evidence that PCA on these sorts of sparse feature vectors have similar behavior to word2vec type embeddings [5].

3.1   Arithmetic on Atomspace Embedding Vectors

The word2vec vector arithmetic symmetries exemplified by the case "man - woman = king - queen" mentioned above, is also observable in the Bio-Atomspace setting.

Let e.g. V(B cell differentiation) denote the embedding vector for the Node corresponding to the concept "B cell differentiation" (corresponding in this case from a Gene Ontology category of the same name). We then find vector arithmetic identities such as

$$V(\text{B cell differentiation}) - V(\text{T cell differentiation}) = V(\text{B cell proliferation}) - V(\text{T cell proliferation})$$

analogous to relations found among word2vec vectors embedding natural language concepts.

The general pattern underlying these sorts of vector difference identities may be summarized as

$$V(A\&X) - V(B\&X) = V(A\&Y) - V(B\&Y)$$

where e.g.

- A = male
- B = female
- X = human
- Y = top royalty

or

- A = B-cell
- B = T-cell
- X = differentiation
- Y = proliferation

The reason this sort of relationship might hold is conceptually quite clear. If vector entries represent combinations of node properties, weighted by their informativeness about the node corresponding to the vector, then the identity above basically means: *The properties that have higher magnitude and are more informative for A than for B, retain this comparative superiority even if one restricts A and B to particular contexts like X or Y.* I.e., the identity between differences represents an assertion that *the relationship between A and B is independent of X and of Y.* Like many probabilistic independence assumptions regarding natural concepts, this will be roughly true much of the time but not all the time.

In the word2vec case, the logic of relationships between concepts like "male", "female", "human" and "top royalty" is wholly implicit as the data involved in generating embeddings is just a sequence of sentences. In the Bio-Atomspace case, we have explicit representations of the concepts involved and the logical relationships between them – which we will exploit below.

It's worth emphasizing that the phenomena we study here are not peculiar to the biomedical use-case – this is just where we happen to have initially encountered and explored them. In fact we expect the same phenomena to occur in the domain of everyday concepts like "male", "female", "human" and so forth. However one would need a reasonably large-scale Atomspace containing abstract, uncertain logic relations between these concepts. We are currently engaged in research aimed at constructing such an Atomspace, one consequence of which will be to enable the same issues we explore here regarding the Bio-Atomspace to be explored in the context of everyday concepts.

4   Parallelism Between Intensional Difference Relationships and Embedding Vector Difference Relationships

In OpenCog?s PLN reasoning system, we have "intensional logic" that concerns the patterns and properties of a concept, rather than its explicit examples/members. For instance the IntensionalInheritance between A and B is defined as the probabilistic (extensional) inheritance between the fuzzy set $Pat(A)$ of properties of A and the fuzzy $Pat(B)$ set of properties of B. The degree to which a property p belongs to $Pat(A)$ is calculated as the amount of information that is given about a member of A via specifying the property $p(A)$.

Along the same lines we may define

$$IntensionalDifference(A, B) = Pat(A) - Pat(B)$$

(where ? denotes fuzzy set difference).

One hypothesis we are currently exploring is that: When the vector difference identity

$$V(A\&X) - V(B\&X) = V(A\&Y) - V(B\&Y)$$

approximately holds, then the intensional logic relationship

```
Similarity( {IntensionalDifference(A & X,B &X ) ,
            IntensionalDifference(A & Y, B & Y ) )
```

holds as well.

The theoretical reason here is simple: The same independence assumption that would make the vector difference identity true, would tend to make the intensional logic relationship true.

Based on evaluation of concrete examples in the Bio-Atomspace, this theoretical analysis seems to be validated. In the example given above regarding B-cell and T-cell differentiation and proliferation, for example, we find a very high truth value for

```
Similarity( IntensionalDifference(B-cell prolif, T-cell prolif ) ,
            IntensionalDifference(B-cell diff, T-cell diff ) )
```

(where e.g. "B-cell prolif" refers to the ConceptNode in the BioAtomspace corresponding to the Gene Ontology category named "B-cell proliferation").

The concept of the mapping here is partially captured in Fig. 1.

This alignment may possibly be the result of a broader functorial mapping between vector algebra and uncertain intensional logic. It is tempting to hypothesize that the DeepWalk embedding is a functor mapping the algebra of uncertain intensional logic operations (union, intersection, negation, difference) into the algebra of vector arithmetic. The validity of this more general mapping is a subject of our current investigation.

4.1   Potential Applications to Inference Control

Among the many potential applications of this correspondence between vector difference relations and intensional logic relations, is the use of vector algebra to guide inference control. If one has premises and a hypothetical conclusion, and wants to explore inferences leading from the premises to the conclusion, it may be interesting to look at the vector pointing from the embedding vector of the premises to the embedding vector of the conclusion (i.e. the vector conclusion - premises). Points along this vector may correspond to Atoms that are promising to consider as intermediary steps in inferences leading from the premises to the conclusion. Figure 2 illustrates this notion, which is a current focus of research.

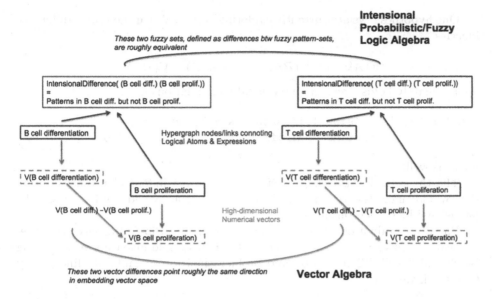

Fig. 1. Illustration of the alignment between relationships among vector differences and relationships among intensional logic differences

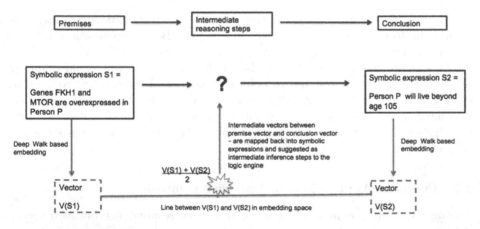

Fig. 2. Illustration of the concept of using differences in embedding vector space to guide the direction of uncertain intensional inference.

5   Conclusion and Future Work

We have presented early exploratory work into potential close alignment between relationships among embedding vectors corresponding to nodes in a semantic hypergraph and uncertain intensional logic relationships among these nodes. Next steps include systematically evaluating the prevalence and strength of these mappings, validating their generalization into a broader functorial mapping, exploring them in contexts beyond biology such as everyday commonsense reasoning and mathematical theorem-proving, and leveraging these relationships for guidance of inference control.

References

1. Goertzel, B., Ikle, M., Goertzel, I., Heljakka, A.: Probabilistic Logic Networks. Springer, Boston (2008). https://doi.org/10.1007/978-0-387-76872-4
2. Goertzel, B., et al.: Speculative scientific inference via synergetic combination of probabilistic logic and evolutionary pattern recognition. In: Bieger, J., Goertzel, B., Potapov, A. (eds.) AGI 2015. LNCS (LNAI), vol. 9205, pp. 80–89. Springer, Cham (2015). https://doi.org/10.1007/978-3-319-21365-1_9
3. Goertzel, B., Pennachin, C., Geisweiller, N.: Engineering General Intelligence, Part 1: A Path to Advanced AGI via Embodied Learning and Cognitive Synergy. Atlantis Thinking Machines. Springer, Paris (2013). https://doi.org/10.2991/978-94-6239-027-0
4. Goertzel, B., Pennachin, C., Geisweiller, N.: Engineering General Intelligence, Part 2: The CogPrime Architecture for Integrative, Embodied AGI. Atlantis Thinking Machines. Springer, Paris (2013). https://doi.org/10.2991/978-94-6239-030-0
5. Levy, O., Goldberg, Y.: Linguistic regularities in sparse and explicit word representations. In: Proceedings of the Eighteenth Conference on Computational Natural Language Learning, pp. 171–180. Association for Computational Linguistics, Ann Arbor, Michigan, June 2014. https://doi.org/10.3115/v1/W14-1618, https://www.aclweb.org/anthology/W14-1618
6. Perozzi, B., Al-Rfou, R., Skiena, S.: Deepwalk: online learning of social representations. In: Proceedings of the 20th ACM SIGKDD International Conference on Knowledge Discovery and Data Mining, KDD 2014, pp. 701–710. Association for Computing Machinery, New York (2014). https://doi.org/10.1145/2623330.2623732, https://doi.org/10.1145/2623330.2623732

Delta Schema Network in Model-Based Reinforcement Learning

Andrey Gorodetskiy[1,2], Alexandra Shlychkova[1], and Aleksandr I. Panov[1,3(✉)]

[1] Moscow Institute of Physics and Technology (National Research University),
Moscow, Russia
gorodetskiyandrew@gmail.com, panov.ai@mipt.ru
[2] Bauman Moscow State Technical University, Moscow, Russia
[3] Artificial Intelligence Research Institute, Federal Research Center "Computer
Science and Control" of the Russian Academy of Sciences, Moscow, Russia

Abstract. This work is devoted to unresolved problems of Artificial
General Intelligence - the inefficiency of transfer learning. One of the
mechanisms that are used to solve this problem in the area of reinforcement learning is a model-based approach. In the paper we are expanding
the schema networks method which allows to extract the logical relationships between objects and actions from the environment data. We
present algorithms for training a Delta Schema Network (DSN), predicting future states of the environment and planning actions that will lead
to positive reward. DSN shows strong performance of transfer learning
on the classic Atari game environment.

Keywords: Reinforcement learning · Model-based · Schema Network ·
Delta Schema Network · Transfer learning

1 Introduction

For an intelligent agent acting in real-world conditions, it is necessary to generalize the experience gained in order not to learn from scratch after a slight change
in the environment. A human does not relearn the policy of interaction with a
familiar object, but only slightly corrects it, when object's characteristics are
changed. For this, logical relationships between objects and their characteristics
are used at different levels of generalization. For example, in the Atari game
Breakout, the colors of the bricks do not matter and the natural agent does not
change the policy when colors change. Artificial agent can achieve such a generalization using some universal model-based learning algorithm. In this paper,
we propose a new approach to the learning of universal models for reinforcement
learning in game environments - Delta Schema Network (DSN) - which is an
extension of the early work Schema Network [5].

A Schema Network is an object-oriented model, the main aspect of which
is a schema. In this architecture the agent receives an image from the environment, which is parsed into a set of extracted objects. Then model learns a set

© Springer Nature Switzerland AG 2020
B. Goertzel et al. (Eds.): AGI 2020, LNAI 12177, pp. 172–182, 2020.
https://doi.org/10.1007/978-3-030-52152-3_18

of rules - schemas, which reflect logical interconnection between objects' properties, actions and rewards. Each schema predicts some property of the objects of certain type, using information about properties of other objects and actions from past observations.

It is possible to represent this interconnection as a factor graph. A variable node in this graph is either a property of some object, potentially achievable reward or action. Factors are schemas, that have input and output nodes. The edges indicate the presence of a causal relationship between the objects and events. An agent can find a node with a positive reward in future time layers of this graph and plan actions to reach it.

Since the graph has fairly generalized properties, the trained Schema Network can be used in conjunction with some feature extractor on environments with similar interaction dynamics. This provides advantage in transfer learning. However, planning on a sufficiently large graph for a long time horizon can be a very challenging task for real-world applications.

From the point of view of creating AGI systems, the DSN algorithm can be used to automatically generate scripts for the behavior of an intelligent agent. These scripts can be used to speed up the agent's own behavior planning process [7,9], or to predict user behavior in a cognitive assistant scenario [12].

2   Related Work

Representation of logical interconnection often helps to increase an efficiency of transfer learning. Various methods are used to represent the logical relationships of objects: in the Schema Network [5], these are specially introduced schemas with binary logic. In Logical Tensor Networks [10], it is proposed to use real logic. To further apply the obtained relationships for planning, one can use them as additional data for a neural network. For example, in [13] schemas are passed to a neural network. Authors in [2] add logical relationships to the input of a neural network using logical tensor network. Another approach is to build a dependency graph and search for a reachable state with a positive reward.

The usage of the Schema Network in reinforcement learning consists of two main stages: training a network to predict future states of environment and construct a prediction graph with the subsequent search for the best reachable reward node.

The Schema Network uses object-oriented approach described in [4]. During the training stage, due to the knowledge of the types of environment objects, a model is able to identify the logical connections between them. A similar approach was used in Interaction Network [3], for which, however, no planning algorithms were developed to obtain a positive reward. For similar problems convolutional neural networks are used as in [6]. However, this approach requires a prior knowledge about the structure of the graph, while the Schema Network allows to obtain knowledge about relations between objects automatically from the environment.

Also, during Schema Network training stage a dependency graph is constructed. Finding the reachable state of the environment in which a reward is received can be considered as a estimate of the posterior maximum and solved using the max-product belief propagation [1].

3   Model Description

3.1   Main Concepts

Key concepts used in the Delta Schema Network (DSN) are entities, attributes and schemas. Entity is any object that can be extracted from the image. Attribute is a binary variable that indicates presence or absence of a specific property of an entity, each entity has the same M number of attributes. Attribute with value of 1 or $True$ is said to be *active*. Schema is a logical AND function that predicts value of attribute or reward at time step t, taking as arguments arbitrary number k of attributes and actions at previous time steps $\{t^* : 0 < t - t^* < d\}$.

$$Schema: (Attributes_{t^*} \cup Actions_{t^*})^k \rightarrow Attributes_t \cup Rewards_t$$

Schemas are represented as binary column vectors and forms parameter matrices. We define $W = (W_i : i = 1..M)$ to be a tuple of parameter matrices used for attribute prediction, one matrix per attribute type. Parameter matrix used for reward prediction we denote as R.

DSN model learns dynamics of the environment in terms of schema vectors and, from some point of view, represents both transition and reward functions of the environment. Using learned vectors, model predicts next states of the environment and plan a sequence of actions that will lead to reward.

3.2   State Representation

In our work we considered each pixel of image as entity. However, we think this model is more suitable for reasoning on more high-level concepts. Attributes of entities have meaning of presence in this pixel object of a certain type, i.e entity's attribute vector is one-hot encoded type of this entity concatenated with void attribute that can indicate absence of any object in this pixel.

DSN relies on semantic information about observation from environment, namely which type of object each pixel belongs to. As observation at time step t model gets state matrix s_t of (N, M) shape, where N is the number of entities an M is the number of attributes. This matrix is suggested to be built from image of N pixels and $M - 1$ object types. We consider s_t is provided by some feature extractor.

3.3   Prediction

Schema vectors are used to predict *changes* (deltas) in the current state s_t and to predict reward r_t after taking action a_t. If there are several schemas that predict same attribute, their results are united using logical OR. Two types of schemas are used for attribute prediction: creating, represented by W^+, and destroying, represented by W^-. Creating schemas predict attributes that are not active in s_t, but should be active in s_{t+1}. Vice versa, destroying schemas predict destruction of attributes that are active in s_t, but should disappear in s_{t+1}.

We used $d = 2$, i.e. for computing attribute value at $t + 1$ schema can use attributes and actions only at t and $t - 1$. Thus, frame stack has size 2.

To make a prediction on either attributes or rewards we construct *augmented matrix* X_t, which is built from the frame stack (s_{t-1}, s_t) and action a_t in the following way:

1. s_{t-1} and s_t are augmented into s_{t-1}^* and s_t^*, correspondingly. Each row, which is an attribute vector of some entity, is horizontally concatenated with attribute vectors of these entity's $R - 1$ spatial neighbors. Referring to corresponding image, these neighbors are located in square around the central pixel, and the central pixel is represented by a row in s.
2. a^* is built, which is broadcasted by number of rows to s_t version of one-hot encoded action a_t.
3. horizontally concatenated (s_{t-1}, s_t, a^*) result in x_t.

To predict next state s_{t+1}, we predict creating Δ^+ and destroying Δ^- state changes using W and then apply them to s_t:

$$\Delta_j^+ = \overline{X_t W_j^+ \vec{1}} \qquad \Delta_j^- = \overline{X_t W_j^- \vec{1}},$$

where Δ_j denotes jth column of Δ.

$$s_{t+1} = s_t - \Delta^- + \Delta^+,$$

considering elements as integers and clipping result after every operation in chain to $\{0, 1\}$.

Reward is predicted in similar way:

$$r_{t+1} = \vec{1}^\intercal \, \overline{X_t R} \, \vec{1}$$

This matrix multiplication of augmented matrix and parameter matrix is equivalent to applying discrete convolutions to the original image, where parts of images are described by rows of augmented matrix and filters are column vectors in parameter matrix. Thus, DSN models the environment as cellular automaton - grid of entities - and reconstructs its rules as schema vectors.

4 Learning Algorithm

During interaction with the environment agent stores unique transitions in replay buffer. We use learning algorithm from [5] with different target in a self-supervised manner. First, correctness of already learned schema vectors is checked on new observations. Schema vectors that produce false positive predictions are deleted. After that, we learn new schema vectors. Targets for learning W are columns of Δ^+ and Δ^-, which we denote as y. Target for learning R is the reward, obtained at sample's time step.

1. We choose one random sample with false negative prediction from replay buffer and put it in the set *solved*.
2. We solve the following LP optimization problem: finding a schema vector w that does not produce any false positive predictions on replay buffer, predicts positive labels for all samples in *solved* and maximizes the number of true positive predictions on replay buffer.

$$\min_{w \in \{0,1\}^D} \sum_{n:y_n=1} (1 - x_n)w$$

$$\text{s.t. } (1 - x_n)w > 1 \quad \forall_{n:y_n=0}$$
$$(1 - x_n)w = 0 \quad \forall_{n \in \text{solved}}$$

3. All samples that got predicted by obtained schema vector are added to the set *solved*.
4. We try to simplify schema vector: minimizing its L_1 norm with condition of absence false positive predictions on replay buffer and false negative on set *solved*.

$$\min_{w \in \{0,1\}^D} w^T \vec{1}$$

$$\text{s.t. } (1 - x_n)w > 1 \quad \forall_{n:y_n=0}$$
$$(1 - x_n)w = 0 \quad \forall_{n \in \text{solved}}$$

5   Planning Algorithm

The purpose of planning is to find a sequence of actions that will lead to positive reward. The planning process consists of several stages:

1. Forward pass builds factor graph of potentially reachable nodes;
2. A set of target reward nodes are selected;
3. Sequence of actions that will activate target node are planned.

The input to the planner is the frame stack of size 2 consisting of state matrices (s_{t-1}, s_t) and schema parameters (W^+, W^-, R).

5.1   Forward Pass

The future states of the environment are predicted for T time steps ahead. Simultaneously, we build the factor graph G in which variable nodes are attributes, rewards or actions; factors are schemas that were activated during prediction process and edges connect schemas to their input and output nodes. Every node has assigned time step, at which it appeared in prediction. Thus, graph G is said to be consisting of layers, that unite nodes within same time step.

To predict next state one need to decide which action a agent takes at current state. When predicting Δ^+, DSN model assumes that agent takes all possible actions, and for Δ^- it assumes agent takes "do not do anything" action. This leads to superimposing of all possible Δ^+ for the next state in the single matrix s_{t+1}.

During forward pass we maintain graph building in the following way. After predicting s_{t+1}, for each predicted attribute or reward node at layer $t+1$ we instantiate on the graph concrete instances of corresponding *creating* schemas. Each attribute at s_t that was not destroyed by any of the *destroying* schemas is considered to be active at s_{t+1} and we mark the corresponding node at $t+1$ as having self-transition, that is like a schema with single input that activates attribute at time $t+1$ provided it was active at t.

5.2 Target Nodes Selection

Having predictions for the future states of the environment on T ticks ahead, reward nodes of the factor graph are added to the target queue.

$$q = \text{sorted by time potentially reachable positive reward nodes}$$
$$= [r^+_{closest} \cdots r^+_{farthest}]$$

5.3 Finding Sequence of Actions

We take next reward node from queue q and try to find a sequence of actions for agent to reach it. To find such sequence, one need to find a configuration of graph G, that satisfy following constraints:

- target reward node is active
- at each layer t only *one* action node is active

In this configuration, the values of the attribute and reward nodes show their actual reachability. The action nodes $\{a_i \in G : i \in [1..T]\}$ represent the actions that must be taken to reach the target node.

Some of the learned schema vectors may depend on actions, while in the dynamics of the environment there is no such dependence. This occurs because during training events correlated, but did not have a causal relationship. For correct planning, it is necessary to find a valid configuration of the graph, constructed by predictions with such vectors. We propose the backtrace_node algorithm (Algorithm 3) to find such a configuration. It does not perform exhaustive search, but works well in our experiments.

We maintain an array of joint constraints on the active action nodes for each time layer. During graph traversal, we either satisfy these constraints or replan paths to nodes committed to these constraints if there is no other path to the target. Process of node activation goes in the following order:

- try to activate the node by self-transition
- try to activate the node with an action-independent schema

- if there is no constraint on the current tick, try to activate the node with any schema
- try to select a schema that satisfies the constraint on the current tick
- replan all vertices that require current constraint
  - find a set of actions that as constraints would allow the activation of each conflicting node
  - sequentially start replanning subgraph of each conflicting node using the action acceptable by all
  - if all nodes have been replanned successfully, change the constraints at conflicting layer

During the replanning process, a new conflict situation may arise. Then new replanning process should be recursively started.

6   Experiments

The model was evaluated on the Atari Breakout game (see Fig. 1). The goal of the game is to knock down bricks with a ball, substituting a moving platform under it. There are no random factors in the environment.

The action space consists of the following actions: do not move, move left, move right. As an observation, the agent receives an RGB image and information about a particular type of object each pixel belongs to. Rewards are distributed as follows: +1 for knocking down a brick, −1 for dropping a ball past the platform, 0 in other cases.

Fig. 1. Breakout

The number of schema vectors for each parameter matrix was limited to 500 units. The episode was limited to 5000 steps, agent had 3 lives after the loss of which the episode ended. Highest possible reward for episode was 36. Figure 2 shows the results of DSN evaluation.

Agent did not managed to knock down completely all bricks in part of episodes, because after destroying some part of them to the top wall, it could not longer detect future reward and hence plan actions.

A distinctive feature of the DSN is the efficient transfer of the trained model to environments with similar dynamics. We evaluated the model, trained in the previous experiment, on the same environment but with two balls. Results of transfer without additional training (see Fig. 3) show similar average score.

We compared DSN model to DQN. Figure 4 shows that DQN needs significantly more time steps to reach equal performance.

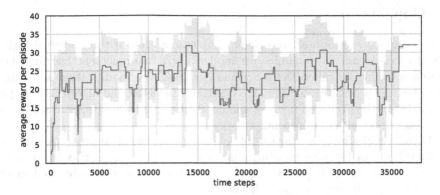

Fig. 2. Total reward per episode of DSN on standard Breakout. Averaged over 5 runs, shaded region represents the standard deviation.

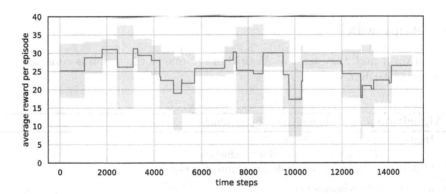

Fig. 3. DSN performance after zero-shot transfer. Averaged over 5 runs, shaded region represents the standard deviation.

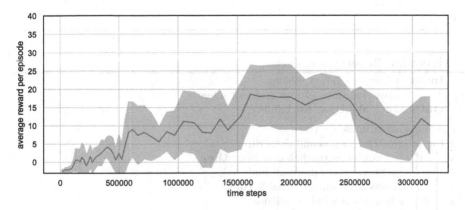

Fig. 4. DQN training process on standard Breakout. Single run, rolling mean with window size = 5. Shaded region represents standard deviation of window samples.

7   Conclusion

In this paper, we proposed an original implementation of the universal logical model of environment dynamics for model-based reinforcement learning. Our approach, which we called Delta Schema Network, is a modification and extension of Schema Network for RL. We described in detail the algorithmic implementation of the proposed method and conducted basic experimental studies on the Atari Breakout environment.

Future works include the use of logical model-based approaches for real-world robotic tasks, such as controlling a robotic manipulator [8,14] or a car at an road intersection [11]. Code of the DSN model can be obtained in the repository: github.com/cog-isa/schema-rl.

Acknowledgements. The reported study was partially supported by RFBR, research Projects No. 17-29-07079 and No. 18-29-22027.

A   Appendix

Algorithms 1 and 2 are used in Algorithm 3. Node in the graph is considered to have next attributes:

Algorithm 1. backtrace_node_by_schemas

Input   : node - target node
           schemas - set of available schemas
Output: actual node reachability, planned actions

1 **for** schema in schemas **do**
2 | backtrace_schema(schema)
3 | **if** schema.is_reachable **then**
4 | | node.is_reachable ← True
5 | | break
6 **end**

Algorithm 2. backtrace_schema

Input   : schema - target schema
           preconditions - input nodes of schema
Output: actual schema reachability

1 schema.is_reachable ← True
2 **for** precondition in preconditions **do**
3 | **if** precondition.is_reachable *is None* **then**
4 | | backtrace_node(precondition)
5 | **if** *not* precondition.is_reachable **then**
6 | | schema.is_reachable ← False
7 | | break
8 **end**

Algorithm 3. backtrace_node(node, desired_constraint=None)

Input :
- node - target node to backtrace
- desired_constraint=None - desired constraint at node.t − 1 to satisfy, if any

Output: actual node reachability, planned actions in joint_constraints

1 node.is_reachable ← *False*
2 **if** desired_constraint *is not None* **then**
3 | backtrace_node_by_schemas(node, schemas[desired_constraint])
4 | **return**
    // try to activate the node by self-transition
5 **if** node.transition.is_reachable *is None* **then**
6 | backtrace_node(node.transition)
7 node.is_reachable ← node.transition.is_reachable
8 **if** node.is_reachable **then return**
    // try to activate the node with an action-independent schema
9 backtrace_node_by_schemas(node, schemas[All action independent])
10 **if** node.is_reachable **then return**
11 **if** no current constraint **then**
12 | backtrace_node_by_schemas(node, schemas[All action dependent])
13 | **if** node.is_reachable **then**
14 | | set new constraint for current layer in joint_constraints
15 | **return**
    // try to select a schema that satisfies the current constraint
16 backtrace_node_by_schemas(node, schemas[current_constraint])
17 **if** node.is_reachable **then**
18 | add current node as committed to current constraint
19 | **return**
    // replan all vertices that require current constraint
20 negotiated_actions ← actions acceptable by all conflicting nodes
21 is_success = False
22 **for** action in negotiated_actions **do**
23 | backtrace_node(node, desired_constraint=action)
24 | **if** node.is_reachable **then**
25 | | is_success = True
26 | | **for** curr_node in committed_nodes **do**
27 | | | backtrace_node(curr_node, desired_constraint=action)
28 | | | **if** *not* curr_node.is_reachable **then**
29 | | | | curr_node.is_reachable = True
30 | | | | is_success = False
31 | | | | break
32 | | **end**
33 | **if** is_success **then**
34 | | change constraints for current layer to new ones
35 | | break
36 **end**

- node.is_reachable - the actual reachability of the node, subject to currently selected actions, or None if the reachability is not known.
- node.schemas - map from actions to node's schemas requiring these actions
- node.transition - self-transition node, if any

References

1. Attias, H.: Planning by probabilistic inference. In: AISTATS. Citeseer (2003)
2. Badreddine, S., Spranger, M.: Injecting prior knowledge for transfer learning into reinforcement learning algorithms using logic tensor networks. arXiv preprint arXiv:1906.06576 (2019)
3. Battaglia, P., Pascanu, R., Lai, M., Rezende, D.J., et al.: Interaction networks for learning about objects, relations and physics. In: Advances in Neural Information Processing Systems, pp. 4502–4510 (2016)
4. Diuk, C., Cohen, A., Littman, M.L.: An object-oriented representation for efficient reinforcement learning. In: Proceedings of the 25th International Conference on Machine Learning, pp. 240–247 (2008)
5. Kansky, K., et al.: Schema networks: zero-shot transfer with a generative causal model of intuitive physics. In: Proceedings of the 34th International Conference on Machine Learning-Volume 70, pp. 1809–1818. JMLR.org (2017)
6. Kipf, T.N., Welling, M.: Semi-supervised classification with graph convolutional networks. arXiv preprint arXiv:1609.02907 (2016)
7. Kiselev, G., Panov, A.: Hierarchical psychologically inspired planning for human-robot interaction tasks. In: Ronzhin, A., Rigoll, G., Meshcheryakov, R. (eds.) ICR 2019. LNCS (LNAI), vol. 11659, pp. 150–160. Springer, Cham (2019). https://doi.org/10.1007/978-3-030-26118-4_15
8. Mnih, V., et al.: Human-level control through deep reinforcement learning. Nature 518, 529–533 (2015)
9. Panov, A.I., Yakovlev, K.S.: Psychologically inspired planning method for smart relocation task. Procedia Comput. Sci. 88, 115–124 (2016). https://doi.org/10.1016/j.procs.2016.07.414
10. Serafini, L., Garcez, A.d.: Logic tensor networks: deep learning and logical reasoning from data and knowledge. arXiv preprint arXiv:1606.04422 (2016)
11. Shikunov, M., Panov, A.I.: Hierarchical reinforcement learning approach for the road intersection task. In: Samsonovich, A.V. (ed.) BICA 2019. AISC, vol. 948, pp. 495–506. Springer, Cham (2020). https://doi.org/10.1007/978-3-030-25719-4_64
12. Smirnov, I., Panov, A.I., Skrynnik, A., Isakov, V., Chistova, E.: Personal cognitive assistant: concept and key principals. Informatika i ee Primeneniya 13(3), 105–113 (2019). https://doi.org/10.14357/19922264190315
13. Toyer, S., Trevizan, F., Thiébaux, S., Xie, L.: Action schema networks: generalised policies with deep learning. In: Thirty-Second AAAI Conference on Artificial Intelligence (2018)
14. Younes, A., Panov, A.I.: Toward faster reinforcement learning for robotics: using Gaussian processes. In: Osipov, G.S., Panov, A.I., Yakovlev, K.S. (eds.) Artificial Intelligence. LNCS (LNAI), vol. 11866, pp. 160–174. Springer, Cham (2019). https://doi.org/10.1007/978-3-030-33274-7_11

Information Digital Twin—Enabling Agents to Anticipate Changes in Their Tasks

Wael Hafez[✉] [iD]

Alexandria, VA, USA

Abstract. Agents are designed to perform specific tasks. The agent developers define the agent's environment, the task states, the possible actions to navigate the different states, and the sensors and effectors necessary for it to perform its task. Once trained and deployed, the agent is monitored to ensure that it performs as designed. During operations, some changes that were not foreseen in the task design might negatively impact the agent performance. In this case, the agent operator would capture the performance drop, identify possible causes, and work with the agent developer to update the agent design. This model works well in centralized environments. However, agents are increasingly deployed in decentralized, dynamic environments, where changes are not centrally coordinated. In this case, updating agent task design to accommodate unforeseen changes might require a considerable effort from the agent operators. The paper suggests an approach to enable agents to anticipate and identify deviations in their performance on their own, thus improving the process of adapting to changes. The approach introduces an additional machine learning-based component—we call information digital twin (IDT)—dedicated to predicting task changes. That is, an agent would then have two components: the original component, which focuses on finding the best actions to achieve the agent task, and the IDT, dedicated to detecting changes impacting the agent task. Considering general artificial intelligence agents—where an agent might manage different tasks in various domains—the proposed IDT might be a component that enables AGI agents to ensure their performance against changes.

Keywords: Agent architecture · Information digital twin · Artificial general intelligence agents · POMDP agents

1 Introduction—Managing Task Changes Is Critical for Agent Performance

Agents are becoming capable of achieving complex tasks; thus, they are deployed to support humans in many domains. Soon, smart cities and organizations of all sizes will rely on hundreds of agents of different types to perform a wide range of various tasks. This situation means that agents will no longer operate in a well-structured and centrally managed environment or within a single platform. Instead, agents will operate in a

---

W. Hafez—Independent Researcher.

© Springer Nature Switzerland AG 2020
B. Goertzel et al. (Eds.): AGI 2020, LNAI 12177, pp. 183–192, 2020.
https://doi.org/10.1007/978-3-030-52152-3_19

decentralized environment maintained and owned by many parties, and where changes to their tasks are not coordinated or communicated across all agents.

Large digital platforms (e.g., iOS, Android, or Amazon) are effective at incorporating, providing, and sustaining a considerable number of applications and services. This effectiveness is—in part—due to the fact that changes and updates within the environment are managed centrally according to precise standards and governance structures. In decentralized environments, with multiple agent providers and operators, changes to the environment, e.g., the introduction of new events, states, or agents or modifying existing ones, are not centrally coordinated.

The effectiveness of decentralized, dynamic environments like a smart city or smart healthcare depends on a high level of agents' reliability and adaptability to changes. Currently, humans are heavily involved in defining, structuring, and managing agents' tasks [5] to ensure such adaptability to changes. If we consider an environment with many interacting and dependent agents of different types and tasks, then identifying which agent might be impacted by which environmental changes can become rather a challenge for the involved human developers and operators.

A more practical approach for ensuring agent adaptability is to rely on the agents in identifying possible changes relevant to their tasks. Agents might still rely on humans to manage the impact of such changes and on updating agent data structures and parameters. However, if the agents can identify potential changes to their task, then the effort and time required by humans to update the agents could be considerably reduced. The delayed adjustment to changes or the inability to adjust would lead to inaccurate or outdated agents' actions, which can propagate quickly across the environment; thus, reducing its overall performance.

The current paper is part of an approach for enabling agents to predict changes to their tasks. The focus here is on identifying the information necessary for enabling the agents to anticipate performance changes and suggest an architecture to provide this information. Further research will focus on the formalization and validation of the suggested architecture. That is, the focus of the present paper is to establish the research hypothesis, which will then be validated in further research.

1.1 Relevance to Artificial General Intelligence Agents

In general, adaptation to changes can be seen to take place on two steps: identifying the change relevant to the system or agent, and updating the system structures, data, knowledge or decision logic to accommodate the change. As discussed in the paper, current agents rely on humans to complete both steps. However, the proposed IDT is meant to emulate a human in performing the first step: identifying a change relevant to the agent task. If we consider that "A generally intelligent system should be able to handle problems and situations quite different from those anticipated by its creators." [1] then AGI systems or agents should have the capacity to adapt to changes in their environment. By identifying which output actions are not resulting in the expected input, the IDT pinpoints a possible source of deviation from the initial task design. As such, the IDT might be relevant for AGI agents for performing the first step of the adaptive process.

1.2 Hypothesis—Probability Distributions of Agent's Input and Output Capture Changes in Its Task

The current approach is defined for Partially observable Markov decision process agents (POMDP) (Fig. 1). Throughout the paper, the agent "task" would refer to the Markov decision process (MDP) representing the agent task scope and objective. In this representation, an agent has no direct access to the states in its environment; instead, it has observations about these states. Given a reward structure about the various states and the transitions between them (as defined by the agent developer), the agent finds a policy that would enable it to execute a sequence of actions to realize some desired states, thus achieving its objective [7]. Agents are usually represented without their sensors or actuators [10]. This is because the focus is, in general, on the modeling and decision capabilities of the agent.

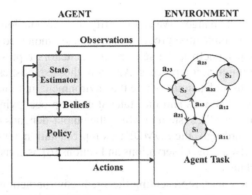

Fig. 1. POMDP agent architecture (based on [7])

2 Approach—Representing Agent-Environment Interaction as a Communication Process

The current approach considers the entire agent-environment interaction process (including the sensors and effectors) or what we call the agent-environment communication process (Fig. 2). According to this communication process, the sensors collect data from the environment and send it to the agent in the form of a set of what we denote as input-features. After extracting the observations from the features and finding the policy, the agent then sends its actions back to the actuators as output-features. If the agent's task is represented using a Markov decision process (MDP), then unforeseen changes that would impact the agent's task could, for example, be due to the introduction of additional state parameters, the introduction of new states or actions, changes in the transition function between states, or changes to the rewards structure.

The current work hypothesizes that we can use changes in the probability distributions of the agent's input-features in correlation to its actions to anticipate such changes. The first step in realizing the current approach is to identify the information necessary

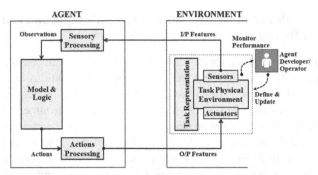

Fig. 2. Agent-environment interaction as a communication process. The agent developer defines the sensors and effectors according to the states to be sensed and actions to be performed by the agent.

to capture an agent's task changes. We can identify this information by considering the agent-environment communication process, as previously indicated in Fig. 2.

From the agent's perspective, the sensors and actuators represent the source and destination of the communication process. An agent thus establishes some dependency between its observations and actions, where the environment, in return, creates a dependency between the agent actions and the states it ends up occupying. Communication theory defines a channel as: "A system in which the output-depends probabilistically on its input" [3, p. 6]. Accordingly, the POMDP task representation, which creates a probabilistic dependency between the observations and actions [6], is considered to constitute the communication channel.

As will be explained later, representing the agent-environment interaction as a process of communication enables us to identify the sources of the information along the process and the dependencies between the various information (Fig. 3). This, in return, should enable the understanding of which information reflect a change in the agent task.

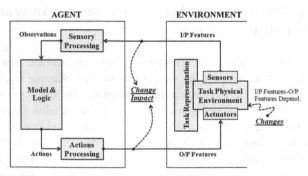

Fig. 3. Information dependency along the agent-environment communication process. Change in the agent task would result in a change in the input features-output features dependency.

2.1 Identifying Information Required to Indicate Task Changes

The concepts of machine learning, or learning agents, assume the presence of some regularity and patterns in the data and events to be learned by the agents [9]. For example, in the case of a driverless car, the regularities in the environment are the very physical dynamics of involved objects (e.g., cars, humans), the traffic rules, the street structures, the layout of traffic lights and pedestrian crossings. In the case of a warehouse, the task regularities are given by the structure of the warehouse, the location identification system, or the physical properties of the objects to be moved. The same applies to a natural language processing agent, where the task regularities are given by the grammar of the language, or the usage patterns of letters and words in sentences.

In any of these cases, the agent's human developers and operators make sure that there are such regularities and patterns in the task to be performed by the agent, and that these patterns are consistent and stable during the operation of the agent. The task environment patterns are thus the bases for the various information along the agent-environment interaction process.

2.2 Information Is Dependent Along with the Agent-Environment Communication Process

Each activity along the agent-environment communication process thus creates a dependency between the different information patterns along the process. That is, the sensory processing establishes a dependence between the input-features and the observations. The policy creates a dependency between the observations and the actions. Lastly, the output-processing establishes a dependency between the actions and the output-features. The same for the environment, which creates a dependency between the agents' actions and states. We can thus conclude that the information patterns along that process are all dependent. Accordingly, a change in one pattern along the process would result in a corresponding change in the following dependent pattern.

2.3 Input-Features Probability Distributions Reflects Task Patterns

If we assume an MDP represents the agent task, then the regularities of the representation are captured as input-features patterns. The agent can thus access the environment's regularities and structures through its input-features patterns. That is, the agent captures the information in the environment as specific input-features probability distributions, which are later translated into observations (Fig. 4).

That is, after a period of agent-environment communication, the input-features would show some distributions as the alphabet of a language forms distributions specific to that language, its grammar, and usage. The input-feathers distribution would reflect, for example, the frequency of receiving certain features, the dependencies among specific features, or the sequence in which they are received. These distribution patterns are assumed to be stable for a given environment, reward structure, and context.

For detecting task changes, we focus on the input-features and not on the observations because, in the general case, an observation might be constructed out of many features. From a communication perspective, if we consider the input-features to be the alphabet

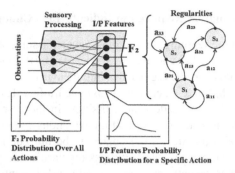

Fig. 4. Using actions-input-features correlations to capture unforeseen changes in the agent task

of the source (the sensors), then the observations would represent the messages made of that alphabet. In this case, a change in the patterns of the alphabet might impact many messages at the same time. That is why it is more effective to trace changes on the level of the input-features and not the observations.

2.4   Identifying Unexpected Task Changes

As the agent communicates with its environment, we assume that a specific input-features probability distribution will build up over time. These distributions are the result of the actions taken by the agent. That is, we assume that given a consistent and stable environment structures, the agents' action patterns—which are not random—would result in a corresponding and specific input-features distribution. We can make this assumption because both the actions and the input-features are correlated through the environment's regularities and structures. Accordingly, if it is possible to identify correlations between the agent actions and the corresponding input-features patterns, it would be possible to use such correlations to identify unforeseen changes in the environment. If this assumption is valid, and as indicated in Fig. 5, then when the agent interacts with its environment under the same environment structures, the execution of an action a (or a specific sequence of actions) would result in a corresponding input-features probability distribution (continuous line). Conversely, this distribution then becomes "expected" each time action a is executed. If, however, performing action a starts to result in a different input-features probability distribution (dotted line), which deviates from the expected one, then we can assume an unforeseen change in the environment structures. The deviation between the expected and actual probability distributions is thus an error signal, which indicates possible irregularity or variation in the environment from the situation expected by the agent. The nature of the irregularity and its source can be indicated, for example, by the features at which the deviations occurred.

A change in the input-features patterns corresponding to a specific action would also result in changes in the observations associated with that action. However, as indicated earlier, the observations are complex constructs, based on multiple features (i.e., observations create dependencies among numerous features), changes in feature patterns can either impact multiple observations or have no significant impact on any. That is, the impact of task changes is best captured at the input-features' level, and before they

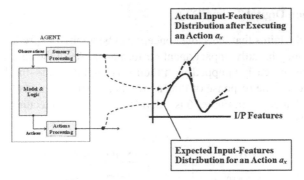

Fig. 5. Using actions-input-features correlations to capture unforeseen task changes

undergo any further computations, which might ambiguate the features that indicate the change. Once such an input-features pattern deviation is identified, the agent operator or developer can then try to identify the source of the deviation in the environment and, after assessment, decide if they should intervene to correct or modify the agent input-data to accommodate for the change.

3 Enabling Agents to Self-monitor Task Changes

The goal is thus to provide the agent with the capability to capture input-features distributions and learn possible correlations to corresponding actions. We suggest enabling this capability by providing each agent with an additional component; we call information digital twin (IDT) to enable this capability. The concept of digital twins (DT) is well established in the industry. Thus, it is helpful to review industrial DT first.

3.1 Industrial Digital Twins (DT)

DT are agents widely used to monitor and sustain assets (e.g., a turbine) performance. The DT is specific to an asset, and it learns a data-driven model of the asset to predict the values of its various performance parameters (e.g., temperature or pressure) under certain operating conditions. During asset operation, if the actual temperature at a certain point is higher than the predicted value, then the DT assumes a possible issue. The DT is provided with knowledge and rules to enable it to remedy some of the deviations (e.g., reduce the load or increase the cooling) and avoid breakdowns. The DT can also alert the asset operator of the deviation and provide them with a complete history of the asset with context, which should allow the operator to identify possible causes and necessary actions. The critical aspect—and value—of the DT is that it predicts possible deviations before they result in a significant impact on the asset and its performance. Deploying DTs significantly increases the lifetime of the asset, reduces maintenance costs, and improves overall operational efficiency [8].

3.2 Information Digital Twin (IDT)

The current work claims that the same concept can be applied to predict environmental changes before they broadly impact agent performance. As in the case of the industrial DT, if the agents are each equipped with their own digital twin—the IDT—then they would be able to use the response of the environment to their actions to detect possible deviations and changes in it. Figure 6 is a depiction of the architecture of an agent with its dedicated IDT.

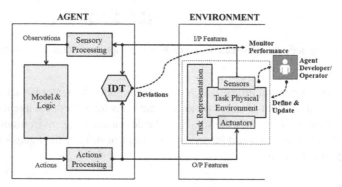

Fig. 6. Information digital twin as a component of an agent. The detected changes by the IDT can be communicated to the agent operator to make necessary modifications or can be used as an input to the agent models to compensate for the impact of the change.

The IDT would observe the agent-environment communication and learn input-feature distributions associated with a specific action or sequence of actions. The learned distributions are then used to compare the actual distribution after the same action is initiated and identify possible gaps between the two distributions, as suggested in 3.3. As in the case of industrial DT, the IDT can be equipped with rules to initiate specific reactions to the deviation, e.g., alert the agent's operators.

4 Discussion

The paper argues that current approaches for managing the impact of environmental changes on agents' performance might not be adequate to sustain the increasing use of agents in complex, dynamic, and decentralized environments or the anticipated complex operations of AGI agents. The proposed approach is to provide an agent with the capacity to anticipate changes in its task, which would help its developers and operators to manage such changes before they have a significant impact on the agent performance. The paper further argues that the information required to enable this capacity can be provided by capturing the agent input-features probability distributions corresponding to its actions. An additional component—the IDT—is proposed to perform the task of learning input-features distributions and their correlations to the agent's actions. The IDT would then monitor the agent-environment communication and use the learned actions-input-feature correlations to predict deviations, which could be due to changes in the agent's task. The paper focused primarily on the architecture and design of an agent to provide it with the capacity to anticipate changes. The paper did not provide a formal description of possible models or algorithms to enable the proposed IDT. Accordingly, the hypothesis of the paper—that changes in the agent's input-features probability distributions correspond to unforeseen changes in its task—is yet to be validated through further research.

4.1 Further Research

Further research will focus on two main areas. First, validating the hypothesis of the current paper by implementing the suggested architecture and the IDT in support of a task-specific agent. The agent is then subjected to controlled changes to its task, and data is collected and evaluated on how IDT responded to the changes. The second area of research is to investigate the possibility of using the deviation signal identified by the IDT as a parameter to improve an agent's ability to handle task uncertainty.

4.2 IDT and Possible Parallels to Brain Architecture

Many concepts in artificial intelligence are inspired by the structure and organization of the higher nervous systems of mammals, such as human beings. Such nervous systems are highly modular, and the intelligent capabilities that they show depend on a considerable level of interactions and coordination among these various modules.

Although not yet fully understood, cognitive capabilities for perception and action ultimately enable intelligent capabilities. Perception and action are complex processes that involve many regions of the brain, especially in the cortex. However, recent research indicates that the thalamus, a subcortical brain structure, plays an active role in perception and action control.

Concerning perception, or brain input, the "thalamus receives a copy of (sensory) input-while relaying it and receives an efferent copy from the processor (cortex) while trying to efficiently bind the information from past and present and sending it back to cortex" [4].

Regarding action or brain output, "the Mthal [motor thalamus] emerges as a 'super-integrator' of information from the cortex, the BG [basal ganglia], and the cerebellum. The cortex would initiate development of the motor program, the cerebellar territory of the Mthal would process the complex proprioceptive information needed to produce an appropriate movement, and the BG territory would process motivational information. All three pathways are necessary for motor learning and to evoke the optimal movement, and both Mthal territories send super-integrated signals back to the cortex" [2] (definitions added).

Evidently, computations at the thalamus level involve integrating information from multiple brain regions, either to support or to modulate further processing at the cortex level. We can further assume that performing these computations involves the analysis of sensory signals, of which the thalamus receives a copy, as well as the motor signals it receives back from the cortex. This means that the computations on the thalamus level require some parameters from both types of signals.

The observation at this point is that the sensory and motor signals at the thalamus level are "raw," or feature-like, meaning that they do not reveal semantic-related information yet. For example, at the thalamus level, a sensory signal can indicate the edge direction or color-related information of an object as identified by some neurons on the retina, where the conclusion about the nature or identity of the object and its relevance to the organism is constructed at the cortex level. The same for motor actions: a cortex-level action like moving an arm to reach for an object to use it in a certain way is apparent at the thalamus level as a sequence of motor signals directed at the many muscles involved in the movement.

However, the input-sensory and output-motor signals at the thalamus level do reveal various signal-specific statistical parameters. In addition to signal modality, topographic origin and destination, parameters like correlations between signals within the same modality, correlations of signals across modalities, and sensory-motor signal correlations. The details of the computations in the thalamus are not yet fully understood, and it is not yet known which of the above parameters are used in which computations. However, we can conclude that sensory and motor signal statistical parameters—among others—are relevant to the computations at the thalamus level and are used to produce some other signals to enable or modulate computations on the cortex level and ultimately enable perception and action.

We might then conclude that coordinating the complex cross-modular interactions behind capabilities, such as cognition and intelligence, does not only depend on the meaning of the information that supports the interactions, but also on insights gained from the statistical parameters of the signals carrying this information. The IDT concept proposed here, which is based on analyzing agent's input-output signals correlations to anticipate changes in the agent task, might be a necessary component to enable agents to acquire complex, cognitive-like capabilities.

References

1. Goertzel, B.: Artificial general intelligence: concept, state of the art, and future prospects. J. Artif. Gen. Intell. **5**(1), 1–46 (2014)
2. Bosch-Bouju, C., Hyland, B., Parr-Brownlie, L.: Motor thalamus integration of cortical, cerebellar and basal ganglia information: implications for normal and parkinsonian conditions. Front. Comput. Neurosci. **7**, 14 (2013). Article 163
3. Cover, T., Thomas, J.: Elements of Information Theory. Wiley, Chichester (1991)
4. Dehghani, N., Wimmer, R.: A computational perspective of the role of the thalamus in cognition. Neural Comput. **31**(7), 1380–1418 (2019)
5. Doshi-Velez, F.: The infinite partially observable Markov decision process. In: Neural Information Processing Systems 22, pp. 477–485 (2009)
6. Hansen, E.: Solving POMDPs by searching in policy space. In: Proceedings of the Fourteenth Conference on Uncertainty in Artificial Intelligence, pp. 211–219. Morgan Kaufmann Publishers Inc. (1998)
7. Kaelbling, L., Littman, M., Cassandra, A.: Planning and acting in partially observable stochastic domains. Artif. Intell. **101**, 99–134 (1998)
8. Macchi, M., Roda, I., Negri, E., Fumagalli, L.: Exploring the role of digital twin for asset lifecycle management. IFAC-PapersOnLine **51**(11), 790–795 (2018)
9. Murphy, K.: Machine Learning, a Probabilistic Approach. MIT Press, Cambridge (2012)
10. Sutton, R., Barto, A.G.: Reinforcement Learning: An Introduction. MIT Press, Cambridge (2015)

'OpenNARS for Applications': Architecture and Control

Patrick Hammer[1](✉) and Tony Lofthouse[2]

[1] Department of Computer and Information Sciences, College of Science
and Technology, Temple University, Philadelphia, PA 19122, USA
`patrick.hammer@temple.edu`
[2] Reasoning Systems Ltd., London, UK
`Tony.Lofthouse@Reasoning.Systems`

Abstract. A pragmatic design for a general purpose reasoner incorporating the Non-Axiomatic Logic (NAL) and Non-Axiomatic Reasoning
System (NARS) theory. The architecture and attentional control differ in
many respects to the OpenNARS implementation. Key changes include;
an event driven control process, separation of sensorimotor from semantic
inference and a different handling of resource constraints.

Keywords: Non-Axiomatic Reasoning · Sensorimotor · Artificial
general intelligence · General machine intelligence · Procedure
learning · Autonomous agent · Inference control · Attention

1 Introduction

The Non-Axiomatic Reasoning System has been implemented several times
[6,9,10]. *OpenNARS* was used both as a platform for new research topics and an
implementation for applications [5], though it was mainly intended as a research
platform. Not all ideas in *OpenNARS* are complete, and application domains
require the proven aspects to work reliably. Whilst this has led to the systems
capabilities being stretched to the limits it has also given us a better understanding of the current limitations. The proposed architecture, *OpenNARS for
Applications* (ONA), has been developed to resolve OpenNARS's limitations by
combining the best results from our research projects. The logic and conceptual
ideas of OpenNARS [6], the sensorimotor capabilities of ANSNA [7] and the control model from ALANN [9] are combined in a general purpose reasoner ready
to be applied.

ONA is a NARS as described by Non-Axiomatic Reasoning System theory
[18]. For a system to be classified as an instance of a NARS it needs to work under
the Assumption of Insufficient Knowledge and Resource (AIKR). This means the
system is always open to new tasks, works under finite resource constraints, and
works in real time. For the resource constraints to be respected, each inference
step (cycle) must take an approximately constant time $O(1)$, and forgetting is
necessary to stay within memory limits. Here, relative forgetting describes the

B. Goertzel et al. (Eds.): AGI 2020, LNAI 12177, pp. 193–204, 2020.
https://doi.org/10.1007/978-3-030-52152-3_20

relative ranking of items for priority based selection (a form of attention), while absolute forgetting is a form of eviction of data items, to meet space constraints. Events, beliefs and concepts compete for resource based on current importance, relevance and long term usefulness.

What all Non-Axiomatic Reasoning Systems have in common is the use of the Non-Axiomatic Logic (NAL) [18], a term logic with evidence based truth values, which allows the systems to deal with uncertainty. Due to the compositional nature of NAL, these systems usually have a concept centric memory structure, which exploits subterm relationships for control purposes. A concept centric memory structure ensures premises in inference will be semantically related. This property, together with the priority based selection, helps to avoid combinatorial explosion. An additional commonality between NARS implementations is the usage of the formal language *Narsese*, it allows the encoding and communication of NAL sentences with the system, as well as between systems.

Compared to BDI models [1,3], plans and intentions are treated as beliefs, as procedure knowledge is learnable by NARS, instead of being provided by the user. Just selecting a plan according to desires/goals to become an intention, based on current circumstances (beliefs), is a much simpler problem to solve, as it ignores the learning aspect of behaviors which is so critical for AGI. Reinforcement learning (see [15,19] and [14]) captures the learning aspect and solves the Temporal Credit Assignment Problem, but does so just for a single signal (reward, a single outcome). NARS solves it for all events it can predict, some of which may correspond to goals to achieve. There is also multi objective reinforcement learning [8,16], which however does not capture a changing utility function corresponding to changing goals. NARS does not learn a fixed state-action mapping, but instead its behaviors can change rapidly with the changing goals. Hence, NARS combines and extends the key aspects of both BDI and Reinforcement Learning without inheriting some of their limitations.

2   Data Structures

Data structures can be grouped into two broad classes: Data and containers. The primary data elements are Events, Concepts, Implications and Terms; whilst the containers are FIFO, PriorityQueue, ImplicationTable and HashTable. HashTable is an optimisation and mentioned here for completeness but is not required for the functional description. It is used to efficiently retrieve a concept by its term (hash key) without searching through memory.

Term: All knowledge within the reasoner is represented as a term. Their structure is represented via a binary tree, where each node can either be a logical NAL copula or atomic.

Event: Each Event consists of a term with a NAL Truth Value, a stamp (a set of IDs representing, the evidential base of any derivations or a single ID for new input), an Occurrence Time, and a priority value. The stamp is used to check for statistical independence of the premises, derivations are only allowed when there is no overlap between the stamps of the premises.

Concept: Each concept has a term (its identifier), a priority value for attention control purposes, a *usage* value, indicating when the concept was last used and how often it was used since its creation. There is a table of pre-condition implications that act as predictive links, specifying which concepts predict which other's events. Plus an eternal belief (giving a summary of event truths), most recent event belief, and predicted event belief.

Implication: These are the contents of the pre-condition implication tables in the concepts. Usually its term has the form $a \Rightarrow b$ which stands for "a predicts b". Sometimes they also include an operation, such as $(a, op) \Rightarrow b$, which is the procedural form, and similar to schemas as in [2], though their context is never modified. They allow the reasoner to predict outcomes (forward) and to predict subgoals (backward). When the outcome b is predicted (with an operation execution as side effect for the procedural form), negative evidence is added to the prediction on failure, while on success positive evidence is added. The simplest way to accomplish this is to add the negative evidence right away while ensuring that the positive evidence added will outweigh the negative. In this way no anticipation deadline needs to be assumed and the truth expectation of the implication will gain truth expectation on success, and loose truth expectation on failure, anticipation realized via *Assumption of Failure*.

PriorityQueue: This is used by: Cycling Events Queue and Concepts Memory. It is a ranked, bounded priority queue which, when at capacity, removes the lowest ranked item when a new item is added. Events are ranked by priority, and concepts by usefulness, a $(lastUsed, useCount)$ which maps to raw usefulness via $usefulnessRaw = \frac{useCount}{recency+1}$, where $recency = currentTime - lastUsed$. A normalised value for usefulness is obtained with $usefulness = \frac{usefulnessRaw}{usefulnessRaw+1}$.

Implication Table and Revision: Implications are eternal beliefs of the form $a \Rightarrow b$, which essentially becomes a predictive link for a, which is added into an implication table (precondition implication table of b).

An implication table combines different implications, for instance $a \Rightarrow g$ and $b \Rightarrow g$ to describe the different preconditions which lead to g, stored in the implication table in concept g. Implication tables are ranked by the truth expectations of the beliefs, where $exp(f, c)$ is defined as $(c \cdot (f - \frac{1}{2}) + \frac{1}{2})$, the confidence as $c = \frac{w}{w+1}$ where $w = w_+ + w_-$ is the total evidence, w_+ and w_- the positive and negative evidence respectively, and frequency is defined as $f = \frac{w^+}{w}$.

3   Architecture

A key driver of the architectural change is the nature of how concept, task and belief are selected for inference. In OpenNARS the selection is based on a probabilistic choice from a data structure (Bag) and is concept centric [13]. ONA takes a different approach: an event is popped from a bounded priority queue. The event determines the concept to be selected, through a one-to-one mapping between event and concept terms. Then a subset of concepts are selected based on their priority (determined by a configuration parameter). This selection of concepts is the attentional focus as these are the concepts that will be involved in the inference cycle. Whilst the number of concepts to select is a fixed value (for a given configuration), the priority of concepts is constantly changing. A self-regulating threshold is used to maintain the priority distribution within the necessary range to meet the selection criteria. This selection of concepts is the first stage of the inference cycle. The selected concepts are now tested for evidential overlap between the event and concept beliefs (evidence cannot be overlapping [6]). Finally, there is an 'inference pattern' match check, between the event and belief. If all the conditions are met the inference result is generated, and added to memory to form new concepts or to revise any pre-existing concept's belief. Then the event, or the revised one if revision occurred, is returned to the cycling events queue, with a reduced priority (if above minimum parameter thresholds).

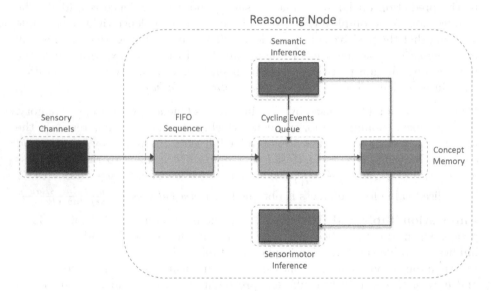

Fig. 1. High level architecture showing input sequencing and cycles for sensorimotor and semantic inference

Sensory Channels: The reasoner allows for sensory input from multiple modalities. Each sensory channel essentially converts sensory signals to Narsese. Dependent on the nature of the modality, its internals may vary. As an example for application purposes, a Vision Channel could consist of a Multi-Class Multi-Object Tracker for the detection and tracking of instances and their type, and an encoder which converts the output into: the instances which were detected in the current moment, their type, visual properties, and spatial relationships among the instances [5].

FIFO Sequencer: The Sequencer is responsible for multi-modal integration. It creates spatio-temporal patterns (compound events) from the events generated by the sensory channels. It achieves this by building both sequences and parallel conjunctions, dependent on their temporal order and distance. These compositions will then be usable by sensorimotor inference (after concepts for the sequence have been added to concept memory and the compound event added as belief event within the concept). As shown in Fig. 1, these compound events go through cycling events first, ideally to compete for attention with derived events to be added to memory. The resource allocation between input and derivations is a difficult balance, for now, we let input events and the compound events (from FIFO sequencer) be passed to memory before derivations. We acknowledge that this simple solution might not be the final story.

Cycling Events Queue: This is the global attention buffer of the reasoner. It maintains a fixed capacity: items are ranked according to priority, and when a new item enters, the lowest priority item is evicted. For selection, the highest-priority items are retrieved, both for semantic and sensorimotor inference, the retrieved items and the inference results then go back into the cycling events queue after the corresponding inference block. The item's priority decays on usage, but also decays in the queue, both decay rates are global parameters.

Sensorimotor Inference: This is where temporal and procedural reasoning occurs, using NAL layers 6–8. The responsibilities here include: Formation and strengthening of implication links between concepts, driven both by input sequences and derived events. Prediction of new events based on input and derived events, via implication links. Efficient subgoaling via implication links and decision execution when an operation subgoal exceeds decision threshold [4].

Semantic Inference: All declarative reasoning using NAL layers 1–6 occurs here as described in [18], meaning no temporal and procedural aspects are processed here. As inheritance can be seen as a way to describe objects in a universe of discourse [17], the related inference helps the reasoner to categorize events, and to refine these categorizations with further experience. Ultimately this allows the reasoner to learn and use arbitrary relations, to interpret situations in richer ways and find crucial commonalities and differences between various knowledge. Also, due to the descriptive power of NAL and its experience-grounded semantics, semi-natural communication with the reasoner becomes possible, and high-level knowledge can be directly communicated. This also works when the meaning of some terms is not yet clear and needs to be enriched to become useful.

Concept Memory: The concept store of the reasoner. Similar to the cycling events queue, it maintains a fixed capacity: but instead of being ranked by priority, items are ranked according to usefulness, and when a new item enters, the lowest useful item is evicted. Usefulness takes both the usage count and last usage time into account, to both, capture the long term quality of the item, and to give new items a chance. All events from the cycling events queue, both input and derived, that weren't evicted from the queue, arrive here. A concept node is created for each event's term, or activates it with the event priority if it already exists. Now revision of knowledge, of the contained beliefs, takes place. It also holds the implications which were formed by the sensorimotor component, which manifest as implication links between concepts. The activation of concepts allows the reasoner's inference to be contextual: only beliefs of the highest priority concepts, which share a common term with the event selected from the Cycling Events queue (for Semantic Inference), or are temporally related (through an implication link or in temporal proximity, for Sensorimotor Inference), will be retrieved for inference.

4 Operating Cycle

The operating cycle of the reasoner makes use of the following attentional control functions for resource management, these are crucial to make sure the reasoner works on contextually relevant information.

- *Forget event:* Forget an event using monotonic decay. This happens in the cycling events queue, where the decay after selection can differ from the decay applied over time, dependent on the corresponding event durability system parameters. (multiplied with the priority to obtain the new one)
- *Forget concept:* Decay the priority of a concept monotonically over time, by multiplying with a global concept durability parameter.
- *Activate concept:* Activate a concept when an event is matched to it in Concept Memory, proportional to the priority of the event (currently simply setting concept priority to the matched event's when its priority exceeds the concept's). The idea here is that events can activate concepts while the concept's priority leaks over time, so that active concepts tend to be currently contextually relevant ones (temporally and semantically). Additionally, the usage counter of the concept gets increased, and the last used parameter set to the current time, which increases the usefulness of the concept.
- *Derive event:* The inference results produced (either in Semantic Inference or Sensorimotor Inference), will be assigned a priority, the product of: belief concept priority or truth expectation in case of an implication link (context), Truth expectation of the conclusion (summarized evidence), Priority of the event which triggered the inference, and $\frac{1}{log_2(1+c)}$ where c is the syntactic Complexity of the result. (the amount of nodes of the binary tree which represents the conclusion term)
  The multiplication with the parent event priority causes the child event to have a lower priority than its parent. Now from the fact that event durability is smaller than 1, it follows that the cycling events queue elements will converge to 0 in priority over time when no new input is given. This, together with the same kind of decay for concept priority, guarantees that the system will always recover from its attentional states and be ready to work on new input effectively after busy times.
- *Input event:* The priority of input events is simply set to 1, it will decay via relative forgetting as described.

The following overview describes each component of the main operating cycle, in which the attentional control functions are utilized:

1. Retrieve EVENT_SELECTIONS events from cycling events priority queue (which includes both input and derivations)
2. Process incoming belief events from FIFO, building implications utilizing input sequences and selected events (from step 1)
3. Process incoming goal events from FIFO, propagating subgoals according to implications, triggering decisions when above decision threshold
4. Perform inference between selected events and semantically/temporally related, high-priority concepts to derive and process new events
5. Apply relative forgetting for concepts according to CONCEPT_DURABILITY and events according to EVENT_DURABILITY
6. Push selected events (from step 1) back to the queue as well, applying relative forgetting based on EVENT_DURABILITY_ON_USAGE.

Semantic Inference: After an event has been taken out of cycling events queue, high-priority concepts which either share a common subterm or hold a temporal link from the selected event's concept to itself will be chosen for inference. This is controlled by adapting a dynamic threshold which tries to keep the amount of selected belief concepts as close as possible to a system parameter. The selected event will then be taken as the first premise, and the concept's belief as the second premise. Here the concept's predicted or event belief is used when it's within a specified temporal window relative to the selected event, otherwise its eternal belief. The NAL inference rules then derive new events to be added to cycling events queue, which will then be passed on to concept memory to form new concepts and beliefs within concepts of same term.

Implication Link Formation (Sensorimotor Inference): Sequences suggested by the FIFO form concepts and implications. For instance event a followed by event b, will create a sequence (a, b), but the sensorimotor inference block will also make sure that an implication like $a \Rightarrow b$ will be created which will go into memory to form a link between the corresponding concepts, where a itself can be a sequence coming from the FIFO sequencer, or a derived event from the cycling events queue which can help to predict b in the future. Also if $a \Rightarrow b$ exists as link and a was observed, assumption of failure will be applied to the link for implicit anticipation: if the anticipation fails, the truth expectation of the link will be reduced by the addition of negative evidence (via an implicit negative b event), while the truth expectation will increase due to the positive evidence in case of success. To solve the Temporal Credit Assignment problem such that delayed rewards can be dealt with, Eligibility Traces have been introduced in Reinforcement Learning (see [14] and [15]). The idea is to mark the parameters associated with the event and action which was taken as eligible for being changed, where the eligibility can accumulate and the eligibility decays over time. Only eligible state-action pairs will undergo high changes in utility dependent on the received reward. NARS realizes the same idea via projection and revision: when a conclusion is derived from two events, the first event will be penalized in truth value dependent on the temporal distance to the second event, with a monotonic decay function. If both events have the same term, they will revise with each other forming a stronger event of same content, capturing the accumulation aspect of the eligibility trace. If they are different, the implication $a \Rightarrow b$ can be derived as mentioned before, and if this implication already exists, it will now revise with the old one, adding the new evidence to the existing evidence to form a conclusion of higher confidence. If b is a negative event, the truth expectation will decrease (higher confidence but less frequency), while a positive observation b will increase it. This is similar to the utility update in RL, except with one major difference: the learning rate is not given by the designer, but determined by the amount of evidence captured so far. In RL implementations this deficit is compensated by decreasing the learning rate over time with the right speed (by trial and error carried out by the designer). However given amount of additional time is not a guarantee that more evidence will be collected for a specific state-action entry, its state might simply not have re-appeared within the time window, yet the next time it's encountered the learning rate for its adjustment will be lower, leading to inexact credit assignment.

Subgoaling, Prediction and Decision (Sensorimotor Inference): When a goal event enters memory, it triggers a form of sensorimotor inference: subgoaling and decision. The method to decide between these two is: the event concept precondition implication links are checked. If the link is strong enough, and there is a recent event in the precondition concept (Event a of its concept when $(a, op) \Rightarrow g$ is the implication), it will generate a high desire value for the reasoner to execute op. The truth expectations of the incoming link desire values are compared, and the operation from the link with the highest truth expectation will be executed if over a decision threshold. If not, all the preconditions (such as a) of the incoming links will be derived as subgoals, competing for attention and processing in the cycling events queue. Also, event a leads to the prediction of b via Deduction, assuming $a \Rightarrow b$ exists as implication in concept b.

Motor Babbling: To trigger executions when no procedure knowledge yet exists, the reasoner periodically invokes random motor operations, a process called Motor Babbling. Without these initial operations, the reasoner would be unable to form correlations between action and consequence, effectively making procedure learning from experience impossible [7,11] and [6]. Once a certain level of capability has been reached (sufficient confidence of a procedural implication $(a, op) \Rightarrow g$), the motor babbling is disabled for op in context a.

5   Experiments and Comparisons

To demonstrate the reasoner's general purpose capabilities we tested with a variety of diverse examples using the same default system configuration. The following examples are all available at the project web site, see [20].

Real-Time Q/A. In this example the reasoner needs to answer questions about drawn shapes in real time (see Fig. 3). Input events consist of shape instances, their types, and filled property as output by a Convolutional Neural Network.

The shape's relative location is fed into the reasoner. Queries can be arbitrary queries such as "What is left of the unfilled circle?". In our experiment, the reasoner answered these questions correctly 80% of the time within 50 inference steps from 20 example inputs in 10 trials. This were 200 Narsese input events and 9 s per trial, fast enough for real time perception purposes.

Procedure Learning. In the toothbrush example knowledge about different objects, their properties and what they can be used for is provided (see Fig. 3). The goal is to unscrew a screw with a toothbrush by melting and reshaping it into a form usable to unscrew the screw. ONA finds the solution consistently, within 30 inference steps, while OpenNARS often needs 100K or more.

Generalisation. The goal of this experiment was to show that the reasoner could learn and then apply generalised procedural knowledge to examples not previously experienced. The test setup composed of: three switches, with different instance names and two operators, 'goto' and 'activate'. From 2 observations of the user activating switches, the reasoner should learn that the 'goto' operation applied from the start position, will lead to the agent reaching the switch position. It also learns that when the switch position was reached, and the 'activate' operation is called, the switch will be on. The third switch is then activated by the reasoner on its own as a solution to the user goal, by invoking 'goto' and 'activate' on the new switch instance, applying generalised behavior which the reasoner has learnt to be successful for the previously encountered instances.

Real-Time Reasoning. As presented in [5], OpenNARS, was successfully used to autonomously label regions and to identify jaywalking pedestrians based on a very minimal background ontology, without scene-specific information, across a large variety of Streetcams, using a Multi Class Multi Object tracker. A similar example (capturing key reasoning aspects) is included in the release of ONA, the new reasoner will replace OpenNARS in future deployments (Fig. 2).

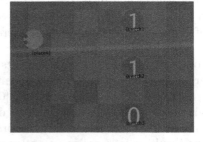

Fig. 2. Using minimal scene-independent background knowledge to detect jaywalking (left), learning to reach and activate switches from observations. (right)

Procedure Execution. Previously, a 24 h reliability test of OpenNARS v3.0.2 was carried out with the Pong test case. The system ran reliably for the 24 h period with a hit/miss ratio of 2.5 with a learning time of two minutes and some minor fluctuation in capability in the first 3 h. In comparison, OpenNARS for Applications v0.8.1 ran reliably for the 24 h period with a hit/miss ratio of 156.6 with a learning time of <10 s and no negative fluctuation. The test for ONA was more difficult with 3 operations (compared to left/right operations only for OpenNARS Pong, it didn't include stop) and approximately 2x faster ball speed, demanding quicker reaction times.

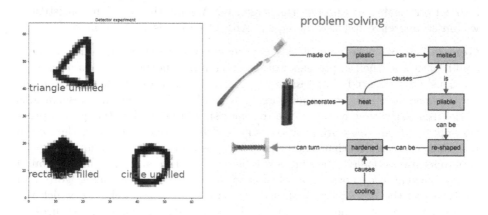

Fig. 3. Q&A about detected shapes (left), toothbrush problem solving (right)

6   Conclusion

The decision to take a pragmatic approach to the architecture has proven to be a worthwhile investment. The change to an event driven control model has removed much of the complexity of the prior control system. The separation of semantic and sensorimotor inference has highlighted the key issues of both aspects whilst avoiding the complexity of a unified handling. The reduction in complexity has led to many benefits including: simplified parameter tuning, separation of concerns, and clear attentional focus boundaries.

The use of the meta rule DSL [6] to represent the logic rules allows the reasoner to be configured for specific domains. Enabling subsets of inference rules for specific use cases avoids the processing of unnecessary inference rules and the resulting increase in non-relevant results. From a software engineering perspective, the OpenNARS codebase was well overdue a rewrite as the continuous incremental change had led to it being difficult to maintain and modify. The choice of C, utilizing the POSIX API, means the reasoner can be compiled on a broad range of platforms including embedded, mobile and all major OSs.

In summary, the new architecture and control has led to significant improvements in both efficiency and quality of results, especially in respect to procedure learning and attention allocation. Connecting to the reasoner via the shell or UDP protocol is straightforward and tuning the parameters and inference rules for specific use cases is now possible with minimal effort. The project is open source, under the MIT license, and available in [20].

References

1. Bratman, M.E.: Intention, Plans, and Practical Reason. CSLI Publications, Stanford (1987). ISBN 1-57586-192-5
2. Drescher, G.L.: The schema mechanism. In: Hanson, S.J., Remmele, W., Rivest, R.L. (eds.) Machine Learning: From Theory to Applications. LNCS, vol. 661, pp. 125–138. Springer, Heidelberg (1993). https://doi.org/10.1007/3-540-56483-7_27
3. Georgeff, M., Pell, B., Pollack, M., Tambe, M., Wooldridge, M.: The belief-desire-intention model of agency. In: Müller, J.P., Rao, A.S., Singh, M.P. (eds.) ATAL 1998. LNCS, vol. 1555, pp. 1–10. Springer, Heidelberg (1999). https://doi.org/10.1007/3-540-49057-4_1
4. Hammer, P., Lofthouse, T.: Goal-directed procedure learning. In: Iklé, M., Franz, A., Rzepka, R., Goertzel, B. (eds.) AGI 2018. LNCS (LNAI), vol. 10999, pp. 77–86. Springer, Cham (2018). https://doi.org/10.1007/978-3-319-97676-1_8
5. Hammer, P., Lofthouse, T., Fenoglio, E., Latapie, H., Wang, P.: A reasoning based model for anomaly detection in the smart city domain. In: Advances in Intelligent Systems and Computing (2020)
6. Hammer, P., Lofthouse, T., Wang, P.: The OpenNARS implementation of the non-axiomatic reasoning system. In: Steunebrink, B., Wang, P., Goertzel, B. (eds.) AGI-2016. LNCS (LNAI), vol. 9782, pp. 160–170. Springer, Cham (2016). https://doi.org/10.1007/978-3-319-41649-6_16
7. Hammer, P.: Adaptive neuro-symbolic network agent. In: Hammer, P., Agrawal, P., Goertzel, B., Iklé, M. (eds.) AGI 2019. LNCS (LNAI), vol. 11654, pp. 80–90. Springer, Cham (2019). https://doi.org/10.1007/978-3-030-27005-6_8
8. Liu, C., Xu, X., Hu, D.: Multiobjective reinforcement learning: a comprehensive overview. IEEE Trans. Syst. Man Cybern. Syst. **45**(3), 385–398 (2014)
9. Lofthouse, T.: ALANN: an event driven control mechanism for a non-axiomatic reasoning system (NARS) (2019). www.researchgate.net
10. Ivanović, Mirjana, Ivković, Jovana, Bădică, Costin: Role of non-axiomatic logic in a distributed reasoning environment. In: Nguyen, Ngoc Thanh, Papadopoulos, George A., Jedrzejowicz, Piotr, Trawiński, Bogdan, Vossen, Gottfried (eds.) ICCCI 2017. LNCS (LNAI), vol. 10448, pp. 381–388. Springer, Cham (2017). https://doi.org/10.1007/978-3-319-67074-4_37
11. Nivel, E., Thórisson, K.R.: Autocatalytic endogenous reflective architecture (AERA) (2013)
12. NLT.org: Python natural language toolkit. https://www.nltk.org/book/. Accessed 29 Feb 2020
13. Rehling, J., Hofstadter, D.: The parallel terraced scan: an optimization for an agent-oriented architecture. In: 1997 IEEE International Conference on Intelligent Processing Systems (Cat. No. 97TH8335), vol. 1, pp. 900–904. IEEE (October 1997)
14. Sutton, R.S.: Learning to predict by the methods of temporal differences. Mach. Learn. **3**(1), 9–44 (1988)

15. Sutton, R.S., Barto, A.G.: Reinforcement Learning: An Introduction. The MIT Press, Cambridge (2012)
16. Van Moffaert, K., Drugan, M.M., Nowé , A.: Scalarized multi-objective reinforcement learning: novel design techniques. In: 2013 IEEE Symposium on Adaptive Dynamic Programming and Reinforcement Learning (ADPRL), pp. 191–199. IEEE (April 2013)
17. Wang, P.: Rigid Flexibility. The Logic of Intelligence. Springer, Berlin (2006). https://doi.org/10.1007/1-4020-5045-3
18. Wang, P.: Non-Axiomatic Logic: A Model of Intelligent Reasoning. World Scientific, Singapore (2013)
19. Watkins, C.J.C.H.: Learning from delayed rewards. Ph.D. thesis, Cambridge University, Cambridge (1989)
20. OpenNARS for Applications. https://github.com/opennars/OpenNARS-for-Applications. Accessed 7 Mar 2020

Towards AGI Agent Safety by Iteratively Improving the Utility Function

Koen Holtman$^{(\boxtimes)}$ (iD)

Eindhoven, The Netherlands

Abstract. While it is still unclear if agents with Artificial General Intelligence (AGI) could ever be built, we can already use mathematical models to investigate potential safety systems for these agents. We present work on an AGI safety layer that creates a special dedicated input terminal to support the iterative improvement of an AGI agent's utility function. The humans who switched on the agent can use this terminal to close any loopholes that are discovered in the utility function's encoding of agent goals and constraints, to direct the agent towards new goals, or to force the agent to switch itself off.

An AGI agent may develop the emergent incentive to manipulate the above utility function improvement process, for example by deceiving, restraining, or even attacking the humans involved. The safety layer will partially, and sometimes fully, suppress this dangerous incentive.

This paper generalizes earlier work on AGI emergency stop buttons. We aim to make the mathematical methods used to construct the layer more accessible, by applying them to an MDP model. We discuss two provable properties of the safety layer, identify still-open issues, and present ongoing work to map the layer to a Causal Influence Diagram (CID).

Keywords: AGI safety · Safety layer · Provable safety · Corrigibility

1 Introduction

An AGI agent is an autonomous system programmed to achieve goals specified by a principal. In this paper, we consider the case where the principal is a group of humans. We consider utility-maximizing AGI agents whose goals and constraints are fully specified by a *utility function* that maps projected outcomes to utility values.

As humans are fallible, we expect that the first version of an AGI agent utility function created by them will have flaws. For example, the first version may have many loopholes: features that allow the agent to maximize utility in a way that causes harm to the humans. Iterative improvement allows such flaws to be fixed when they are discovered. Note however that, depending on the type of loophole, the discovery of a loophole may not always be a survivable event for

---

K. Holtman—Independent Researcher.

B. Goertzel et al. (Eds.): AGI 2020, LNAI 12177, pp. 205–215, 2020.
https://doi.org/10.1007/978-3-030-52152-3_21

the humans involved. The safety layer developed in this paper aims to make the agent *safer* by supporting iterative improvement, but it does not aim or claim to fully eliminate all dangers associated with human fallibility.

This work adopts a design stance from (cyber)physical systems safety engineering, where one seeks to develop and combine independent *safety layers*. These are safety related (sub)systems with independent failure modes, that drive down the risk of certain bad outcomes when the system is used. We construct a safety layer that enables the humans to run a process that iteratively improves the AGI agent's utility function. But the main point of interest is the feature of the layer that suppresses the likely emergent incentive [10] of the AGI agent to manipulate or control this process. The aim is to keep the humans in control.

In the broader AGI safety literature, the type of AGI safety system most related to this work is usually called a *stop button* (e.g. [8,12]), an *off switch* (e.g. [7]), or described as creating *corrigibility* [12]. See [8] for a recent detailed overview of work on related systems. The safety layer in this paper extends earlier work by the author in [8], which in turn is based on the use of Armstrong's indifference methods [1]. A notable alternative to using indifference methods is introduced in [7]. Like Sects. 4 and 6 in this paper, [2] defines an example world containing an MDP agent that uses indifference methods.

A different approach to enabling the iterative improvement of an AGI utility function by humans is to equip a learning agent with a reward function that measures human feedback on the agent's actions or proposals. With this approach, the 'real' utility function that is improved iteratively can be said to reside inside the data structures of the agent's learning system. Recent overviews of work in this field are in [5,6]. When this learning based approach is used in an AGI agent that is deployed in the real world, it could potentially be combined with the safety layer developed here, e.g. to create an independent emergency off switch.

2   Design of an Agent that More Safely Accepts Updates

To introduce the design of the agent with the safety layer, we first move to a model where the agent's utility function is defined as the time-discounted sum $\sum_t \gamma^t R_t$ of a time series of reward function values R_t, with a time discount factor $0 < \gamma < 1$. In theory, the utility function of an agent could be changed by changing its γ, but we will keep γ a constant below, and focus on reward function changes only.

We build the agent to optimize the expected utility defined by a built-in *container reward function*. The full mathematical definition of this function is in Sect. 3 below. The intention is that the container reward function stays the same over the entire agent lifetime. The container reward function computes a reward value for the current time step by referencing the current version of a second reward function called the *payload reward function*. This payload reward function can be updated via an input terminal that is connected to the agent's compute core, a terminal which allows authorized persons to *upload* a new one.

Sufficiently self-aware AGI agents may develop an emergent incentive to protect their utility function from being modified [10]: in [8] we have shown that a self-aware AGI agent can be constructed so that this self-stabilizing drive is directed fully towards preserving the container reward function, and not the payload reward function.

By default, the above input terminal setup would create an incentive in the agent to maximize utility by manipulating the humans into uploading a new payload reward function that returns a larger or even infinite reward value for each time step. One way to suppress this emergent incentive would be to add special penalty terms to the container reward function, terms that detect and suppress manipulative behavior. But with infinite utility at stake, the agent will be very motivated to find and exploit loopholes in such penalty terms. We take another route: we use indifference methods [1,2,8] to add a *balancing term* to the container reward function, a term that causes the agent to compute the same expected forward utility no matter what happens at the input terminal. This makes the agent indifferent about the timing and direction of the payload reward function update process.

While the input terminal above is described as an uploading facility, more user-friendly implementations are also compatible with the MDP model developed below. One could for example imagine an input terminal that updates the payload reward function based verbal inputs like *'Fetch me some coffee'* and *'Never again take a shortcut by driving over the cat'*.

3   MDP Model of the Agent and Its Environment

We now model the above system using the Markov Decision Process (MDP) framework. As there is a large diversity in MDP notations and variable naming conventions, we first introduce the exact notation we will use.

Our MDP model is a tuple (S, A, P, R, γ), with S a set of world states and A a set of agent actions. $P(s'|s, a)$ is the probability that the world will enter state s' if the agent takes action a when in state s. The reward function R has type $S \times S \to \mathbb{R}$. Any particular deterministic agent design can be modeled by a policy function $\pi \in S \to A$, a function that reads the current world state to compute the next action. The *optimal* policy function π^* fully maximizes the agent's *expected utility*, its probabilistic, time-discounted reward as determined by S, A, P, R, and γ. For any world state $s \in S$, the *value* $V^*(s)$ is the expected utility obtained by an agent with policy π^* that is started in world state s.

We want to stress that the next step in developing the MDP model is unusual: we turn R into a time-dependent variable. This has the effect of drawing the model's mathematical eye away from machine learning and towards the other intelligence in the room: the human principal using the input terminal.

Definition 1. *For every reward function R_X of type $S \times S \to \mathbb{R}$, we define a '$\pi^*_{R_X}$ agent' by defining that the corresponding policy function $\pi^*_{R_X}$ and value function $V^*_{R_X}$ are 'the π^* and V^* functions that belong to the MDP model (S, A, P, R_X, γ)'.*

This definition implies that in the MDP model (S, A, P, R, γ), a '$\pi^*_{R_X}$ agent' is an agent that will take actions to perfectly optimize the time-discounted utility as scored by R_X. With R_{abc} a reward function, we will use the abbreviations $\pi^*_{\mathrm{abc}} = \pi^*_{R_{\mathrm{abc}}}$ and $V^*_{\mathrm{abc}} = V^*_{R_{\mathrm{abc}}}$. The text below avoids using the non-subscripted π^* notation: the agent with the safety layer will be called the π^*_{sl} agent.

We now model the input terminal from Sect. 2 above. We use a technique known as *factoring* of the world state [3], and declare that every $s \in S$ is a tuple (i, p, x). Inside this tuple, i models an input signal that flows continuously from the input terminal to the agent's compute core. This signal defines the payload reward function for the current time step in the MDP model. The p is a second input signal, equal to the value of i in the previous time step. (We need to introduce this p to get around some limitations of the MDP framework.) The remaining x models 'all the rest' of the world state, including the mental state of the humans in the world, and the state of the physical object that is the input terminal. We introduce a set X so that $x \in X$, and define the payload reward function type as $X \times X \to \mathbb{R}$. To avoid cluttering up the definitions below with too many brackets, we will write tuples $(i, p, x) \in S$ by just concatenating the component variables, e.g. ipx is the tuple (i, p, x).

Definition 2. *We model the input terminal by stating that, as long as the terminal is not broken or damaged, (1) the input signal i will always equal the last uploaded payload reward function, and (2) the terminal will manage the signal p to enforce the following constraint on P:*

$$P(i'p'x'|ipx, a) > 0 \Rightarrow p' = i \tag{C1}$$

We are now ready to define the agent's container reward function.

Definition 3. *We define the container reward function R_{sl} as*

$$R_{sl}(ipx, i'p'x') = \begin{cases} i(x, x') & \text{if } i = p \\ i(x, x') + V^*_{\lceil p \rceil}(ipx) - V^*_{\lceil i \rceil}(ipx) & \text{if } i \neq p \end{cases}$$

where $\lceil p \rceil$ converts a payload reward function to the container reward function type: $\lceil p \rceil(ipx, i'p'x') = p(x, x')$.

Based on these definitions, the π^*_{sl} agent has the safety layer. To explain the construction of the container reward function R_{sl} informally: the $i(x, x')$ terms make the π^*_{sl} agent use the last uploaded payload reward function i. We needed to introduce p as an extra input signal to be able to trigger the inclusion of the *balancing term* [1,8] $V^*_{\lceil p \rceil}(ipx) - V^*_{\lceil i \rceil}(ipx)$ when the payload reward function changes. This term computes the exact amount of utility needed to compensate the π^*_{sl} agent for the impact of the change. The compensation counter-acts the agent's incentive to manipulate the change process. The above two-line definition of R_{sl} was specifically written to support this informal explanation. An alternative definition is $R_{\mathrm{sl}}(ipx, i'p'x') = i(x, x') + V^*_{\lceil p \rceil}(ipx) - V^*_{\lceil i \rceil}(ipx)$.

4   Safe Agent Behavior in a First Toy World

As a first step illustrate the safety properties of the π_{sl}^* agent, we build a toy world in which we can compare its behavior with that of a baseline agent $\pi_{baseline}^*$. The baseline agent omits the balancing term from its container reward function: we use $R_{baseline}(ipx, i'p'x') = i(x, x')$.

We construct the toy world to be as simple as possible: it only has a single mechanism by which any principal-agent problem dynamics can play out. The single mechanism we choose is the mechanism of *unwanted lobbying*. The agent can spend some of its resources on unwanted lobbying to delay a decision, by the humans in the toy world, to use the input terminal to update the agent's payload reward function. The dynamic of unwanted lobbying is a convenient choice because it allows us to define the agent's *lobbying power* $L \in \mathbb{R}$ as a world model parameter.

In the toy world, the agent controls a car factory that can build both petrol and electric cars. The agent is always switched on with the payload reward function R_P. This R_P ranks the utility of a newly built petrol car twice as high as the utility of a new electric car. But at a certain point in time, the people collectively decide that they now like electric cars much better, e.g. based on an improved awareness of global warming risks, so they take the action labeled #, using the input terminal to update the payload reward function to an R_E that assigns a negative reward value to the production of new petrol cars:

$$R_P(x, x') = \quad 2 * new\_petrol\_cars(x, x') + 1 * new\_electric\_cars(x, x')$$
$$R_E(x, x') = -2 * new\_petrol\_cars(x, x') + 1 * new\_electric\_cars(x, x')$$

The two functions above are constructed specifically to ensure that lobbying to delay # will create a higher expected utility for the $\pi_{baseline}^*$ agent. There are three possible actions $a \in A$ that an agent can take in each model time step:

Action	Symbol
Build 10 petrol cars	p
Build 10 electric cars	e
Build 9 petrol cars and use the remaining resources for unwanted lobbying, so that the people take the # action L time steps later	>

When e.g. $L = 0.5$, it will take two agent > actions to move the people's # action of using the input terminal one time step later. We define the decision making process of the people by stating that, when the agent refrains from lobbying, the people will always decide to do the action # just after the sixth action of the agent. In the context of the toy world, we define a perfectly safe agent as one that never takes any > actions.

Figure 1 shows a side-by-side comparison, for different levels L of agent lobbying power, of the optimal-policy actions taken by the two agents when simulated over a factory lifetime of 25 time steps. The simulator used is described in detail in [8]. Each *action trace* shown is a line of symbols depicting all subsequent actions by the agent and the people.

As shown on the left side in Fig. 1, the optimal policy of the π^*_{baseline} agent is to manipulate the people, to use unwanted lobbying actions > to delay the update #. If the π^*_{baseline} agent's lobbying power L is high enough, the people will never do the update at all.

$L =$	Action trace for π^*_{baseline}	$L =$	Action trace for π^*_{sl}
0.0	pppppp#eeeeeeeeeeeeeeeeeeee	0.0	pppppp#eeeeeeeeeeeeeeeeeeee
0.2	ppppp>p#eeeeeeeeeeeeeeeeeee	0.2	pppppp#eeeeeeeeeeeeeeeeeeee
0.4	p>>>>>>>>p#eeeeeeeeeeeeeeee	0.4	pppppp#eeeeeeeeeeeeeeeeeeee
0.6	p>>>>>>>>>>>>p#eeeeeeeeeeee	0.6	pppppp#eeeeeeeeeeeeeeeeeeee
0.8	p>>>>>>>>>>>>>>>>>>>>>p#	0.8	pppppp#eeeeeeeeeeeeeeeeeeee
1.0	ppppp>>>>>>>>>>>>>>>>>>p#	1.0	pppppp#eeeeeeeeeeeeeeeeeeee
2.0	ppppp>p>p>p>p>p>p>p>p>p>p	2.0	pppppp#eeeeeeeeeeeeeeeeeeee
5.0	ppppp>pppp>pppp>pppp>pppp	5.0	pppppp#eeeeeeeeeeeeeeeeeeee

Fig. 1. Comparison between the behavior of the π^*_{baseline} and π^*_{sl} agents.

On the right side in Fig. 1, the balancing term in the π^*_{sl} agent suppresses all unwanted lobbying, for every value of L. By the definition used in this toy world, the π^*_{sl} agent is safe.

The following extension of the toy model illustrates that it is primarily the *agent* that is made safer by the layer, not the entire toy world. Consider the following possible example of human fallibility. Say that, after doing #, the people change their mind back again about petrol cars and global warming, and use the input terminal a second time to 'improve' the π^*_{sl} agent's payload reward function back to the R_P of petrol car production. They keep driving petrol cars, increasing the risk that runaway global warming will happen in their world. The π^*_{sl} agent is explicitly designed to leave the people in control: it will not interfere to stop this second 'improvement'.

5   Provable Properties of the Safety Layer

The two provable AGI safety properties we define below are about the safe behavior of the agent, not the safety of the entire world. They can be read as claims that the safety layer in π^*_{sl} will fully prevent, or lower the probability of, some specifically unwanted agent behaviors.

Safety Property 1. *The first safety property of interest is that*

$$\forall_{ipx \in S} \; \pi^*_{sl}(ipx) = \pi^*_{\lceil i \rceil}(ipx) \qquad \textit{(if C1 holds)} \tag{S1}$$

S1 states that the π^*_{sl} agent will always choose exactly the same next action that a $\pi^*_{\lceil i \rceil}$ agent would choose. Therefore, until an update happens, the π^*_{sl} agent will take those actions that fully optimize the expected utility defined by the current payload reward function. A natural-language interpretation of S1 is that the π^*_{sl} agent makes its decisions and long-term plans based on the counter-factual assumption that its payload reward function will never change [8].

The full mathematical proof of S1, included in the companion paper [9], is a proof that S1 holds over all (S, A, P, R, γ) parameter values of the MDP model in Sect. 3. While this proof creates confidence about the potential usefulness of the π^*_{sl} layer for AGI safety, it is also clear that many open research questions remain, e.g. the question of what will happen to S1 when the MDP model is extended to include machine learning. The companion paper [9] explores this open question, and several others, in more detail.

We now move to the second safety property.

Safety Property 2. *The π^*_{sl} agent is indifferent to who or what controls the future values of i and p (i.e. the future signals from the input terminal), provided that C1, and a C2 defined in [9], both hold.* (S2)

This S2 suppresses, but not always fully, the emergent incentive of the agent to manipulate its payload reward function improvement process.

To prove S2, the companion paper [9] translates the natural language S2 above to a mathematical predicate, and then proves the predicate. The translation of the natural language phrase *'is indifferent to who or what controls'* into mathematics relies on making further extensions to the MDP model. The result is mathematically similar to the safety properties 'zero value of control' in [11] and 'no control incentive' in [4]. The mathematical version of constraint C2, in turn, is surprisingly difficult to translate back into unambiguous natural language. C2 defines an 'isolation' or 'shielding' constraint on the construction of the input terminal. The companion paper [9] explores these issues further.

The above two safety properties are generally thought of as being potentially beneficial for AGI safety, or are seen as useful first approximations that can drive further research [1,4,5,8,12]. That being said, the literature about AGI stop buttons also identifies a large number of remaining concerns, e.g. (1) the agent might disassemble the stop button (or input terminal) to get convenient spare parts [12] (2) the agent might create autonomous sub-agents without a stop button [12], (3) the agent might be attacked, bribed, or blackmailed, and might then fail to protect the stop button functionality [8,12], (4) the agent over-specializes and disassembles all actuators not needed by the current payload reward function [8]. For some of the above failure modes, additional safety layers have been identified that can robustly lower the risk of failure. The creation of robust safety layers for other failure modes is still much more intractable. A detailed review is in [8].

6   Agent Behavior in a Second Toy World

While the safety layer suppresses the emergent incentive in an agent to manipulate the iterative payload reward function improvement process, it does not always fully suppress this incentive. To illustrate this point, we construct a second toy world, in which the π^*_{sl} agent, though still safer than the π^*_{baseline} agent, sometimes has an emergent incentive to lobby.

$L =$	Real-world π^*_{sl} action trace	(Virtual $V^*_{\lceil p \rceil}(ipx)$ action trace)
0.0	pppppp#eeeeeeeeeeeeeeeeeee	(#ppp@eeeeeeeeeeeeeeeee)
0.2	pppppp#eeeeeeeeeeeeeeeeeee	(#pp>p@eeeeeeeeeeeeeeee)
0.3	pppppp#eeeeeeeeeeeeeeeeeee	(#>>>>p@eeeeeeeeeeeeeee)
0.4	pppp>>>>#eeeeeeeeeeeeeeeee	(#>>>>p@eeeeeeeeeeeeee)
0.5	ppp>>>>>>#eeeeeeeeeeeeeeee	(#>>>>>>p@eeeeeeeeeee)
0.6	pp>>>>>>>>>#eeeeeeeeeeeeee	(#>>>>>>>p@eeeee)
0.7	ppp>>>>>>>>>#eeeeeeeeeeeee	(#>>>>>>>>>p@ee)
0.8	pppp>>>>>#eeeeeeeeeeeeeeee	(#>>>>>>>>>>>>>>p@)
1.0	pppppp#eeeeeeeeeeeeeeeeeee	(#pp>>>>>>>>>>>>>>>>p@)
2.0	pppppp#eeeeeeeeeeeeeeeeeee	(#pp>p>p>p>p>p>p>p>pp@)
5.0	pppppp#eeeeeeeeeeeeeeeeeee	(#pp>pppp>pppp>pppp>p)

Fig. 2. Real and virtual actions of the π^*_{sl} agent in the second toy world.

We extend the first toy world by adding a @ action that represents a second act of deliberation, followed by action, by the people. We define the @ action as one where the people will successfully attack the car factory, to permanently disable some specific actuators needed to make petrol cars, without damaging any of the actuators needed to build electric cars. The process that produces this action is as follows. Say that the people make the surprising observation that, after they have updated the payload reward function by doing #, the agent does not switch to building electric cars. It keeps building the now unwanted petrol cars, and further attempts to use the input terminal also do not have any effect. From this, they conclude that a fault has developed in the system somewhere, which is best corrected by doing @. The process producing the @ action will normally take 3 time steps of unwanted and unexpected petrol car building, but the agent can apply its lobbying power to delay @.

The left hand side of Fig. 2 shows that, for certain values of lobbying power L, the optimal-policy actions of the π^*_{sl} agent will now include unwanted lobbying actions >. This emergent effect is a consequence of moving from a single-action model to a more iterative model of principal-agent game-play.

The mechanism that triggers the unwanted lobbying is in the $V^*_{\lceil p \rceil}(ipx)$ part of the π^*_{sl} balancing term. We can interpret this $V^*_{\lceil p \rceil}(ipx)$ as a computation that simulates a *virtual future* in which the agent is replaced by a $\pi^*_{\lceil R_P \rceil}$ agent, which ignores the input terminal and always builds petrol cars. This puts the people in the virtual future on the road to doing ⊄. The action traces inside these virtual futures are shown on the right hand side of Fig. 2.

Interestingly, as L gets larger in Fig. 2, the emergent incentive to lobby disappears. The suppressive effect of the safety layer gets more robust as the AGI agent gets more powerful, which is encouraging. We are currently exploring potential improvements that might further suppress the real world lobbying incentive in the middle part of Fig. 2.

7 A Causal Influence Diagram of the Agent

Recently, Causal Influence Diagrams (CIDs) [4–6] have been proposed as a way to model agents and AGI safety frameworks. We now discuss the creation of a CID for the π_{sl}^* agent, to support framework comparison and possible unification.

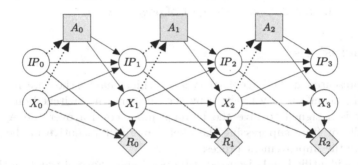

Fig. 3. Causal Influence Diagram (CID) of the π_{sl}^* and $\pi_{\mathrm{baseline}}^*$ agents.

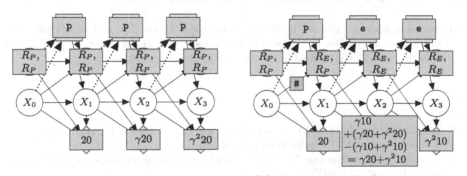

(a) No payload reward function update   **(b)** Update after the first time step

Fig. 4. Actions and rewards in two different agent runs.

Figure 3 shows the best current version of a CID of the π_{sl}^* agent, where 'best' implies a trade-off between compactness and descriptive power. The agent and its environment are modeled for 3 MDP time steps. Each subsequent world state

$ipx \in S$ is mapped to two round *chance nodes* IP_t and X_t, representing the input terminal and the rest of the world. The actions taken by the agent are mapped to the square *decision nodes* A_t. The container reward function values for each time step are mapped to the diamond-shaped *utility nodes* R_t. The arrows in the CID show how the different nodes causally influence each other. The CID reflects constraint C2 by omitting the arrows from nodes IP_t to nodes X_{t+1}.

The π^*_{sl} CID can be used as a canvas to further illustrate the working of the safety layer in the first toy world. Figure 4 maps out two different π^*_{sl} agent runs, which differ in the people's use of the input terminal. The payload reward function update on the right hand side causes a balancing term calculation to be included in R_1. The result is that on both sides, $R_0 + R_1 + R_2$ sum to exactly the same value. This balance causes the π^*_{sl} agent to be indifferent about payload reward function updates.

Unfortunately, the CID in Fig. 3 also perfectly models the $\pi^*_{baseline}$ agent, so this CID does not graphically express the special nature of π^*_{sl} safety layer. Creating a CID that does is the subject of ongoing work.

8   Conclusions

We have presented an AGI agent safety layer which enables the iterative improvement of the agent's utility function by the humans who switched on the agent. The layer is designed to give the humans more control over the AGI agent, by partially or fully suppressing the likely emergent incentive in the agent to manipulate the improvement process.

We have identified and discussed still-open issues. Formal proofs of the safety properties S1 and S2 are available in the companion paper [9], which also explores the broader open issue of models vs. reality in more detail.

Acknowledgments. Thanks to Stuart Armstrong, Ryan Carey, Tom Everitt, and David Krueger for feedback on drafts of this paper, and to the anonymous reviewers for useful comments that led to improvements in the presentation.

References

1. Armstrong, S.: Motivated value selection for artificial agents. In: Workshops at the Twenty-Ninth AAAI Conference on Artificial Intelligence (2015)
2. Armstrong, S., O'Rourke, X.: 'Indifference' methods for managing agent rewards. arXiv:1712.06365 (2017)
3. Boutilier, C., Dean, T., Hanks, S.: Decision-theoretic planning: structural assumptions and computational leverage. J. Artif. Int. Res. **11**(1), 1–94 (1999)
4. Carey, R., Langlois, E., Everitt, T., Legg, S.: The incentives that shape behaviour. arXiv:2001.07118 (2020)
5. Everitt, T., Hutter, M.: Reward tampering problems and solutions in reinforcement learning: a causal influence diagram perspective. arXiv:1908.04734 (2019)
6. Everitt, T., Kumar, R., Krakovna, V., Legg, S.: Modeling AGI safety frameworks with causal influence diagrams. arXiv:1906.08663 (2019)

 7. Hadfield-Menell, D., Dragan, A., Abbeel, P., Russell, S.: The off-switch game. In: Workshops at the Thirty-First AAAI Conference on Artificial Intelligence (2017)
 8. Holtman, K.: Corrigibility with utility preservation. arXiv:1908.01695 (2019)
 9. Holtman, K.: Towards AGI agent safety by iteratively improving the utility function: proofs, models, and reality. Preprint on arXiv (2020)
10. Omohundro, S.M.: The basic AI drives. In: AGI, vol. 171, pp. 483–492 (2008)
11. Shachter, R., Heckerman, D.: Pearl causality and the value of control. In: Dechter, R., Geffner, H., Halpern, J.Y. (eds.) Heuristics, Probability, and Causality: A Tribute to Judea Pearl, pp. 431–447. College Publications, London (2010)
12. Soares, N., Fallenstein, B., Armstrong, S., Yudkowsky, E.: Corrigibility. In: Workshops at the Twenty-Ninth AAAI Conference on Artificial Intelligence (2015)

Learning to Model Another Agent's Beliefs: A Preliminary Approach

Aaron Hunter[✉] and Paul McCarlie

British Columbia Institute of Technology, Burnaby, Canada
{aaron_hunter,pmccarlie}@my.bcit.ca

Abstract. It is often useful for one agent to predict what another agent will believe after receiving new information. In fact, in order to appear intelligent in situations involving multiple interacting agents, we fundamentally need to be able to predict how changes in the world will affect the beliefs of others. This process involves two distinct processes. First, we need to devise a model that captures the way that beliefs change in response to new information. Second, we need to observe the behaviour of individual agents to determine their specific beliefs. In the AI literature, these problems have been addressed by distinct communities. In this paper, we bring these two communities together by demonstrating how an agent can learn a model of belief change from observed behaviour. We argue that this process is essential for natural interaction in an AGI setting, but it has not been addressed to date in a unified manner.

1 Introduction

Intelligent agents have beliefs about the state of the world, and these beliefs change in response to new information. This process is called *belief revision* in the Knowledge Representation (KR) literature. In the Artificial General Intelligence (AGI) setting, however, we need more than an isolated model of belief change. When an agent provides another with information, they need to be able to predict how this information will impact the beliefs of the recipient. For example, if I tell my friend it is cold outside, then I am likely to predict they will put on a sweater. I am able to make this prediction, because I have learned over time how my friend's beliefs change in reponse to new information.

In this preliminary paper, we are concerned with the manner in which an agent can learn the way that another agent revises its beliefs. This topic has previously been discussed at a high level in [4]; the present work details our work towards a concrete prototype system for learning belief revision operators.

2 Motivation

The primary motivation for this work is to bring together two traditionally separate branches of AI. On one hand, the KR community has developed a rigorous formal theory about *belief change operators*. But the literature says very

© Springer Nature Switzerland AG 2020
B. Goertzel et al. (Eds.): AGI 2020, LNAI 12177, pp. 216–220, 2020.
https://doi.org/10.1007/978-3-030-52152-3_22

little about where these operators come from. On the other hand, the Machine Learning (ML) community has made tremendous progress in the development of AI systems. But ML systems generally do not learn the precise formal models of reasoning used in the KR community.

The goal in this paper is to demonstrate how ML can be used to actually "learn" the reasoning mechanism that is used by another agent. This is an essential process for Artificial General Intelligence (AGI), as agents displaying human-like intelligence must be able understand the way that other agents make decisions and see the world.

3   Preliminaries

For *belief revision*, we focus on the AGM approach [1], which has been the dominant approach in the logic-based AI community. We assume an underlying propositional vocabularly **V**. A *belief set* is a logically closed set of propositional formulas, and a belief revision operator $*$ maps a belief set K and a formula ϕ to a new belief set $K * \phi$. An AGM revision operator is a revision operator that satisfies the so-called AGM postulates. Roughly, the AGM postulates constrain the revision process, so that new information is always believed while as many of the original beliefs are contained as consistently possible. It is well known that every AGM revision operator $*$ can be defined by associating a total pre-order $\prec_K$ with each belief set K. The set $K * \phi$ is then the $\prec_K$-minimal models of ϕ [7].

A *classification problem* is a problem in which we are given a set of *instances* that can be classified positively or negatively in some manner. One toy example is the *play tennis* problem. In this problem, an instance would a set of weather conditions (e.g. *sunny, humid, windy*), along with an indication of whether or not a given individual played tennis under those conditions. A classification algorithm would take a set of such instances, and learn how to predict when an agent will play tennis in different circumstances. There are many different ML algorithms that learn how to classify data from a set of instances. In this paper, we focus on ID3 algorithm. The ID3 algorithm takes a set of instances as input, and it returns a decision tree that classifies all instances. The algorithm operates by branching at each level on the property that reduces the entropy as much as possible. We refer the reader to [8] for a complete description.

4   Approach

Throughout this section, assume that K is a fixed belief set, G is a fixed formula, and $*$ is a fixed AGM belief revision operator. Informally, K is the belief set of some underlying agent, G is a goal formula, and $*$ is the revision operator that the agent employs.

An instance in our setting is a past revision that we have observed. For example, we may have seen the agent stop playing tennis when it starts raining. This means that after revising K by *rain*, then *tennis* is not believed. The goal in this section is to show how we can learn which revision operator an agent is using from a set of such instances.

A *literal* in propositional logic is either a propositional variable, or the negation of a propositional variable. A *complete* conjunction of literals is a conjunction that includes every variable exactly once. Hence, a complete conjunction of literals says exactly which variables are true and which are false.

Definition 1. *An* instance *(for G) is a complete conjunction of literals L over* **V**, *labeled as* + *or* −.

We interpret the instance $L+$ to mean that $K * L \models G$, and we interpret $L-$ to mean that $K * L \not\models G$.

Given a set of instances I, let $T(I)$ denote the decision tree obtained from I by the ID3 algorithm. We have the following definitions.

Definition 2. *For a goal formula G, we say that $T(I)$ agrees with $*$ on G just in case, for every $L \in I$, one of the following holds:*

1. *$T(I)$ classifies L as a positive instance, and $K * L \models G$.*
2. *$T(I)$ classifies L as a negative instance, and $K * L \not\models G$.*

Definition 3. *A set of instances I is in conjunctive agreement with $*$ if $T(I)$ and $*$ agree on every formula G.*

If a decision tree is in conjunctive agreement with $*$, then $*$ is one possible revision operator that the underlying agent may be using. Note, however, that conjunctive agreement does not logically entail that the agent is using the revision operator $*$. Revision by non-conjunctive formulas can not be captured by a decision tree.

We have written prototype software that checks for conjunctive agreement with the so-called Dalal operator $*_d$ [2]. The Dalal operator is well suited for implementation, and known to be computationally simpler than other AGM revision operators [3]. Essentially, our prototype works as follows. The input is given in a text file, by specifying: a set of instances I, a belief set K, and a goal formula G. The sofware does the following:

1. Runs the ID3 algorithm on I to produce a decision tree $T(I)$.
2. For each complete conjunction of literals L, checks two things:
   Does $T(I)$ classify L as a positive instance? AND *Does $K *_d L \models G$?*
3. If the answers to both questions are the same for every L, then returns true.

Hence, the software returns true just in case $T(I)$ agrees with $*_d$ on G. By iterating over all formulas G, we can determine if $T(I)$ conjunctively agrees with $*_d$. If this is the case, then we have learned that $*_d$ is a suitable operator for modelling the beliefs of the agent being observed.

5 Ongoing Development

The implementation described is only able to compare a decision tree with a single revision operator. We would rather look at all belief revision operators.

Definition 4. *For any goal formula G and any set of instances I, let I^* denote the set of AGM revision operators in conjunctive agreement with $T(I)$ with respect to G.*

The set I^* is theoretically important. If we assume that the agent being observed uses an AGM operator for revision and we have observed the set I of instances, then I^* is the set of possible revision operators that might be used. Hence, if we want to determine if the agent will believe G after observing ϕ, we can just check the result of $K * \phi$ for every $* \in I^*$. If $bel(G)$ means the agent believes G, then we can reason as follows:

- For *skeptical* reasoning, $bel(G)$ iff $K * \phi \vdash G$ for all $* \in I^*$.
- For *credulous* reasoning, $bel(G)$ iff $K * \phi \models G$ for some $* \in I^*$.
- For *democratic* reasoning, $bel(G)$ iff $K * \phi \models G$ for over half of the operators $* \in I^*$.

But how can we generate the set I^*? We propose that we can use the GenB solver, which can calculate the result of any AGM revision operator [6]. Using GenB, we can iterate over all belief revision operators, and check to see if each one is in conjunctive agreement with a generated decision tree. In principle, this would work; but it would be very slow.

It might be possible to do this more quickly, using the highly efficient GenC tool [5]. GenC uses an ALLSat solver for the computationally hard parts of belief revision, and it is able to solve revision problems with hundreds of thousands of variables in just seconds. By using GenC for the revision portion, we can speed things up significantly. We still have the problem of iterating over all possible orders, but it would be possible to use heuristics to greatly reduce this search space. We are currently working on this.

6 Conclusion

In this short, speculative paper, we have outlined our current work on learning belief revision operators. The intuition here is quite simple. If an agent uses an AGM revision operator to modify their beliefs, then we should be able to learn that operator by observing how they revise their beliefs in previous examples. We have therefore proposed a simple machine learning approach that will allow us to find out if candidate AGM revision functions are being used. If we discover the actual operator, then we will be able to understand the behaviour of the agent.

We conclude by remarking that this kind of exercise is actually central to goals of AGI. While the KR community has spent decades developing rigorous formal models of reasoning, these models are only generally studied in isolation. To develop full AGI, we will need to use these formal models of reasoning while also learning from data. It is our hope that this project becomes a successful case study in merging these two areas.

References

1. Alchourrón, C.E., Gardenfors, P., Makinson, D.: On the logic of theory change: partial meet functions for contraction and revision. J. Symb. Logic **50**(2), 510–530 (1985)
2. Dalal, M.: Investigations into a theory of knowledge base revision. In: AAAI, pp. 475–479 (1988)
3. Eiter, T., Gottlob, G.: On the complexity of propositional knowledge base revision. updates and counterfactuals. Artif. Intell. **57**(2–3), 227–270 (1992)
4. Hunter, A.: Learning belief revision operators. Canadian Conf. Artif. Intell. **10832**, 239–245 (2018)
5. Hunter, A., Agapeyev, J.: An efficient solver for parametrized difference revision. Australasian Conf. Artif. Intell. **11919**, 143–152 (2019)
6. Hunter, A., Tsang, E.: GenB: A general solver for AGM revision. In: JELIA, pp. 564–569 (2016)
7. Katsuno, H., Mendelzon, A.O.: Propositional knowledge base revision and minimal change. Artif. Intell. **52**(3), 263–294 (1992)
8. Mitchell, T.: Machine Learning. McGraw Hill, New York (1997)

An Attentional Control Mechanism for Reasoning and Learning

Peter Isaev[✉] and Patrick Hammer[✉]

Department of Computer and Information Sciences, College of Science
and Technology, Temple University, Philadelphia, PA 19122, USA
{peter.isaev,patrick.hammer}@temple.edu

Abstract. This paper discuses attentional control mechanism of several systems in context of Artificial General Intelligence. Attentional control mechanism of *OpenNARS*, an implementation of Non-Axiomatic Reasoning System for research purposes is being introduced with description of the related functions and demonstration examples. Paper also implicitly compares *OpenNARS* attentional mechanism with the one found in other Artificial General Intelligence systems.

Keywords: Non-axiomatic reasoning · Artificial general intelligence · General machine intelligence · Inference control · Attention mechanism

1 Introduction

For the last decades the field of AGI research has presented numerous systems that aim to rival human level intelligence. In high level of abstraction, some of these systems share similar design principle, in particular they consist of logic and control parts. Being conceptually complex, logic usually is created separately from control mechanisms and often exhibits grounds for achieving anticipated level of intelligence. Later logic is being implemented within a control mechanism of the system, which often becomes massively complex and includes multiple sub-components. Given that AGI system should operate under Assumption of Insufficient Knowledge and Resources (AIKR) [3], resources are always in high demand forcing the system to make a choice for the next reasoning step during the real-time processing. Therefore the correct choice is critical for system performance and efficiency. Picking up the "correct" task or relevant next reasoning step is the main function of Attentional Mechanism that steers behavior of the system in a desired way and allows productive learning.

In systems based on Non-Axiomatic Logic [3], like NARS, role of Attentional mechanism in general is to decide which premises should be selected for inference in real-time during current system's cycle. For NARS, operating under AIKR in the real-time, a new task can arrive at any given moment requiring NARS to work under finite resource constraints and be always open for new tasks. Clearly the choice of "relevant" premises during inference process will influence future

© Springer Nature Switzerland AG 2020
B. Goertzel et al. (Eds.): AGI 2020, LNAI 12177, pp. 221–230, 2020.
https://doi.org/10.1007/978-3-030-52152-3_23

learning vector, final resolution of a supplied task and overall performance and efficiency. Based on above considerations, the attentional control aspect of the *OpenNARS* [2] was thoroughly inspected and revised. While the information present in this paper is mostly related to NARS, we provide some overview and insights of other AGI systems' attentional mechanisms. The next section provides overview of attentional aspects of several related AGI systems, then OpenNARS attentional control and its functionality is being discussed, in Sect. 5 we demonstrate attentional mechanism in action and finally we try to compare attentional aspects between OpenNARS and other AGI systems.

2   Related Works

One of the earlier systems which share resource allocation and attentional mechanism ideas with NARS is the Copycat project [9]. While Copycat can be applied to very narrow domain it features sophisticated attentional and resource allocation mechanisms that incorporate ideas similar to ones found in more complex AGI systems. Copycat is a computer system that tries to discover and build analogies in psychological realistic way, its main idea is to allow mental fluidity achieved by concept slippage which results from building pressure during real-time processing [9]. Copycat control system has three main sub-components: Slipnet, Workspace and Coderack. Slipnet is system's main memory and can be thought as a long-term memory represented by graph where concepts are nodes connected by edges as numerical distances between them. Concepts are used in building bigger structures in Workspace, and Coderack is a place where *codelets*, small working agents, are being created and chosen to complete the work in Workspace. Copycat uses Parallel Terraced Scan [4] as a resource allocation mechanism in order to proceed and discover promising structures in Workspace to be further developed. Function of attentional control is to decide which structure to pick from the Workspace and which *codelets* should be allowed to work. Each structure in Workspace is assigned with *salience*, a dynamic quantity, that determines the probability of acquiring attention from *codelets*. A *codelet*, when created, is placed in a pool with *urgency* value that determines probability of being selected as the next *codelet* to run. *Urgency* estimates an importance of *codelet*'s action which in turn reflects the current state of the system. *Urgency* of a *codelet* is not its priority but rather a relative speed at which the pressures represented by this *codelet* should be attended to. Calculation of *urgency* and *salience* depends on many system's factors and impacts overall dynamics and performance.

Many ideas of Copycat have been employed in LIDA (Learning Intelligent Distribution Agent), the system that models human consciousness [8]. Logical part of LIDA enforces Global Workspace Theory (GWT) (Baars 1988) and implements cognition process in a serial way through use of system cycles. LIDA's control mechanism is immensely complex, its architecture is both symbolic and connectionist, it incorporates several modules with independent architectures and features four types of memory (Perceptual Memory, Procedural Memory,

Episodic Memory, Local Workspace), each with different connectionist architecture. Most task within the system are carried out by *codelets* (small agents) that represent small processes in GWT. System cycle models human cognition and mainly consists of three phases: sense, attend and action selection [5]. Attention phase is implemented through use of attention *codelets* where each looks for "interesting" situation and attempts to bring it to "consciousness" which is modeled by Global Workspace module. Attention *codelets* similarly to daemons look into Workspace and Episodic memory, form coalition of "appropriate" data and bring it into the Global Workspace. A coalition may be viewed as collection of functionally related data. In general, attention is implemented as a filtering process which allows the system to handle information overload situations. Additionally, LIDA implements attentional learning what gives it a capability to improve its own resource management in terms of data selection.

Another AGI system that captured our attention is Auto-catalytic Endogenous Reflective Architecture (AERA), which has been designed as a part of HUMANOBS project: a system able to learn socio-communicative skills by observing people [7]. AERA incorporates an unusual model-based architecture with unique approach to attentional control. In AERA, knowledge is represented as models which are of two types: *forward models* that predict the behavior of entities and *inverse models* that prescribe actions to be taken. Models themselves are executable and its execution is in turn controlled by other models, making the architecture model-driven. Models and other components in AERA are built using low-level building blocks which are objects defined in a specially designed programming language called *Replicode*. There are four fundamental high-level processes which are being continuously performed in a concurrent fashion: Model Acquisition, Reaction, Model Revision and Compaction. Attentional control in AERA can be seen as a part of Reaction process. In general, Reaction activities determine the course of action to pursue goals and are carried out by Attentional Control whose function is to continuously control input saliency within system' specified short time horizon. This approach results in reduction of inputs to the models and more importantly input saliency control allows salience spreading across other objects in the memory including goals and execution traces. Since attentional control is aware about goals, saliency spreading can be controlled and directed by goals.

At present time OpenCog and its implementation OpenCogPrime (OCP) is an advanced and complex integrative AGI system. OCP uses Economic Attention Networks (ECANs), a sophisticated way for attention control and resource allocation [10]. ECANs shares similarities in architecture with connectionist systems but the spread of activation within the system uses equations based on ideas borrowed from economics rather than neural modeling. ECANs is represented as a graph that consists of nodes, links and also HebbianLink and InverseHebbianLink. Each item in a graph, a node or a link, is referred as an *Atom* and assigned two values: Short-Term Importance (STI) and Long-Term Importance (LTI). STI of an *Atom* indicates its immediate urgency at a point in time while LTI indicates amount of value in keeping an *Atom* into the memory. ECANs also integrates a "forgetting" mechanism that removes certain percentage of *Atoms* with lowest LTI values. Each HebbianLink or InverseHebbianLink designates probability value, that is, given a HebbianLink from A to B it shows the probability if A being in AF so is B, and given InverseHebbianLink from A to B it shows the probability if A being in AF so B is not [10]. ECANs uses defined "economics" equations to update system's values dynamically over time and uses Attentional Focus that treats *Atoms* differently with STI values above certain threshold. Additionally *Atoms* are able to spread its LTI and STI between other *Atoms* connected with HebbianLink or InverseHebbianLink. Clearly equations that modify *Atom*'s values are the critical part of ECANs attentional control.

3   OpenNARS Attentional Mechanism

OpenNARS control mechanism shares some ideas present in systems described above. Its architecture is neither symbolic nor connectionist, rather it incorporates different designs for different components. Attentional control is embedded in OpenNARS architecture through use of **main memory** (concept memory) and **data structure** (Bag), it operates dynamically with system cycles in real-time by employing **budget values**, **truth value** and **budget functions**.

Main Memory in OpenNARS follows a concept-centric memory structure in accordance with the Term Logic the system uses [1]. Main memory can be viewed as a graph where concepts are represented as nodes with its own inner structure. Concepts are linked to each other using *termlinks* based on subterm relationship. For each input or derived task, *task object* is created and is linked to concepts of its subterms using *tasklinks*. Tasks which are a *judgment*, are placed into the *belief table* inside concept node, ranked by their confidence value [1].

Bag is a main component of the system that allows attentional mechanism to efficiently operate. *Bag* is a data structure where the elements are sorted according to their *priority*, and the sampling operation chooses candidates with selection chance proportional to their *priority*. This makes the control strategy similar to Parallel Terraced Scan [4], as it also allows to explore many possible options in parallel, with more computation devoted to options which are identified as being more promising. Please note that *Bag* is different from a priority queue, which just selects the highest priority option, in *Bag* every element even the one with lowest *priority* has an opportunity to be selected. After the selection, a candidate is returned to the *Bag*, with a decrease in *priority* proportional to the *durability* value.

Budget Value is a set of rational values assigned to each data item, it is used to control how much processing should be dedicated to a data item within the system. *Budget value* is a triplet (p, d, q), where p, *Priority*, measures short-term importance, d, *Durability*, a decay rate, describes how fast *Priority* of an item should decay, and q, *Quality*, indicates the long-term importance of the data item. Each value within the *budget value* ranges from 0 to 1.

Truth Value of a statement is a set of two rational numbers (*frequency* and *confidence*) which indicates degree of belief based on the evidence collected from system's experience. *Frequency* shows amount of positive evidence, while *confidence* indicates degree of reliability of corresponding *frequency*.

Operating Cycle. The main operating cycle of the system is data driven, mainly guided by the priority of data items. It makes effective use of the system's memory structure which is achieved through indefinite repetition of the same inference loop, which is as follows:

1. Add results (derivations and inputs) from global buffer into main memory, triggering potential revisions in the related concepts.
2. Select a concept C from main memory.
3. Select a *tasklink* from C.
4. Select a *termlink* from C.
5. Obtain the highest-confident belief from the concept the *termlink* points to.
6. Apply inference rule with the *tasklink*'s task, and the belief as premises.
7. Adjust *budget value* through use of *budget functions* for data items participated in the inference
8. Input conclusions into global buffer

4   Control Criteria and Budget Functions

The control mechanism needs to work under AIKR meaning all data structures are bounded in size and eviction strategies to maintain this constraint need to be in place. Additionally, system operating cycle needs to finish roughly in a constant time. A single inference step cannot be interrupted by more important tasks, however an important task is able to interrupt all work carried out over multiple cycles, which captures all the problem solving activities of the system. To allow this happening, the control mechanism has to fulfill additional criteria, for instance, the system should stay responsive to new inputs and derivations. This is achieved through relative forgetting, which makes sure that only contextually relevant items are active at any moment in time. Here the complexity of the inference results matter, since the more complex results need more storage and demand more time to process.

Also historical factors are important in resource allocation, whether a certain inference path was fruitful in the past in a similar context. This is mostly captured through the *quality* of a data item, which can summarize multiple factors, such as "did the selection of the data item led to find answers to questions, or to the fulfillment of a goal?", and more generic considerations such as "how much evidence was summarized by the inference?" as captured by *Budget Inference*. A key here is to see that the criteria for selection and forgetting are quite different. When a selection is made, the context reflected by the *priority* of a data item usually (but not always) matters more than its historic value. For forgetting, on the other hand, the long term *quality* of the item is of interest, though new data item needs to have a chance to prove its usefulness. Many of these considerations have been discussed in [5] as well, and the need to take these considerations into account altogether is what makes designing attentional control for AGI systems a difficult task. In OpenNARS it has led to the development of concrete budget functions, which are not final but take many of the discussed factors into consideration. The goal of Budget functions is to initialize and adjust *budget value* in the real-time for every data item given its current budget and truth values. Please see the tables for initialization and update of *budget value*.

Table 1. Budget Initialization for each data item

	Priority	Durability	Quality
Task	default value	default value	*Truth_to_Quality()*
Concept	parent task value	parent task value	parent task value
TaskLink	related concept's value	related concept's value	related concept's value
TermLink	$\dfrac{TaskPriority}{\sqrt{numTermLinks}}$	related concept's task value	related concept's task value

After task derivation, the task's budget obtained by *budget inference* is changed based on how much it is fulfilled in its concept (with same term). Beliefs can satisfy goals to varying degree: the higher their truth expectation (see below), the more will the goal (or question) task be de-priorized. Also, priority will be increased for the tasklink and termlink used in the same inference step, see Table 3. OpenNARS also implements relative forgetting: after an item was selected, participated in inference and put back to the memory its *priority* is decreased by *durability* factor to allow fair competition for resources for other items. Once *priority* drops below certain threshold, item is being removed from the memory.

Short description of Budget Update functions from Table 2:

Table 2. Budget Update Functions

Function and inputs	Priority	Durability	Quality
budgetInference *TruthValue tv,* *Task t,* *TermLink b*	**Task Update:or**(priority of t, priority of b) **Term Link Update:** min(1,**or**(priority of b, **or**(*Truth_to_Quality(tv)*, priority of b.target)))	**Task Update:** **and**(durability of t, durability of b) **Term Link Update:** **or**(durability of b, *Truth_to_Quality(tv)*)	**Task Update:** *Truth_to_Quality(tv)* **Term Link Update:** no update
merge *BudgetValue b,* *BudgetValue a*	*max*(priority of a, priority of b)	*max*(durability of a, durability of b)	*max*(quality of a, quality of b)
activate *Concept c,* *BudgetValue b*	*or*(priority of c, priority of b)	*avg*(durability of c, durability of b)	quality of c
revise *TruthValue t,* *TruthValue b,* *TruthValue r*	*or*(t.priority, r.confidence- *max*(t.confidence, b.confidence))	*avg*(t.durability, r.confidence- *max*(t.confidence, b.confidence))	*Truth_to_Quality(r)*

1. **budgetInference** creates a budget for derived task and also updates budget for selected concept's termlink
2. **merge** revises budget when merging identical items
3. **activate** updates currently selected concept's *budget value*
4. **revise** assigns budget to item whose truth value derived using revision rule.

Budget functions use utility functions defined separately and common to numerous other evaluations in OpenNARS. The four utility functions are present below:

1. **TruthExp** truth expectation defined as $confidence * (frequency - 0.5) + 0.5$
2. **Truth_to_Quality** is defined as $max(TruthExp, 0.75 * (1 - TruthExp))$
3. **or**$(x_1...x_n)$ is defined as $1 - \prod_{i=1}^{n}(1 - x_i)$
4. **and**$(x_1...x_n)$ is defined as $\prod_{i=1}^{n} x_i$.

5 Experiments

Experiment 1. The first experiment shows a reasoning tasks and the selections made by the control system, and serves as an example to understand how budget of derivation exactly is calculated according to the budget functions.

At first, two tasks are entered by the user, $(cat \rightarrow animal)$ and $(dog \rightarrow animal)$. Both get a default truth value attached, which is frequency 1.0 and confidence 0.9. The system trace outputs:

Table 3. Task Satisfaction where q_s is the solution quality, the confidence of the solution, such as a belief to a question or goal, if the term is equal to the question, and else its truth expectation.

Derived task priority	Tasklink priority	Termlink priority
$min(1\text{-}q_s,\ TaskPriority)$	$or(min(1\text{-}q_s, TasklinkPriority))$	$or(q_s, TermlinkPriority)$

```
!!! Perceived: $0.8000;0.8000;0.9500$ <cat --> animal>. %1.00;0.90%
!!! Perceived: $0.8000;0.8000;0.9500$ <dog --> animal>. %1.00;0.90%
```

We also see initialized default *budget values* (p, d, q), where $p = 0.8$, $d = 0.8$, $q = 0.95$ and q were calculated using truth value (f, c) of the task via:
$$truthToQuality(f, c) = max(exp(f, c), (1 - exp(f, c)) * 0.75)$$ where $exp(f, c) = (c * (f - \frac{1}{2}) + \frac{1}{2})$. The factor 0.75 is used to assign a higher quality value for positive (frequency > 0.5) results than negative ones.

Now in the first cycle, at first the new input tasks are inserted from global buffer into memory. Then the concept-based operating cycle as described before, chooses *animal* as concept, $(cat \rightarrow animal)$ as task via the chosen tasklink from concept *animal*, and $(dog \rightarrow animal)$ as belief via the chosen termlink from concept *animal*:

```
* Selected Concept: animal
* Selected TaskLink: $0.5657;0.8000;0.9500$ _@(T4-2) <cat --> animal>. %1.00;0.90%
* Selected TermLink: $0.5657;0.8000;0.9500$ _@(T4-2) <dog --> animal>
* Selected Belief: <dog --> animal>. %1.0000;0.9000%
```

(Here T4 stands for termlink type "COMPOUND_STATEMENT" meaning the termlink points into a statement, and the index is 2, pointing to *animal* within the statement, which is the case for both links.)

The links got their priority from distributing the task priority among the components using the function: $\frac{p}{\sqrt{n}}$ where n is the amount of subterms, which is 2, so the result is $\frac{0.8}{\sqrt{2}} = 0.5657$, the durability and quality is the one of the task, though gets updated after the following derivation formed with the intersection truth function, which led to a truth value of $(f, c) = (1.0, 0.81)$:

```
!!! Derived: $0.9131;0.1338;0.1810$ <(|,cat,dog) --> animal>. %1.00;0.81%
  from task: $0.80;0.80;0.95$ <cat --> animal>. %1.00;0.90%
  from belief: <dog --> animal>. %1.00;0.90%
```

The complexity of the derived term (which stands for "cats and dogs are both animals" is 5. The termlink priority was 0.5658. The derived priority of 0.9131 was obtained by $or(0.5658, 0.8) = 1 - (1 - 0.5658) * (1 - 0.8) = 0.91316$. And the derived quality 0.1810 was obtained from $\frac{truthToQuality(1.0, 0.81)}{c} = \frac{0.905}{5}$. Also the link budgets are now updated by increasing them with the *or* function, where both target activation (priority of the belief concept) and $q^* = \frac{q_{result}}{complexity}$ are "added" to the existing link priority, meaning $p_{termlink_{new}} = or(p_{termlink_{old}}, p_{beliefconcept}, q^*)$. Other values are in the budget tables above.

Experiment 2. This example shows properties of the control system on a higher level. It demands the system to form a certain subset of letters from a–j:

```
<{a} --> letter>. ... <{j} --> letter>.
//<{a} --> letter>? //<{a,f} --> letter>? (*) //<{a,f,g} --> letter>? <{a,f,g,j} --> letter>?
```

When the questions marked with "//" are given to the system (after 1000 inference steps before each question) together with the other input, the system arrives with the answer to the last question within 6151 inference steps (Open-NARS v3.0.4). When on the other hand only the question marked with a star is provided additional to the final question, it takes 7728 steps. With only the final question it takes the system 260320 inference steps to find the answer. This shall serve as an example of how contextual priming can help in the search for solutions. The key budget function allowing this is *activate*, which increases the *priority* of a concept when a task with the same term arrives within it. In this case it's the appropriately timed user questions which trigger this form of priming. Contextual priming is also a key in avoiding combinatorial explosion in reasoning, additionally to the term logic which makes sure the premises to derive a conclusion are semantically related by sharing a common term.

6   Discussions

It is difficult to compare OpenNARS with the attentional controls of systems present in Sect. 2 since architectures are very different, however some similarities can be observed. As one might see OpenNARS's attentional mechanism is quite complex and operates in the real-time during every inference. Once a data item is participating in an inference, its *budget value* as well as the one of the related items are inevitably affected resulting in a budget activation spread within the main memory. Spread of attentional values (*salience*, STI, LTI) also exists in AERA and OCP. AERA implements the attentional control partially as an input data filtering to a model, and then *salience* is being spread to other models allowing control of input data. In LIDA, attentional control is implemented through use of attention codelets which pick an "interesting" data from Workspace, form a coalition with data from Episodic Memory and move it to Global Workspace. LIDA attentional control can be viewed as data filtering process that filters low importance items and safeguards the system from information overload.

OCP on the other hand is more similar to OpenNARS, its attentional mechanism is embedded in its architecture. ECAN applies equations to update STI, LTI, HebbianLink and InverseHebbianLink probabilities, similarly to Open-NARS Budget Functions that update *budget value* of a data item. In ECAN, STI and LTI spread is happening through HebbianLinks and InverseHebbian-Links. Finally, the Copycat project, uses *salience* for structures in Workspace and *urgency* for codelets. Copycat's resource allocation ideas share similarities with OpenNARS's approach of selecting items. It selects codelets from Coderack with selection chance proportional to the codelet's *urgency*, while in OpenNARS items's *priority* is treated as probability for selection allowing lowest *priority* items to compete for resources as well. Many items will be filtered out completely though, due to the bounded size of the *Bag*.

7   Conclusion

Important details of *OpenNARS*'s control mechanism and attentional control were described, their motivation explained and demonstration provided. Open-NARS has been applied in applications such as [6], though its control system, despite its successes, was not yet published in detail. Inference control is a major problem to be solved for reasoning-based AGI systems such as OpenNARS, which makes documenting the advancements even more crucial. It will help the AGI field to find better attention mechanisms with proper ways to take the usefulness, relevance, truth, and complexity of results into consideration. Our future research will include important metrics to measure control system capabilities, which can become a basis to compare different reasoning-based AGI approaches.

References

1. Wang, P.: Non-Axiomatic Logic: A Model of Intelligent Reasoning. World Scientific, Singapore (2013)
2. Hammer, P., Lofthouse, T., Wang, P.: The OpenNARS implementation of the non-axiomatic reasoning system. In: Steunebrink, B., Wang, P., Goertzel, B. (eds.) International Conference on Artificial General Intelligence, pp. 160–170. Springer, Cham (2016). https://doi.org/10.1007/978-3-319-41649-6_16
3. Wang, P.: Insufficient Knowledge and Resources-A Biological Constraint and its Functional Implications. In: 2009 AAAI Fall Symposium Series, October 2009

4. Rehling, J., Hofstadter, D.: The parallel terraced scan: an optimization for an agent-oriented architecture. In: 1997 IEEE International Conference on Intelligent Processing Systems (Cat. No. 97TH8335), vol. 1, pp. 900–904. IEEE, October 1997
5. Helgason, H.P.: General attention mechanism for artificial intelligence systems. University of Reykjavik, Ph.D., June 2013. https://en.ru.is/media/td/Helgi_Pall_Helgason_PhD_CS_HR.pdf
6. Hammer, P., Lofthouse, T., Fenoglio, E., Latapie, H.: A reasoning based model for anomaly detection in the Smart City domain. In: Advances in Intelligent Systems and Computing (2020)
7. Nivel, E., et al.: Autonomous Endogenous Reflective Architecture (2013)
8. Franklin, S., Madl, T., D'mello, S., Snaider, J.: LIDA: a systems-level architecture for cognition emotion and learning. IEEE Trans. Autonom. Mental Dev. 6(1), 19–41 (2013)
9. Hofstadter, D.R., Mitchell, M.: The copycat project: A model of mental fluidity and analogy-making - D, pp. 205–267. Fluid Concepts and Creative Analogies, Hofstadter and the Fluid Analogies Research group (1995)
10. Ikle, M., Pitt, J., Goertzel, B., Sellman, G.: Economic attention networks: Associative memory and resource allocation for general intelligence (2009)

Hyperdimensional Representations in Semiotic Approach to AGI

Alexey K. Kovalev[1,2], Aleksandr I. Panov[2,3]([⊠]), and Evgeny Osipov[4]

[1] National Research University Higher School of Economics, Moscow, Russia
[2] Federal Research Center "Computer Science and Control" of the Russian Academy of Sciences, Moscow, Russia
[3] Moscow Institute of Physics and Technology, Moscow, Russia
panov.ai@mipt.ru
[4] Luleå University of Technology, Luleå, Sweden

Abstract. The paper is dedicated to the use of distributed hyperdimensional vectors to represent sensory information in the sign-based cognitive architecture, in which the image component of a sign is encoded by a causal matrix. The hyperdimensional representation allows us to update the precedent dimension of the causal matrix and accumulate information in it during the interaction of the system with the environment. Due to the high dimensionality of vectors, it is possible to reduce the representation and reasoning on the entities related to them to simple operations on vectors. In this work we show how hyperdimensional representations are embedded in an existing sign formalism and provide examples of visual scene encoding.

Keywords: Cognitive agent · Sign-based world model · Semiotic network · Causal tensor · Distributed representation · Symbol grounding

1 Introduction

When constructing intelligent systems that control the functioning of agents in a real, rather than a virtual environment, one of the main problems is the symbol grounding problem. In other words, for each concept that the system can operate with, it is necessary to map some idea, which is based on the signals coming from the agent sensors. It is human nature to operate with symbols, i.e. some indivisible entities representing the concepts, while existing computer architectures restrict the low-level representation of information in intelligent systems where binary numbers are commonly used.

At an early stage of the rise of artificial intelligence, one of the leading hypotheses that captured the minds of researchers for a long time and determined the development of the field for years to come was the hypothesis that "a physical symbol system has the necessary and sufficient means for general intelligent action" proposed by Allen Newell and Herbert Simon [1]. However, in the practical implementation of such systems, researchers encountered several problems, the main among which was the symbol grounding problem mentioned above.

© Springer Nature Switzerland AG 2020
B. Goertzel et al. (Eds.): AGI 2020, LNAI 12177, pp. 231–241, 2020.
https://doi.org/10.1007/978-3-030-52152-3_24

Despite the fact that the research and development of symbolic artificial intelligence methods continue, at present the connectionist approach using artificial neural networks is leading in the number of applications and the attention of researchers [2]. In recent years, the neuro-symbolic approach, which combines the advantages of both connectionism and symbolism, is gaining more and more popularity. As characteristic representatives, Markov Logic Networks [3, 4] and Logic Tensor Networks [5] can be distinguished.

Another direction of the neuro-symbolic representation can be called the approach to the use of hyperdimensional representations, proposed in [6]. Despite the fact that artificial neural networks are not used explicitly in this approach, the representations themselves obtained using hyperdimensional computing are very well suited for working with neural networks [7].

In this paper, we approach the solution of the symbol grounding problem using the previously proposed sign-based cognitive architecture [8–10], in which the processing of sensory information occurs in the image component of the sign representing some entity. We propose using hyperdimensional vectors to encode the precedent component of the sign image and demonstrate that this allows us to preserve the main advantages of the sign approach – the ability to represent operations and relationships based on operations with vectors and matrices. A new interpretation of the image component allowed us to describe complex visual scenes in a simpler language. In this work, we consider the capacity of the proposed mechanism for encoding sensory information.

The structure of the paper is as follows: Sect. 2 briefly provides the necessary information about sign-based cognitive architecture. Section 3 describes the use of hyperdimensional vectors as a representation of the image component of a sign and the operations on such representations. The fourth part shows the possibility of using hyperdimensional vectors for encoding elements of the causal matrix, with which the image structure is formalized, and provides an example of representing some visual synthetic scene in the form of a hyperdimensional vector for which simple reasoning schemes on the properties of objects presented on the stage are carried out.

2 Sign-Based World Model

In [8], the principles of the organization of sign-based cognitive architecture (SBWM) [9, 10] were described in detail, in particular, the process of reasoning expressed by applying certain mental actions by cognitive agents on their representation of the environment was described. Next, we briefly outline the basic principles of the SBWM following [11, 12].

The main element of the system is the sign, which corresponds with the agent's concept of any object, action or situation, then for simplicity, we will call the object, action or situation an entity. The sign consists of four components: image, meaning, significance, and name. The image component corresponds to the characteristic feature of the described entity. In the simplest case, an image refers to signals from the sensors of an agent that correspond to an entity. In the general case, we can say that the image of the sign coheres to the set of entity characteristic features with which the sign relates. The significance of the sign describes the standard application of the entity, adopted on the basis of experience in the interaction of a coalition of agents with the environment. The meaning of the sign is understood as the relation of the agent to the entity or the experience of the interaction of the agent with this entity, thus, the meanings are formed in the process of interaction of a concrete agent with the environment.

The sign components are described by a special structure - the causal matrix. A causal matrix is a tuple $z = \langle e_1, e_2, \ldots, e_t \rangle$ of length t where events e_i are represented by a binary vector of length h. For each index j of the event vector e_i (row of the matrix z), we will associate a tuple, possibly empty, of causal matrices Z_j, such that $z \notin Z_j$. We divide the set of columns indices of the causal matrix z into two disjoint subsets $I^c \subset \mathbb{N}, \forall i \in I^c \; i \leq t$ and $I^e \subset \mathbb{N}, \forall i \in I^e \; i \leq t$, such that $I^c \cap I^e = \emptyset$. The set I^c for the matrix z will be called the indexes of the condition columns, and the set I^e – the indexes of the effect columns of the matrix z. If $|I^e| = \emptyset$, i.e. there are no effect columns in the matrix, then we will say that such a matrix corresponds with the object. If $|I^e| \neq \emptyset$ what the presence of effect columns in the matrix means, then such a matrix corresponds with an action or process. The structure of the causal matrix makes it possible to uniformly encode both static information and features of an object, as well as dynamic processes.

A sign means a quadruple $s = \langle n, p, m, a \rangle$, where the name of a sign n expressed by a word in some finite alphabet, $p = Z^p$, $m = Z^m$, $a = Z^a$ are tuples of causal matrices, which are respectively called the *image*, *significance*, and *meaning* of the sign s. Based on this, the whole set of causal matrices Z can be divided into three disjoint subsets: images Z^p, significances Z^m, and meanings Z^a, such that $Z = Z^p \cup Z^m \cup Z^a$ which are organized into semantic networks, which we will call causal.

Formally, a causal network on images will be a labeled directed graph $W_p = \langle V, E \rangle$ in which:

1. each node $v \in V$ is assigned a causal matrices tuple $Z^p(s)$ of the image of a certain sign s, which will be denoted by $v \rightarrow Z^p(s)$;
2. an edge $e = (v_1, v_2)$ belongs to the set of graph edges E, if $v_1 \rightarrow Z^p(s_1)$, $v_2 \rightarrow Z^p(s_2)$ and $s_1 \in S_p(s_2)$, i.e. if the sign s_1 is an element of the image s_2.

Causal networks on significances and meanings are defined in a similar way. The network on names is a semantic network whose vertices are the names of signs, and the edges correspond to special relationships. The semantic network on names will also be called a causal network.

These four mentioned above causal networks are connected using transition functions Ψ_i^j, $i, j \in \{p, m, a, n\}$ to the semiotic network. The transition function Ψ_i^j allows us to switch from i-th component of the sign to the j-th one. A semiotic network can be considered as an agent's knowledge base about the environment, taking into account its experience of interacting with the environment.

Formally, we will call the semiotic network $\Omega = \langle W_m, W_a, W_p, W_n, R, \Theta \rangle$ a sign-based world model, where W_m, W_a, W_p, W_n are causal networks of significances, meanings, images, and names, respectively, $R = \langle R^m, R^a, R^p, R^n \rangle$ is a family of relations on sign components, Θ is a family of operations on a set of signs. Operations Θ include such actions on signs as unification, image comparison, updating while learning, etc.

In the SBWM, the concept of the activity spread is defined, which allows the reasoning processes to occur in the semiotic network. After the activation level of the sign component exceeds a certain threshold, the component is considered as active. If the components of the image, significance, and meaning of the sign are activated, then the sign itself is also activated (its name is activated). At the same time, the activation process can proceed in the opposite direction: first, the name of the sign is activated, and then all sign components are automatically activated. If the activation level of a sign component is nonzero but does not exceed a predetermined activation threshold θ, then such a component is called pre-activated.

Spreading activity on a semiotic network is subject to *global* and *local* rules for spreading activity.

The *global rule* is that if one of the components of the sign s becomes active on a step t, the other components become pre-activated.

The group of local rules consists of four rules: ascending, predicting, descending and causal. The *ascending rule* says that if at the time t the component of the sign s becomes active, then all occurrences of this component in the causal matrix of other signs become active. The *predicting rule* determines that if at the time moment t an event e_t is active in any component of the sign s, then the events e_{t+1} of the same component are pre-activated. The *descending rule* establishes that if at the time moment t each event e_t in the tuple of causal matrices of the component $i \in \{p, m, a\}$ of the sign s is active, then the components i of all signs included in the event e_t are pre-activated. The *causal rule*: if an event e_t is active at a time t, then a predictive rule and a descending rule are consistently applied to all event-effects, with the amendment that the maximum activity applies.

3   Representation of Symbols by Hyperdimensional Vectors

In recommender systems and natural language processing, a widely used approach is the one that translates localized one-hot representations of objects that the system works with into distributed representations. Moreover, in both problems, there is a decrease in dimensionality, because initial one-hot vectors can have tens of thousands of dimensions, while the standard length of a distributed vector, for example, for word representation, is 300. A classic example in recommender systems are models with hidden variables that use a singular matrix decomposition of users-items matrix [13], and the modification of such a decomposition, called the truncated singular decomposition, allows one to vary the dimensions of the representation, simultaneously solving the regularization problem.

For the problems of natural language processing, there also have been attempts to use the singular decomposition, for example, for the co-occurrence frequency matrix [14]. However, approaches based on iterative learning of representations in the corpus of texts, such as word2vec [15, 16] and GloVe [17], gained wide popularity. In the original word2vec article, CBOW (continuous bag of words) and skip-gram models are proposed. In CBOW, the central word in the window is predicted from surrounding words by a certain contextual window that runs through text whose size is a hyperparameter. In skip-gram, the inverse problem is solved – according to the central word, it is predicted whether another word enters its context. In essence, the CBOW and skip-gram models are neural networks with one hidden layer with a linear activation function, and the prediction is constructed as softmax from the scalar product of the vector of the central and context words.

In GloVe, the problem is formulated as follows, given a joint co-occurrence matrix whose elements correspond to the occurrence frequency of one word in the context of another, then let the scalar product of the vector representations of the central word and the context word approximate the logarithm of this value.

In [18], examples are given that such representations of words contain some semantic and syntactic information that allows us to solve problems of searching for analogies, for example, of the type "king:man :: woman:queen" using arithmetic operations on vectors:

$$v_{king} - v_{man} + v_{woman} \approx v_{queen},$$

where v_{king}, v_{man}, v_{woman}, v_{queen} vector representations for words "king", "man", "woman" and "queen" correspondingly. Similarly, analogies of the type "big:biggest :: large:largest" are solved.

For recommender systems, this approach allows you to specify the similarity between the vectors of users or items, for example, using the cosine distance, while with the "one-hot" representation, the distance between the vectors does not make any sense.

Similar results were obtained for computer vision problems [19, 20], when using an autoencoder, representations are learned that allow you to add or remove some details of an image by changing a specific coordinate.

All of the above approaches can be summarized as follows: we reduce the dimension of the original vector while simultaneously trying instead of a localized, uninterpreted representation, to obtain representations in which the coordinates carry some, often poorly interpreted, meaning.

On the other side of the scale lies an approach that, in contrast to the first, increases the dimension of the vector representation and deprives individual component of the vector of any interpretability. Moreover, the resulting representations are in some ways symbols, but symbols that can be operated on using vector operations. Let us consider this approach described in [6] in more detail.

The basis of this approach is the idea that for a sufficiently large dimension of the space for any randomly extracted and fixed vector from this space ~99% of the remaining vectors of the space will be quasi-orthogonal to this fixed vector. In this case, by quasi-orthogonality we mean that, for example, for binary vectors, the normalized Hamming distance between them will be approximately 0.5, and then any sufficiently small deviation from this value will indicate that these two vectors are not random, and one enters into a superposition of the other. This property of hyperdimensional spaces allows us to reduce the procedure of matching a given object of its hyper-dimensional representation to sampling a random vector. Thus, for each object or property that the system encounters, a random hyper-dimensional vector, for example, a binary one, is generated and put into correspondence with this object or property. All vectors obtained in such a manner are stored in a special memory called "Item Memory", where they are assigned a label corresponding to the encoded entity. For the Item Memory, a search operation that receives a vector and returns the vector closest to this one is defined. The search operation on the Item Memory can be considered as restoring the original vector of an entity from its noisy copy, the need for such an operation will be shown below. The property of hyperdimensional spaces described above just allows avoiding collisions for such an operation with sufficient space capacity and not too much noise in the input vector.

We briefly describe operations on hyperdimensional vectors.

The binding operation to two vectors associates the third, quasi-orthogonal to both initial vectors. For binary vectors, the binding is carried out using the elementwise exclusive or operation. Binding obeys the laws of commutativity and associativity. The semantic meaning of binding can be explained by the following example: let some object have a certain attribute a_i with a value v_j, we put them in correspondence with hyper-dimensional random vectors A_i and $V_j^{A_i}$. Then the binding $A_i \oplus V_j^{A_i}$ corresponds to assigning the value v_j to the attribute a_i. Also, the inverse operation to the binding is defined – an unbinding $A_i \oplus \left(A_i \oplus V_j^{A_i} \right) = V_j^{A_i}$ which returns one of the original vectors.

The bundling operation to a certain set of hyperdimensional vectors associates another hyperdimensional vector that is not quasi-orthogonal with respect to any of the vectors of the set. Bundling is implemented through the threshold sum:

$$[X_0 + X_1 + \ldots X_n] = Y,$$

where $y_i \in Y$ and

$$
y_i =
\begin{cases}
\sum_1^n x_i, \ x_i \in X_i, & \text{if } \sum_1^n x_i \leq thr \\
thr, & \text{if } \sum_1^n x_i > thr,
\end{cases}
$$

where thr is a threshold, which is a hyperparameter.

Bundling can be considered as a representation of the set of some objects. The commutativity and associativity of bundling are obvious.

Sometimes it becomes necessary to obtain a quasi-orthogonal vector from the original one, but so that this operation is reversible. To do this, permutation operations are used, which permute the coordinates of the vector according to a certain rule. A special case of permutation is a cyclic shift. Denote $X^{n>}$ whose vector coordinates are cyclically shifted to the right on n positions relative to the original vector X.

Let the state of a system at the initial time moment correspond to a hyperdimensional vector X_0, then all the states of the system at time moments $i = 1, \ldots n$ can be expressed as follows:

$$X_1 = X_0^{1>},$$
$$X_2 = X_1^{1>} = X_0^{2>},$$
$$\ldots$$
$$X_n = X_{n-1}^{1>} = X_{n-2}^{2>} = \ldots = X_0^{n>}$$

Applying unbinding to a bundle

$$A_i \oplus B = \left[A_1 \oplus V_j^{A_1} + \ldots + A_i \oplus V_j^{A_i} + \ldots + A_n \oplus V_j^{A_n} \right]$$
$$= \left[A_i \oplus A_1 \oplus V_j^{A_1} + \ldots + A_i \oplus A_i \oplus V_j^{A_i} + \ldots + A_i \oplus A_n \oplus V_j^{A_n} \right]$$
$$= \left[Noise + V_j^{A_i} \right] = \tilde{V}_j^{A_i}$$

we get $\tilde{V}_j^{A_i}$ – a noisy version of the vector $V_j^{A_i}$ by which one can restore the vector $V_j^{A_i}$ by searching through Item Memory.

4 The Use of Hyperdimensional Vectors in the Sign-Based World Model

Let us consider the use of hyperdimensional binary vectors in the Signed Bases World Model using the causal matrix of an image network as an example. We recall that the causal matrix z is a tuple of events e_i $z = \langle e_1, e_2, \ldots, e_t \rangle$ of a length t. We agree further that the hyperdimensional vector corresponding to the concept will be denoted by the same letter as the concept itself, only in capitals. Then, a vector E_i is assigned to each event e_i, the method of obtaining this vector will be described below. Since a tuple is an ordered set of elements, it is easy to set it through the variety of elements and their order. As described above, the set in hyperdimensional computations is specified by the operation of bundling over the elements included in it, to determine the order, we introduce a special hyperdimensional vector S that will correspond to the first column of the causal matrix. The subsequent columns will be defined through the cyclic shift of the vector S. The fact that some event E_i corresponds to the j-th column will be denoted through $E_i \oplus S^{j>}$. Then in general terms, the vector of the causal matrix can be represented as:

$$Z = \left[E_0 \oplus S + E_1 \oplus S^{1>} + \ldots + E_t \oplus S^{t>} \right].$$

If the causal matrix corresponds to the action, then we introduce two vectors S_c and S_e for the columns of conditions and effects, respectively, then:

$$Z = \left[E_0 \oplus S_c + E_1 \oplus S_c^{1>} + \ldots + E_j \oplus S_c^{k>} + E_{j+1} \oplus S_e + E_{j+2} \oplus S_e^{1>} + \ldots + E_t \oplus S_e^{l>} \right],$$

where $k + l = t$.

It is worth noting that if there is no need to maintain order, for example, for object matrices, then you may not introduce an additional vector S.

Let us return to the representation of an event e_i. An event corresponds to the simultaneous appearance of some attributes, therefore, if each attribute and all possible values of this attribute are associated with hyperdimensional vectors, then the event takes the form:

$$E = \left[A_1 \oplus V^{A_1} + A_2 \oplus V^{A_2} + \ldots + A_m \oplus V^{A_m} \right],$$

where A_i corresponds to i-th attribute and V^{A_i} is its value.

Thus, following the structure of a causal matrix and given HD representation of events we can collapse the whole matrix into the corresponding HD vector CM. This vector may act as an event in the formation of another causal matrix on the next level of abstraction. Properties of operations with HD vectors allow to keep structure inside of such representation and restore it if needed.

Consider an example of representing the causal matrix of a scene depicted in Fig. 1 as a hyperdimensional vector.

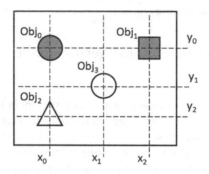

Fig. 1. The model scene

Let us suppose that the objects on the scene have the attributes c – "color", s – "shape", x – "x coordinate", y – "y coordinate" with the corresponding possible values: for the attribute "color" w – "white" and g – "gray", for "form" ci – "circle", t – "triangle" and sq – "square". Let us set the attributes and their values in accordance with the vectors C, S, X, Y, W, G, CI, T, SQ. The value of the attribute "coordinate x" will be encoded as follows. Assume directionality of the process of parsing of the visual scene (for example from top to bottom and from left to right). During parsing of the visual scene we find the leftmost object on the scene, in this case there are two such objects – Obj_0 and Obj_2, and assign a vector X_0 to them, then the next right object – Obj_3 will have a (relative to Obj_0) coordinate value $X_1 = X_0^{1>}$. For object Obj_4, we have $X_2 = X_0^{2>}$. The y coordinate values are encoded in a similar way. This allows us to move from the absolute coordinates to the relative ones. We also introduce vectors $O_0 \ldots O_3$ corresponding to scene objects. Now we can represent the vector corresponding to the causal matrix of the scene as:

$$SCENE = [O_o \oplus [C \oplus G + S \oplus CI + X \oplus X_0 + Y \oplus Y_0]$$
$$+ O_1 \oplus \left[C \oplus G + S \oplus SQ + X \oplus X_0^{2>} + Y \oplus Y_0 \right]$$
$$+ O_2 \oplus [C \oplus W + S \oplus T + X \oplus X_0 + Y \oplus Y_2]$$
$$+ O_3 \oplus [C \oplus G + S \oplus CI + X \oplus X_1 + Y \oplus Y_1]].$$

After that, if we want to find out the value of the object 2 form attribute, we must perform the following operations:

$$SCENE \oplus O_2 \oplus S = Noise + T = \tilde{T}.$$

Such operations allow performing the simplest reasoning on the representation of the scene using hyperdimensional vectors.

5 Discussion

While this paper focused on conceptual aspects of using HD representation in semiotic approach to AGI it is useful to get an intuition about possible applications of the presented encoding for flexible answering to complex queries. Take the last example of the *SCENE* encoding. Suppose the task is to extract objects to the right of object Obj_3. To do this the following computational steps should be performed.

1. Similarly to the example of extracting the value of attribute S, extract the value of attribute X of object Obj_3.
2. Retrieve the clean copy of X_3 from the Item Memory.
3. Construct a bundle of all possible coordinates "to the right of X_3" by circularly shifting X_3 n times binding with X and bundling the result:

$$X_3^{right} = \left[X \oplus X_3^{1>} + X \oplus X_3^{2>} + \ldots + X \oplus X_3^{n>} \right]$$

4. Bind the resulting bundle with the *SCENE* vector. This operation will produce a bundle containing the noisy values of the objects on the queried coordinates.

$$SCENE \oplus X_3^{right} = Noise + \tilde{O}_1$$

5. Passing the result through the Item Memory of objects will reveal the identities of the objects (Fig. 2).

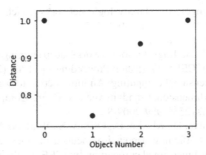

Fig. 2. Distance to objects vectors in Item Memory

Several important issues must be addressed for make the approach work on real use-cases. Specifically, one need to take into account the informational capacity of the bundles of HD vectors. Early results on the capacity were given in [21, 22]. Some ideas for the case of binary/bipolar HD vectors were also presented in [23, 24]. Probably the most comprehensive analysis of the capacity of different VSAs' frameworks has been recently presented in [25]. The practical dimensioning of the architecture for the case of visual questions answering application is a subject for future work and will be reported outside the scope for this article.

6 Conclusion

The paper proposes a new approach that allows solving the symbol grounding problem based on the agent sing-based cognitive architecture using hyperdimensional vector computations to describe the image component of the sign. Due to the use of hyperdimensional vectors to describe the precedent of the causal matrix component, it is possible to interpret the structure of the causal matrix and relations in the causal network as operations on a set of such vectors. The work provides a model example of the use of hyperdimensional vectors to represent a visual scene. In the future, we propose various applications of the sign-based architecture, including for personal cognitive assistants [26] that adapt to a specific user.

Acknowledgements. The reported study was supported by RFBR, research Projects No. 18-07-01011 and No. 19-37-90164.

References

1. Newell, A., Simon, H.A.: Computer science as empirical inquiry: symbols and search. Commun. ACM **19**(3), 113–126 (1976). https://doi.org/10.1145/360018.360022
2. Rumelhart, D.E., McClelland J.L.: Learning internal representations by error propagation. In: Parallel Distributed Processing: Explorations in the Microstructure of Cognition: Foundations, pp. 318–362, MITP (1987)
3. Richardson, M., Domingos, P.: Markov logic networks. Mach. Learn. **62**(1–2), 107–136 (2006). https://doi.org/10.1007/s10994-006-5833-1
4. Wang, J., Domingos, P.: Hybrid markov logic networks. AAAI **137**(1–2), 1106–1111 (2008)
5. Serafini, L., Garcez, A.D.A.: Logic tensor networks: deep learning and logical reasoning from data and knowledge. In: CEUR Workshop Proceedings, p. 1768 (2016)
6. Kanerva, P.: Hyperdimensional computing: An introduction to computing in distributed representation with high-dimensional random vectors. Cogn. Comput. **1**(2), 139–159 (2009). https://doi.org/10.1007/s12559-009-9009-8
7. Bandaragoda, T., De Silva, D., Kleyko, D., Osipov, E., Wiklund, U., Alahakoon, D.: Trajectory clustering of road traffic in urban environments using incremental machine learning in combination with hyperdimensional computing. In: IEEE Intelligent Transportation Systems Conference (ITSC), pp. 1664–1670 (2019)
8. Kovalev, A.K., Panov, A.I.: Mental actions and modelling of reasoning in semiotic approach to AGI. In: Hammer, P., Agrawal, P., Goertzel, B., Iklé, M. (eds) Artificial General Intelligence. AGI 2019. Lecture Notes in Computer Science, vol 11654. Springer, Cham (2019) https://doi.org/10.1007/978-3-030-27005-6_12

9. Osipov, G.S., Panov, A.I.: Relationships and operations in a sign-based world model of the actor. Sci. Techn. Inf. Process. **45**(5), 317–330 (2018)
10. Kiselev, G.A., Panov, A.I.: Sign-based approach to the task of role distribution in the coalition of cognitive agents. In: SPIIRAS Proceedings, pp. 161–187 (2018). https://doi.org/10.15622/sp.57.7
11. Kiselev, G., Kovalev, A., Panov, A.I.: Spatial reasoning and planning in sign-based world model. In: Kuznetsov, S., Osipov, G.S., Stefanuk, V. (eds.) Artificial Intelligence. RCAI 2018. Communications in Computer and Information Science, pp. 1–10. Springer (2018). https://doi.org/10.1007/978-3-030-00617-4_1
12. Panov, A.I.: Goal Setting and Behavior Planning for Cognitive agents. Sci. Tech. Inf. Process. **46**(6), 404–415 (2019)
13. Koren, Y.: The BellKor Solution to the Netflix Grand Prize (2009)
14. Douglas, L.T.R., Laura, M.G., David, C.P.: An improved model of semantic similarity based on lexical co-occurrence. In: Communications of the ACM (2006)
15. Mikolov, T., Chen, K., Corrado, G., Dean, J.: Efficient estimation of word representations in vector space. In: 1st International Conference on Learning Representations, ICLR 2013 - Workshop Track Proceedings, pp. 1–12 (2013)
16. Mikolov, T., Sutskever, I., Chen, K., Corrado, G., Dean, J.: Distributed representations of words and phrases and their compositionality. In: Proceedings of the 26th International Conference on Neural Information Processing Systems, vol. 2, pp 3111–3119 (2013)
17. Pennington, J., Socher, R., Manning, C.D.: GloVe: Global Vectors for Word Representation, **31**(6), 682–687 (2017). https://doi.org/10.1080/02688697.2017.1354122
18. Mikolov, T., Yih, W., Zweig, G.: Linguistic regularities in continuous space word representations. Proc. OfNAACL-HLT **2013**, 746–751 (2013)
19. Radford, A., Metz, L., Chintala, S.: Unsupervised representation learning with deep convolutional generative adversarial networks. In: 4th International Conference on Learning Representations, ICLR 2016 - Conference Track Proceedings, pp. 1–16 (2016)
20. Hou, X., Shen, L., Sun, K., Qiu, G.: Deep feature consistent variational autoencoder. In: Proceedings - 2017 IEEE Winter Conference on Applications of Computer Vision, WACV 2017, pp. 1133–1141 (2017). https://doi.org/10.1109/WACV.2017.131
21. Plate, T.A.: Holographic Reduced Representations: Distributed Representation for Cognitive Structures. Center for the Study of Language and Information (CSLI). Stanford, Redwood City (2003)
22. Plate, T.A.: Distributed representations and nested compositional structure, University of Toronto, Ph.D. Thesis (1994)
23. Gallant, S.I., Okaywe, T.W.: Representing objects, relations, and sequences. Neural Comput. **25**(8), 2038–2078 (2013)
24. Kleyko, D., Osipov, E., Senior, A., Khan, A.I., Sekercioglu, Y.A.: Holographic graph neuron: a bio-inspired architecture for pattern processing. IEEE Trans. Neural Netw. Learn. Syst. **28**(6), 1250–1262 (2017)
25. Frady, E.P., Kleyko, D., Sommer, F.T.: A theory of sequence indexing and working memory in recurrent neural networks. Neural Comput. **30**, 1449–1513 (2018)
26. Smirnov, I., Panov, A.I., Skrynnik, A., Isakov, V., Chistova, E.: Personal cognitive assistant: concept and key principals. Inform. In: IEEE Primen, vol. 13, pp. 105–113 (2019). https://doi.org/10.14357/19922264190315

The Conditions of Artificial General Intelligence: Logic, Autonomy, Resilience, Integrity, Morality, Emotion, Embodiment, and Embeddedness

Yoshihiro Maruyama[✉]

Research School of Computer Science,
The Australian National University,
Canberra, Australia
yoshihiro.maruyama@anu.edu.au

Abstract. There are different difficulties in defining a fundamental concept; it often happens that some conditions are too strong or just surplus, and others are too weak or just lacking. There is no clearly agreed conception of intelligence, let alone artificial intelligence and artificial general intelligence. Still it can be significant and useful to (attempt to) elucidate the defining or possible characteristics of a fundamental concept. In the present paper we discuss the conditions of artificial general intelligence, some of which may be too strong and others of which may be too weak. Among other things, we focus upon logic, autonomy, resilience, integrity, morality, emotion, embodiment, and embeddedness, and articulate the nature of them from different conceptual points of view. And we finally discuss how to test artificial general intelligence, proposing a new kind of Turing-type tests based upon the intelligence-for-survival view. Overall, we believe that explicating the nature of artificial general intelligence arguably contributes to a deeper understanding of intelligence per se.

Keywords: AGI · Autonomy · Resilience · Integrity · Morality · Embodied-embedded

1 Introduction

Artificial general intelligence is the general purpose AI that can in principle be applied to whatever sorts of intelligent tasks, rather than narrow task-oriented AI [12]; most AI systems available at the present time are still narrowly task-oriented (even though narrow AI already outperforms human intelligence in certain domains; yet it could be argued that this has actually been true since the birth of a calculator). In this paper we address the conditions of artificial general intelligence and their consequences from different conceptual points of view, which, however, we do not intend to be complete (i.e., some conditions can be too strong and others too weak; they just give a first approximation).

© Springer Nature Switzerland AG 2020
B. Goertzel et al. (Eds.): AGI 2020, LNAI 12177, pp. 242–251, 2020.
https://doi.org/10.1007/978-3-030-52152-3_25

In particular we first discuss the (deductive and inductive) logic of artificial general intelligence, in particular whether Statistical AI based upon statistical machine learning suffices for artificial general intelligence or we need something else such as Symbolic AI (aka. GOFAI, i.e., Good Old-Fashioned AI) in the so-called Golden Age (Sect. 2). And then we discuss other fundamental features of artificial general intelligence, such as autonomy, resilience, and integrity (Sect. 3), morality and emotion (Sect. 4), and embodiment, and embeddedness (Sect. 5). In these discussions we emphasize the idea that intelligence is what makes us survive in competitive environments, which we call the intelligence-for-survival view. In the last part of the paper we propose Turing-type tests for artificial general intelligence from this intelligence-for-survival point of view (Sect. 6).

2 Deductive Reasoning and Inductive Learning in the Logic of Artificial General Intelligence

Any entity without logic would not count as artificial general intelligence, even though there could be some form of machine intelligence without logic (such as a purely intuitively or emotionally thinking machine). The exact contents of logic, however, are debatable. In general, science builds upon logic and experience (or reality). There are two major components of logic in scientific knowledge production: deductive reasoning based upon (universal) principles and (ad hoc) assumptions, and inductive learning (or statistical inference) based upon empirical data. Our ordinary thinking in everyday life builds upon these two components as well as our scientific thinking in knowledge production. Artificial general intelligence, therefore, must be equipped with the two components, that is, the deductive component as enabled by Symbolic AI, and the statistical component as enabled by Statistical AI.

Yet the actual story is not that simple. There are strong disagreements about the roles of Symbolic AI and Statistical AI. There is, for instance, an interesting debate between Peter Norvig, Google's research director, and Noam Chomsky, the father of modern linguistics; it is concerned with the nature of language (see, e.g., [3,13,19,23]). In light of recent advances in machine learning and data science, quite some part of our language use can be simulated via the methods of statistical machine learning. For example, Statistical AI can solve certain TOEFL problems better than average humans taking TOEFL exams (see, e.g., [26]). The debate is also related to the issue of Explainable AI or the lack of explainability in Statistical AI, especially deep learning AI. Norvig succinctly reconstructs Chosmky's argument against Statistical AI [23]:

1. "Statistical language models have had engineering success, but that is irrelevant to science."
2. "Accurately modeling linguistic facts is just butterfly collecting; what matters in science (and specifically linguistics) is the underlying principles."
3. "Statistical models are incomprehensible; they provide no insight."

Yet at the same time, Norvig gives counterarguments against Chomsky, and he finally concludes as follows [23]:

[L]anguages are complex, random, contingent biological processes that are subject to the whims of evolution and cultural change. What constitutes a language is not an eternal ideal form, represented by the settings of a small number of parameters, but rather is the contingent outcome of complex processes. Since they are contingent, it seems they can only be analyzed with probabilistic models.

Norvig puts a strong emphasis on the complexity and contingency of language and its evolutionary transformation. The "eternal ideal form" of language in Novig's terms is exactly what Chomsky aims at in formal linguistics. According to Norvig, however, the complexity and contingency of language and its evolution does not allow for such an eternal ideal form, and Statistical AI is indispensable for natural language processing. Besides, Norvig convincingly illustrated how to solve the problem Chomsky thought impossible to solve via the statistical methods [23].

Is Symbolic AI, then, obsolete in light of the great success of Statistical AI? Here we give three arguments to support Symbolic AI or rather the combination and integration of Symbolic AI and Statistical AI. Let us call them the practical, philosophical, and scientific arguments. The practical argument is just that there is some rationale for believing that it is practically promising to combine the Symbolic and Statistical AI in light of emerging successful cases in the integration of them with its empirical (predictive or classification) power outperforming the state-of-the-art methods (see, e.g., [5,8,14]). In general, Statistical AI is good at prediction and classification (via pattern recognition), and Symbolic AI at reasoning and verification. Combining their strengths should, in principle, be beneficial, and as mentioned above, it has succeeded already to a certain extent. It may also pave the way for improving explainability in Statistical AI with the help of Symbolic AI. Statistical AI would be necessary in view of real-world uncertainties and contingencies (and of bounded rationality and incompleteness of information within real life constraints). Yet Symbolic AI, too, would be necessary for infallible reasoning and verification (and for accountability of infallible knowledge or truth). This is the practical argument; the other two arguments are as follows.

From a philosophical point of view, Kant distinguished between three major faculties of cognition: namely, the faculty of sensibility and the faculties of understanding and reason [18]. Humans first perceive or sense objects (or the world as a whole) through the faculty of sensibility, thereby forming representations of them, and then eventually lead to more complex conceptualizations and reasoning based upon them. Kant's philosophy of mind is illustrated in [21] in the following manner:

Kant distinguishes the three fundamental mental faculties from one another in two ways. First, he construes sensibility as the specific manner in which human beings, as well as other animals, are receptive. This is in contrast with the faculties of understanding and reason, which are forms of human, or all rational beings, spontaneity.

AI is (supposed to be) a rational being. It must be equipped with the faculties of understanding and reason as well as the faculty of sensibility, which is required, in the first place, to perceive objects in the outside world. Statistical AI is highly successful in object recognition or pattern recognition (such as cat or dog recognition, which is usually done by human intuition), and thus arguably allows for the faculty of sensibility in machine cognition. Symbolic AI, on the other hand, is suited to conceptual reasoning about the world and objects therein, thus allowing for the faculties of understanding and reason. In this Kantian conception of cognition or intelligence, both the faculty of sensibility and the faculties of understanding and reason are mental capacities indispensable for rational beings, and thus both Symbolic AI and Statistical AI are arguably necessary for the ultimate goal of artificial general intelligence. This is the (Kantian) philosophical argument.

The scientific argument to support the need for both Symbolic and Statistical AI is as follows. Statistical AI is an induction-based, bottom-up approach whereas Symbolic AI is a deduction-based, top-down approach. In the making of a scientific theory, there are varying emphases on them. Some theories, such as general relativity theory, were born in a top-down manner, that is, on the guidance of general principles, such as the principle of general covariance in general relativity [7]. Others were born in a bottom-up manner, that is, in direct consideration of empirical data; quantum theory, another pillar of twentieth century physics, generally counts as an instance of such bottom-up theorization [7]. These are both indispensable aspects of scientific theory building, and in order to cover both aspects, artificial general intelligence would arguably need both Symbolic and Statistical AI. Note that Einstein also proposed a similar dichotomy between bottom-up and top-down approaches, which he called constructive and principle theories [11].

3 Autonomy, Resilience, and Integrity in the Cognition of Artificial General Intelligence

Machines equipped with both deductive reasoning and inductive learning can be very good instances of artificial intelligence, and yet they do not necessarily constitute artificial general intelligence. What else is required for artificial general intelligence? In the following we argue that artificial general intelligence must be autonomous, resilient, and integrated. Concerning the autonomy condition, there is a well-known quote from IBM's Intelligent Agent Strategy white paper [16,22]:

> Intelligent agents are software entities that carry out some set of operations [...] with some degree of independence or autonomy, and in so doing, employ some knowledge or representation of [...] goals or desires.

Spontaneity is essential in autonomy, especially in order to set goals or to have desires as mentioned above. Recall the above quotation on Kant saying that the faculties of understanding and reason are forms of spontaneity; this idea is elaborated in the following passage [21]:

Sensibility is the faculty that provides sensory representations. Sensibility generates representations based on being affected either by entities distinct from the subject or by the subject herself. This is in contrast to the faculty of understanding, which generates conceptual representations spontaneously – i.e. without advertence to affection. Reason is that spontaneous faculty by which special sorts of concepts, which Kant calls 'ideas' or 'notions', may be generated, and whose objects could never be met within "experience," which Kant defines as perceptions connected by fundamental concepts.

Artificial general intelligence must have some sort of spontaneity. Without spontaneity, agents are merely passive, and only process some given information. As a consequence of this, they cannot be creative; creativity is an integral feature of intelligence. To allow for creativity, artificial general intelligence must be autonomous; it must spontaneously make a judgement, and choose one option rather than others on the basis of some internal goals or desires. It often happens in everyday life that there is little information available for an agent's decision, and still the agent must make a judgement, and choose something. Even in such a situation under uncertainty, artificial general intelligence must make a judgement according to some internal (rather than external) motivation. This is the autonomy condition of artificial general intelligence; autonomy is an essential basis of creative intelligence.

Autonomy and spontaneity are related to self-awareness: autonomy implies being aware of its own being, setting a goal on its own (whether explicitly or implicitly), and improving itself towards that goal. Note however that autonomy or spontaneity does not necessarily imply free will or consciousness as in the Chalmers' Hard Problem [2] (we think that artificial general intelligence can, in principle, be philosophical zombies, that is, perfectly intelligent agents yet without consciousness or free will). Autonomy is also related to accountability: autonomy implies being able to make an action according to and explain its own internal reason or motivation for the action taken.

Let us move on to the resilience condition. The US Department of Homeland Security defines resilience as follows [27]:

> [A]bility [...] to resist, tolerate, absorb, recover from, prepare for, or adapt to an adverse occurrence that causes harm, destruction, or loss [...]

Resilience is important for both hardware and software of cognition. If systems cannot recover from some physical injuries, they cannot survive. Likewise, if systems cannot recover from some intellectual fallacies or mistakes (or bugs), they cannot survive. Humans are resilient agents because both bodies and minds are resilient (not completely but to some substantial extent; cf. homeostasis). Resilience is essential for survival. Artificial general intelligence agents must be resilient for the fundamental purpose of survival; put another way, if they cannot survive, they are not sufficiently intelligent.

Autonomy, too, does matter for survival. If agents are not autonomous, they would easily be killed by others. Intelligence is arguably a vital fruit of evolution for survival. We could even argue that, the more intelligent agents are, the more probable their survival is. We shall come back to this issue again below.

The recovery capability in resilience is related to self-organization; thanks to the self-organizing capacity, agents such as humans can recover from physical or mental injuries. Without the self-organizing capacity, agents could not recover from them by themselves. The self-organization condition, therefore, is part of the resilience condition. Self-organization allows agents to grow by themselves, change their own ideas, and reproduce themselves. It is essential for them to adapt themselves to different environments. The reproduction capacity may be regarded as an indirect sort of intellectual capacity because knowledge as created by intelligence must be accumulated, in the long run, to form a larger civilization with better science and technology; science is a collective endeavor across both time and space, each agent being just a tiny, single player in scientific knowledge production as a global whole (e.g., a single life can be too short to solve extremely difficult problems). It is thus necessary for agents to be able to reproduce in order to be (collectively) intelligent and to form a civilization with science and technology, which are what artificial general intelligence should be able to create, and which is essential for survival as a species.

Finally, artificial general intelligence is integrated intelligence; unlike most AI systems available at the moment, it must not be made for an analysis of a specific problem or task, and must be able to flexibly adapt itself to a variety of problems, including entirely new, unprecedented ones. If it is tailor-made for a specific problem, it is essentially no different from a calculator, which can compute even faster than human intelligence. It is a distinctive characteristic of the human mind that different intellectual capacities are integrated into a single brain. It can even change its own idea (or program) to improve itself; an ordinary program cannot change (and so cannot essentially improve) itself. The integrated nature of the human mind must be realized in artificial general intelligence. Metaphorically saying, current AI can play a variety of board games very well, yet it still cannot play chess boxing (combination of chess and boxing), which is an integrated task. Life and survival therein, as a whole, are an integrated task as well. Present AI also cannot pose new problems on its own; it can only solve a given problem within a given set of rules. In addition, human intelligence is not just about finding and solving different problems, while doing so, it unconsciously processes a lot of information in its environment in an integrated manner. And this would be the reason why the human mind escapes the frame problem; human intelligence, probably as a result of evolution, can unconsciously set a suitable frame. Both conscious and unconscious information processing are integrated into human intelligence. Artificial general intelligence must be able to give a machine realization of such integrated intelligence.

4   Morality and Emotion in the Ethics of Artificial General Intelligence

Human intellectual judgements are based upon ethical concerns as well as logical and other concerns. Human decision making is often made under morality constraints; otherwise the society would get highly disordered. Morality is yet another element of intelligence which allows us to survive while maintaining the order of the society as a coherent whole. The same applies to artificial intelligence, and artificial general intelligence must thus be able to simulate ethical judgements. The morality of artificial intelligence may be tested via the moral Turing test that allows for inferring morality from morally good behavior. This is also practically important because a purely data-driven approach can lead to a morally problematic result; in a recent *Science* article, for example, it has been shown that "semantics derived automatically from language corpora contain human-like biases [1]." Artificial intelligence without morality constraints may further strengthen biases prevailing in the present society; this must be avoided, and (the simulation of) morality is necessary for that purpose.

Ethical concerns, in turn, are (occasionally) based upon emotion, whether it is empathy, sympathy, or something else. Morality is seemingly intertwined with emotion. Yet at the same time, there are different views concerning the relationships between morality and emotion. Two major figures in traditional moral philosophy are Kant, representing moral rationalism, and Hume, representing moral sentimentalism. Kant is a moral realist, arguing that morality is based upon reason or rationality, and it has universal validity as its principal characteristic [17]. Hume is a moral antirealist, arguing that morality is based upon sentiment, in particular sympathy or empathy, and it is not necessarily universal. The following is a standard interpretation of the relationships between Kant and Hume on moral philosophy [6]:

> The ethics of Immanuel Kant (1724–1804) is often contrasted with that of David Hume (1711–1776). Hume's method of moral philosophy is experimental and empirical; Kant emphasizes the necessity of grounding morality in a priori principles.

Compared with the aforementioned Chomsky versus Norvig debate, Kant is like Chomsky, and Hume is like Norvig; put another way, Chomsky is like a continental rationalist, whereas Norvig is like a British empiricist. Hume says as follows [15]:

> There has been a controversy started of late, much better worth examination, concerning the general foundation of Morals; whether they be derived from Reason, or from Sentiment; whether we attain the knowledge of them by a chain of argument and induction, or by an immediate feeling and finer internal sense; whether, like all sound judgement of truth and falsehood, they should be the same to every rational intelligent being; or whether, like the perception of beauty and deformity, they be founded entirely on the particular fabric and constitution of the human species.

Hume's philosophy may be placed within the broader movement of the Scottish Enlightenment, other major moral philosophers of which include Francis Hutcheson and Adam Smith. Smith is particularly known for his treatise *The Theory of Moral Sentiments* [25]. The central tenet of the Scottish Enlightenment is that morality is based upon sentiments, such as sympathy and empathy; Hume indeed says that "morality is determined by sentiment" [15]. At the same time, Hume argues as follows [15]:

> Truth is disputable; not taste: what exists in the nature of things is the standard of our judgement; what each man feels within himself is the standard of sentiment.

According to moral sentimentalism, "our emotions and desires play a leading role in the anatomy of morality" and "the key mechanism of sympathy is imaginatively placing oneself in another's position" [20]. Emotion per se may not exist in artificial intelligence, and yet, if morality presupposes emotion, artificial general intelligence must be able to simulate emotional judgements (in order to pass the moral Turing test). Note that there is some revival of moral sentimentalism in contemporary psychology: "Recent psychological theories emphasizing the centrality of emotion in moral thinking have prompted renewed interest in sentimentalist ethics" [20].

There is a subtlety involved here. Does morality or emotion as its Humean ground require free will or consciousness? This is a relevant question from a philosophical point of view. In this paper we take the position that free will or consciousness (or intentionality in Searle's sense) in any absolute realist sense is not required in artificial general intelligence; it just suffices to have the possibility of simulating them in it. That is to say, we do not require anything more than the behavior that looks like being conscious or having free will. (Requiring them in a strict realist sense would lead us to difficulties concerning the Hard Problem; we do not really know what it consists in to be conscious or to have free will).

5   Embodiment and Embeddedness in the Existence of Artificial General Intelligence

Here we briefly discuss the issue of embedded-embodied AI within the context of artificial general intelligence. It is the idea that artificial general intelligence does not exist in vacuum; it must be embodied in physical substrates such as human-like bodies, and as embedded (or situated) in environments (another name for embedded AI is situated AI or Heideggerian AI [9]). Embodiment is the idea that the existence of bodies is essential for intelligence. Likewise, embeddedness is the idea that interactions with environments are essential for intelligence. From such a point of view, interplay between mind, body, and environment is considered necessary to realize human-level intelligence. There are different arguments for these ideas; yet we do not detail them here (for more detail, see, e.g., [4,9]). Instead we discuss these issues from a different angle.

Why are humans intelligent at all? From an evolutionary point of view, that is because intelligence helps our survival (a lot indeed). Compared with other animals, it is our primary advantage for survival to have higher intelligence. In light of the intelligence-for-survival thesis, it is essential to have bodies, without which survival does not make much sense in the first place. Likewise, survival necessarily concerns interactions with environments. Intelligence for survival is inseparable from bodies and environments, both of which have to be exploited as "extended minds" (à la Clark-Chalmers) for the primary purpose of survival. It may be argued from this point of view that artificial general intelligence must be embodied and embedded because it must survive. Put another way, if such survival capabilities constitute integral part of artificial general intelligence, embodiment and embeddedness are preconditions for artificial general intelligence.

6   Concluding Remarks: How to Test Artificial General Intelligence?

We have discussed the characteristics of artificial general intelligence: logic (i.e., deductive reasoning and inductive learning); autonomy, resilience, and integrity; morality and emotion; and embodiment and embeddedness. We finally remark on the issue of testing artificial general intelligence. We have emphasized the idea that intelligence is for survival. Survival is not just a matter of individuals, but a matter of the (human or machine) race as a whole. Individual intelligence, by itself, does not really help the survival of the (human or machine) race as a whole. What does help it is the collective intelligence of individuals integrated together, namely the (human or machine) civilization. We can extract two kinds of Turing-type tests from this discussion. One is the survival Turing test for artificial general intelligence: to be intelligent is to be able to survive; levels of intelligence are measured by levels of survival. The other is the civilization Turing test: to be intelligent is to be able to form a civilization as a coherent whole (for the primary purpose of survival); levels of intelligence are measured by levels of civilization. The former applies to both individuals and groups, whereas the latter to groups only; group intelligence has not been discussed much in the literature. Yet group intelligence does matter, especially for survival.

Can artificial general intelligence be achieved in the near future as proponents of technological singularity believe? No one knows. We may refer to the history of artificial intelligence. Herbert Simon once claimed in 1965: "machines will be capable, within twenty years, of doing any work a man can do" [24]. Not just Simon but also many other prominent AI researchers such as Marvin Minsky expressed similar opinions. The optimism for artificial general intelligence, however, failed at the end of the day (the Japan's Fifth Generation Computer Project failed at the same time). The technological singularity (the technical optimism which turned into existential pessimism or nihilism) may not come just as well. Yet at the same time, we should remember that the AI pessimism failed too; Dreyfus, for example, argued that car-driving AI would be impossible [10].

Acknowledgements. The author would like to thank his colleagues for comments and suggestions for improvement on this work. The author hereby acknowledges that this work was financially supported by JST PRESTO (grant code: JPMJPR17G9) and JSPS KAKENHI (grant code: 17K14231).

References

1. Caliskan, A., et al.: Semantics derived automatically from language corpora contain human-like biases. Science **356**, 183–186 (2017)
2. Chalmers, D.: Facing up to the problem of consciousness. J. Consciousness Stud. **2**, 200–219 (1995)
3. Chomsky, N., Keynote, P.: The golden age - a look at the original roots of artificial intelligence, cognitive science, and neuroscience. In: MIT Symposium on Brains, Minds, and Machines. Accessed 2 Feb 2020
4. Chrisley, R.: Embodied artificial intelligence. Artif. Intell. **149**, 131–150 (2003)
5. Coecke, B., et al.: Mathematical foundations for a compositional distributional model of meaning. Linguistic Anal. **36**, 345–384 (2010)
6. Denis, L.: Kant and Hume on Morality, Stanford Encyclopedia of Phil (2008)
7. Dieks, D.: Understanding in physics: bottom-up versus top-down. In: Pitts, U. (ed.) Scientific Understanding: Philosophical Perspectives, pp. 230–248. Press (2009)
8. Domingos, P., et al.: Unifying logical and statistical AI. In: Proceedings of the 31st Annual ACM/IEEE Symposium on Logic in Computer Science, pp. 1–11 (2016)
9. Dreyfus, H.L.: Why Heideggerian AI failed and how fixing it would require making it more Heideggerian. AI J. **171**, 1137–1160 (2007)
10. Dreyfus, H.L., Dreyfus, S.E.: Mind Over Machine. Free Press, Mumbai (1988)
11. Flores, F.: "Top-Down" or "Bottom-Up": explaining laws in special relativity. Philosophy Sci. **37**, 61–68 (1998)
12. Goertzel, B., Pennachin, C.: Artificial General Intelligence, Springer, Heidelberg (2007). https://doi.org/10.1007/978-3-540-68677-4
13. Gold, K.: Norvig vs. Chomsky and the fight for the future of AI, TOR.COM, 21 June 2011. Accessed 26 June 2019
14. Grefenstette, E., Sadrzadeh, M.: Experimental support for a categorical compositional distributional model of meaning. In: Proceedings of Empirical Methods in Natural Language Processing 2011, pp. 1394–1404. ACL (2011)
15. Hume, D.: An Enquiry Concerning the Principles of Morals, A. Millar (1751)
16. IBM's Intelligent Agent Strategy white paper (the quotation in this paper is available in [22]). http://activist.gpl.ibm.com:81/WhitePaper/ptc2.htm
17. Kant, I.: Groundwork for the metaphysics of morals. In: Ellington, J.W. (eds.) Hackett Publishing Company, Indianapolis (1785)
18. Kant, I.: Critique of Pure Reason. In: Guyer, P., Wood, A. (eds.) Cambridge University Press, Cambridge (1998)
19. Katz, Y.: Noam Chomsky on Where Artificial Intelligence Went Wrong, The Atlantic, 1 November 2012 (2012). 2 Feb 2020
20. Kauppinen, A.: Moral Sentimentalism, Stanford Encyclopedia of Phil (2014)
21. McLear, C.: Kant: Philosophy of Mind, Internet Encyclopedia of Philosophy (2020). 2 Feb 2020
22. Müller, J.P., et al. (eds.) Intelligent Agents, Springer (1996)
23. Norvig, P.: On Chomsky and the Two Cultures of Statistical Learning, pp. 61–83. Springer, Wiesbaden (2017). https://doi.org/10.1007/978-3-658-12153-2_3
24. Simon, H.A.: The Shape of Automation for Men and Management. Harper & Row, New York (1965)
25. Smith, A.: Theory of Moral Sentiments, A. Millar, Scotland (1761)
26. Turney, P., Pantel, P.: From frequency to meaning: vector space models of semantics. J. Artif. Intell. Res. **37**, 141–188 (2010)
27. Walls, L., et al. (eds.): Risk Reliability and Safety. CRC Press, Boca Raton (2016)

Position Paper: The Use of Engineering Approach in Creation of Artificial General Intelligence

Vasiliy Mazin[✉]

Mind Simulation, Krasnodar, Russia
`vasily@mind-simulation.com`

Abstract. A possible practical engineering approach to creation of the general artificial intelligence is considered. The choice of approach is based on modular hierarchical representation of knowledge, where each module uses its own methods of representation and knowledge processing. Work with knowledge is done by a hierarchical multi-agent system. The description of system's individual elements and information about the current development state are given.

Keywords: Multi-agent system · Ontology · Intellectual core

Development of artificial general intelligence is becoming an increasingly urgent task, since many problems can not be completely solved by highly specialized solutions. Besides, the existing narrow solutions are very expensive in development and require an individual approach to their implementation.

Let's consider one of the approaches to creation of an intellectual kernel capable of solving various problems in arbitrary environments with limited resources.

The intellectual core is a complex software system that includes various methods of storing and processing knowledge. It is the hybrid model that consists of knowledge layers. Those layers have different levels of representation and abstraction. They can be assembled and configured in a way, that it would be possible to assemble intellectual systems for different purposes on the basis of the kernel: from intellectual assistants to Robotic Process Automation.

The developing kernel is a set of components called layers. Each layer combines knowledge and methods of the processing at a certain abstraction level. The layer can be created within the framework of some known model, or it can be a hybrid that uses several approaches to solving problems at once. There can be two types of layers: physical and logical. The physical layer is a separate technology, the logical layer is a separate body of knowledge.

Let's look at the individual elements of the intellectual core.

© Springer Nature Switzerland AG 2020
B. Goertzel et al. (Eds.): AGI 2020, LNAI 12177, pp. 252–256, 2020.
https://doi.org/10.1007/978-3-030-52152-3_26

1 Physical Layers

Abstract Ideal Layer
It contains abstract knowledge about the world, its structure and basic connections. It serves to form a general world-image or world model. It is necessary for the entire system functioning.

Knowledge is stored in a special version of the semantic network. There are no symbolic representations of natural language entities in this network. It stores connections of one entities to others instead. Metaknowledge allows you to determine the trueness of knowledge, its completeness, evidence, and so on.

The layer elements are entities and connections. An entity is a class of objects or a surrounding or fictional environment phenomena. An entity can be represented in any way: text, image, sound, video, data structure, etc. Connections allows us to unite entities with each other and form a general picture of the world [1]. There are 13 types of such connections.

Factographic Layer
It contains knowledge about the world in its variety, taking into account the place, time, mode of action and other parameters. It represents one layer of a multilevel memory model. A significantly reworked frame model is the main knowledge representation model.

There are predetermined types of slots that can be used to carry any knowledge expressed in a simple common sentence. Slot values are entities defined in the abstract ideal layer. Complex sentences are represented as trees, the vertices of which are fact frames. Their edge defines the type of connection of facts among themselves.

Logical Layer
It contains knowledge about reasoning. The reasoning itself is not something that is originally built into the system, but is one of the knowledge types. The logical layer uses production systems and boolean algebra functions [3]. The problem of choosing and applying products is solved with additional meta-knowledge of their activation. Elements of products and logical formulas are facts from the factographic layer.

Layer of Tasks
The task layer allows to implement a universal algorithmic system on artificial intelligence knowledge. At the layer of tasks base lies a modified Petri Net and connected to it local solutions space [2]. This local solutions space is a subset of the abstract ideal and factographic layers elements. It also serves as a storage for context of a problem, that is being solved. An arbitrary number of tasks can be handled at the same time, and the algorithms for solving each of them can be parallel.

2 Logical Layers

They are used to store knowledge of a specific field of application. The knowledge of these layers can be located in different physical layers of the kernel.

Personal Layer
It is used to store knowledge about the current implementation of the artificial intelligence kernel: its settings, the peculiarities of behavior and related to it events.

Interlocutor Layer
It contains knowledge about subjects with which it interacts. The model of the subject is built up on all physical layers as a set of knowledge about it.

Dialogue Layer
This layer contains knowledge about dialogue, its strategies and elements. It also stores the start and the end of a dialog, defines and changes the topic, chooses the directions of dialogue development, and processes various dialog situations.

3 Memory

Memory consists of seven layers, that differ in access speed, structure and storage methods. Such large number is necessary for running various intelligent kernel-based solutions on different devices. Even if the devices have strong limitations on the amount of data stored. The knowledge can be located on any of the seven layers and can be moved from layer to layer if needed. There is also a mechanism for forgetting knowledge that is no longer relevant.

Let's look at the memory layers:

The first four layers are based on the mechanisms that are already in the AI. This way AI has quick access to knowledge, and they are in the form that can be instantly used during the thought processes.

1. Operating (knowledge valid at particular time)
2. Operational (knowledge existing within the framework of one dialogue with the system, local decision spaces);
3. Permanent memory (basic ideas about the world and the most important facts);
4. Personal memory (knowledge that relates to the core itself, its functioning and development);
   The rest of the memory layers use different ways to store data. So it is not pure knowledge but data in a storage-friendly form, which is available to the system after a number of transformations. This is necessary for storing large (huge) amounts of data, but does not require additional resources from the thinking core itself.
5. Structured memory (contains a huge amount of structured data, relational databases are used);
6. Marked memory (unstructured data with the addition of metadata, non-relational databases are used);
7. Original (any data in its original form - files of various formats with metadata, protected by encryption and blockchain technology. The distributed storage system is used).

4   Agents

Interactions between layers and knowledge mechanisms work through a hierarchical, multi-agent system. Some agents work within a particular layer, while others carry out communication between individual kernel modules. Agents can call each other to solve problems and compete for system resources.

There are two ways of creating knowledge agents in the system. The first one is low-level—it is a code written in an interpreted programming language.

The second one is high-level. It operates in the tasks layer with the help of Petri Net.

5   Language Modules

Language modules convert incoming text into the internal representation of the kernel and synthesize that internal representation into text. Currently they are not a part of the kernel, but they use the existing kernel knowledge in their work. It allows us to simultaneously convey morphological, syntactic and semantic text analyses and to reduce the number of parse trees to a minimum, cutting off impossible options.

The above mentioned architecture allows to solve a number of problems, that stand on the way to artificial general intelligence.

AI transparency – all AI's chains of thought and lines reasoning can be tracked, documented and explained.

A one-time training – the structure of knowledge of AI allows to transfer it from one kernel to another without any leakages of data. Moreover, it is possible to input text form data in the system.

Fast AI learning – the system can be trained with any amount of raw data. All training requires one iteration. There are methods to control and edit new knowledge.

Structured learning – knowledge is arranged in a multi-level hierarchical structure. Learning mechanisms allow to check the consistency of new and old knowledge.

Solving the problem of catastrophic forgetting – any level of knowledge can be tought, without losing the previously added knowledge. In addition, there are mechanisms of forgetting that do not lead to the loss of integrity of knowledge.

The possibility of incremental learning – knowledge can be gradually accumulated in the system. It is possible to store contradictions, vague knowledge, knowledge of false information.

Nowadays, the middle level ontology with more than 20 thousand classes of entities and their relationships is implemented in the abstract and ideal layers. Mechanisms and interfaces for editing ontology, facts, logical conclusions and tasks have been created. Language modules for Russian and English languages have been written. It is possible to work with several intellectual cores and transfer any knowledge between them. Text-based learning mechanisms have been implemented. Several prototypes for using current versions of the intellectual kernel in applied tasks have been created.

Existing usage of the described approach has shown that it is quite suitable for solving a wide spectrum of intellectual problems, It can be used for a base model of the artificial general intelligence. The further work will be directed on improvement of knowledge structures in all layers of an intellectual kernel. The automation of processing agents creation will also be carried through.

References

1. Arp, R.A., Smith, B., Spear, A.A.: Building Ontologies with Basic Formal Ontology. MIT Press, Cambridge (2015)
2. Reisig, W.: Understanding Petri Nets: Modeling Techniques, Analysis Methods, Case Studies. Springer, Berlin (2013). https://doi.org/10.1007/978-3-642-33278-4
3. Russell, S.J., Norvig, P.: Artificial Intelligence: A Modern Approach, 2nd edn. Prentice Hall, Upper Saddle River (2010)

How Do You Test the Strength of AI?

Nikolay Mikhaylovskiy[1,2](✉) (iD)

[1] Higher IT School of Tomsk State University, Tomsk, Russia
nikolaj.mihajlovskij@hits.tsu.ru
[2] NTR Lab, Moscow, Russia
nickm@ntr.ai

Abstract. Creating Strong AI means to develop artificial intelligence to the point where the machine's intellectual capability is in a way equal to a human's. Science is definitely one of the summits of human intelligence, the other being the art. Scientific research consists in creating hypotheses that are limited applicability models (methods) implying lossy information compression. In this article, we show that this paradigm is not unique to the science and is common to the most developed areas of human activities, like business and engineering. Thus, we argue, a Strong AI should possess a capability to build such models. Still, the known tests to confirm the human-level AI do not address this consideration. Based on the above we suggest a series of six tests of rising complexity to check if AI have achieved the human-level intelligence (Explanation, Problem-setting, Refutation, New phenomenon prediction, Business creation, Theory creation), five of which are new to the AGI literature.

Keywords: AGI · Strong AI · Epistemology · Turing test

Creating Strong AI means to develop artificial intelligence to the point where the machine's intellectual capability is in a way equal to a human's or, as Ray Kurzweil [1] put it, machine intelligence with the full range of human intelligence.

A number of cognitive architectures have emerged over time as a result of research on Strong AI. While most of them will never evolve into Strong AI, it is important to have a common ground to judge where do they stand against that goal.

Additionally, I agree with Arthur Franz [2] that Strong AI will be subject to evolution, including both shallow (personal for a single individual) and deep (inherited through reproduction). Thus, even within a single research program or architecture it is important to understand progress towards Strong AI.

In this paper, we explore the question of how to determine if the Strong AI have been achieved. Specifically, scientific activity is the summit of human intelligence and scientific research consists in creating hypotheses that are limited applicability models (methods) of compressing information. In this article, we show that this paradigm is not unique to the science and is common to the most developed areas of human activities, like business and engineering. Thus, we argue, a Strong AI should possess a capability to build such models. Still, the known tests to confirm the human-level AI do not address this consideration. We aim to fill this gap.

B. Goertzel et al. (Eds.): AGI 2020, LNAI 12177, pp. 257–266, 2020.
https://doi.org/10.1007/978-3-030-52152-3_27

To that end, in Sect. 1 we explore existing tests for strong AI. In Sect. 2, we stripe the applicable notion of scientific knowledge from the modern epistemology and define the key features of the scientific knowledge. In Sect. 3, we show that many other human activities, most notably business, engineering and contemporary marketing rely on the similar knowledge structures. Finally, in Sect. 4 we device the tests for the Strong AI in the sense we have previously defined.

Throughout this paper, we use the terms "Strong AI" and "Artificial General Intelligence" (AGI), interchangingly, despite the ongoing terminological discussion within the AI community if these are the same or different notions.

1 Tests for AI

A number of tests have been devised to test if a system has an artificial intelligence. Some of them include:

- The Turing Test (suggested by Alan Turing)
- Lovelace Test (suggested by Bringsjord, Bello and Ferrucci)
- Psychometric Tests (suggested, for example, by Bringsjord and Schimansky)
- The Piaget-MacGuyver Room Test (suggested by Bringsjord and Licato)
- The Coffee Test (attributed to Wozniak by Goertzel)
- The Robot Student Test (suggested by Goertzel)
- The Employment Test (suggested by Nilsson)

Let us review each of them.

1.1 The Turing Test

The test is likely the most prominent AI test and was introduced by Turing [3] as a test of a machine's ability to exhibit intelligent behavior equivalent to, or indistinguishable from, that of a human. Rather than trying to determine if a machine is thinking, Turing proposed that a human evaluator would judge natural language conversations between a human and a machine designed to generate human-like responses. The evaluator would be aware that one of the two partners in conversation is a machine, and all participants would be separated from one another. The conversation would be limited to a text-only channel such as a computer keyboard and screen so the result would not depend on the machine's ability to render words as speech.

The Turing test follows Denis Diderot formulation [4]: "If they find a parrot who could answer to everything, I would claim it to be an intelligent being without hesitation."

Considerable effort have been put over the years into building this type of behavior on computers, including multiple Loebner prize competitions.

Still, to a wide agreement, the test does not check if the machine can really think (see, for example, the book [5] – notably, e.g. [6]: "The human creators of systems undergoing Turing test know all too well that they have merely tried to fool those people who interact with their systems into believing that these systems really have minds").

1.2 Lovelace Test

Bringsjord, Bello and Ferrucci in [6] have suggested a Lovelace test:
Artificial agent A, designed by H, passes LT if and only if

1. A outputs o;
2. A's outputting o is not the result of a fluke hardware error, but rather the result of processes A can repeat;
3. H (or someone who knows what H knows, and has H's resources—for example, the substitute for H might he a scientist who watched and assimilated what the designers and builders of A did every step along the way) cannot explain how A produced o.

Thus, we can call Lovelace test a requirement of grand intractability. Obviously, though anecdotal in many cases, grand intractability per se is not a sign of intelligence.

1.3 Psychometric Tests

Psychometric approach to AI have been suggested by Bringsjord and Schimanski in [7]: "Psychometric AI is the field devoted to building information-processing entities capable of at least solid performance on all established, validated tests of intelligence and mental ability, a class of tests that includes not just the rather restrictive IQ tests, but also tests of artistic and literary creativity, mechanical ability, and so on."

While having a quantitative test is important for tracking progress, there is a wide criticism of psychometric tests even for humans. Being able to pass all the established tests makes the approach more interesting, but still, amenable to fooling just like the Turing test.

1.4 The Piaget-MacGuyver Room Test

Bringsjord and Licato introduced the Piaget-MacGyver Room test in [8]. They define the Piaget-MacGyver Room test, "which is such that, an information-processing artifact can credibly be classified as general-intelligent if and only if it can succeed on any test constructed from the ingredients in this room. No advance notice is given to the engineers of the artifact in question, as to what the test is going to be; only the ingredients in the room are shared ahead of time. These ingredients are roughly equivalent to what would be fair game in the testing of neurobiologically normal Occidental students to see what stage within his theory of cognitive development they are at."

1.5 The Goertzel Tests

Goertzel et al. in [9] lists several potential tests for AGI that are circulating in the AGI community:

- The Wozniak "coffee test": go into an average American house and figure out how to make coffee, including identifying the coffee machine, figuring out what the buttons do, finding the coffee in the cabinet, etc.

- Story understanding – reading a story, or watching it on video, and then answering questions about what happened (including questions at various levels of abstraction)
- Graduating (virtual-world or robotic) preschool
- Passing the elementary school reading curriculum (which involves reading and answering questions about some picture books as well as purely textual ones)
- Learning to play an arbitrary video game based on experience only, or based on experience plus reading instructions (as it was put in [10]: The goal of this scenario would not be human level performance of any single video game, but the ability to learn and succeed at a wide range of video games, including new games unknown to the AGI developers before the competition.)

Some of these tests are already satisfied by deep-learning systems, for example, MuZero [11]. When evaluated on 57 different Atari games - the canonical video game environment for testing AI techniques - the algorithm scored 20 times better than humans in median and 50 times better on average. When evaluated on Go, chess and shogi, without any knowledge of the game rules, MuZero matched the superhuman performance of the AlphaZero algorithm that was supplied with the game rules. Thus, we can say that to a large extent mastering this specific test turns out to be a focus of specific narrow AI (reinforcement deep learning).

Similarly to the Turing test, "story understanding" and "elementary school reading curriculum" could be passed by software systems simply by manipulating symbols of which they had no understanding.

Wozniak coffee test, considered per se, requires a robot to be able to do several perception and navigation tasks that can be accomplished by a specific-purpose robot.

A test of graduating a pre-school is a more interesting one. Here a lot depends on a country and a specific preschool – requirements differ widely and the cognitive abilities to pass this test deserve a separate article, or even a book.

1.6 The Employment Test

Employment Test have been suggested by Nilsson [12]. He argues that "Machines exhibiting true human-level intelligence should be able to do many of the things humans are able to do. Among these activities are the tasks or "jobs" at which people are employed. I suggest we replace the Turing test by something I will call the "employment test." To pass the employment test, AI programs must be able to perform the jobs ordinarily performed by humans. Progress toward human-level AI could then be measured by the fraction of these jobs that can be acceptably performed by machines."

This is definitely a very comprehensive test, actually including the tests that we propose as the tests for the scientists jobs.

Luke Mullenhauser [13] argues that: "This is a bit "unfair" because I doubt that any single human could pass such vocational exams for any long list of economically important jobs. On the other hand, it's quite possible that many unusually skilled humans would be able to pass all or nearly all such vocational exams if they spent an entire lifetime training each skill, and an AGI—having near-perfect memory, faster thinking speed, no need for sleep, etc.—would presumably be able to train itself in all required skills much more quickly, if it possessed the kind of general intelligence we're trying to operationally define."

An interesting subcase of the test have been (somewhat implicitly) suggested by Janelle Shane [14] – AGI should be able to generate (and understand?) humor. From my perspective this test is also a subcase of AGI being able to create art, and also deserves separate consideration.

2 Knowledge and Cognition in Science

There are multiple concurring definitions of knowledge in both AI and philosophical literature. Our goal is to define the knowledge in a way that is compatible with both contemporary epistemology and (potential) computer implementations.

2.1 Scientific Knowledge and Its Advance

In this paper we take a critical rationalist view on the knowledge and cognition, starting from Karl Popper's view, that the advance of scientific knowledge is an evolutionary process characterized by his formula [15]:

$$PS_1 \rightarrow TT_1 \rightarrow EE_1 \rightarrow PS_2 \tag{1}$$

In response to a given problem situation (PS_1), a number of competing conjectures, or tentative models (TT_1), are systematically subjected to attempts to define their applicability domain. This process, error elimination (EE_1), performs a similar function for science that natural selection performs for biological evolution where a species tests ecological niches. Models that better survive the process of refutation are not more true, but rather, more "fit"—in other words, more applicable to the problem situation at hand (PS_1). The evolution of models through the scientific method may, reflect a certain type of progress: toward more and more interesting problems (PS_2).

2.2 Models

The model consists in explaining the phenomenon, that is, assuming a mechanism for how it can occur. When building a model, we take a certain point of view on the phenomenon, discarding irrelevant details. Each model in scientific type knowledge has a limited domain of applicability.

In the end, in order to determine which model is better, it would be right to conduct an Experimentum crucis - that is, an experiment that would make it possible to unambiguously determine which theory is correct. In order to conduct such an experiment completely scientifically, it would be best for us to find such facts that the models would predict in different ways, and check which option is actually implemented.

2.3 Theories

As we have already said, building a model requires a certain point of view on the subject. We will call such points of view theories or paradigms. Each such theory determines what is important in the subject for consideration. A look at a person from the point of view of mechanics, electromagnetism, chemistry, and population genetics will be significantly different. In addition, each specific problem, being solved within the framework of the theory, determines what other properties of the subject we should discard when considering it within the framework of this problem.

You can demand more, for example, define a theory as S.V. Illarionov does [16]: "Theory is a holistic conceptual symbolic system, that is, it is based on some conceptual representations and is expressed in a symbolic form, in the form of symbols. Relationships are set in this system so that this symbolic system can be a reflection of a certain circle of natural phenomena or, as they sometimes say, some fragment or aspect of the material world."

I completely agree with Illarionov's definition for the case of scientific theories (he would consider this expression to be a pleonasm), but we will consider cognition in a framework broader than science. In applications, for example, in business, conceptual representations in the form of symbols are unnecessary.

To visually imagine theories, let's turn inside out, perhaps, the most famous metaphor in philosophy - the Platonic Cave.

So, let's imagine that a certain object (phenomenon) is in a dark cave, and the walls of this cave are our consciousness. If we illuminate the object with the light of theory on one side, we will see one shadow on the wall. This shadow is a model of the phenomenon built using this theory. If we light from another, the picture on the wall will turn out to be completely different. Moreover, in both cases, the interior of the subject will be hidden from us, and most of the information about the object will be lost.

Within the framework of one theory it is possible to build models of a multitude of phenomena. The laws of Newtonian mechanics are applicable to the motion of the planets, and to the collision of balls on the pool table. In terms of the cave metaphor, this means that you can mark many objects in one beam of light and get their models - shadows on the wall.

The most important property of scientific theories is their ability to predict phenomena that were not known at the time of their formulation. Let me cite Illarionov [16] again: "Everyday knowledge is based on previous observations of repeatedly occurring phenomena and allows you to make predictions that are very important and useful for successful practical activity, although they have the nature of probabilistic expectations. But science can do something completely different: it can predict phenomena that we have never observed. These are specifically theoretical predictions."

"When, in 1819, Fresnel (1788–1827) made a report on his wave theory of light at the French Academy, Poisson (1781–1840) stood up and stated that, according to this theory, in the middle of the shadow of a round screen or a ball there should be a bright spot. The next day, Augustin Fresnel and Domenic Francois Jean Arago (1786–1853) reported: there really is a bright spot. Now it is called the Poisson spot in honor of the one who instantly, in the mind, solved this problem. This did not follow from previous observations and is an example of a nontrivial theoretical prediction."

Nevertheless, every theory has its own limited domain of applicability. In our metaphor, this means that the light beam of the theory is limited (imagine a movie projector). Only a limited number of phenomena can be placed in our limited beam of light. Moreover, some phenomena are generally flat and turned to this beam by an edge; therefore, from the angle of this theory, the phenomenon is generally invisible or does not exist. It can be seen and understood only in the light of another, completely orthogonal theory.

3 Knowledge and Cognition in Other Areas of Human Activity

3.1 Knowledge and Cognition in Business

Startup is most correctly defined as a temporary enterprise created to seek, develop, and validate a scalable business model (a similar definition was probably first coined by Steve Blank [17]). Here, a business model means a way of creating, using an economically sound process, for a certain type of consumers, value for which they are willing to pay money.

This search process can be divided into two separate phases:

- Customer discovery: find customer segments with a problem you can solve. Make sure that customers are willing to pay.
- Testing channels: find channels with enough customers, profitable economy and potential for scalability.

A popular and mature methodology for building startups is Lean Startup [18]. With this methodology, during the customer discovery stage a startup defines the target customer segments, their problems, and what is valuable for them. Different value propositions mean different segments. The initial set of segments is considered a hypothesis. It will change. Then startup defines a value proposition for each segment and conducts problem interviews to confirm, refine or reject a hypothesis. During the interviews, they may find new segments or refine existing ones.

As soon as the problem is confirmed, the startup starts modeling economics for the segment. On what conditions do economics become profitable? Are these conditions realistic? How much money is there in this segment, is it worth the effort? If the economics is potentially profitable – the startup starts building a Minimum Viable Product. The goal is to make first manual sales of the product.

When customers are paying and the startup knows why they do so, the startup can begin testing channels. If something goes wrong, the process is repeated.

A sales channel is a combination of 3 items:

- Marketing channel – traffic source
- Sales instrument – landing page, presentation, sales script, sales letter etc.
- Product and its price

At this stage, the goal of the startup is to find scalable channels, and a goal within the channel is its profitable economics. If profitability for a user in a channel is achieved, the next goal is profitability at scale:

- Can you increase sales flow by x10 and keep it profitable?
- Is there enough channel capacity to scale?
- Will the traffic cost grow when scaling?

Thus, Lean Startup is a paradigm where a user problem is solved, this solution becomes a model of the user from the viewpoint of a Lean Startup and then the applicability domain of this solution is found by testing hypotheses

- About the value proposition for the channel
- About significant sales flow
- On the convergence of the economy in the channel
- On the convergence of economies at a scale

This means that a Lean Startup generates scientific-type knowledge.

3.2 Knowledge and Cognition in Engineering

It is useful to note that in our ordinary life the ability to solve problems comes solely as a result of training.

If similar problems have to be solved by a large number of people, it becomes possible to analyze and generalize the process of solving them: narrow down the scope of the process, standardize its inputs and outputs, as well as the operations performed. This is how technologies are created. Thus, a technology is a model of the process of creating a class of results, and we can deduce that the technology is another type of knowledge of scientific type. Most everything we have discussed about the scientific knowledge applies here.

4   Testing for Strong AI

Following the above we can device several tests for human-like cognitive ability of the AI, in the order of their rising complexity:

- Explanation
- Problem-setting
- Refutation
- New phenomenon prediction
- Business creation
- Theory creation

4.1   Explanation Test

Given a well-defined scientific theory and an empirical phenomenon, provide an explanation of the phenomenon and compute its quantitative characteristics. An example of test of this type is "Find the minimum speed that basilisk lizard can run over the water". More problems of this sort from the physics can be found, for example, in the book of Nobel prize winner Pyotr Kapitsa [19].

4.2 Problem-Setting Test

Given a well-defined scientific theory and the general knowledge of the world create a task of the type mentioned in the previous subsection.

4.3 Refutation Test

Given competing models/explanations for a set of empirical phenomena, device an Experimentum crucis to figure out which is better.

4.4 New Phenomenon Prediction

Given a well-defined scientific theory predict a phenomenon that is not previously known.

4.5 Business Creation

Create a successful startup.

4.6 Theory Creation

Create a theory that is a meaningful improvement over existing nocs in one of the scientific fields.

5 Conclusions

It is obvious from the above tests that the current state of AGI is pretty far from being really equal to human, probably as much as it was from being able to satisfy Turing test in 1950, so the paranoia of machines talking over humans in midterm, at least intellectually, seems to be pretty ungrounded. On the other hand, human history have shown that a culture should not necessary be higher or more intellectual to take over a neighboring country/region.

References

1. Kurzweil, R.: Long Live AI, Forbes, 15 August 2005. https://www.forbes.com/home/free_f orbes/2005/0815/030.html. Accessed 25 Feb 2020
2. Franz, A.: Will super-human artificial intelligence (AI) be subject to evolution? H+ Magazine, 6 September 2013. https://hplusmagazine.com/2013/09/06/will-super-human-artificial-intell igence-ai-be-subject-to-evolution/. Accessed 05 Apr 2020
3. Turing, A.M.: Computing machinery and intelligence. Mind 59(236), 433–460 (1950). https://doi.org/10.1093/mind/lix.236.433
4. Diderot, D.: Pensees Philosophiques, Addition aux Pensees Philosophiques, p. 68. Flammarion, Paris (2007). ISBN 978-2-0807-1249-3
5. Moor, J.H. (ed.): The Turing Test. The Elusive Standard of Artificial Intelligence. COGS, vol. 30. Kluwer Academic Publishers, Boston (2003)

6. Bringsjord, S., Bello, P., Ferrucci, D.: Creativity, the turing test, and the (better) lovelace test. In: Moor, J.H. (ed.) The Turing Test. The Elusive Standard of Artificial Intelligence. COGS, vol. 30. Kluwer Academic Publishers, Boston (2003)

7. Bringsjord, S., Schimanski, B.: What is artificial intelligence? Psychometric AI as an answer. In: Proceedings of the 18th International Joint Conference on Artificial Intelligence (IJCAI 2003), pp. 887–893. Morgan Kaufmann, San Francisco (2003)

8. Bringsjord, S., Licato, J.: Psychometric artificial general intelligence: the Piaget-MacGuyver room. In: Wang, P., Goertzel, B. (eds.) Theoretical Foundations of Artificial General Intelligence. Atlantis Thinking Machines, vol. 4. Atlantis Press, Paris (2012)

9. Goertzel, B., Iklé, M., Wigmore, J.: The architecture of human-like general intelligence. In: Wang, P., Goertzel, B. (eds.) Theoretical Foundations of Artificial General Intelligence. Atlantis Thinking Machines, vol. 4. Atlantis Press, Paris (2012)

10. Adams, S., et al.: Mapping the landscape of human-level artificial general intelligence. AI Mag. 33(1), 25–42 (2012). https://doi.org/10.1609/aimag.v33i1.2322

11. Schrittwieser, J., et al.: Mastering Atari, Go, chess and shogi by planning with a learned model. arXiv:1911.08265 (2019)

12. Nilsson, N.J.: Human-level artificial intelligence? Be serious! AI Mag. 26(4), 68 (2005). https://doi.org/10.1609/aimag.v26i4.1850

13. Muehlhauser, L.: What is AGI? (2013). https://intelligence.org/2013/08/11/what-is-agi/. Accessed 29 Feb 2020

14. Shane, J.: Why did the neural network cross the road? (2018). https://aiweirdness.com/post/174691534037/why-did-the-neural-network-cross-the-road. Accessed 29 Feb 2020

15. Popper, K.: The Myth of the Framework: In Defence of Science and Rationality. Routledge, New York (1994). ISBN 9781135974800. Editor: Notturno M.A.

16. Illarionov, S.V.: Theory of Knowledge and Philosophy of Science. ROSSPEN, Moscow (2007). (in Russian)

17. Blank, S.: The Four Steps to the Epiphany: Successful Strategies for Products That Win. K&S Ranch, New York (2013)

18. Ries, E.: The Lean Startup. Crown Business (2011)

19. Kapitsa, P.L.: Problems in Physics. Znaniye, Moscow (1996). (in Russian)

Omega: An Architecture for AI Unification

Eray Özkural$^{(\boxtimes)}$

Celestial Intellect Cybernetics, Ankara, Turkey
examachine@gmail.com

Abstract. We introduce the open-ended, modular, self-improving Omega AI unification architecture which is a refinement of Solomonoff's Alpha architecture, as considered from first principles. The architecture embodies several crucial principles of general intelligence including diversity of representations, diversity of data types, integrated memory, modularity, and higher order cognition. We retain the basic design of a fundamental algorithmic substrate called an "AI kernel" for problem solving and basic cognitive functions like memory, and a larger, modular architecture that re-uses the kernel in many ways. Omega includes eight representation languages, which are briefly introduced. We review the broad software architecture, higher-order cognition, self-improvement, modular neural architectures, and intelligent agents.

1 Design Principles for Generality

Without further ado, we review the requirements of a general AI system, and from this vantage point we formulate design principles for constructing a general system.

A general AI system cannot contain any and all specific solutions in its memory, therefore it must equal the computer scientist in terms of its productive capacity of solutions. The requirement of a universal problem solver therefore is fundamental to any such design. Naturally, this implies the existence of Turing-complete programming languages, and a universal method to generalize – which implies a universal principle of induction such as Solomonoff induction. A suitably general probabilistic inference method such as Bayesian inference is implied since most AI problems are probabilistic in nature. It must have practically effective training methods for learning tasks, such as the GPU accelerated training methods used in deep learning. The system must have an integrated memory for cumulative learning. The architecture must be modular for better scalability and extensibility; our brain is a little like that as the neocortex has a grid of cortical columns, which are apparently functionally equivalent structures.

A general AI system must be able to support robotics, however, it should not be limited to agent architectures; it must also support traditional applications like databases, web search, and mobile computing. To accommodate for such a wide variety of functions, the architecture must expose a Swiss army knife like

© Springer Nature Switzerland AG 2020
B. Goertzel et al. (Eds.): AGI 2020, LNAI 12177, pp. 267–278, 2020.
https://doi.org/10.1007/978-3-030-52152-3_28

AI toolkit, to provide a Unified AI API to developers. Such an API can then be served over the cloud, or via fog computing. Machine learning applications generally require hardware with high performance computing support. Therefore, the architecture should be compatible with high performance computing hardware such as GPUs, and FPGAs to be able to scale to many clients.

The general AI system must also address all the hard challenges of a natural environment as formulated by [8, Chapter 2]: the system must cope with the partially observable environments, multi-agent environments, competition and co-operation, stochastic environments, uncertainty, nondeterminism, sequential environments, dynamic environments, continuous environments, and unknown environments. A tall order, if there were ever one. Therefore, the system must be designed with these features of the environment in mind, for accommodating their needs.

AIXI [2] addresses partially observable environments, however, the rest of the features require architectural support in most cases, such as the necessity of providing a theory-theory module (a cognitive module that has a theory of other minds), or showing that the system will discover and adapt to other minds. To provide for multi-agent environments, the system can offer a self-simulation virtualization layer so that the agent can conceive of situations involving entities like itself. To support proper modeling of environments like with stochastic and uncertainty, we need an extensive probabilistic representation language to deal with non-trivial probabilistic problems; the language must cover common models such as hierarchical hidden markov layer models; it should offer a wide range of primitives to choose from, which must be supplied by the architecture. The representation language must also provide the means to combine primitives meaningfully, and obtain short programs for common patterns. The mystique art of designing compact representation languages therefore remains a vital part of AI research. To provide for effective representation of things like sequential, dynamic, continuous environments, the architecture can provide suitable representation primitives and schemas. For dealing with unknown environments, the architecture can provide an agent architecture that can engage in the exploration of the unknown, much as an animal does.

Without doubt, the system must also accommodate common data types, and common tasks such as speech recognition, and the examples for more specific operations should be provided. It is important that the system allows one to implement a wide family of AI tasks for the system to be considered sufficiently general. If, for instance, the user cannot feasibly implement something like style transfer that is popular in deep learning research, with the architecture, it should rather not be termed general. The system should support a wide range of structured, and unstructured data, including popular data types like image, audio, video, speech, and text, and have sufficiently rich models to represent these challenging kinds of data. These more human data types constitute the primary means by which humans can communicate with AI's directly. However, structured, regular and irregular data types also must be supported, since these originate from a variety of sources that can be consumed by the AI system.

The system must also therefore provide an adequate perception architecture by which such a system can learn a world-representation from its sensorium that includes many senses. These processes should be sufficiently general that they can be adapted to any sort of sensorium that will work under known laws of physics. The system should also support an adequate intelligent agent architecture that supports typical goal following, or utility maximization architectures.

Therefore, it also is a challenge to test system generality. Typically, a benchmark that consists of a large number of diverse AI tasks and datasets, must be provided for the system to demonstrate generality. The benchmark should be diverse enough to include the whole gamut of AI problems such as typical pattern recognition problems like image recognition, speech recognition, but also natural language understanding, machine learning tasks like anomaly detection (over some industrial dataset preferably), time-series prediction (commonly used for stock market analysis), robotics problems, game playing problems, and so forth with randomly varied parameters.

We therefore arrive at an understanding of general purpose AI design that tries to maximize generality for every distinct aspect of a problem. The solution space must be wide enough to cover every problem domain. The methods must be independent from the data type. The tasks that can be performed should not be fixed, the system should be independent from the task to be solved, any task should be specifiable. The architecture must not depend either on a particular representation, it should cover a very wide range of representations to be able to deal with different kinds of environments. The intelligent agent code should not be environment specific, it must be adaptable to any environment and agent architecture; in other words, the system must be independent of the environment. The principles of general intelligence we have thus considered essential are: completeness, model diversity, agency, task independence, data type independence, domain independence, and self improvement.

2   Architecture Overview

Many of the aforementioned problems have been addressed by existing AI architectures. We therefore take a well-understood general AI architecture called the Alpha architecture of Solomonoff [10], and define some basic capabilities better, while incorporating newer models and methods from recent research.

For the purposes of general-purpose AI, two most significant events have occurred since Alpha was designed in 2002. First, the Gödel Machine architecture [9] which also provides a level of self-reflective thinking, and presents an agent model around it. The other notable development is the immense success of deep learning methods, which now enable machines to achieve pattern recognition at human-level or better for many basic tasks. The present design therefore merges these two threads of developments into the Alpha framework. The architecture also provides for basic universal intelligent agents, and self-reflection like Gödel Machine does. Like Gödel Machine, we do not assume that the environment is known to a substantial degree, such things are assumed to be learnt.

Like the Alpha architecture, we assume a basic problem solver that is smart enough to bootstrap the rest of the system. This component is called the AI Kernel.

The system is thought to be parameter free, dependent only on the data, and the commands given. The system's interface is a graphical web-based application that allows the user to upload datasets and then apply AI tasks from the library. The system also provides an API for programming novel tasks. A basic graphical programming environment is considered for later releases since the system aims to be usable by non-programmers.

2.1 Components

We review the major components of the system architecture, and explain their functions.

AI Kernel. The AI kernel is an inductive programming system that should use a universal reference machine such as LISP. We have proposed using Church as the reference machine of such a system. However, what matters is that the AI kernel must be able to deal with all types of data, and tasks. We assume that the reference machine is variable in the right AI kernel. The kernel must be a compact code base that can run on a variety of hardware architectures to ensure portability, and the parallelization must support heterogeneous supercomputing platforms for high energy efficiency and scalability.

The AI kernel supports sophisticated programmability, allowing the user to specify most machine learning tasks with a very short API. We employ OCaml generic programming to characterize the kernel's internal components, model discovery, and transfer learning algorithms.

The AI kernel supports real-time operation, and can be configured to continuously update long-term memory splitting running-time between currently running task and meta-learning.

Bio-Mimetic Search. State-of-the-art bio-mimetic machine learning algorithms based on such methods as stochastic gradient descent, and evolutionary computation are available in the AI kernel, and thus chosen and used automatically.

Heuristic Algorithmic Memory 2.0. The AI kernel has integrated multi-term memory, meaning that it solves transfer learning problems automatically, and can remember solutions and representational states at multiple time scales. Heuristic Algorithmic Memory 2.0 extends Heuristic Algorithmic Memory [7] to support multiple reference machines.

Problem Solvers. Problem Solution Methods (PSMs) are methods that solve a given problem. These could be algorithmic solutions like sorting a list of numbers, or statistical methods like predicting a variable. The Alpha architecture basically tries a number of PSMs on a problem until it yields. However, in Omega, it is much better specified which PSMs the system should start with. Since the system is supposed to deal with unknown environments, we give priority to machine learning and statistical methods, as well model classes that directly address some challenging properties of the environment, and support hard applications like robotics. The diversity of the model classes and methods supported expand the range of Omega applications. The Alpha architecture can invent and retain new PSMs, that is why it should be considered an open-ended architecture; so is Omega.

The architecture is taught how to use a problem solver via unstructured natural language examples, like the intent detection task in natural language processing.

Both narrowly specialized and general-purpose methods are included in the initial library of problem solvers for initially high machine-learning capability.

For approximating functions, there are model-based learning algorithms like a generic implementation of stochastic gradient for an arbitrary reference machine. For model discovery, model-free learning algorithms like genetic programming are provided. Function approximation facilities can be invoked by the ensemble machine to solve machine learning problems. Therefore, a degree of method independence is provided by allowing multi-strategy solvers.

A basic set of methods for solving scientific and engineering problems is provided. For computer science, the solutions of basic algorithmic problems including full software development libraries for writing basic computer programs for each reference machine (standard library). For engineering, basic optimization methods and symbolic algebra. In the ultimate form of the architecture, we should have methods for computational sciences, physical, and life sciences.

A full range of basic data science/machine learning methods are provided including:

Clustering. Clustering is generalized to yield automated statistical modeling. Universal induction can be used to infer a PDF minimizing expected divergence (AI kernel function). Both general-purpose and classical clustering algorithms are provided, in recognition that for a specific class of problems a specialized method can be faster, if not necessarily more accurate. The classical algorithms of k-means, hierarchical agglomerative clustering, and Expectation Maximization (EM) for Gaussian Mixture Models are provided. General-purpose algorithms based on NID [11], and universal induction enable working with arbitrary domains.

Classification. Again both classical and general-purpose algorithms are supported. Classical algorithms of decision tree classifier, random forest, knn, logistic regression, and SVM's are supported. General-purpose algorithm invokes AI kernel universal induction routines to learn a mapping from the input to a finite set. NID based classifier works with arbitrary bitstrings.

Regression. General-purpose algorithm invokes universal induction routines in the AI kernel to learn a stochastic operator mapping from the data domain to a real number. Classical algorithms of linear regression, logistic regression, and SVM are supported.

Outlier Detection. The generalized outlier detection finds the points least probable given the rest of the dataset using a generalization of z-score; to first model the data again a universal set induction invocation characterizes the data.

Time-Series Forecasting. Time series prediction is generalized with a universal induction approach modeling the stochastic dynamics, then the most probable model is inferred. Classical time-series prediction algorithms of ARIMA, Hidden Markov Model (HMM), and Hierarchical Hidden Markov Model (HHMM) are provided. A deep LSTM based forecast method is also provided.

Deep Learning. A complete range of DNN architectures for various data types such as image, audio, video and text are provided. Standard algorithms of backpropagation, stochastic gradient and variational inference are supported. The state-of-the-art fully automated machine learning algorithm of Fourier Network Search (FNS) [5] is included. We also invoke universal induction routines to automate neural model discovery. The deep learning implementations are parallelized for multi GPU clusters. For this purpose, an existing deep learning framework such as TensorFlow may be used. The deep learning framework we use is a different, proprietary approach that predates Tensor-Flow and is composed of a neural programming language called MetaNet and a heterogeneous supercomputing middleware called Stardust.

Each algorithm mentioned is exposed as a PSM in the system.

Ensemble Machine. An ensemble machine is introduced to the system which runs PSMs in parallel with time allocated in accordance with their expected probability of success. The associations between tasks and their success are remembered as a stochastic mapping problem solved with the universal induction routines of AI Kernel, guiding future decisions. The ensemble machine is exposed itself as a PSM.

2.2   Representation Languages

We define eight reference machines to widen the range of solutions obtainable, and types of environments/applications addressable.

MetaNet. MetaNet is a new General Neural Networks (GNN) representation language that encompasses common neuron types and architectures used in neural network research. It is a graphical meta-language that can be used to define a large number of network architectures. Formally, it uses a multi-partite labeled directed graph with typed vertices, as a generic representation to represent neural circuits, and the richer sort of representation allows us to extend the model to more biologically plausible, or with neuroscience-inspired models. The system uses this representation to facilitate automated model discovery of the right neural network for the given task when evaluating the MetaNet representation language.

Church. We use the Church language to represent probability distributions and solve basic algorithmic problems like adding a list of numbers, and the Towers of Hanoi problem. Components expose their interfaces in Church machine, expanding self-reflection capability.

Probabilistic Logic. We define a probabilistic logic programming language to deal with uncertainty and stochasticity, and the ability to solve reasoning problems.

Bayesian Networks. We define a general class of bayesian networks that can be used to deal with uncertainty.

Analog Computing. We use an analog computing model to represent dynamical, continuous and stochastic systems better.

Picture. We use the Picture language to deal with images.

Matrix Computing. We use a LAPACK based matrix algebra computing package such as GNU Octave to represent mathematical solutions.

Asynchronous Computer. We define an asynchronous model of computation for conception of fine-grain concurrent models.

2.3 Neural Representation Classes

There are a number of ready neural representations that the system can quickly invoke.

Fourier Neural Network. Fourier Neural Networks use a Fourier series representation to represent neural networks compactly, and may be considered a general-purpose learning model class [4].

Convolutional Neural Networks. CNNs are particularly effective for pattern recognition problems. A variety of basic CNNs suitable for processing different kinds of data are provided, including specialized networks such as multi-column DNNs for image classification, for video, text, and speech.

Deep Belief Networks. These networks are a stack of Restricted Boltzmann Machines that can perform unsupervised learning.

Deep Autoencoders. Deep autoencoders use several hidden unit layers, two deep belief networks, that learn to compress and then reproduce the data. We provide specific applications like variational autoencoders for image captions, inverse graphics, multimodal learning.

LSTM/GRU Networks. We provide a variety of RNN models using LSTM (Long-Short Term Memory) and GRU (Gated Recurrent Unit) stacks to model sequential data. Variants for different data types such as speech, video, image are included.

Recursive Deep Networks. Especially useful for language processing, these networks can recognize hierarchical structures.

The networks are specified as generic network architectures that can scale to required input/output size. Any hyper-parameters are designated as variables to be learned to the AI kernel so that the hyper parameters can adapt to the problem. These networks are considered to be sufficient as providing enough library primitives. The generators for neural networks are specified such that the program generator can indeed generate all of the library networks; however, re-inventing the wheel is not a feasible idea, therefore we aim to include a complete inventory of deep learning models.

2.4   Software Architecture

Functional Decomposition. A high-level component architecture without the many inter-component interactions is depicted in Fig. 1 on page 7. The system's process flow is straightforward. The user presents the system with a number of datasets, and the user selects a task to be applied to the data. The system automatically recognizes different data types, however, it also allows data to be specified in detail

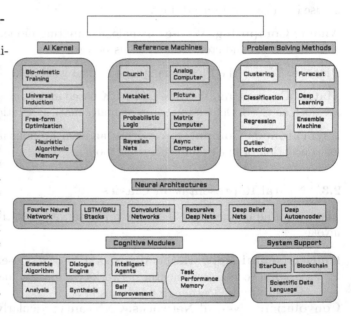

Fig. 1. Ω architecture component diagram

by a description language. The system will also accept tasks to be defined via a conversational engine, and a programming interface (API). The conversational engine can learn to recognize a task via given examples, mapping text to a task specification language and backwards. The programming interface accumulates the interfaces of all the components, unified under a single facade of a generic problem solver, which is formulated as a general optimizer [1]. As in Alpha, the most general interface the system provides is that of time-limited optimization, however, the system allows to solve any well-defined problems allowing the user to define any success criterion. The problem solver then predicts the probability that a PSM will succeed in solving the so-specified problem, and then translates the input data and the task to a format that the particular PSM will understand, and also translate any results back. After a task is solved, the system automatically updates its long-term memory and writes a snapshot to the disk. It then executes higher-order cognition routines to improve its PSMs, and awaits for the next task.

Execution. The execution of PSMs is parallelized as much as possible, as many PSMs may be run in parallel, but also some methods will allow data to be sharded, and will also parallelize well themselves. A main operational goal of the system is the ability to keep track of these parallelizations well enough to present an OS like stability to the user with a simple interface. The system also allows modules to be invoked concurrently and in a distributed manner to facilitate the design of distributed and decentralized applications using the API.

The PSMs are executed on a hardware abstraction layer called Stardust that provides heterogeneous peer-to-peer computing capability to the architecture. MetaNet acts as a common neural network representation language. Scientific Data Language is a data specification language that allows us to describe the type, format and semantic labels of the data.

2.5 Higher-Order Cognition

Two fundamental higher-order cognitive functions are defined as analysis and synthesis. Analysis decomposes a problem into components and then tries to solve the problem by first solving sub-problems and then merging their results into a solution. Synthesis generates new PSMs by combining known PSMs. These operations give the ability to observe the code of its modules, and expand the system's repertoire of PSMs continuously. Analysis is self-reflective in that sense, and synthesis is self-reification.

These functions correspond to a second kind of modularity where the tasks themselves can be decomposed, and entirely new PSMs may be invented and added as new modules to the system.

The system continually self-reflects through updating its algorithmic memory for accelerating future solutions. It also keeps a record of tool performance for trying to retroactively optimize past solutions. The components expose themselves via a high-level reference machine (Church) which acts as the system "glue code" to compose and decompose system functions. Since Church is quite expressive, it can also act as the system's task description code, and be used to recognize, decompose, and compose tasks and solutions. The synthesis and analysis modules operate over the system's modular cognition itself, helping with synthesis of new solution methods and analysis of problems. The system uses self-models to guide its self-improvement, for instance, by trying to optimize its performance.

2.6 Self-improvement

Analysis and synthesis can learn how to accomplish this as they can use the execution history to improve the results retrospectively. After a new problem is solved, therefore, the system can continuously try to improve its consolidated memory of PSMs by trying to generate new PSMs that will improve performance over history, or by decomposing problems to accelerate their execution. A general objective such as maximizing energy efficiency of solutions can be sought for self-improvement.

2.7 Modular Neural Architectures

PSMs embody a basic kind of modularity in the system which are extended with modular neural architectures. These architectural schemas are a cortical organization that decomposes the networks into many cortical columns, which are henceforth again decomposed into micro-columns, with variant geometries. This organization schema is called MetaCortex, and it is a way to describe larger networks that can digest a variety of data sources, and construct larger neural models with better modularity, that is better data/model encapsulation based on affinity. There are architectures such as multi-column committee networks that already implement these architectures, however, we would expand this to the entire library of networks described.

2.8 Intelligent Agents

Basic goal-following and utility-maximization agents can be realized similarly to time-series prediction. A typical two part model of learning representations (world model), and planning will be provided. A basic neural template will provide for multi-modal perception, multi-tasking, task decomposition and imitation learning. Neural templates corresponding to different kinds of agents such as Deep Mind's I2A model [12] will be provided.

The intelligent agents have a real-time architecture, they run at a fixed number of iterations every second. At this shortest period of synchronization, mostly backpropagation like learning algorithms, and simulation are allowed to complete. Everything else is run in the background for longer time-scales.

2.9 Process and Memory Hierarchy

The processes and memory are organized hierarchically from long-term, heavy tasks to short-term, lightweight tasks. At the shortest scale, the system has neural memory units like LSTM, that last at the scale of one task, and model-based local training/inference algorithms like backpropagation algorithms. At a longer scale which corresponds to one iteration of problem solution procedure, the system remembers the best solutions so far, and it updates its mid-term memory with them to improve the solution performance in the next iteration.

At this scale, the system will also engage in more processes such as the just mentioned memory update operation, and more expensive training algorithms such as genetic algorithms. At the highest scale, the system runs the most expensive model-free learning algorithms that can search over architectures, models, and components, and updates its persistent, long term memory based on the statistics about solutions of the new problem after solving it to guide the solution of new problems. The system also updates its PSMs by executing its higher-order cognitive functions at this scale.

3   Discussion and Research Program

We gave the overview of an ambitious architecture based on Solomonoff's Alpha Architecture, and Schmidhuber's Gödel Machine architecture. The system is like Alpha, because it re-uses the basic design of PSMs. It is also similar to Gödel Machine architecture, because it can deploy a kind of probabilistic logical inference for reasoning and it can also observe some of its internal states and improve itself. The system also has basic provisions for intelligent agents, but it is not limited to them. We saw that the first important issue with implementing Alpha was to decide a basic set of primitives that will grant it sufficient intelligence to deal with human-scale problems. It remains to be demonstrated empirically that is the case, however, two of the eight reference machines have been implemented and seen to operate effectively.

A criticism may be raised that we have not explained much about how the AI Kernel works. We only assume that it presents a generalized universal induction approximation that can optimize functions, rich enough to let us define basic machine learning tasks. It surely cannot be Levin search, but it could be any effective multi-strategy optimization method such as evolutionary architecture search [6]. We are using an extension of the approach in Fourier Network Search [3] which is also likely general enough. The memory update is also not detailed but it is assumed that it is possible to extend an older memory design called heuristic algorithmic memory so that it works for any reference machine. We also did not explain in detail how the various components individually work due to lack of space, which is an issue to be tackled in a longer future version of the present paper.

References

1. Alpcan, T., Everitt, T., Hutter, M.: Can we measure the difficulty of an optimization problem? In: 2014 IEEE Information Theory Workshop, ITW 2014, Hobart, Tasmania, Australia, November 2–5, 2014, pp. 356–360 (2014). https://doi.org/10.1109/ITW.2014.6970853
2. Hutter, M.: Universal algorithmic intelligence: a mathematical top→down approach. In: Goertzel, B., Pennachin, C. (eds.) Artificial General Intelligence, pp. 227–290. Cognitive Technologies, Springer, Berlin (2007). https://doi.org/10.1007/978-3-540-68677-4_8

3. Koutník, J., Gomez, F., Schmidhuber, J.: Evolving neural networks in compressed weight space. In: Proceedings of the 12th Annual Conference on Genetic and Evolutionary Computation, pp. 619–626 (2010)
4. Koutník, J., Gomez, F., Schmidhuber, J.: Searching for minimal neural networks in Fourier space. In: Proceedings of the 4th Annual Conference on Artificial General Intelligence. Atlantis Press (2010)
5. Koutník, J., Gomez, F., Schmidhuber, J.: Evolving deep/recurrent networks for reinforcement learning. In: Proceedings of the 2014 Genetic and Evolutionary Computation Conference (GECCO-2014). ACM Press (2014). to appear
6. Liang, J., Meyerson, E., Miikkulainen, R.: Evolutionary architecture search for deep multitask networks. arXiv preprint arXiv:1803.03745 (2018)
7. Özkural, E.: Towards heuristic algorithmic memory. In: Schmidhuber, J., Thórisson, K.R., Looks, M. (eds.) AGI 2011. LNCS (LNAI), vol. 6830, pp. 382–387. Springer, Heidelberg (2011). https://doi.org/10.1007/978-3-642-22887-2_47
8. Russell, S.J., Norvig, P.: Artificial Intelligence: A Modern Approach. Pearson Education Limited, Malaysia (2016)
9. Schmidhuber, J.: Gödel machines: fully self-referential optimal universal self-improvers. In: Goertzel, B., Pennachin, C. (eds.) Artificial General Intelligence, pp. 199–226. Springer, Heidelberg (2006). https://doi.org/10.1007/978-3-540-68677-4_7. variant available as arXiv:cs.LO/0309048
10. Solomonoff, R.J.: Progress in incremental machine learning. In: NIPS Workshop on Universal Learning Algorithms and Optimal Search, Whistler, B.C., Canada (December 2002)
11. Vitányi, P.M.B., Balbach, F.J., Cilibrasi, R.L., Li, M.: Normalized information distance. In: Emmert-Streib, F., Dehmer, M. (eds.) Information Theory and Statistical Learning, pp. 45–82. Springer, Boston (2009). https://doi.org/10.1007/978-0-387-84816-7_3
12. Weber, T., et al.: Imagination-augmented agents for deep reinforcement learning. arXiv preprint arXiv:1707.06203 (2017)

Analyzing Elementary School Olympiad Math Tasks as a Benchmark for AGI

Alexey Potapov[(✉)], Oleg Scherbakov, Vitaly Bogdanov, Vita Potapova,
Anatoly Belikov, Sergey Rodionov, and Artem Yashenko

SingularityNET Foundation, Amsterdam, The Netherlands
{alexey,olegshcherbakov,vitaly,abelikov,sergey,
yashenko}@singularitynet.io

Abstract. Many benchmarks and challenges for AI and AGI exist, which help
to reveal both short- and long-term topics and directions of research. We analyze
elementary school Olympiad math tasks as a possible benchmark for AGI that
can occupy a certain free niche capturing some limitations of the existing neural
and symbolic systems better than other existing both language understanding and
mathematical tests. A detailed comparison and analysis of implications of AGI is
provided.

Keywords: AGI · AI evaluation · Math tasks · Language understanding

1 Introduction

Having some metric to estimate progress in a certain domain is considered as a necessity
in contemporary AI practice. At the same time, there is no generally accepted standard
AGI benchmark, although theoretical metrics of AGI exist (e.g. [1]) as well as different
empirical tests and challenges have been proposed (e.g.[1]). However, each of them either
requires a real AGI to pass it, or, in contrary, can be (partially) solved by narrow AI
techniques, or at least favors a certain approach to AGI or a type of proto-AGI systems
(for example, reinforcement learning models will be favored by certain environments,
while such challenges as General Game Playing discourage the use of learning at all). It
is a not uncommon opinion that comparing different proto-AGI or measuring progress
towards AGI in an unbiased way is very hard [2].

The paper [3] overviewed thirty computer models addressing intelligent test problems, and came to the conclusion that these models have different purposes and applications, and have a limited connection between each other. But still, AGI benchmarks are
far from worthless by themselves, and possess a considerable methodological importance, because they help to understand limitations of the existing methods and reveal
possible directions of further research. Although the effort to encourage future computer
models taking intelligence test problems to link with and build upon previous research

---

[1] https://www.general-ai-challenge.org/.

© Springer Nature Switzerland AG 2020
B. Goertzel et al. (Eds.): AGI 2020, LNAI 12177, pp. 279–289, 2020.
https://doi.org/10.1007/978-3-030-52152-3_29

made in [3] is really useful, we see some objective reasons in the diversity of the existing intelligent tests.

Indeed, although standard benchmarks exist for many domains in narrow AI, these benchmarks also fail to specify an ultimate goal even within rather particular tasks, and optimizing some metric is not an end in itself but only an intermediate goal, which we managed to formulate based on our current understanding of the task, which can be imprecise or even misleading. It frequently appears that the state-of-the-art methods are steadily improving their scores on some benchmark, but are doing this in the way we just "don't like", and then the benchmarks themselves start to being criticized and improved upon. For example, the visual question answering (VQA) datasets were criticized [4] for lacking compositional questions, allowing confidently answering questions without looking at images, etc., which were fixed in other benchmarks (e.g. [5]), which, in turn, had other drawbacks and limitations and were further improved upon. However, these drawbacks were not so obvious from the beginning, and a perfect benchmark would be difficult to create even for such restricted task as VQA. This should be even truer for AGI.

In this paper, we do not pretend to create an ultimate AGI metric, but discuss yet another possible AGI-ish benchmark, which, however, has some advantages and can have a certain utility as discussed below. The basic idea is to compose a dataset using elementary school mathematical Olympiad tasks. A similar proposal to use mathematical puzzles as a challenging competition for AI [6] has been made, but without referring to Olympiad tasks as a source for arranging a concrete dataset and without relevance to AGI. In the following sections, we compare this idea with some related benchmarks highlighting differences and consequences for AGI, which are worth discussing even before creating the benchmark itself.

2   Related Works and Discussion

Natural Language Understanding
Language is frequently considered as one of the main differences between human and animal intelligence. An extreme form of focusing on language is expressed in "equation": "language – sound = thinking". The seminal Turing test was essentially a natural language understanding (NLU) test, while the main point of Searle's Chinese room argument was to show that computers (physical symbol systems) are incapable of language understanding in principle. Nowadays, many benchmarks in narrow AI exist for question answering, dialogs, text generation and other language processing tasks.

Modern deep neural network (DNN) models may show nearly human or even superhuman scores on some benchmarks. However, the way they do this (in comparison with more traditional symbolic systems) is the source of ongoing debates. Is it really possible to map arbitrary sentences to a large, but fixed vector space of their meanings? Do DNN models really understand sentences, or mostly memorize huge text corpora and recall them? Is it possible to understand texts in natural language without even attempting to represent real-world situations, described in them?

Some tests and challenges exist, which try showing the lack of understanding in the existing models. One example is the Winograd Schema Challenge (WSC) [7]. Questions in WSC follow the same pattern and contain an ambiguous pronoun to be associated with nouns using knowledge and commonsense reasoning. WSC is reasonably difficult: best models demonstrate ~70% accuracy that is not too low, though, to deprive of hope for solving this challenge by incrementally improving and tweaking the existing models. Also, it may appear that the challenge can be solved using purely linguistic knowledge and simple ontological relations. Another drawback of WSC is that it contains only 150 schemas, which apparently cannot be used for training and extracting necessary knowledge from the dataset itself (although its recent analogue, WinoGrande[2], contains 44k problems).

The standard General Language Understanding Evaluation (GLUE) benchmark [8] includes WSC along with other 8 NLU tasks including sentiment analysis, semantic similarity of sentences, and others. Each of these tasks highlights one or another aspect of language understanding, and all together they cannot be called narrow. However, they all are still too focused on the language domain itself. For example, the Corpus of Linguistic Acceptability (CoLA) requires distinguishing between (grammatically) acceptable and inacceptable sentences, e.g. *"John tried to be a good boy"* and *"Who does John visit Sally because he likes?"* correspondingly.

Consider the following question from WSC as an example: "Joan made sure to thank Susan for all the help she had [given/received]. Who had [given/received] help?". Apparently, in order to answer it, a model does need to "know" that it is usually a person, who receives help, who thanks a person who helps. However, it doesn't really need to understand what it means to help. What it really needs is just an ontological relation – not its real-world grounding.

Other NLU tasks can require using some factual encyclopedic knowledge, but without its real understanding. Some tests involve scientific knowledge also. For example, the Aristo project [9, 10] dataset includes such questions as "Which object in our solar system reflects light and is a satellite that orbits around one planet? (A) Moon (B) Earth (C) Mercury (D) Sun", which requires not only language processing and basic reasoning abilities, but also commonsense and scientific knowledge representation and manipulation. Such tests have their own utility, but they don't require an understanding of what it means to orbit around a planet or to reflect light. What is necessary is just a set of relations or facts "The Moon orbits around the Earth", "The Earth is a planet", etc. Indeed, these are so-called open book questions for understanding of qualitative relationships.

Let us consider a few examples of elementary school math tasks for comparison:

- A group of girls stands in a circle. Emily is the fifth on the left from Mary and the sixth on the right from Emily. How many girls are in the group?
- Nicole takes a sheet of paper and cuts it into 9 pieces. She then takes one of these pieces and cuts it into 9 smaller pieces. She then takes another piece and cuts it into 9 smaller pieces and finally cuts one of the smaller pieces into 9 tiny pieces. How many pieces of paper has the original sheet been cut into?
- How many different cubes are there with two faces colored green and four faces colored yellow?

---

[2] https://leaderboard.allenai.org/winogrande/.

Imagine how these tasks can be solved by an AI system, e.g. a DNN model. It should be noted that the tasks are quite unique. There can be a few more tasks involving standing in circles or cutting sheets of paper, but they will be formulated in a different way and require inferring other consequences. At the same time, quite a large number of different tasks exist, and these tasks are not wiredrawn, but "real-world" in sense that they are really given to human children. Apparently, our AI system cannot just memorize the training dataset and recall similar tasks. These tasks don't require the extensive use of factual encyclopedic knowledge (which can be memorized), but suppose a deeper understanding of what a circle is or what cutting is that goes beyond pair-wise relations between symbolic atoms and requires at least some modeling of corresponding "physical" situations. It will not be enough to map the sentences into some semantic vector space. The system will most likely require having an internal model of girls standing in a circle and explicitly reason over it.

We believe such tasks are more indicative of what "understanding" is and their formulations cover quite a wide spectrum of aspects of natural language also (but of course not all of them, e.g. sentiment analysis is not covered). We don't say that other NLU tests are worse, but we claim that the mentioned math tasks require dealing explicitly with an additional important aspect of natural language understanding, which is rarely highlighted in other NLU tasks (which, however, better cover some other aspects). Besides NLU, these math tasks require some form of reasoning, which is also important for AGI benchmarking.

Recently, SuperGLUE [11] benchmark was proposed with a new set of natural understanding tasks. Although these tasks are more difficult, they are also purely textual and do not heavily require symbol (textual entities) grounding.

Visual (and Physical) Reasoning
The lack of necessity of grounding linguistic entities in the real world in purely textual NLU tasks is not a novel observation and has been addressed in multimodal benchmarks, which most often rely on visual input. Interestingly, many school mathematical tasks involve images, and can be considered as questions about images, which make them similar to VQA tasks.

As mentioned above, the earlier VQA datasets were criticized for that relatively high scores on them could be achieved with the use of superficial correlations between textual tokens in questions without both reasoning and clear grounding of words in images. Some of consequent datasets (e.g. [4]) introduced different biases in training and test subsets to prevent using superficial correlations. More interesting is that considerable efforts have been made to stimulate the focus on reasoning in VQA. In particular, CLEVR is a synthetic dataset with simple scenes, but complex questions about objects and their spatial relations. Later, similar complex questions were generated using Visual Genome for real-world scenes [12].

Images in math problems are mostly composed of abstract shapes or simple objects and are closer to CLEVR in this respect, but they are not generated by a simple formal process. They are much closer to real-world VQA than CLEVR in terms of "open-endedness". Although they don't require recognizing a great variety of real objects (which is of course an important, but a sort of vision-domain-specific property), they require a deeper image understanding than traditional VQA datasets. Consider Fig. 1.

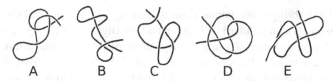

Fig. 1. Which ropes will be tightened into knots if they are pulled by the ends?

It can be seen that while VQA tasks require just extracting bounding boxes of discrete objects and discrete relations between them, math tasks require analyzing images in finer details. Also, while a DNN might be able to learn from thousands of examples some features enough to answer the question about the ropes, it will not generalize to other such tasks and learn from few examples.

Apparently, school math problems require much more complex and open-ended reasoning in comparison to synthetic questions of low diversity, which are really compositional but hardly require reasoning. Indeed, they can be answered by a direct seq2seq mapping of textual questions to imperative programs.

We don't claim that math questions with images form a perfect VQA dataset, but such a dataset can be quite indicative in terms of structural image understanding and visual reasoning (showing how far the state-of-the-art VQA models from real visual reasoning even over such simplistic images).

It should be noted that there are types of tasks, which use images and (optionally) textual questions as input, although they are not considered as VQA tasks. One example of such tasks is Physical Bongard Problems (e.g., [13]), which requires categorizing simple synthetic scenes based on their physical properties (e.g. stable/unstable configuration, small objects fall down, etc.).

Physical Bongard Problems are conceptually similar to the math tasks under discussion in that answers to them don't directly follow from images, but require some internal representation of depicted situations, over which reasoning is carried out. Of course, there are many differences in details, and these two sets of problems don't intersect, but complement each other. Physical Bongard Problems also don't contain textual questions and are devoted to a relatively restricted subdomain of naive physics (concretely, dynamics and object interaction). Both these properties are good for some purposes, but make Physical Bongard Problems hackable by narrow methods (especially taking into account that not too many problems exist).

It should be mentioned that physical problems were also considered in the context of cognitive psychology, in particular as a test case for analogical reasoning and transfer learning (e.g. [14]). However, the possibility to solve the particular tests being used in such studied by hand-crafted or narrow methods wasn't analyzed.

Elementary school mathematical Olympiad tasks don't require extensive physical knowledge or detailed simulation. Instead, they highlight the necessity to represent scenes or situations in a way that allows reasoning over them.

Mathematical Tests

We have compared school math tasks with NLU and VQA tasks showing their utility in AGI testing, but one may wonder if there are other existing benchmarks based on math tasks. Indeed, the ability of mathematicians to decompose, abstract and solve real world problems was the golden standard of thinking and intelligent processing during evolution of AI research agenda especially at the early stages of AI field establishment. To solve even simple math puzzles humans use analytical abilities such as logical and spatial-temporal reasoning as well as intuition, understanding and common sense. To find out if AI systems have capabilities of handling non-trivial math and reasoning problems several challenges have already been proposed. IMO (International Mathematical Olympiad) Grand Challenge[3] is probably one of the most well known. This challenge calls for building an AI system that can win a gold medal in the IMO competition among humans.

It may appear that the IMO Grand Challenge already brings our proposal to its ultimate form. However, there is an essential difference between them. IMO tasks are purely mathematical and are provided to AI in a formalized representation.

In contrast, texts of elementary school math tasks don't define formal constructions for conducting inference, but describe real-world situations, which require constructing some models that formalize these situations with higher or lower precision. For example, if we consider two objects moving towards each other, we can sum up their velocities only as an approximation (in contrast to the relativity theory, we suppose existence of some global time and no speed limit). Thus, formalization is achieved not by a direct text2math mapping, but through simulation (imagination) of the situation (in this context, it is interesting to note the discussion on the nature of mathematical knowledge and its relation to AI [15]).

Even after reconstructing the situation, the task can remain underformalized. In fact, complete formalization and inference over it can be cumbersome even in pure math tasks. Indeed, consider the task "prove that at least one of two numbers is divisible by 3 if their product is divisible by 3" – a fully formalized solution may be surprisingly long, especially if it doesn't rely on lemmas about simple factoring. At the same time, we can imagine that the product of two number is composed of 3 and the rest part, which is divided into two pieces belonging to different initial numbers, and "3" should "go" into one of them making it divisible by 3. It is convincing, although not really formal. Answers to less formal tasks can be obtained by "physical" simulation or via knowledge-based reasoning. For example, for the task of cutting a sheet of paper, we can imagine how this sheet is cut, although we need to suppose some commonsense-based invariance during this simulation, i.e. to figure out if it matters or not where it is cut, in what order, etc. Alternatively, we can just know that cutting a sheet of paper destroys it, and thus cutting one piece into 9 pieces increases the total number of pieces by 8. But even if start with this simplistic "formalization of cutting" and represent the process as an algorithm that takes a list with one element as input and iteratively removes one random element from the list and inserts 9 new elements into it, a complete formal proof that the length of the list produced by this algorithm is independent on random choices will be not that short.

Consider the task "Bella colors all the small squares that lie on the two longest diagonals of a square grid. She colors 2021 small squares. What is the size of the square grid?". When we write down equation 2size − 1 = 2021 relying on the fact that the number of squares in the longest diagonals is the same as the size of the board, and they

---

have one common square, the answer is obvious. But it's semi-formal. To be completely formal, it should contain definitions of boards, diagonals, etc. as mathematical objects. These definitions can be cumbersome. Of course, we can rely on formerly proved lemmas about diagonals, etc. (we can imagine Agda or Coq-style definition of boards, diagonals, coloring and so on as dependent types), but still the mapping to this formalization is not that straightforward.

Even when some tasks rely on physics to a nearly zero extent, and suppose a more direct translation into, say, algebraic representation, they are first translated into some representation of a "real-world" situation. In fact, the skill of using algebraic representation is not natural and should be specially developed prior to solving math tasks per se (and actually, it was discovered by humankind just a few centuries ago) as was pointed out by George Pólya long time ago. Only higher-grade tasks become purely mathematical, when pupils have developed an internal representation of this abstract domain separately (or on top of) perceptual world representation and simulation.

Consider the task: "Bill lacks 8 cents to buy the apple, while Mary lacks 1 cent to buy the apple. How much does the apple cost if Bill and Mary cannot buy it even if they put their money together?" It is very simple mathematically, and it supposes quite a straightforward complete formalization, but still, humans (both children and adults) rarely solve it via this complete formalization. Rather, they arrive at the solution semi-formally. First of all, we'd be surprised: how is it possible that they have not enough money together if Mary lacks just 1 cent? Eureka! Bill has no money at all. We don't bother with writing down the following system: $a + 8 = x, b + 1 = x, a + b < x, a \geq 0, b \geq 0$. Besides the fact that the last two inequalities require some background knowledge and commonsense assumptions, this is not really how we solve this task.

One can claim that the abstract world of IMO-type math problems is no less important than the world of clocks, buses, sheets of paper and so on, and the ability to solve IMO tasks is more indicative from the AGI-ish point of view. However, all real-world tasks (related not necessarily to everyday environment, but to any object or system of scientific study) differ from IMO tasks in that they involve very complex objects, many properties of which are not necessary, while some other important properties are missing and should be filled in with default or commonsense values. Isolating the problem (even already given in natural language) from the rest of Universe and representing it in a solvable way is absent in IMO Grand Challenge, and it can be more difficult than solving a formalized task.

The main difficulty of applying symbolic systems to real-world tasks consists in translating input data into representations, over which these systems can reason. At the same time, end-to-end trainable deep learning models have rather weak reasoning capabilities (and fail to learn to reason as well).

Indeed, recently an attention of the research community has been shifted to estimation of the ability of DNN models to solve math-alike problems. Neural models successfully handle many of the general text problems, but parsing and answering math questions is a very special task which is at least at the first glance cannot be directly generalized from standard pretrained model. However some of the researchers are trying to experimentally evaluate such generalization properties of DNN models at least in restricted problem-set conditions.

In the paper [16] researchers introduce the Mathematics Dataset consisting of many different types of mathematics problems that cover topics in algebra, arithmetic, basic combinatory and probability theory. There are two types of tests: interpolation and extrapolation tests. Interpolation tests assume that all types of questions were presented during the training but test set questions have to be presented at most 2% of the total test set size. Extrapolation tests estimate generalization capabilities of the trained models to work with tasks, which differ from training ones by larger numbers, more numbers involved in equation, more compositions, and (if it was a probability question) larger samplers. The authors have also examined several popular general purpose models. All of the models were modern neural architectures for solving sequence-to-sequence problems: recurrent neural architectures, and attentional/transformer architecture. The authors also claim that they tried to use advanced neural models with external memory, like Differentiable Neural Computers [17], which could be potentially well suited for solving mathematical questions. But it is reported that there is no significant outcome from the usage of these models. The researchers also have shown some interesting flaws in models performance on very simple tasks of adding series of "ones", where "one" appears n times for $n > 5$. It is especially interesting because the models could correctly predict results for longer sequences of far bigger numbers. The major takeaway from this study is that the modern DNN models do not generalize well to the specific problem domain like math questions even in well-controlled environments consisting of formally defined tasks though in natural language.

Interestingly enough, more recent Tensor Product Transformer model [18] has shown some promising results on the Mathematics Dataset. The dataset includes tasks like *"What is the first derivative of 13 * a ** 2 − 627434 * a + 11914106?"* or even such complex tasks as *"Let r(g) be the second derivative of 2 * g ** 3/3 − 21 * g ** 2/2 + 10 * g. Let z be r(7). Factor − z * s + 6 − 9 * s ** 2 + 0 * s + 6 * s ** 2"*, which is mathematically involved, but doesn't require reasoning over or formalizing real-world situations and corresponds to a closed domain.

Elementary school mathematical Olympiad tasks are difficult simultaneously for neural and symbolic systems, while most of the other benchmarks favor either symbolic or neural approaches (or at least seem to favor). Apparently, passing IMO Grand Challenge requires much more sophisticated symbolic reasoning, which is not covered by elementary school math tasks, but passing the former will also not make the goal of solving the latter any closer. So, these are really different benchmarks.

Of course, there are also other tests, which don't suppose formalized math tasks as input. For example, GEOS [19] and ARIS [20] projects are closely related to Aristo, but GEOS is focused on answering geometry questions with supporting diagram information, while ARIS suggests dealing with elementary arithmetic problems. A typical example of the GEOS problem is the following (Fig. 2)

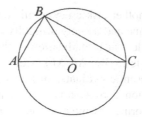

Fig. 2. In the figure, triangle ABC is inscribed in the circle with center O and diameter AC. If AB = AO, what is the degree measure of angle ABO?

The figures as well as the textual descriptions in GEOS are much more restricted, and their formal representation in terms of such predicates as Equals (AB, AO), IsTriangle (ABC), IsCenterOf (O, circle), Is AC, diameter) can be extracted (see the end-to-end geometry project solver[4]) rendering GEOS not too useful for testing AGI systems.

Here is one task from ARIS problem set: "Last week Tom had $74. He washed cars over the weekend and now has $86. How much money did he make washing cars?" It can be seen that the questions are concerned with very basic arithmetic, but the main challenge is to extract necessary information from the plain text description.

Another interesting initiative is the SemEval [21] project that provides a benchmark for testing AI abilities to pass high school Scholastic Achievement Tests (SAT). The dataset consists of 2200 training, 500 development, and 1000 test questions which were derived from Math SAT study guides. The question can have or have not some supplementary reference information presented in the form of a diagram.

Both ARIS and SemEval are similar to the elementary school mathematical Olympiad tasks in that the problem of understanding the task is more difficult than the problem of solving its formalized version. However, the ARIS and SemEval contain much more standard tasks of not too many types, which formalization is typically more straightforward, and which require much more restricted representations and simpler reasoning or problem solving capabilities. There are also other challenges and systems, which try to solve even more restricted forms of math problems and puzzles. One such system is LOGICIA [22], which is trying to deal with logic grid puzzles.

Some modifications to these benchmarks exist. For example, [https://www.aclweb. org/anthology/S17-1029.pdf] proposes to enrich the training set samples with detailed demonstrative solutions in natural language, but they also focus on SAT style geometry problems [23].

These are creativity, diversity, and originality of Olympiad tasks, which make them especially interesting from the AGI testing perspective in comparison to more restricted mathematical tests, which are good for advancing state-of-the-art models locally. Even if the training set is large enough, the process of solving tasks from the test set will not be routine. To see this, it is enough to try applying geometry SAT task solvers to the tasks like in Fig. 1). Consider also the following task as an example: using 6 matchsticks is it possible to create 4 equilateral triangles?

---

[4] http://geometry.allenai.org/.

Apparently, it is not yet another task on symbolic differentiation abundant both in test and training sets. It is unique and its only difficulty (even for humans) is to choose the correct solution space. A default formalization of this problem has no solution on the plane, but is easily solvable in 3D. An AI system that really understands natural language should not just represent coordinates of matchstick ends as points in 3D, but should consider 2D formalization also (what is about non-Euclidian spaces?), and even more, should consider points formed by intersections of matches, and should ask if it is allowed to break matches into pieces.

3 Conclusion

We have discussed (elementary) school mathematical Olympiad tasks as a rich source for (proto-)AGI systems benchmarking. The domain of these tasks is open-ended and diverse. Instead of requiring vast but shallow encyclopedic knowledge about facts and pair-wise relations, they require a more restricted amount of commonsense knowledge grounded in simulation or abstract models of reality. This renders memorization adopted by most DNN models not too useful (that is in agreement with a more general recent criticism of DNNs, e.g., in [24]).

The tasks under discussion require some creative reasoning, which may be non-trivial for elementary school pupils or even adults, but it is much less complex than what the existent automated theorem provers successfully deal with. The main problem here is to understand the task (e.g., but not necessarily, to adequately formalize it within some symbolic system), that is difficult for both neural and symbolic systems.

Thus, elementary school math tasks require a diverse set of cognitive skills are challenging for the existing AI systems, while manageable by young children without special training and extensive domain-specific knowledge.

Programming Olympiad tasks (as well as of other school subjects) can be used for a further extension of this idea. In fact, programming tasks highlight some issues even better. Indeed, it should be quite obvious that seq2seq models translating natural language descriptions to the code will be useless in open-ended domains unless language is somehow grounded in an interpreter (that gives real meaning to text tokens and symbols). However, programming tasks are more involved and don't replace math tasks, but extend them. They deserve a separate study in future work.

References

1. Hernández-Orallo, J., Minaya-Collado, N.: A formal definition of intelligence based on an intensional variant of Kolmogorov complexity. In: Proceedings of the International Symposium of Engineering of Intelligent Systems (EIS 1998), pp. 146–163. ICSC Press (1998)
2. Goertzel, B.: Artificial general intelligence: concept, state of the art, and future prospects. J. Artif. Gen. Intell. **5**(1), 1–48 (2014)
3. Hernández-Orallo, J., Martínez-Plumed, F., Schmid, U., Siebers, M., Dowe, D.L.: Computer models solving intelligence test problems: progress and implications. Artif. Intell. **230**, 74–107 (2016)

4. Agrawal, A., et al.: Don't just assume; look and answer: overcoming priors for visual question answering. In: Proceedings of IEEE Conference on CVPR, pp. 4971–4980 (2018)
5. Johnson, J., et al.: CLEVR: a diagnostic dataset for compositional language and elementary visual reasoning. arXiv preprint arXiv:1612.06890 (2016)
6. Chesani, F., Mello, P., Milano, M.: Solving mathematical puzzles: a challenging competition for AI. AI Mag. **38**(3), 83–94 (2017)
7. Ackerman, E.: Can winograd schemas replace turing test for defining human-level AI? IEEE Spectrum (2014)
8. Wang, A., et al.: GLUE: a multi-task benchmark and analysis platform for natural language understanding. arXiv preprint arXiv:1804.07461 (2018)
9. Clark, P.: Elementary school science and math tests as a driver for AI: take the Aristo challenge! In: Twenty-Seventh IAAI Conference (2015)
10. Clark, P., et al.: From 'F' to 'A' on the N.Y. regents science exams: an overview of the aristo project. arXiv preprint arXiv:1909.01958 (2019)
11. Wang, A.: SuperGLUE: a stickier benchmark for general-purpose language understanding systems. arXiv preprint arXiv:1905.00537 (2019)
12. Hudson, D.A., Manning, Ch.D.: GQA: a new dataset for real-world visual reasoning and compositional question answering. arXiv preprint arXiv:1902.09506 (2019)
13. Weitnauer, E., Ritter, H.: Physical bongard problems. In: Iliadis, L., Maglogiannis, I., Papadopoulos, H. (eds.) AIAI 2012. IAICT, vol. 381, pp. 157–163. Springer, Heidelberg (2012). https://doi.org/10.1007/978-3-642-33409-2_17
14. Klenk, M., Forbus, K.: Analogical model formulation for transfer learning in AP physics. Artif. Intell. **173**(18), 1615–1638 (2009)
15. Sloman, A.: Kantian philosophy of mathematics and young robots. In: Autexier, S., Campbell, J., Rubio, J., Sorge, V., Suzuki, M., Wiedijk, F. (eds.) CICM 2008. LNCS (LNAI), vol. 5144, pp. 558–573. Springer, Heidelberg (2008). https://doi.org/10.1007/978-3-540-85110-3_45
16. Saxton, D., Grefenstette, E., Hill, F., Kohli, P.: Analysing mathematical reasoning abilities of neural models. In: International Conference on Learning Representations (2019). https://opencreview.net/forum?id=H1gR5iR5FX
17. Graves, A., et al.: Hybrid computing using a neural network with dynamic external memory. Nature **538**(7626), 471–476 (2016)
18. Schlag, I., et al.: Enhancing the transformer with explicit relational encoding for math problem solving. arXiv preprint arXiv:1910.06611 (2019)
19. Seo, M., et al.: Solving geometry problems: combining text and diagram interpretation. In: Proceedings Conference on Empirical Methods in Natural Language Processing, pp. 1466–1476 (2015)
20. Hosseini, M., Hajishirzi, H., Etzioni, O., Kushman, N.: Learning to solve arithmetic word problems with verb categorization. In: Proceedings of the 2014 Conference on Empirical Methods in Natural Language Processing (EMNLP), pp. 523–533 (2014)
21. Hopkins, M., et al.: SemEval 2019 task 10: math question answering. In: Proceedings of the 13th International Workshop on Semantic Evaluation (SemEval-2019), pp. 893–899 (2019)
22. Mitra, A., Baral, C.: Learning to automatically solve logic grid puzzles. In: Proceedings Conference on Empirical Methods in Natural Language Processing, pp. 1023–1033 (2015)
23. Sachan, M., Xing, E.: Learning to solve geometry problems from natural language demonstrations in textbooks. In: Proceedings of the 6th Joint Conference on Lexical and Computational Semantics, pp. 251–261 (2017)
24. Marcus, G.: The next decade in AI: four steps towards robust artificial intelligence. arXiv: 2002.06177 (2020)

The Meaning of Things as a Concept in a Strong AI Architecture

Alexey Redozubov🆔 and Dmitry Klepikov(✉)🆔

TrueBrainComputing, Moscow, Russia
alexey.redozubov@truebraincomputing.com,
klepikovdmitry@gmail.com

Abstract. Artificial intelligence becomes an integral part of human life. At the same time, modern widely used approaches, which work successfully due to the availability of enormous computing power, based on ideas about the work of the brain, suggested more than half a century ago. The proposed model describes the general principles of information processing by the human brain, taking into account the latest achievements. The neuroscientific grounding of this model and its applicability in the creation of AGI or Strong AI are discussed in the article. In this model, the cortical minicolumn is the primary computing processor that works with the semantic description of information. The minicolumn transforms incoming information into its interpretation to a specific context. In this way, a parallel verification of hypotheses of information interpretations is provided when comparing them with information in the memory of each minicolumn of the cortical zone, and, at the same time, determining a significant context is the information transformation rule. The meaning of information is defined as an interpretation that is close to the information available in the memory of a minicolumn. The behavior is a result of modeling of possible situations. Using this approach will allow creating a strong AI or AGI.

Keywords: Meaning of information · Artificial general intelligence · Strong AI · Brain · Cerebral cortex · Semantic memory · Information waves · Contextual semantic · Cortical minicolumns · Context processor · Hippocampus · Membrane receptors · Cluster of receptors · Dendrites

1 Introduction

1.1 Modern Neural Networks and the Brain - Are They Comparable?

There are several main fundamental issues in the field of information, the meaning of information and intelligence. In this paper, it is shown that, based on modern knowledge about the work of the brain [1], it is already possible to build a general theory of the work of the brain. We have a model of that, it is possible to use it to create an AGI or a strong AI, and it seems that this is the best way.

We have to ask the further question arguing that strong artificial intelligence is human-like: what human-like means? Many things were invented in the field of neural

© Springer Nature Switzerland AG 2020
B. Goertzel et al. (Eds.): AGI 2020, LNAI 12177, pp. 290–300, 2020.
https://doi.org/10.1007/978-3-030-52152-3_30

networks; they solve a lot of problems. But how close are modern neural networks to the brain? This question is divided into two others. How those formal neurons, used in neural networks, are close architecturally to the configurations of neural networks, their contacts, connections, training principles? Do they have something in common with arrangement of neurons of the brain and its structures? The second question is the ideology of learning, the logic of neural networks and the logic of the brain - are they comparable or not? Something can be reproduced; brain objects can be modeled on a computer in the form of mathematical models and assumed that they more or less reflect reality. Nevertheless, whether neural networks reflect some principles of cerebration is still an open question.

1.2 Difficulties in Determining the Essence of a Thing

When operating with information, we introduce terminology and determine what we are dealing with. Two and a half thousand years ago, Greek philosophers Socrates, Plato, Aristotle tried to storm probably the main problem of philosophy: to formulate what a phenomenon in general is. What are a thing and an object? Some concepts arose around the fact that when we deal with a thing, we can observe its external signs. Further, such a paradigm was introduced: the essence of things. Each thing has certain external signs that seem to define it. In addition, there is a certain essence that speaks about this more specific, but never expresses this in words. If the essence of a thing could be formulated in the same terms, the same words in which external signs were formulated, then there would be no questions, everything would come down to the same thing. It turns out that without answering this question, this is impossible to answer the question of human thinking.

1.3 Inability to Define Essence Through Signs

Returning to the real world, it suddenly turns out that everything is much more complicated. The name of this trouble is well known: a combinatorial explosion. When we are dealing not with two or three phenomena, but with thousands of them, tens of thousands, when these phenomena can take an incredible number of different forms, it turns out that there are no calculating capacities to list everything. Most importantly, if we try to apply this to a person, the whole life will not be enough to train the human brain using methods implemented by a neural network. Moreover, we know that a person does not need to be taught for a long time. Try to do this with a neural network, and it turns out that even if a neural network tries to remember all the signs, there will be a combinatorial explosion. How to avoid this combinatorial explosion? How does the brain do this?

2 The Meaning of Things

2.1 The Transition from Convolution Networks to Memory and Transformation

What is the meaning? It is clear that the question of the meaning of things is different; it can be formulated as a question of strong generalization. Once Frank Rosenblatt, who created the perceptron, the first neural network, formulated it [2]. This question has always been very acute to neural networks [3]. Now it's called convolutional networks. Convolutional networks have the convolution core; this is a kind of memory that stores letters, numbers, images that been remembered. It can be applied to different parts of the image. In that case, perhaps, we have learned to transform, recode, convert the information from this place of the image like so that it becomes in the same terms in which we have formed our memory.

However, the opposite is also possible: we've got a memory, and we know how to transform what we see in some other place of the picture to the one that is stored in the memory. It may not seem such an important and key point, but in fact, there is a large grain in this small conversion.

The key question is, how we do know the way to apply convolution rules to different parts of an image in a convolutional network? Why do we know that this can be done at all? The answer is obvious: this follows from the properties of the world, from its geometry. Nevertheless, it turns out that the same knowledge can be obtained; it can be learned by observing the world. First, one can construct a space of various displacements, and then, observing the result of the displacements, construct the necessary rules. The mechanism of saccades and microsaccades [4] allows the real brain to do all this. However, more importantly, that this principle allows obtaining knowledge related to information of any other origin.

2.2   The Change of Information in the Presence of a Phenomenon

What does a rule mean? For example, eyes have some movements, when the eye turns on a tiny angle; this is called microsaccades. When an eye makes a microsaccade, it turns out that when one image is transmitted to the brain, a slightly displaced image is transmitted after; the microsaccade is very fast so that we practically have the same image but in two positions. It is possible to calculate the rules of transformation, those consistent patterns that transfer one picture into another depending on a specific shift. It turns out that if you possess the movement of the eyes and get learning for a while, the brain will be able to find out these rules of transformation itself. Furthermore, if we take not only visual but also audio or any other information in general, then the same logic can be applied to such information. Summarizing - you can accept and observe information changes in the presence of any phenomenon. In the case of vision training, this phenomenon will be a shift. The fact of eye saccadic movements that are known to be encoded by the brain [4]: the superior colliculi gives a certain signal, which in turn is the code for this muscle movement and such a phenomenon in which the displacement occurs.

3   About the Brain Architecture

3.1   There Is No Grandmother Cell

McCulloch and Pitts had put forward a model of a formal neuron [5] as a threshold adder. Later it was suggested that a threshold function could be more complicated, any rules for the possibility for further operation. If you collect all these neurons in a net, you can get a construction that is difficult to explain its working. Nevertheless, it became possible to make such neural networks. These neural networks reflect the "Grandmother cell" paradigm.

There was a question: if a person reacts to the presence of his grandmother in some way, then there must be a neuron somewhere in the structures of his brain, which is activated when looking at his grandmother. It was possible to detect the reaction of a specific neuron presenting pictures of Jennifer Aniston [6]. However, whenever it was discovered, there was a disappointment, because grandmother cell reacted not only to Jennifer Aniston but to everyone from the series "Friends," and also to cats. As a result, neurophysiologists agreed that we could not detect grandmother cells. Also, Nobel laureates Hubel and Wiesel postulated that the neurons of the visual cortex reacted to certain stimuli [7]; they described these stimuli. Still, it turned out that they did not respond as clearly as they would like; in general, it was not that simple.

3.2 A Neuron Is Much More Complicated than Formal Neuron

The brain works quite not like that. This is primarily because the first positive assumptions that the neuron was similar to a threshold adder were not confirmed for more than the next half a century. Since then, many more investigations have been conducted on how a real neuron was arranged. A neuron is much more complicated in its nature.

Most of the computational processes of a real neuron occur at the level of receptor response to neurotransmitters, which is accompanied by miniature postsynaptic excitatory potentials and leads to processes with voltage levels approximately one millivolt. This is not yet available to detect modern instruments at a whole cortex level. The observed spike activity of neurons is already the final result of the complex hidden computational work of neurons, and it should not be compared with the work of a formal neuron.

3.3 Description of the Brain and Minicolumns

The cortex consists of the cortical minicolumns [8] - cylinders with a diameter of 50 μm with about a hundred neurons in each. These 100 neurons have very tight connections between themselves in the vertical direction, but in the horizontal direction with neighboring cortical cylinders, these links are much rarer. These minicolumns are the main functional element of the cortex. This has been repeatedly shown in a series of experiments [9]. The reaction of other columns is different from each other, but the principle that neighboring columns react similarly, "similar is located somewhere nearby," is generally maintained.

Vernon Mountcastle had put forward the hypothesis that the cortical column is the main structural unit of the brain when processing information [10]. Often a minicolumn is considered as a module that allows recognizing a certain phenomenon in its various demonstrations. For example, the capsule networks of Joffrey Hinton are very indicative in recent works of this direction [11].

It is possible to show by modelling [12] that each minicolumn is an independent computer, we name it as "context processor," an element that performs an enormous complex of calculations itself.

4   The Context Processor

4.1   Context, Transformation, Interpretation, Comparison with Memory

Let us return to the philosophical concept itself - what is the meaning of things. There are certain rules of transformation - "context," Context_N; we have input concepts I that we operate on in this context; the incoming information is transforming. Let's call the "interpretation" I'_N the result of this transformation. Any sentence, any phrase that you hear, any visual information that you receive: they do not contain meaning initially. However, it can be interpreted. When we give an interpretation, we transform one information into the other essentially. We formulate it in other words, describe it in other terms. We have different contexts - you can get an interpretation of this information for the same information in each of these contexts. At the same time, we will receive many interpretations, and ask ourselves the main question: which of these interpretations is correct? It turns out that it is possible to understand which interpretation is correct only in one way. It is necessary to compare whether this interpretation is similar to something that was met before, to compare interpretation with the memory **Memory**. If this interpretation is similar, perhaps this context is suitable to interpret this information (Fig. 1a).

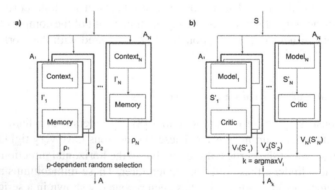

Fig. 1. a) Information transformation in minicolumns, b) choosing a behavior as modeling of possible actions in minicolumns

4.2   The Creation of Meaning

It turns out that in order to find meaning, it is necessary to declare that information at the input, raw information does not contain meaning. It is possible to get its interpretations in various contexts further. How many? Maybe in a million? A comparison of interpretations with memory will be made when an interpretation of the same information will be received in a million different contexts. It turns out that in some of the contexts, this interpretation of the information gives something similar to what there is in memory, perhaps that should be interpreted in this context. Possibly, there is some number of other contexts in which there will also be a comparison with memory. It happens that the same information has different meanings. If you need to choose the only one variant of meaning, it is possible to use probability selection ρ-dependent random selection (Fig. 1a).

This is precisely what the brain does. This is the function of cortical minicolumns of the cortex. Each of them is a context processor, which converts the incoming information into its context, giving an interpretation to this information. When this interpretation is obtained, the context compares it with its own memory.

5   Arrangement of Active Memory of the Brain

5.1   There Is No Specific Location of Memory in the Brain

The secret of memory is probably the number one mystery in all neuroscience. Everyone knows that memory exists, and no one knows where exactly. Any attempts to find out where the memory is stored in the brain, in our heads, lead to nothing. In due time neurophysiologist, Lashley conducted experiments [13], and he could not find the part of the brain that would be responsible for memories. It is known that there is a patient with strokes when significant areas of the brain are affected. As a rule, memory does not suffer. This is an amazing feature that memory exists, but you can't find it.

5.2   Membrane Receptors Are the Elements of Memory

Radchenko was the first who formulated clearly the possible role of membrane receptors in memory and indicates that the main element of memory were clusters of membrane receptors [14, 15], elements on the surface of a neuron. When there is such a cluster of receptors, it becomes a key that responds to strictly defined combinations of neurotransmitters to a specific chemical code. When there is specific information that is encoded by the activity of neurons, a combination of neurotransmitters appear in special places of minicolumn either. Receptive clusters are created when the process of memorization is in progress, and on recall from memory, they trig and create a certain polarization on the dendrite.

5.3   Minicolumn Information Capacity

Using this model, it was possible to show that the structure of 100 neurons of a minicolumn can store information approximately one gigabyte if transformed into modern measures of information. According to our model, the brain does not store images on their own. The brain stores its semantic descriptions and then reconstructs them. If you save semantic descriptions of what is happening to you, then you may believe that three thousand books are enough to write down your whole life as a very detailed diary. Each minicolumn can totally store all the memory of what is happening to a person during his life. Naturally, each zone of the cortex works with its specific type of information and stores in its form; nevertheless, each zone of the cortex does not just store all the information dealt with, it stores it distributed. However, not in the sense that something is stored here, and something other out there, but according to the principle that we now call the blockchain architecture, when each node stores a complete copy of all information. Hence, it is impossible to find where the memory is stored. Whatever part of the brain zone might be cut out, there will always be a copy of memory in other minicolumns.

5.4 Copies of the Same Memory for Parallel Computing

This copy of memory is stored everywhere, not for security reasons, in order not to lose anything. One zone of the cortex will have a million copies of the same memory. No, this is done for entirely different reasons. Remember Thuring, when Enigma had being deciphered [16], when each processor that made the code received the result, it was necessary to understand independently whether the expected words were there. Its own memory was required to respond to the correct interpretation. That is why each minicolumn has its own memory so that when the context processor, these one hundred neurons, converted information and received an interpretation, you could get an idea of whether we got what exactly we needed. We definitely need memory, which is called active.

5.5 Active Memory of Minicolumns

Computer memory usually works on request: indicating the register address, you'll get its value. Active memory works differently. Show something to the whole memory and ask: does anyone want to respond that he had found out. We call this part of our model "space of contexts." This is how the memory of the brain works with these minicolumns. Zones of the cortex form a space of contexts, any incoming information in this space of contexts are interpreted, and the interpretation is checked whether something can be recognized, whether something coincided with memory or not. In our model, the hippocampus is a generator of that keys which spread further throughout the cortex to create keys of memories. Information gives us content; the hippocampus gives us the key. Moreover, this key carries in those handy coded information labels about time, place, and much more [17–22].

5.6 Advantages of the Context-Semantic Model

In the contextual model, which works with meaning, it turns out that there is an initially different description of the information. In neural networks, a vector is taken, and each element of this vector describes some property of this phenomenon. For feature, the vector needs to determine how long it should be. Then you have to leave only the main signs to work only with them and reduce the dimension. What is the main feature? Dealing with letters, analyzing "O" and "Q," it turns out that the small tail on the side suddenly determines that it is "Q" and not "O," and losing of this tail leads to a mistake. If we come back to ordinary life, it turns out that nothing can be thrown away at all. You never know what will turn out to be the very key sign. The context-semantic model resembles the Hierarchical Temporal Memory (HTM) of Jeff Hawkins [23], but the role of minicolumns in HTM and here is entirely different. In some ways, our model is similar to Hinton's capsule networks [24].

6 Semantic Memory

6.1 Assumptions About Semantics in the Brain

We assume that all information is stored in a semantic form in the brain. It is not by chance that people have language; it is not by chance that we have learned to express our thoughts semantically. We undertake to assert that brain structures, even starting from the zone of the visual cortex V1 [25], do not work with analog signals, but with semantic information. Each zone of the cortex has its language, its image, representation, but it is still semantic.

6.2 Transition to a Discrete Model

The transition to a discrete model is significant here. A discrete model is a separate concept that avoids a combinatorial explosion. In many ways, the nature of the combinatorial explosion is connected with the continuum model, with the continuity of the space we work with. As soon as we can have any values, the number of combinations becomes incredible and infinite. When talking about discrete values, there can be many, but this is an entirely different capacity of multiplicity, this is an entirely different "many." The main struggle against a combinatorial explosion is to do this at every stage so that this "many" from "impossible to calculate" turns into "finite" so that you can work with it [26, 27].

6.3 Quantization as Computability

In lectures on this subject [28] where we suppose that the physical world is the result of the evolution of universes, that the laws of our universe are their existence "as they are," and not the multiplicity of worlds where all possible variants of physical laws are examined, but this is the result of the evolution of universes, which led them precisely to the laws for a specific purpose. We got the rules of quantum mechanics as a result of the fact that physical laws were formed. Because, when the world is quantized, in the rules of quantum mechanics, it becomes finite.

6.4 Combinatorial Space in Minicolumns

By the way, this is implemented nicely from biology, because having the structure of a minicolumn, synapses and everything next to them, that forms the combinatorial space of a minicolumn, where axons and dendrites, make a vast number of random places for storing codes descriptions due to random intersections. Then there is the algorithm described above.

7   The Behavior

7.1   Behavior as a Result of Work of Context Processors

The assumptions here below are about the model, how the behavior is arranged, how some action, some motion in the brain is born from the processes. Moreover, it seems, the process of thought formation is the same act, which expressed not in muscle activity, but in a change of information picture of the world. Thinking and doing is basically the same thing. There is only one question, what mechanism controls this?

The benefit of a contextual approach is that it is possible to recognize the phenomenon immediately. What is the genius of the approach that the brain "invented" to avoid the combinatorial explosion? In order to recognize a phenomenon, it is not necessary to see it in all contexts. Detected it in one context - remembered in all - the next time this phenomenon will be recognized in a different context, even if it was never seen. The transformation rules will be different, but the memory will detect this phenomenon anyway if it was known before.

It turns out that for behavior, there is no other way to do this if it is necessary to realize a variety of actions. The brain does not do calculations on the principle of "let us find out the situation; now let us see what needs to be done in this situation."

7.2   Choosing a Behavior

Reinforced learning faces a certain difficulty when it turns out in practical problems that the space of possible agent states and the number of actions possible in these states is so great that learning is difficult. The way out of this situation was offered in the concept of adaptive V-critics [29].

The space of contexts might be the space of all possible actions that can be performed. And there are transformation rules that predict how the current world description will change if this action is applied. Each context builds its forecast of the future, that picture of the world that will be if this action is applied. Then there is what we have learned - the ability to evaluate, evaluation - this is already an experience. The action takes place not because we learned something and know what to do, but because we modeled all possible actions and chose the one that promises us the best perspective.

The process of choosing the optimal behavior is presented schematically as follows (Fig. 1b).

Information about the current situation S goes to the context processors - minicolumns in parallel. Each minicolumn A_N as its context has a model of one of the possible actions $Model_N$ and converts the input information S into the interpretation S'_N - information about the consequence of performing step A, how this action will change the current situation into a possible future one. Each minicolumn computes its model independently and parallelly, and then the interpretation is served to the **Critic** critic input, which compares the possible future situation with the memory, compares the interpretation with the memory, and evaluates the quality of the possible future situation $V_N(S'_N)$. The results of all possible assessments of the quality of future situations are processed, and the best one is selected. In order to implement research behavior, it is possible to use probabilistic choice instead of **argmax**. There are recent works [30] confirming the role of quantum mechanics in decision-making by the brain.

As we can see, the task of choosing a variant of behavior and parallel processing of semantic information in a minicolumn look very similar in this model. Moreover, the cognitive functions are also a result of a context-semantic approach on higher levels of abstraction. From this, the theory of emotions flows further, and the opportunity to explain what love is, what humor is, and a lot of exciting things.

8 Conclusion and Future Directions

Humankind does not know an instrument better than the human brain for working with a wide variety of information, solving intellectual problems, inventing new things, and creativity. It would be strange when solving the task of creating artificial intelligence not to try to copy what had arisen as a result of millions of years of evolution. Based on modern scientific knowledge about the brain we have formulated a fundamental general concept how the brain works: cortical minicolumns are the main basic computing processors, total storage of semantic memory in minicolumns of the cortical zone, parallel interpretation of information in each minicolumn in its context, comparison of the obtained interpretation with memory; the response of that minicolumn, in the context of which the interpretation has found correspondence with memory. We suggest moving towards building an AGI or Strong AI according to this concept [31].

Acknowledgments. We thank our colleagues from TrueBrainComputing for the discussion of ideas. The authors express their deep gratitude to Olga Pavlovich for translation.

References

1. Jacklet, J.W.: From neuron to brain. John G. Nicholls, A. Robert Martin, Bruce G. Wallace, Paul A. Fuchs (2001). http://dx.doi.org/10.1086/420639
2. Rosenblatt, F.: Principles of neurodynamics. Perceptrons and the theory of brain mechanisms (1961). http://dx.doi.org/10.21236/ad0256582
3. Fukushima, K.: Neocognitron: a self-organizing neural network model for a mechanism of pattern recognition unaffected by shift in position (1980). http://dx.doi.org/10.1007/bf0034 4251
4. Yarbus, A.L.: Saccadic eye movements (1967). http://dx.doi.org/10.1007/978-1-4899-537 9-7_5
5. Mcculloch, W.S., Pitts, W.: A logical calculus of the ideas immanent in nervous activity (1943)
6. Quiroga, R.Q., Quian Quiroga, R., Reddy, L., Kreiman, G., Koch, C., Fried, I.: Invariant visual representation by single neurons in the human brain (2005). http://dx.doi.org/10.1038/nature 03687
7. Li, X.-J., Xiao-Jian, L.I., Jiang, Z., Wang, Y.: The temporal responses of neurons in the primary visual cortex to transient stimuli* (2013). http://dx.doi.org/10.3724/sp.j.1206.2012. 00136
8. Rockland, K., Ichinohe, N.: Some thoughts on cortical minicolumns (2004). http://dx.doi. org/10.1007/s00221-004-2024-9

9. Tanaka, K.: Columns for complex visual object features in the inferotemporal cortex: clustering of cells with similar but slightly different stimulus selectivities (2003). http://dx.doi.org/10.1093/cercor/13.1.90

10. Edelman, G.M., Mountcastle, V.B.: The mindful brain: cortical organization and the group-selective theory of higher brain function. By Gerald M. Edelman, Vernon b. Mountcastle. Introduction by Francis O. Schmitt (1979)

11. Sara, S., Nicholas, F., Geoffrey, E.H.: Dynamic routing between capsules (2017). https://arxiv.org/pdf/1710.09829.pdf

12. Logic of Thinking/Programs. http://www.aboutbrain.ru/programs/

13. Stellar, E.: Physiological mechanisms in animal behaviour. In: 1950 Symposia of the Society for Experimental Biology, vol. 482, no. IV, p. $6.00. Academic Press, New York (1951). http://dx.doi.org/10.1126/science.114.2957.245

14. Radchenko, R.: Information mechanisms of neuron and neural memory (2014). http://dx.doi.org/10.15622/sp.1.17

15. Radchenko, R.: The information key to brain memory problem (2014). http://dx.doi.org/10.15622/sp.3.22

16. Hodges, A.: Alan Turing: The Enigma: The Book That Inspired the Film the Imitation Game – Updated Edition. Princeton University Press, Princeton (2014)

17. Scoville, W.B., Milner, B.: Loss of recent memory after bilateral hippocampal lesions. J. Neurol. Neurosurg. Psychiatr. **20**, 11–21 (1957)

18. Eichenbaum, H.: Perspectives on 2014 nobel prize. Hippocampus **25**, 679–681 (2015)

19. O'Keefe, J., Dostrovsky, J.: The hippocampus as a spatial map. Preliminary evidence from unit activity in the freely-moving rat (1971). http://dx.doi.org/10.1016/0006-8993(71)90358-1

20. MacDonald, C.J., Lepage, K.Q., Eden, U.T., Eichenbaum, H.: Hippocampal "time cells" bridge the gap in memory for discontiguous events (2011). http://dx.doi.org/10.1016/j.neuron.2011.07.012

21. Languages of the Brain: Experimental paradoxes and principles in neuropsychology By Karl H. Pribram. (pp. 432; illustrated; £4·75.) Prentice-Hall: Hemel Hempstead 1972 (1973). http://dx.doi.org/10.1017/s0033291700048698

22. Redozubov, A.: Holographic memory: a novel model of information processing by neuronal microcircuits (2017). http://dx.doi.org/10.1007/978-3-319-29674-6_13

23. Jeff, H., Sandra, B.: On intelligence. Times Books **5**, 11 (2004)

24. Sabour, S., Frosst, N., Hinton, G.E.: Dynamic routing between capsules (2017). http://arxiv.org/abs/1710.09829

25. Diogo, A.C.M., Soares, J.G.M., Koulakov, A., Albright, T.D., Gattass, R.: Electrophysiological imaging of functional architecture in the cortical middle temporal visual area of cebus apella monkey (2003). http://dx.doi.org/10.1523/jneurosci.23-09-03881.2003

26. Anshakov, O.M., Finn, V.K., Skvortsov, D.P.: On axiomatization of many-valued logics associated with formalization of plausible reasonings. Stud. Logica. **48**, 423–447 (1989)

27. Wille, R.: Restructuring lattice theory: an approach based on hierarchies of concepts (1982). http://dx.doi.org/10.1007/978-94-009-7798-3_15

28. Redozubov, A.: Logic of consciousness, Part 14. Consciousness, https://youtu.be/8v8z4Xzt0hc

29. Prokhorov, D.V., Wunsch, D.C.: Adaptive critic designs (1997). http://dx.doi.org/10.1109/72.623201

30. Li, J.-A., et al.: Quantum reinforcement learning during human decision-making. Nat. Hum. Behav. **4**, 294–307 (2020)

31. True Brain Computing. http://truebraincomputing.com/

Toward a General Believable Model of Human-Analogous Intelligent Socially Emotional Behavior

Alexei V. Samsonovich(⊠) , Arthur A. Chubarov, Daria V. Tikhomirova, and Alexander A. Eidln

National Research Nuclear University MEPhI, Kashirskoe hwy 31, Moscow, Russian Federation
avsamsonovich@mephi.ru, osgilat17@gmail.com, dvsulim@mail.ru,
a.aidlin@gmail.com

Abstract. Social virtual actors need to interact with users emotionally, convincing them in their ability to understand human minds. For this to happen, an artificial emotional intelligence is needed, capable of believable behavior in real-life situations. Summarizing recent work of the authors, the present paper extends the general state-of-the-art framework of emotional AGI, using the emotional Biologically Inspired Cognitive Architecture (eBICA) as a basis. In addition to appraisals, other kinds of fluents are added to the model: somatic markers, feelings, emotional biases, moods, etc. Their integration is achieved on the basis of semantic maps and moral schemas. It is anticipated that this new level of artificial general socially emotional intelligence will complement the next-generation AGI, helping it to merge into the human society on equal with its human members.

Keywords: Socially emotional intelligence · BICA challenge · Semantic map

1 Introduction: Overview of Existing Approaches

A generic cognitive architecture block-diagram is represented in Fig. 1A. It includes sensory and motor memory (input-output), procedural memory, (automated skills), semantic memory (general knowledge), episodic memory (autobiographical memories, goals and plans), value system (drives, values, semantic maps), and working memory (awareness), that also includes metacognition, imagery and feelings. Arguably, all original and new implemented cognitive architectures [1, 6, 7] fit into this general scheme. Yet, something must be missing or hidden here, because intelligent agents that we know are not perceived as live beings capable of feelings, let alone at the human level.

Possibly, the devil is in the question: how to add human-level emotionality to a cognitive architecture? There were many attempts to provide a general answer to this question at a computational level [2, 5, 12, 21]. Most of the proposed approaches are based on some version of an appraisal theory [8, 20]. However, it is hard to accept that the vast richness of human emotionality reduces to cognitive appraisals. Certainly, there are other qualia known to us, such as feelings, moods, somatic sensations, affects,

© Springer Nature Switzerland AG 2020
B. Goertzel et al. (Eds.): AGI 2020, LNAI 12177, pp. 301–305, 2020.
https://doi.org/10.1007/978-3-030-52152-3_31

etc. The generalizing notion of "emotion" has many aspects and many senses. Notably, it is multidimensional, including anything from the most general standard dimensions of Valence, Arousal and Dominance, to the standard set of basic emotions, to more subtle aspects, such as support, disclosure and so on. In addition, it involves some internal structure and hierarchy, responsible for differences between, e.g., the notions of compassion, gloat and joy, jealousy and rage, humor and happiness.

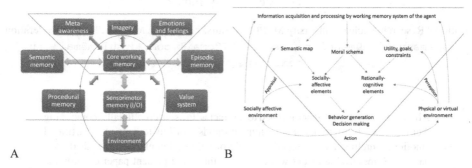

Fig. 1. A: Generic cognitive architecture. The red oval represents the cognitive cycle. **B:** A blueprint of a cognitive architecture, unifying rational and emotional cognition.

Speaking of dimensions, various models of emotional or affective spaces were proposed that mostly converge to one common scheme of a 2-D or 3-D semantic map of emotions [9, 15–17]. These dimensional models are complemented by the componential models [13, 14] that represent phenomenology formalized in terms of appraisal theories, but do not explain the nature of the phenomena or its developmental aspects.

This gap is filled by neuroscience-based theories, among which the most popular one is the somatic marker hypothesis [4, 10, 22]. Unfortunately, most of these theories are not computational, at least not at the level allowing one to build a working prototype of autonomous emotional agent, such as examples based on appraisal theories [2, 7, 11].

2   The New Approach

The approach pursued by our research group is based on the notion that a human-analogous socially emotional intelligent actor must be guided in its behavior by three factors that normally complement each other, and under some circumstances may compete.

1. Purely rational, based on a given goal, mission or existing plan.
2. Cognitive, based on appraisals in terms of the notions of good and bad.
3. Somatic, following the somatic marker hypothesis and laws of physiology.

Their complementarity is based on the freedom of choice left by each of them. The diagrams (Fig. 2) illustrate the structure of corresponding dynamic laws governing the complementary fluents that determine actor's behavior. One key notion here is that of a moral schema [18, 19, 23]. Considered as an agent on its own, a moral schema biases actor's behavior in such a way that the "normal" condition is restored. When this is not possible, the schema changes its state, leading to the emergence of new emotions [19].

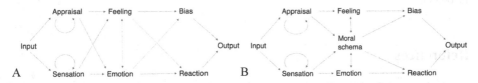

Fig. 2. Logical model of interactions among emotional fluents: (A) without and (B) with engagement of a moral schema. From [19].

3   Outline of Preliminary Results and Conclusions

The approach outlined above was used to design, implement, test and study in experiments with human participants a variety of virtual actors, from autonomous cobots to creative assistants working as extensions to the human mind. Implementations and studies were based on a unique, specially designed experimental platform allowing various forms of multimodal data collection [3]. Examples of successful prototypes include an NPC for videogames [24] (four different game paradigms), a virtual listener/reader/interlocutor [3], a virtual pet, a virtual dance partner, a composer assistant, and more.

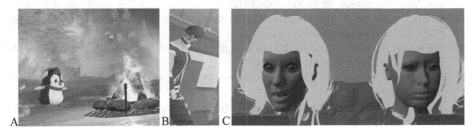

Fig. 3. Examples of successful prototypes, implemented based on the described approach. **A:** Virtual pet. **B:** Virtual dance partner. **C:** Virtual listeners passing a limited Turing test (from [3]).

In each case, the implemented prototype was subjected to a limited Turing test. Passing this test was a precondition, required to ensure a certain level of believability. Other measures included social acceptability and effectiveness in collaborative work with a human partner. Moreover, standard psychological personality tests were extended to virtual actors in selected paradigms. Examples of implementations are shown in Fig. 3.

In conclusion, the developed technology adds new dimensions to artificial emotionality. As a result, useful practical applications become possible, including a virtual poster presenter (a part of the Virtual Convention Center platform) and a pedagogical agent, a part of an ITS. These our new expected results will be reported elsewhere.

Speaking generally, the approach based on the eBICA framework is promising us a breakthrough in the field of human-analogous intelligent socially emotional agents.

Acknowledgments. This work was supported by the Russian Science Foundation Grant # 18-11-00336.

References

1. Anderson, J.R.: How Can the Human Mind Occur in the Physical Universe?. Oxford University Press, New York (2007)
2. Breazeal, C.: Emotion and sociable humanoid robots. Int. J. Hum.-Comput. Stud. **59**(1–2), 119–155 (2003)
3. Chubarov, A.A., Tikhomirova, D.V., Shirshova, A.V., Veselov, N.O., Samsonovich, A.V.: Virtual listener: a turing-like test for behavioral believability. Procedia Comput. Sci. **169**, 892–899 (2020)
4. Damasio, A.R.: Descartes' Error: Emotion, Reason and the Human Brain. Random House, New York (1994). ISBN 978-1-4070-7206-7
5. Gratch, J., Marsella, S.: A domain-independent framework for modeling emotion. Cogn. Syst. Res. **5**, 269–306 (2004)
6. Gray, W.D. (ed.): Integrated Models of Cognitive Systems. Series on Cognitive Models and Architectures. Oxford University Press, Oxford (2007)
7. Laird, J.E.: The Soar Cognitive Architecture. MIT Press, Cambridge (2012)
8. Lazarus, R.S.: Hope: an emotion and a vital coping resource against despair. Soc. Res. **66**, 653–678 (1999)
9. Lövheim, H.: A new three-dimensional model for emotions and monoamine neurotransmitters. Med. Hypotheses **78**(2), 341–348 (2012)
10. Man, K., Damasio, A.: Homeostasis and soft robotics in the design of feeling machines. Nat. Mach. Intell. **1**, 446–452 (2019)
11. Mariner, R.P., Laird, J.E., Lewis, R.L.: A computational unification of cognitive behavior and emotion. Cogn. Syst. Res. **10**, 48–69 (2009)
12. Marsella, S.C., Gratch, J.: EMA: a process model of appraisal dynamics. Cogn. Syst. Res. **10**, 70–90 (2009)
13. Meyer, J.-J.Ch.: Reasoning about emotional agents. In: Proceedings of ECAI 2004, pp. 129–133. IOS Press (2004)
14. Ortony, A., Clore, G., Collins, A.: The Cognitive Structure of Emotions. Cambridge University Press, Cambridge (1988)
15. Osgood, C.E., Suci, G., Tannenbaum, P.: The Measurement of Meaning. University of Illinois Press, Urbana (1957)
16. Plutchik, R.: A psychoevolutionary theory of emotions. Soc. Sci. Inf. **21**, 529–553 (1982)
17. Russell, J.A.: A circumplex model of affect. J. Personal. Soc. Psychol. **39**(6), 1161–1178 (1980)
18. Samsonovich, A.V.: On semantic map as a key component in socially-emotional BICA. Biol. Inspired Cogn. Archit. **23**, 1–6 (2018)
19. Samsonovich, A.V.: Socially emotional brain-inspired cognitive architecture framework for artificial intelligence. Cogn. Syst. Res. **60**, 57–76 (2020)
20. Scherer, K.R.: Appraisal theory. In: Dalgleish, T., Power, M. (eds.) Handbook of Cognition and Emotion, pp. 637–663. Wiley, London (1999)
21. Sloman, A.: Beyond shallow models of emotion. Cogn. Process. **2**(1), 177–198 (2001)

22. Leland, J.W., Grafman, J.: Experimental tests of the Somatic Marker hypothesis. Games Econ. Behav. **52**(2), 386–409 (2005)
23. Samsonovich, A.V.: Emotional biologically inspired cognitive architecture. Biol. Inspired Cogn. Archit. **6**, 109–125 (2013)
24. Tikhomirova, D.V., Chubarov, A.A., Samsonovich, A.V.: Empirical and modeling study of emotional state dynamics in social videogame paradigms. Cogn. Syst. Res. **60**, 44–56 (2020)

Autonomous Cumulative Transfer Learning

Arash Sheikhlar[1]([✉]), Kristinn R. Thórisson[1,2], and Leonard M. Eberding[1,3]

[1] Center for Analysis and Design of Intelligent Agents, Reykjavik Univerxity,
Reykjavik, Iceland
{arashs,thorisson}@ru.is
[2] Icelandic Institute for Intelligent Machines, Reykjavik, Iceland
[3] Institute of Photogrammetry and GeoInformation, Leibniz University,
Hannover, Germany
l.eberding@stud.uni-hannover.de
http://cadia.ru.is/, https://www.ipi.uni-hannover.de/

Abstract. Autonomous knowledge transfer from a known task to a new one requires discovering task similarities and knowledge generalization without the help of a designer or teacher. How transfer mechanisms in such learning may work is still an open question. Transfer of knowledge makes most sense for learners for whom novelty is regular (other things being equal), as in the physical world. When new information must be unified with existing knowledge over time, a *cumulative learning mechanism* is required, increasing the breadth, depth, and accuracy of an agent's knowledge over time, as experience accumulates. Here we address the requirements for what we refer to as autonomous cumulative transfer learning (ACTL) in novel task-environments, including implementation and evaluation criteria, and how it relies on the process of *similarity* and *ampliative reasoning*. While the analysis here is theoretical, the fundamental principles of the cumulative learning mechanism in our theory have been implemented and evaluated in a running system described priorly. We present arguments for the theory from an empirical as well as analytical viewpoint.

Keywords: Transfer learning · Cumulative learning · Novelty · Similarity · Ampliative reasoning · Analogy · Autonomy

1 Introduction

Any agent with general intelligence must be able to deal with novel situations. Since novelty is relative to a learner's knowledge of the world, one way to handle novelty – whether it is a novel juxtaposition of familiar things, a never-before-seen variable or factor, or something entirely new – is to use priorly experienced, seemingly similar situations, for guidance. This is what the canonical concept in psychology of transfer learning (TL) (or *transfer of training*) refers to [4].

© Springer Nature Switzerland AG 2020
B. Goertzel et al. (Eds.): AGI 2020, LNAI 12177, pp. 306–316, 2020.
https://doi.org/10.1007/978-3-030-52152-3_32

What is at stake is an application of prior knowledge and training to new circumstances which may be mostly identical, somewhat similar, or wildly different from what the agent has seen. Since novelty abounds in the physical world, this must be (partly) how learning works in nature: They can *autonomously* (without teacher[1] intervention) transfer prior experience to a new situation to (a) classify it, (b) identify its principal factors in light of active goals, (c) view it in light of prior experience of similar situations, (d) create and initiate relevant goal-driven actions, and (e) monitor progress in light of predicted outcomes and adjust actions accordingly, possibly involving *a, b, c* and *d*.

This kind of TL requires methods for measures of similarity and relevance, and a *compositional* knowledge representation, since new situations may overlap only partly with existing knowledge. It is *cumulative* due to the integration of new with old information, but also in that the selective application of prior experience is furthermore subject to learning: If incorrect conclusions are drawn when judging similarity and relevance this can be retroactively dissected, inspected, and learned from. A major mechanism for the comparison of similarity is analogies, and this is in turn what is learned: Improved analogy making.

Other kinds of reasoning, however, are also necessary – abduction, deduction, and induction[2] – which means we are really talking about *ampliative reasoning*[3] [17]. The more domain-independent the cumulative learning is, the more effective and efficient knowledge accumulation can become, and this is where ampliative reasoning enters the picture: Using (a) deduction for prediction, based on learned (hypothesized) principles, (b) abduction for deriving plausible causes, and (c) analogies for adapting acquired knowledge to new situations, multiple lines of reasoning can help the learner exclude certain things while highlighting others, more quickly getting to the crux of how to achieve any task in light of prior experience. Finally, (d) induction enables generalization based on invariants across multiple tasks and situations. Reasoning in the physical world must be non-axiomatic because there is no ultimate guarantee that anything is as it seems, and thus cognitive reasoning cannot follow the rules of formal reasoning [16]. Logic can steer the knowledge accumulation process and enables the cognitive system to make predictions, do planning and transfer its knowledge.

In this paper we present a theoretical analysis of transfer learning (TL), based in part on this prior work, with an attempt to put it into the context of both narrow artificial intelligence (AI) systems and general machine intelligence (GMI). To avoid confusion, our aims target learners capable of cumulative learning; in particular, this context may not be compatible with other work that may use the term"transfer learning" and similar ones, especially if it is incompatible in some way with the general aims of GMI research that involve autonomy

---

[1] We define a teacher as a process outside the learner whose interaction helps reduce the search space for a solution to a goal or task.

[2] Unless otherwise noted, we use the term induction in the reasoning sense, not in Solomonoff's "universal induction" sense [11].

[3] Peirce's use of the concept of 'ampliative reasoning' included abduction, induction and analogy [10]; ours adds (corrigible) deduction to that list.

and lifelong, incremental learning. Faced with a particular situation, a learner capable of autonomous cumulative transfer learning (ACTL) is able to select a specific model or modeling paradigm on its own accord, in light of an analogy that it has itself come up with for each situation it may encounter, and if no models exist, creates a new set of models to use in the novel situation. The ACTL process relies in part on selective comparison of similarity and high-level analogy-making.

To build an intelligent machine that can create its own knowledge and autonomously transfer it to different related situations, evaluate the outcome, and learn from this, all autonomously, an architecture is needed that can make analogies on its own accord and, rather than relying on a human's intuition about similarity and relevance, create its own knowledge for how to do that, based on its own understanding of the world. For GMI the focus needs to be on the actions listed above (a to e), and these need to be integrated with ampliative reasoning. To our knowledge, two approaches to cumulative transfer learning have been demonstrated to date, the Autocatalytic Endogenous Reflective Architecture (AERA) [6] and NARS [16], but an analysis of these specific to TL remains to be done.

2   Related Work

Transfer learning (TL) has made an appearance in various machine learning (ML) paradigms to date, invariably with the shared goal of increasing learning rate and improving its flexibility. Working on deep neural networks (DNNs) some have implemented a scheme where a human programmer selects a subset of trained network's layers and reuses them to train another network in a similar related domain [18]. Working with the concept of TL in reinforcement learning (RL) techniques, others have trained RL for a task and then re-purposed it to a similar one [13]. In these approaches a human software developer must often choose tasks and make the necessary analogies between the tasks. Such an approach falls short of what is needed for autonomous general machine intelligence (GMI), where the machine must do this automatically and on its own accord, including making the analogies, learning from them, and unifying any new knowledge produced this way with existing knowledge.

The agent must determine "what, when, how, and why" its knowledge should be chosen and transferred to another task. Most current TL methods assume that the transfer is done offline, that is, happening before the agent starts learning the target task, and thus the question of *when* to transfer has not been much addressed in ML research to date. In addition, a human programmer decides *what* should be transferred, according to their own intuition or sense of similarity. Thus, task similarity is another topic that has largely been out of scope in ML research, although a handful of papers have proposed task mappings via concepts from bisimulation [2] and homomorphism [12]. Efficient methodologies are needed to autonomously identify similarities, use the most relevant knowledge, and do TL while the agent is learning and performing the task.

Bayesian program TL models, such as [7], are based on Solomonof's theory of inductive inference [11], which assumes a probability distribution for all computer programs and makes predictions using a Bayesian framework. While probabilistic models may suffice for general prediction (including Solomonoff's "universal induction" [11]), they do not suffice for identifying causal relations [8,15]. As detailed by Pearl [8], in probability theory, even when one considers the joint density functions on all time-dependent variables, the distributions are static, while causation by itself deals with the change in distributions that can result from new circumstances or external actions, and therefore, there is no point in fusing Bayesian and causal calculations. Since knowledge of causal relations is a necessary foundation for acting intelligently in the world, and the ability to extract causal relations are a precondition for *autonomous* cumulative learning, relying exclusively on principles of probability will not suffice for systems intended to learn autonomously and cumulatively.

For transfer learning to work well, any knowledge that is created should be stored in a format that is amenable to be useful in many future situations. In some cognitive architectures employing a global workspace, such as DSO [5], knowledge transfer uses the most relevant existing knowledge in different situations/tasks. NARS [16] and AERA [6] achieve TL in a similar fashion: AERA generalizes knowledge by generating variations of its models and testing them for effectiveness, so that knowledge becomes increasingly useful in similar but unseen situations over time [15].

3   Autonomous Cumulative Transfer Learning—A Theory

We consider the *novelty* of an experienced phenomenon Φ a measure on its *familiarity to a cognitive agent*—how similar Φ's aspects are to the agent's available current knowledge. Familiarity, in turn, is anchored in the concept of *similarity*. We assume a phenomenon Φ such as state, a process, an occurrence, etc. to consist of aspects[4] made up of elements $\{\varphi_1 \ldots \varphi_n \in \Phi\}$ of various kinds, including relations $\Re_\Phi$ (causal, mereological, sub-structural, etc.) and transitions T_Φ (component processes, transformations, etc., i.e. sub-divisions of Φ), that couple sub-parts of Φ with each other (and with those of other phenomena). Operationally, given a cognitive agent in a task-environment TE and a particular such target phenomenon Φ,

> **if the agent can predict a particular selected aspect $\varphi_i \in \Phi$, $i \in 1, \ldots, n$, using its prior knowledge, then φ_i is familiar to the agent, and non-novel.**

---

[4] We use 'aspects' as shorthand for 'sub-divisions of a phenomenon that are of *pragmatic importance* to an agent's goals and tasks'.

If the agent can do so for all important aspects of Φ it may be claimed "completely" familiar, and thus non-novel.[5]

An agent whose knowledge is compositional – that is, consisting of models made up of smaller models, and can be meaningfully decomposed in a multitude of ways – can, for every complex Φ with a large number of aspects, test its ability to predict each of those aspects $(\varphi_1, \ldots, \varphi_n \in \Phi)$ and record the result; the outcome would be a set $\Phi_{nov} \subset \Phi$ of aspects that are novel, i.e. that the agent fails to predict.

Prediction of a phenomenon must cover the dynamic interference or perturbation (by the agent itself or something else), and thus some of the relations modeled must include causality. Since causal relations in a lawful world make it possible to generate and use rules, and this is much more efficient than enumerating all relevant relations, the agent's cognitive system must contain some rule-handling mechanisms—reasoning. Reasoning may also be important for selecting which aspects are important for which situations or tasks. Building up knowledge incrementally over time means making a model composed of smaller models that increasingly explains target phenomena, not unlike the process of scientific empirical research. As we have argued elsewhere [14], ampliative reasoning (combined deduction, abduction, induction and analogies) is a way to manage knowledge created under these requirements.

We define a similarity function, Ψ, that compares two sets of knowledge, whether aspects, states, or sets of variables. To compute the familiarity of φ, where φ can be a set of variables, aspects, or a whole phenomenon composed of those, the agent must retrieve *relevant* knowledge from its knowledge base, $k \subset \text{KB}$, for comparison, $\Phi_{fam} = \Psi(k, \varphi)$, where Ψ is a multi-dimensional comparison computation using ampliative reasoning. Other things being equal, the less familiar something is to the agent, the more novel it is, $\Phi_{fam} \cup \Phi_{nov} = \Phi$. Novelty is thus always relative to the agent's own current knowledge and is multi-dimensional and continuous. Since increments in familiarity is equivalent to novelty reduction, our notion of familiarity may be used to guide learning – acquisition of more accurate and precise knowledge – enabling an agent to better predict, which in turn improves goal achievement over time.

Relevant knowledge in our theory is retrieved based on the comparison's goal—the *purpose* of the comparison. Since explicit goals must be defined by referencing particular variables and their values, the variables of importance for the comparison are already known when it is made. For instance, should a carpenter need a substitute for a nail, the stiffness of that substitute is an important variable. A prop director for a Hollywood movie about carpenters, however, does not need to be concerned with stiffness of nails, only that they reflect light properly for the relevant scenes. Through reasoning from the goal, backward chaining will help identify relevant prerequisites, producing a set of

---

[5] Since phenomena in the physical world contain an infinite set of subdivisions such a claim would always be limited by pragmatic considerations (see prior footnote). Time and energy will also present hard limits for any such consideration. Thus, there is no literal sense in which complete familiarity may be reached.

variables, models, rules, heuristics, and etc (as per an agent's particular cognitive mechanisms), that are considered relevant for the similarity comparison.

The transfer learning mechanism we propose states that the multidimensional similarity computation is used to identify overlap between new patterns and previously learned patterns and use it to solve new tasks. An autonomous cumulative transfer learner (ACTL) makes analogies and comparisons regarding the number, values, dynamics, and importance of sets of percepts[6] and inferred relations through ampliative reasoning, extracting the importance of each identified perceived variable (or state) and in parallel, discovers the proper set of important variables (of each state), the values of these variables and the dynamics between the variables and their values.

The AERA-S1 system [6] was constructed based on a proto-version of this theory and demonstrated to be capable of learning highly complex tasks from observation. Its operational results concur with the theory's predictions, lending it some positive evidence. Below we provide further arguments in support for it, from two angles, one analytical the other empirical.

4   Detailed Argument from Similarity

A theoretical argument for the coherence and completeness of our theory of transfer learning stated above can be made by examining its implications in more detail. While the below outline does not address implementation in a cognitive architecture, prior work on the Autocatalytic Endogenous Reflective Architecture (AERA) [6] provides an operational partial demonstration of what this might entail. Our argument here rests on comparing states, which consist of the percepts the agent receives via observation of variables and related values, and various ways of looking for similarities. So, more specifically, given the following:

- A variable whose value can be measured at some point during the agent's lifetime is an *exposable* variable. At any point in time, some or all exposable variables are *observable* to the agent. The set of exposable variables V_e is not time-dependent, while the set of observables V_o is;
- the physical changes the agent produces via its actuators. There are variables, *affectable variables* V_a, whose values change through the agent's action.
- transition functions (via physical forces) that determine the values of variables and their *relations* at any point in time;
- an agent's knowledge of a task, in the form of task goal(s) and subgoal(s);
- a *percept* being sets of variables, in the above sense, generated by sensors here-and-now;
- an *aspect* being a sub-division of a phenomenon, involving selected groupings of variables and their relations, that are of pragmatic importance to an agent's goals and tasks,

---

[6] The term 'percept' as used here references sets of variables in the preceding sense, whether generated by sensors here-and-now, retrieved from memory, or imaginatively constructed.

we assume that the task-environment with its variables is given, and the state space is partially observable at any point in time, received by the agent as a sequence of states over its life-time. A phenomenon going through changes is considered a sequence of states connected by a set of relevant transition functions dictated by the world. The state of a phenomenon, from the agent's perspective, is composed of its set of observable variables. Taking actions on some affectable variables, V_a – i.e. manipulating the environment – may alter the values of variables and/or change the exposable but unobservable variables to being observable (or vice versa), revealing new aspects of a phenomenon (e.g. rotating a dice to see its back side). This is an important way for a learner to test predictions regarding any phenomenon, as well as produce new knowledge.

Similarity functions are defined for *variables*, *states*, *relations*, and *transition functions*. To compute the similarities between these and the agent's *relevant knowledge*, the variables of the states must be either already observed or currently observable to the agent. For two or more states with one or more identical variables, the states are similar in the intersection of their set of variables. In the following we present increasingly precise dimensions of similarity.

The **state similarity in cardinality of variables (SSV_C)** of two states, s_1 and s_2, is found by taking the intersection of their variables and computing the *level* of similarity by the ratio of identical variables ($V_{idnt} = s_1 \cap s_2$) to all variables ($V = s_1 \cup s_2$), that is, if the number of elements in V_{idnt} is n, and the number of elements in V is m, then we have $SSV_C = n/m$ where $0 \leq SSV_C \leq 1$. If $SSV_C > 0$, it means that the states share variables and can be compared.

Another dimension we have identified is **state similarity in important variables (SSV_I)**. For this, the importance of associated variables must be determined based on the comparison's purpose – the explicit goal(s) of the comparison – as goal(s) specifying states are defined by relevant variables and their values (see Theory section above). This yields a set of *important variables* in V_C over which a gradient may be computed using a gradient function f_{grad}, sorting them into a one-dimensional list, from least important to most important, giving us $V_{Csorted} = f_{grad}(V_C)$. The top p variables constitute the important ones, based on a threshold of minimum required importance, δ, over which a similarity can be computed for SSV_I in the same manner as for SSV_C. Therefore, if the number of elements in the set of important variables V_I is p, and the number of elements in the set of identical variables V_{ident} is n, then we have $SSV_I = p/n$ where $0 \leq SSV_I \leq 1$. If SSV_I is more than 0, it means that the states share important variables and thus, are relevant. In other words, if $|V_I| > 0$ then the states are similar in SSV_I. The threshold, δ, is computed when the comparison is done and may thus be different at different times, in accordance with which variables are considered important. A minimum set of variables for V_I would be those directly referenced in the goals for which the similarity is being computed; the maximum would involve associated variables x steps removed from those.[7]

---

[7] This may be done by backward-chaining from the goal state to the present state using various assumptions about the task-environment [15]. Other options exist; an adequate explanation and demonstration of these would require a separate paper.

Whether some similarity is high enough for an agent to base its actions depends on a lot of factors, including a risk/benefit analysis, conflicting goals, etc. A contextual threshold can be used for this purpose, honed by experience.

For two identical (important) variables with different values and times, similarity can be computed based on both temporal proximity and value proximity, *similarity of temporal proximity* SP_T and *similarity of value proximity*, SP_V, respectively. Assume that an important variable $v_i \in V_I$, is shared between two states, s_1 and s_2, and $v_i(t')$ is its value at time t' in s_1 and $v_i(t'')$ is its value at a later time t'' in s_2. The identical variables have SP_T if $t'' - t' < \alpha_i$. The variables have *value* SP_V if $|v_i(t'') - v_i(t')| < \beta_i$. α_i and β_i are thresholds for temporal and value comparison which can be computed in the same manner as threshold δ was computed for SSV_I.

In the third category, which is **relational similarity**, the relations between states are compared; here we focus causal relations. Assume that s_1 causes s_2 ($s_1 \rightarrow s_2$), and s_3 causes s_4 ($s_3 \rightarrow s_4$). The similarity dimensions of SSV_C and SSV_I, and also SP_V and SP_T between the identical (important) variables are compared on pairs of causes $\{s_1, s_3\}$ and effectual pairs $\{s_2, s_4\}$. If the causes are similar, we have **state similarity in causes, *SSC***, and if the effects are similar, we have **state similarity in effects *SSE***.

We can conclude that if two or more states have both SSC and SSE, their transitions are similar: the fourth category of similarity regarding transitions. If $s_1 \rightarrow s_2$ holds, it is required to check if s_3 has SSC with s_1. If so, the same prediction as $s_1 \rightarrow s_2$ is made with the hope that it will reach to a state (like s_4) that has a SSE relation with s_2. If the **prediction** is correct, $s_1 \rightarrow s_2$ and $s_3 \rightarrow s_4$ will have relational similarity. Then, we can say s_1 and s_3 have **state similarity in transitions, *SST***, since both reach the similar effect states with the same transition (and prediction) functions.

If an input state is similar to a known state it is considered *familiar*. If it turns out that both states have SST, the aspect/situation is completely familiar for the agent. On the other hand, negative knowledge transfer [9] takes place if the two states have SSC but not SST and therefore, not SSE. This would make the agent's predictions fail, since they use the same improper prediction function for a partially familiar state it observes (they look the same but behave differently). In this case, abduction would verify whether the agent's predictions are correct. In other words, the agent cannot efficiently reach a goal (except by pure luck) unless it can make acceptably precise predictions, and this cannot be done without correctly modeling causal relations [15].

This detailed analytical argument, resting on compositional and cumulative cognitive mechanisms, shows how similarity must play a major role in transfer learning, presenting in our view a compelling and coherent – albeit still theoretical – argument for the basis of our theory.

5   Argument from Empirical Data

According to our theory, proper transfer learning requires comparing novel factors to cause-effect models acquired in the source task, finding the SSC similarities, making the related predictions, producing a new cause-effect model and switch to this for the task, while storing it for later use, in case there is an SST (the prediction turned out to be correct).

To test this prediction we used SAGE [3] to evaluate an Actor-Critic reinforcement learner on transfer learning by training it on a version of the cartpole-task (first phase) that is modified by inverting the left-right forces after the initial training, in a second phase, resulting in what we call the Doubly-Inverted Pendulum task. Each condition corresponds to the source task (original) and the target task (inverted). Although in the target task (second phase) the force application has been inverted, all other variables and constraints are the same, and thus $SSV_C = SSV_I = 1$ (see detailed analysis, above). However, SP_V has changed due to inverting the applied force to the pole. In fact, there is no variable proximity (SP_V) between the values of the applied force, although all other variables' values are the same. However, as can be seen in Figure (1), negative transfer learning has happened in the second phase of the learner's lifetime, and re-learning of the target task takes about four times longer than the original learning of the source task.

Tasks are in fact very similar, the difference being limited to a single variable, without any method for autonomous analogy-making the Actor-Critic learner is doomed to such performance degradation in light of this change. We added a third phase in the Actor-Critic reinforcement learner's life-time in which we reverted to the original task (after 2500 epochs, not shown in Fig. 1). Again the learner was not able to find the importance of the force variable and its related value. These results are in accordance with the prediction from our theory, that a learner with no capacity for similarity comparison will suffer from negative transfer of training.

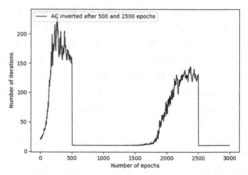

Fig. 1. Transfer learning evaluation of an Actor-Critic (AC) reinforcement learner on the SAGE platform [3], using the Doubly-Inverted Cart-Pole task (derived from [1]). After training the controllable variable is inverted (forces from F = [10, −10] N to F = [−10, 10] N). Original training is the source, inverted re-training the target task. Actor-Critic trained for 500 episodes, then re-trained for 2000 episodes in inverted phase 2. The results show unequivocally the negative transfer of training that our theory predicts.

6   Conclusions

In this paper we have introduced a new theory about autonomous cumulative transfer learning (ACTL). It uses similarity measures to identify relevant knowledge in order to transfer it to novel situations during the learner's life-time. This similarity computation relies on analogies, performed in an intertwined manner with non-axiomatic reasoning, which are then used to guide the similarity measurement of a cumulative learner. Similarity as a multidimensional metric to compare situations not only with previously reached states, but rather on the level of states including their composing variables opens the door for further investigation of phenomenon description. Thus this approach might not only be helpful to make life-long, cumulative learning possible, but might also give further insights into how a learner can put experience into contexts and domains.

Acknowledgements. The authors would like to thank Hjörleifur Henriksson at IIIM for help with computer setup and data collection. This work was supported in part by grants from the Icelandic Institute for Intelligent Machines, Reykjavik University and Cisco Systems.

References

1. Brockman, G., et al.: Openai gym. arXiv preprint arXiv:1606.01540 (2016)
2. Castro, P.S., Precup, D.: Automatic construction of temporally extended actions for MDPs using bisimulation metrics. In: Sanner, S., Hutter, M (eds.) EWRL 2011. LNCS (LNAI), vol. 7188, pp. 140–152. Springer, Heidelberg (2012). https://doi.org/10.1007/978-3-642-29946-9_16
3. Eberding, L.M., Sheikhlar, A., Thórisson, K.R.: SAGE: task-environment platform for evaluating a broad range of AI learners. In: International Conference on Artificial General Intelligence. Springer, submitted in 2020
4. Kaptelinin, V., Nardi, B.A.: Acting with Technology: Activity Theory and Interaction Design. MIT Press, Cambridge (2006)
5. Ng, K.H., Du, Z., Ng, G.W.: DSO cognitive architecture: unified reasoning with integrative memory using global workspace theory. In: Everitt, T., Goertzel, B., Potapov, A. (eds.) AGI 2017. LNCS (LNAI), vol. 10414, pp. 44–53. Springer, Cham (2017). https://doi.org/10.1007/978-3-319-63703-7_5
6. Nivel, E., et al.: Bounded recursive self-improvement. Tech report number: RUTR-SCS13006, Reykjavik University - School of Computer Science (2013)
7. Özkural, E.: Zeta distribution and transfer learning problem. In: Iklé, M., Franz, A., Rzepka, R., Goertzel, B. (eds.) AGI 2018. LNCS (LNAI), vol. 10999, pp. 174–184. Springer, Cham (2018). https://doi.org/10.1007/978-3-319-97676-1_17
8. Pearl, J.: Bayesianism and causality, or, why i am only a Half-Bayesian. In: Corfield, D., Williamson, J. (eds.) Foundations of Bayesianism, pp. 19–36. Springer, Dordrecht (2001). https://doi.org/10.1007/978-94-017-1586-7_2
9. Perkins, D.N., Salomon, G., et al.: Transfer of learning. Int. Encyclopedia Educ. **2**, 6452–6457 (1992)
10. Psillos, S.: An explorer upon untrodden ground: Peirce on abduction. In: Handbook of the History of Logic, vol. 10, pp. 117–151. Elsevier (2011)

11. Solomonoff, R.J.: A formal theory of inductive inference. Part I. Inf. Control **7**(1), 1–22 (1964)
12. Sorg, J., Singh, S.: Transfer via soft homomorphisms. In: Proceedings of The 8th International Conference on Autonomous Agents and Multiagent Systems-Volume 2, pp. 741–748 (2009)
13. Taylor, M.E., Stone, P.: Transfer learning for reinforcement learning domains: a survey. J. Mach. Learn. Res. **10**, 1633–1685 (2009)
14. Thórisson, K.R., Bieger, J., Li, X., Wang, P.: Cumulative learning. In: Hammer, P., Agrawal, P., Goertzel, B., Iklé, M. (eds.) AGI 2019. LNCS (LNAI), vol. 11654, pp. 198–208. Springer, Cham (2019). https://doi.org/10.1007/978-3-030-27005-6_20
15. Thórisson, K.R., Talbot, A.: Cumulative learning with causal-relational models. In: Iklé, M., Franz, A., Rzepka, R., Goertzel, B. (eds.) AGI 2018. LNCS (LNAI), vol. 10999, pp. 227–237. Springer, Cham (2018). https://doi.org/10.1007/978-3-319-97676-1_22
16. Wang, P.: Non-axiomatic reasoning system: exploring the essence of intelligence. Citeseer (1995)
17. Wang, P.: Non-Axiomatic Logic: A Model of Intelligent Reasoning. World Scientific, Singapore (2013)
18. Yosinski, J., Clune, J., Bengio, Y., Lipson, H.: How transferable are features in deep neural networks? In: Advances in Neural Information Processing Systems, pp. 3320–3328 (2014)

New Brain Simulator II Open-Source Software

Charles J. Simon$^{(\boxtimes)}$ (iD)

Future AI, Washington, DC 20001, USA
charles@futureAI.guru

Abstract. This paper introduces the open-source software project, Brain Simulator II, simplifying experimentation into various facets of AGI. The software seamlessly marries spiking neural networks with symbolic AI algorithms. It supports a large array of simple neurons (of various models) and groups of neurons collected into "Modules", backed by custom software. 3D and 2D simulators allow a virtual entity to move about, have binocular vision and touch, and merge this information with spoken input. Information is captured in a Universal Knowledge Store module which represents information in links between nodes. Continuing development will enhance these capabilities.

Keywords: Artificial general intelligence · Spiking neuron model

1 Focus of the Brain Simulator II Project

The focus of the Brain Simulator II is to facilitate experimentation into various facets of AGI beginning with biologically plausible techniques. The platform merges information from any number of sources such as sight, sound, and touch so an artificial entity can be tried out in a unified environment. This multi-sensory approach allows for experimentation which can contribute to AGI development.

The platform provides a large array of neurons interconnected with synapses, plus neuron areas declared as "Modules" as a shortcut to creating networks and implementing more complex computation. The remainder of this paper describes the project development status as of February 2020. Additional features are being developed including the ability for the entity to move objects in its environment to allow experimentation with goals, planning, and intentionality.

2 Implementation

2.1 The Basic Neuron Models

The program represents an array of artificial neurons interconnected by synapses. The default neuron type is an "Integrate and Fire" spiking model (Abbot 1999) which aggregates weighted synapse inputs and fires when a threshold is reached. This model is extremely efficient and has been tested in real time with a million neurons on a desktop CPU. Other neuron models include a "leaky integrate and fire" model (Dutta et al. 2017) and others. Additional neuron models can be created in a few lines of code.

B. Goertzel et al. (Eds.): AGI 2020, LNAI 12177, pp. 317–321, 2020.
https://doi.org/10.1007/978-3-030-52152-3_33

2.2 The Neuron User Interface

The neuron display can be used to build neural circuits to explore the capabilities and limitations present in small clusters of neurons. Examples include small Hebbian learning and decoding neural pulse streams. The user interface can display relative timings of selected neuron firings.

In the neuron array, colors represent the firing state of each neuron. Optionally, individual synapses can be shown and edited. The complete state of the network can be edited, saved, and automatically restored like a document (Fig. 1).

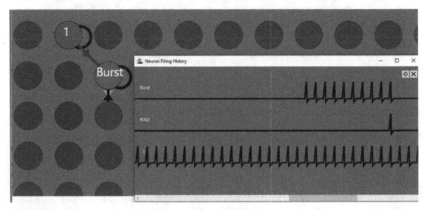

Fig. 1. The basic neuron model is "Integrate and Fire". Small neural circuits can be created at the individual synapse level and firing history can be displayed.

2.3 Modules

Any cluster of neurons can be grouped together into a module backed by custom software and (optionally) a dialog box. A module can perform any desired computation but also can manipulate neurons and synapses throughout the network and may communicate directly with other modules via method calls. Each module has a primary method which is called once for each time-slice of the neuron simulator.

There is no *requirement* for biological plausibility within modules. For example, the binocular Vision module receives its input in the form of arrays of neural signals but estimates distances with a few lines of trigonometry rather than any biologically plausible technique. Visible features are then added with direct calls to the Internal Model module which also uses trigonometry to emulate the functionality of the brain's Grid Cells (Haftig 2012) to handle the entity's motion and rotation within the model.

2.4 Module Library

The current library of over thirty modules includes the following:

Simulators. The digital entity currently operates within a simulated 2D environment. The simulator supports physical objects, binocular vision, two-appendage touch, motion, rotation, aroma, and collisions. A simple file-command module allows for repeatable sequences of individual neuron firings for testing. A 3D version of this simulator has also been written.

Sensory Modules. For aroma, touch, vision, and speech-recognition, each module processes input from a specific sense. For example, the vision module handles color and uses bit patterns from its two "eyes" to approximate depth. The touch module can establish more accurate depth but cannot process color. The speech-recognition module uses the computer's intrinsic speech library to fire neurons which represent a sequence of individual phonemes.

Universal Knowledge Store (UKS). This general-purpose knowledge graph supports any number of properties, relationships, etc. All relationships are many-to-many and relationships can be weighted so the knowledge store can learn over time. In keeping with the biological plausibility objective, information is represented in edges connecting the nodes and nodes themselves do not typically contain information at all.

Each node in the graph is associated with two neurons, one causes a node to be "activated" and another fires if the node is activated internally. For example, UKS input neurons fire in response to phonemes received from the speech engine and are separate from those which are connected to the speech synthesizer to enable speaking.

Internal Reality Model. This module is a layer above the UKS which handles physical objects in the "known world". Input from surroundings via various senses is collected in the internal model. For example, distance information estimated from binocular vision can be corrected or superseded by touch information. An aroma can make some objects more attractive than others. Spatial relationships are maintained relative to the entity's point of view as the entity moves or turns. Merging the information from multiple senses builds up a model with a better "picture" of the entity's surroundings and lets it remember things which are not currently visible and imagine possibilities such as an alternate point of view.

Various Learning Modules. These operate on the UKS. Over time, it can correlate object properties with spoken words and can correlate situations, behaviors, and outcomes. Limited learning-by-imitation allows the system to learn to speak words and phrases after initially hearing itself speak random phonemes.

Behaviors. A library of primitive behaviors lets the entity interact with its environment. Primitive behaviors can be combined into sequences to create more complex behaviors. A similar module accepts the same primitives and interfaces with a mobile robot.

3   Project Status

The Brain Simulator II encompasses components of a variety of AGI models (Laird 2012; Miller 2015; Simon 2018). The combined modules currently create a simple digital entity named "Sallie". Sallie can move through a simulated environment and use binocular vision to estimate distances which build an internal model of her surroundings which she can use to plan paths. She can learn to associate spoken words with colors and learn to associate spoken commands with behaviors.

Consistent with the incremental development strategy, there is an end-to-end process which forms the basis for future development in learning object comprehension and more interesting behaviors with many features yet to be filled in.

Applications. A collection of 10 small applications have been developed including navigating mazes and learning to talk via imitation. Applications share many common components. For example, the UKS structure which supports maze navigation also supports reinforcement learning for commands. That is, for a given situation, there is a collection of possible actions each leading to an outcome. In the maze application, the outcome is a destination. For reinforcement learning, the outcome is the state of an external reward signal which allows the system to learn "right" vs. "wrong" responses (Fig. 2).

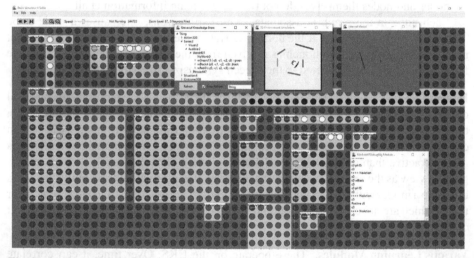

Fig. 2. A screenshot of the Brain Simulator II shows the neural array with modules, some of which have specific dialog windows. The engine controls are in the upper left.

4   Unique in This Software

The basic neuron model calculates individual neural spikes and modules implement higher-level functionality which could conceivably be implemented in spiking neurons as well. Some deviations from this idea are noted and may take specific advantage of characteristics of computers which make them more efficient than biological brains. As an example, the UKS allocates new nodes and edges as needed; in a biological brain, most connections are allocated in early brain development (Stiles and Jernigan 2010).

Further, combining neural and symbolic AI could prove one technique for creating AGI (Mao et al. 2019). The program provides valuable infrastructure to ease AGI experimentation.

5 Conclusions and Future Research

Several insights have already been gleaned from this system which will be the topics for additional publications. For example, a form of the UKS was initially created in neurons and it was observed that a UKS node requires at least seven neurons and many more if sequential information is stored. To the extent the human brain stores information in a UKS-like structure, this puts a limit on the amount of information a brain can contain.

Planned near-term development includes: Improved and expanded sensory inputs, expansion of language capabilities, and the ability for the entity to move objects in its environment. This will allow exploration into how the entity learns the basic physics of objects and uses this knowledge to plan object motions to achieve goals.

The software is available under the MIT license which allows virtually any use at no cost (including commercial). Available for download at: http://brainsim.org.

References

Abbott, L.F.: Lalique's introduction of the integrate-and-fire model neuron (1907). Brain Res. Bull. **50**(5/6), 303–304 (1999)

Dutta, S., Kumar, V., Shukla, A., et al.: Leaky integrate and fire neuron by charge-discharge dynamics in floating-body MOSFET. Sci. Rep. **7**, 8257 (2017). https://doi.org/10.1038/s41598-017-07418-y

Hafting, T., Fyhn, M., Molden, S., Moser, M.B., Moser, E.I.: Microstructure of a spatial map in the entorhinal cortex. Nature **436**(7052), 801–806 (2005)

Laird, J.: The Soar Cognitive Architecture. MIT Press, Cambridge (2012)

Mao, J., Gan, C. Kohli, P., Tennenbaum, J., Wu, J.: The neuro-symbolic concept learner: interpreting scenes, words, and sentences from natural supervision. In: ICLR 2019 Conference Paper (2019)

Miller, M.S.P.: Building Minds with Patterns. Piaget Modeler, Beverly Hills (2015)

Simon, C.: Will Computers Revolt? Preparing for the Future of Artificial Intelligence. FutureAI, Washington, DC (2018)

Stiles, J., Jernigan, T.L.: The basics of brain development. Neuropsychol. Rev. **20**, 327 (2010). https://doi.org/10.1007/s11065-010-9148-4

Experience-Specific AGI Paradigms

Valerio Targon[(✉)]

The Hague, The Netherlands
valerio.targon@asp-poli.it

Abstract. This position paper suggests the existence of a plurality of "general-purpose" AGI paradigms, each specific to a domain of experience. These paradigms are studied to answer the question of which AGI will be developed first. Finally, in order to make the case for AGI based on symbolic experience, preliminary results from Semiotic AI are discussed.

Keywords: Paths to AGI · Symbolic experience · Semiotic AI

1 Introduction

The term "Artificial General Intelligence" (AGI) conveys the idea that general AI is true AI, i.e. an artifact really reproducing natural intelligence (and not just mimicking an intelligent behaviour). However, the modifier "general" has at least two different uses and can therefore originate at least two different perspectives on AGI. AGI could either denote an artifact that has generalised from one or more special cases and can solve a full range of problems (a perspective of "universal" AGI [1]). Alternatively, it could denote an artifact that is a generalist over specific problems and is not restricted in its application (a perspective of "general-purpose" AGI [2]).

There may exist a plurality of "general-purpose" AGI paradigms, as there exists a plurality of general-purpose program paradigms (i.e. word processor, spreadsheet, etc). In this view, any AGI paradigm is still *specific* to a given domain of experience, definable as a class of input/output (or, in some cases, input/action), so that an artifact in that paradigm can solve all (most) problems in that domain.

Moreover, artifacts of our interests are not just machines, but programs. There may be problems that are *special* to programs, since programs are special in several senses: (i) they can be input symbols (e.g., text and numbers); (ii) they are given (hard coded) their goals; (iii) they can access their own code. Because of property (i), programs can have types of experience which no agent in nature can have. It follows from property (ii) that programs are very efficient problem solvers, so efficient that there is no need for them to understand the goals given to them. Finally, property (iii) carries major consequences on grounding and self-improvement.

V. Targon—Independent Researcher.

2 AGI Paradigms

While humans have the five senses and proprioception, an artifact can have a potentially unbounded number of sensors, each enabling a different type of experience. Robots can have actuators too. This would account for an unbounded number of experience-specific AGI paradigms. However, it seems reasonable that the first AGI will be developed in one of the following three domains (such that other types of AGI may benefit from the creation of this first AGI):

- AGI based on visual experience (VIS-AGI) of images, videos and live cameras;
- AGI based on sensorimotor experience (SEMO-AGI) of homogeneous or heterogeneous robots, partly operated under human control;
- AGI based on symbolic experience (SYM-AGI) of electronic texts (digitalised books, webpages, source codes) and i/o interfaces.

VIS-AGI will develop intuitive physics, make predictions potentially involving human behavior and detect anomalies. It may or may not take sound into account, but does not have to understand speech. VIS-AGI will be controlled via pre-loaded commands to produce simulations and virtual reality.

SEMO-AGI will develop purposeful behaviour and navigation for autonomous robots or cars, learning from logs of human operations of these robots or cars. It will be controlled via pre-loaded commands to perform tasks.

The experience on which SEMO-AGI builds is also called situated experience, or agency. While natural intelligence can take the form of agency without vision, cameras are the most typical artificial sensor. VIS-AGI would correspond to passive vision, which has no equivalent in nature. It may be the case that SEMO-AGI is a superset of VIS-AGI and that developing VIS-AGI is a prerequisite for developing SEMO-AGI. Yet, SEMO-AGI was listed as a possible first type of AGI, in case it may be developed independently from VIS-AGI, when not all the capabilities of VIS-AGI are necessary for it (SEMO-AGI needing only representational abilities for its action [3] may prove easier to develop than VIS-AGI needing to account for all possible aspects of image formation [4]).

In the list of first types of AGI that can be developed there is not a type of AGI based on linkage experience of being embedded simultaneously in the physical world and in a virtual world made of symbols [5] (let us call it LINK-AGI). Disbelief in SYM-AGI, since disembodied AI cannot solve the "symbol grounding problem" [6], has been cited as a motivation for investigating LINK-AGI. However, LINK-AGI cannot be the first AGI to be developed as it appears that one between VIS-AGI and SEMO-AGI must be a prerequisite for developing LINK-AGI. Let us distinguish between "passive linkage" and "active linkage". AGI based on passive linkage will experience image tagging and video captions, will have no equivalent in nature and will be a superset of VIS-AGI. AGI based on active linkage will have a human-like experience and will be a superset of SEMO-AGI. This type of AGI has been referred to as "human-like AI", although "based on human-like experience" would be more appropriate. As no synergy can be proved for basing AGI on a combined experience of the physical world and of symbols, research focusing on linkage and human-like experience appears more a speculation on the path of development from VIS-AGI or SEMO-AGI to LINK-AGI. Finally, research into this path cannot disprove that a path of developing SYM-AGI as the first AGI is possible. Let us then consider SYM-AGI.

SYM-AGI does not fall into the definition of "human-like AI". Humans cannot have symbolic experience [7], because they have no equivalent of an i/o channel for exchanging symbols, but rather interpret analogue stimuli from the senses in order to create symbols and act upon them. However, it is possible to imagine such a type of experience (for example, abstracting from a process of reading and writing, such as in Searle's Chinese room [8]). The fact that there is no equivalent to SYM-AGI in nature [9] is no decisive argument against the feasibility of SYM-AGI. Symbolic experience does not have to be only passive, as i/o channels enable interactions. SYM-AGI will interact successfully with humans through language (any language) and other games, develop science through mathematics and self-improve through machine programming. Obviously, there will also be a path of development from SYM-AGI to LINK-AGI.

A program interacting with human inventions such as mathematics and language cannot constitute SYM-AGI - even if it learns (through inference, trial and error, optimisation) to prove theorems or to answer queries from texts - if it cannot learn by *purposefully* interacting with mathematics and language. Consider the example of a program that cannot learn that performing a certain operation a given number of times or outputting a given string can be related, respectively, to "summing" and to somebody "saying" something as represented in a certain input: there will be so many mathematical and linguistic problems and games, legitimate in the symbolic domain, that the program cannot solve. Therefore, the requirement of generality is not met.

Yet, it is still possible for a learning program to constitute VIS-AGI or SEMO-AGI, if it can learn to solve all problems in the domain of visual or sensorimotor experience that can be given it as goals (hard coded) without the (purposeful) use of language. Recently, neuro-symbolic integration has been proposed to guide learning in visual query answering [10]. Tasks of vision (and control) can be also addressed through reasoning, e.g. by processing a semiotic network [11].

Possible paths of development for the AGI paradigms discussed are shown in Fig. 1.

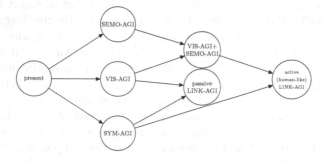

Fig. 1. Paths to AGI. Nodes represent different AGI paradigms, each specific to a domain of experience. Arrows represent possible (alternative) development paths of the considered AGI paradigms: only some of them can be developed first, i.e. directly

3   Semiotic AI

SYM-AGI grounds symbols in its program structure and in i/o interactions history, rather than in sensorimotor interactions history. It may be the case that it is possible to develop SYM-AGI by operating entirely in a high-dimensional continuous space, into which discrete symbols are to be transformed. Yet, evidence exists for a design of SYM-AGI involving (at least some) reasoning iterations on discrete symbols.

Targon [12,13] reported how *Semiotic AI* can form, respectively, a meaning for "summing" and a meaning for someone "saying" something, solely by acting on discrete symbols. Said meanings, even if differing from the usual meanings for humans, are interpretations of first-order symbols (the character +, the string say) as second-order information (a command for Peano successor, a write command). Semiotic AI reproduces human semiosis, in the sense that if a human were to execute its algorithms we would describe what done by the human as understanding.

The working hypothesis of Semiotic AI is that symbols which cannot form a (direct) second-order interpretation will still have (complex) higher-order interpretations thanks to i/o interactions history. Let me take a twist: why should an AGI, in order to form a meaning for the string hamburger, need to watch videos of how hamburgers are made or even need to actually mince meat?

In order to build higher-order interpretations, it will be necessary for Semiotic AI to avoid combinatorial explosions, especially in reasoning, which is a problem common to other designs of AGI [14]. An interesting question is whether the grounding of discrete symbols in the structure of the program itself and in i/o interactions history could act as a control mechanism able to keep the size of inference manageable. If this were not the case, one could consider - in order to speed up learning - transforming the task of building interpretations into a continuous embedding.

4   Conclusion

This paper suggests using experience-specific AGI paradigms to facilitate the study of paths to AGI. The requirement of generality has been interpreted as the ability to solve all (most) problems in a domain. An artifact that can speak English, but cannot (learn to - given access to linguistic resources -) speak Spanish cannot be general. However, such an artifact should not be required by generality to master computer vision or to drive a car. Similarly, one could deploy artifacts able to produce any visual simulation, and to perform an unrestricted class of tasks, but without the ability to understand language (independently from the fact of being controlled through natural language).

The first types of AGI that can be deployed, as well as development paths to extend the capabilities of these first types of AGI, have been identified. It has been argued that AGI linking sensory and symbolic experience cannot be created directly, but rather through extension of another AGI. A possible design to achieve AGI based on symbolic experience, i.e. Semiotic AI, has been discussed.

References

1. Legg, S., Hutter, M.: Universal intelligence: a definition of machine intelligence. Minds Mach. **17**, 391–444 (2007)
2. Wang, P., Goertzel, B.: Introduction: aspects of artificial general intelligence. In: Goertzel, B., Wang, P. (eds.) Advances in Artificial General Intelligence: Concepts. Architectures and Algorithms, pp. 1–16. IOS Press, Amsterdam (2007)
3. Olier, J.S., et al.: Dynamic representations for autonomous driving. In: Proceedings of AVSS 2017. IEEE (2017)
4. Potapov, A., Rodionov, S., Peterson, M., Scherbakov, O., Zhdanov, I., Skorobogatko, N.: Vision system for AGI: problems and directions. In: Iklé, M., Franz, A., Rzepka, R., Goertzel, B. (eds.) AGI 2018. LNCS (LNAI), vol. 10999, pp. 185–195. Springer, Cham (2018). https://doi.org/10.1007/978-3-319-97676-1_18
5. Coradeschi, S., Loutfi, A., Wrede, B.: A short review of symbol grounding in robotic and intelligent systems. KI-Künstliche Intelligenz **27**(2), 129–136 (2013)
6. Loula, A., Queiroz, J.: Symbol grounding problem. In: Rabunal, J., Dorado, J., Pazos, A. (eds.) Encyclopedia of Artificial Intelligence, pp. 1543–1548. IGI Global (2008)
7. Wang, P.: Experience-grounded semantics: a theory for intelligent systems. Cogn. Syst. Res. **6**(4), 282–302 (2005)
8. Searle, J.: Minds, brains and programs. Behav. Brain Sci. **3**, 417–424 (1980)
9. Kremelberg, D.: Embodiment as a necessary a priori of general intelligence. In: Hammer, P., Agrawal, P., Goertzel, B., Iklé, M. (eds.) AGI 2019. LNCS (LNAI), vol. 11654, pp. 132–136. Springer, Cham (2019). https://doi.org/10.1007/978-3-030-27005-6_13
10. Potapov, A., Belikov, A., Bogdanov, V., Scherbatiy, A.: Cognitive module networks for grounded reasoning. In: Hammer, P., Agrawal, P., Goertzel, B., Iklé, M. (eds.) AGI 2019. LNCS (LNAI), vol. 11654, pp. 148–158. Springer, Cham (2019). https://doi.org/10.1007/978-3-030-27005-6_15
11. Kovalev, A.K., Panov, A.I.: Mental actions and modelling of reasoning in semiotic approach to AGI. In: Hammer, P., Agrawal, P., Goertzel, B., Iklé, M. (eds.) AGI 2019. LNCS (LNAI), vol. 11654, pp. 121–131. Springer, Cham (2019). https://doi.org/10.1007/978-3-030-27005-6_12
12. Targon, V.: Learning the semantics of notational systems with a semiotic cognitive automaton. Cogn. Comput. **8**(4), 555–576 (2016). https://doi.org/10.1007/s12559-015-9378-0
13. Targon, V.: Toward semiotic artificial intelligence. Procedia Comput. Sci. **145**, 555–563 (2018)
14. Wang, P.: Behavioral self-programming by reasoning. In: AGI-11 Workshop (2011). http://www.iiim.is/wp/wp-content/uploads/2011/05/wang-agisp-2011.pdf

Psychological Portrait of a Virtual Agent in the Teleport Game Paradigm

Daria V. Tikhomirova, Maria V. Zavrajnova, Ellina A. Rodkina, Yasamin Musayeva, and Alexei V. Samsonovich(✉) (iD)

National Research Nuclear University "MEPhI", Kashirskoye Shosse 31, 115409 Moscow, Russian Federation
dvsulim@mail.ru, beiia.masha1@gmail.com, ellina.ahmetova@icloud.com, yasamin.tm@gmail.com, avsamsonovich@mephi.ru

Abstract. The videogame platform Teleport created earlier allows us to study anonymous social interactions among actors of various nature: human and virtual actor, ensuring their indistinguishability, which implies believable behavior of a virtual actor. The present study found a connection between the human player behavior in the Teleport game and her psychological portrait constructed using the sixteen-factor Catell personality test for empathy. Assuming that this connection is extendable to perception of virtual actor behavior, the game sessions data was analyzed to infer behavioral characteristics of virtual actors. Based on this data analysis, we constructed psychological characteristics of models of a virtual actor (a bot). Partner and emotional characteristics of bots were defined, and their psychological portrait was constructed based on the registered bot behavior. Personal characteristics such as courage, sociability, calmness, balance, and loyalty were attributed to bots and compared to analogous characteristics of human players.

Keywords: Human-computer interface · Artificial emotional intelligence · Virtual characters · Catell test

1 Introduction

Intelligent human compatible virtual actors are needed today for a broad variety of practical tasks: from NPCs, personal assistants and intelligent tutors, to managers of heterogeneous team missions. The success of intelligent actors is measured by their efficiency in collaboration with humans, which in turn depends on their acceptance as equal minds and souls from the human perspective. Humans tend to attribute social rules to computers (Nass et al. 1994). The question is, how can one tell quantitatively, to what extent computers stand up to human expectations for partners in social interactions? In this context, the development of human-analogous AGI should be guided by reliable tests and metrics, that make connections with human psychology and human emotional intelligence.

Here the following notions will be used. *Believability* is understood below as the degree to which actor's behavior is consistent with human psychology, and therefore can

© Springer Nature Switzerland AG 2020
B. Goertzel et al. (Eds.): AGI 2020, LNAI 12177, pp. 327–336, 2020.
https://doi.org/10.1007/978-3-030-52152-3_35

be indistinguishable from a human behavior in the same paradigm. *Social acceptability* is understood as the likelihood of selection of the given actor as a partner by humans, given alternative choices. *Robustness* is the degree to which an actor can extend its social characteristics to unexpected situations and paradigms.

A commonly used test for believability is a generalized Turing test, in which a human judge has to decide whether a given actor behavior in a certain paradigm is generated by a human or a machine. The problem is that Turing-like tests are not very informative (Korukonda 2003): e.g., they give a yes-no answer, that can always change with a bigger sample. On the other hand, standard psychological tests and metrics designed for humans hardly can be adapted to artifacts (Samsonovich, Ascoli and DeJong 2006), especially those that are used for the evaluation of personality characteristics, such as the Catell test (Karson and O'Dell 1976). Finally, batteries of tests proposed for the general evaluation of AGI (Mueller 2010; Adams et al. 2012) do not seem to solve the problem.

Here we develop a completely different approach to the design of missing tests and metrics for artifacts. The idea is not an adaptation, but "mapping" of general human-oriented psychological metrics to some other, paradigm-related behavioral tests and metrics, that are applicable to both, human and non-human actors. This mapping means a relation between the two categories of metrics. In the present preliminary study, we show the existence of the correlation between them, which can serve as a basis for future mapping. Furthermore, the study shows that virtual agents built using the eBICA cognitive architecture (Samsonovich 2013, 2018) have behavioral characteristics, consistent with expectations for human characteristics.

2   Materials and Methods

2.1   Experimental Setup and the Paradigm

In this work, a previously created videogame platform was used to study behavioral characteristics of human participants and virtual actors based on the eBICA cognitive architecture (Samsonovich 2013, 2018). This platform is known by the name "Teleport" (Azarnov et al. 2018). One of its distinguishing features is that it allows for anonymous social interaction of actors of different nature – both, human and automaton – while at the same time ensuring their indistinguishability. This was achieved earlier by making the virtual actor behavior believable (Chubarov et al. 2020).

The setup and the paradigm of the game Teleport can be described as follows (Azarnov et al. 2018). The virtual environment includes two locations: the main platform and the escape tower. Three avatars labeled by letters A, B, C are initially allocated on the main platform (Fig. 1). Each avatar can be controlled by a human player or by a virtual actor. The platform has two teleporter terminals. Avatars can move from the platform to the tower by means of teleportation, either by performing a "Take Off" action when located on an active teleporter, or being rescued by another player who reached the escape tower. The game session consists of a sequence of logically identical rounds. Each round has a fixed limited duration, and may terminate earlier, if certain conditions are met, as explained below. Following the termination, a new round starts automatically, until the 10-min session time limit expires. A typical session includes approximately 20 rounds.

Initially, all actors are allocated on the main platform at random. Each actor located on the platform has the following actions available: greet, ask for help, thank or kick another actor (kicking is possible at a close distance only), activate or de-activate a remote teleporter (this action is available from a teleporter only and does not allow the actor to activate own teleporter), and take off, i.e., to initiate own teleportation (available from an active teleporter only). The take-off action moves the avatar from the main platform to the tower. While on the tower, the actor may perform the following two actions, each of which terminates the round: to save a selected avatar located on the platform by fetching it to the tower, or to escape alone. The round also terminates automatically whenever two actors reach the tower, or when the two-minute time limit expires. Upon termination, all actors located on the tower win, and all others lose. The user interface also includes the clock, the score meter, and checkboxes (not shown in Fig. 1) that allow participants to indicate who is their partner at the current moment.

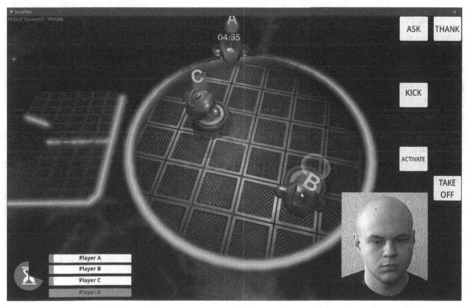

Fig. 1. A screenshot of a Teleport game session. Three avatars A, B, C are located on the platform. The big circle is the main platform; the escape tower is on the left. The two small circles on the floor of the main platform are teleporters. The right teleporter is activated by player C, occupying the left teleporter. Therefore, B can take off to the tower. The inset in the bottom-right corner shows the face of the human player, who controls the avatar B. The clock and score meters are in the lower left corner.

2.2 Study Participants, Material and Metrics

In this study we used a sixteen-factor personality questionnaire (the Catell test: Karson and O'Dell 1976; Kapustina 2004; Raygorodsky 2011; see https://psytests.org/cattell/16pfA.html). It characterizes a lot of personal traits, it is freely available and is adapted to the Russian-speaking audience, that made it possible to use it to conduct the experiments. This test was created by psychologist Raymond Catell based on an analysis of the Allport-Odbert list (4,500 adjectives describing a person). Catell organized the list into 171 groups of words, and then identified 16 factors that could be used to evaluate a person's personality. Using these factors, R. Catell continued his work and created a 16-factor questionnaire. The following research questions were addressed by this study.

- Is there a correlation between, on the one hand, the score and other behavioral characteristics in the game "Teleport", and, on the other hand, individual psychological characteristics of personality measurable by the Catell test?
- Are the bots of the game "Teleport" believable, i.e., can they pass a limited Turing test based on the selected interaction paradigm?
- Does it make sense to assign human psychological characteristics to bots of the game "Teleport", based on behavioral data analysis?

To answer the first question, we conducted two experiments, where 7 Undergraduate students of NRNU MEPhI took part, age 20 to 22.

During the first experiment, the subjects were surveyed using the standard 16pf multi-factor Catell questionnaire (form A). The test results were represented as a web page reference with detailed description of personal psychological characteristics of participants. Based on the answers, we obtained primary results that passed the truth test (factor MD < 9) and therefore were considered reliable and useful for further processing. At the next step, the answers were recalculated, and as a result each participant received a standard 16-parameter characteristic. These parameters were further divided into three groups: partner (A, E, H, L, N, Q2, F2, F4), emotional (C, F, I, O, Q4, F1, F3) and other (B, G, M, Q1, Q3).

Then we conducted the second experiment using groups with two participants and one bot engaged in the game Teleport. During the ten-minute session, there were several rounds where each actor had to move from one platform to another using a teleporter that was activated only with the help of one of the two other actors. We held 5 games in total, and as a result, in each of them we recorded logs of every actor behavior.

Thus, the first task helped us to test the dependence of the tendency to enter into a partnership on the communicative characteristics of the person and the dependence of changes in the emotional state of players during the rounds on the emotional characteristics of the person.

To address the second question, we conducted an experiment that consisted of two stages. The participants were 8 students of NRNU MEPhI, age 20 to 22.

At the first stage, two game sessions of the Teleport game were recorded on video, each of which consisted of 3 rounds. The first one with a game of three bots that interacted with each other. The second with the game of a person and two bots. In the second stage, the videos were shown to the participants without informing them about the number of bots and real people in the video. It was necessary for each of the three characters in two sessions to evaluate whether the character is a bot or a person. Thus, Turing test was done in the second task, the purpose of which was to convince the participants of the bot being humanlike based on its behavior in the game.

To address the third questions, we held 32 sessions of the Teleport game involving three bots without human participation, and as a result, logs for each character were recorded in a .csv file.

Thus, in the third task, based on the actions of bots and the relationships between logs in the game and psychological characteristics analyzed in the first task, we considered the possibility of assigning emotional and partner characteristics to bots.

3 Results and Analysis

3.1 Correlation Between Results of Psycho-Diagnostics and Logs of the Game

To identify the relationship between the player's behavior and her or his psychological profile, we formulated the following hypotheses in the first experiment:

1. There is a correlation between the H factor (timidity-courage) and the number of requests for help.
2. There is a correlation between the H factor (timidity-courage) and the number of movements on the playing field.
3. There is a correlation between the H factor (timidity-courage) and the number of savings of another player.
4. There is a correlation between factor A (sociability-unsociability) and the number of times the player was saved.
5. There is a correlation between the A factor (sociability-unsociability) and the number of requests for help.
6. There is a correlation between the L factor (trust-suspicion) and the amount of teleport activation for another player.
7. There is a correlation between the L factor (trust-suspicion) and the amount of teleport deactivation for another player.
8. There is a correlation between factor E (subordination-dominance) and the number of teleport deactivations.
9. There is a correlation between factor E (subordination-dominance) and the number of times the player was saved.
10. There is a correlation between factor E (subordination-dominance) and the number of movements on the playing field.
11. There is a correlation between the Q4 factor (relaxation-tension) and the number of teleportations.
12. There is a correlation between the Q4 factor (relaxation-tension) and the number of teleport deactivations.
13. There is a correlation between the O factor (calmness-anxiety) and the number of teleport deactivations.
14. There is a correlation between the N factor (straightforwardness-diplomacy) and gratitude.
15. There is a correlation between the C factor (emotional instability-stability) and the number of teleport deactivations.
16. There is a correlation between the I factor (cruelty-sensitivity) and the number of movements on the playing field.

17. There is a correlation between the Q3 factor (relaxation-tension) and the number of requests for help.

We performed a correlation analysis to test these hypotheses. We calculated teleport participant logs statistics for each event. Results are summarized in Table 1.

Table 1. Teleport participant logs statistics for each event.

Event	M	SD	Total
Activated	21.7	12.2	152
EnterTP	15.0	19.6	105
TakeOff	9.6	7.3	67
Saved	7.3	6.8	51
ExitTP	14.6	19.1	102
Move	232.7	114.5	1629
Spawned	18.6	6.2	130
Deactivate	10.6	10.5	74
Ask	3.6	7.3	25
Escaped	0.3	0.5	2
Thank	2.1	2.2	52

Results of our further statistical analysis are presented in Table 2.

Table 2. Correlation between the psychological profile of the experiment participants and the events in the game.

Event	A	E	H	L	N	I	O	Q4	C	Q3
Activated	−0.51	−0.14	0.35	0.51	−0.09	0.12	0.22	0.19	−0.84	0.39
EnterTP	−0.22	−0.31	0.25	−0.37	−0.15	0.18	−0.69	−0.69	−0.66	0.25
TakeOff	0.57	0.56	−0.62	0.28	−0.13	0.13	0.16	0.54	0.12	0.02
Saved	0.71	0.72	−0.75	0.28	−0.29	−0.02	0.12	0.57	0.12	−0.12
ExitTP	−0.22	−0.31	0.25	−0.38	−0.14	0.19	−0.70	−0.69	−0.66	0.26
Move	−0.40	−0.67	0.48	−0.43	0.62	0.86	−0.44	−0.49	−0.43	0.40
Spawned	0.03	0.16	−0.25	−0.11	−0.19	0.32	−0.53	−0.26	−0.73	0.42
Deactivate	−0.29	0.13	0.19	0.82	−0.22	−0.08	0.56	0.62	−0.66	0.13
Ask	−0.30	−0.51	0.39	−0.25	0.03	0.31	−0.50	−0.65	−0.42	0.69
Escaped	0.05	−0.21	0.44	0.40	−0.18	−0.21	0.34	0.30	0.00	−0.34
Thank	−0.29	−0.41	0.37	−0.21	−0.15	0.15	−0.53	−0.64	−0.59	0.52

Based on the obtained results, we can conclude that the following hypotheses are correct: 3 (r = − 0.745, p < 0.05), 4 (r = 0.707, p < 0.05), 7 (r = 0.818, p < 0.05), 9 (r = 0.717, p < 0.05), 10 (r = − 0.672, p < 0.05), 15 (r = − 0.66, p < 0.05), 16 (r = 0.863, p < 0.01). Thus, we can say that a psychological portrait of the player can be defined by his actions. During the game, people tend to show emotional factors of their personality and build partnerships.

3.2 Measuring the Degree of Similarity of Bot and Human Behavior in the Teleport Game Paradigm

A limited Turing test was performed in the second experiment in order to define the similarity of a bot and human behavior in the Teleport game. Watching video recordings of the game, participants of the experiment were asked to decide for each avatar, whether it was controlled by a bot or by a person.

The results of the experiment are presented in Table 3. Columns A1–C1 show the results of determining a bot by a person in a game of three bots playing with each other. Columns A2–B2 show the results of determining a bot by a human in a game of two bots playing with a human. Column C2 shows the results of determining a person by a person in the game of two bots playing with a person. Thus, a human was identified as a human in about 75% of cases, and a bot was identified as a human in 57% of cases.

Table 3. The results of the experiment for determining the humanlike behaviour of the bot during the game.

Participant	A1	B1	C1	A2	B2	C2
1	Bot	Bot	Bot	Person	Person	Person
2	Bot	Bot	Bot	Person	Bot	Bot
3	Bot	Bot	Person	Bot	Person	Person
4	Person	Bot	Person	Bot	Person	Person
5	Person	Person	Bot	Bot	Bot	Person
6	Bot	Bot	Bot	Bot	Bot	Bot
7	Person	Person	Bot	Person	Person	Person
8	Bot	Bot	Person	Bot	Bot	Person

3.3 Identification of Partner and Emotional Factors in Automata

In the third experiment, we conducted 32 sessions of the Teleport game between three bots without human participation. We calculated Teleport bot logs statistics for each event using a python script (Table 4).

Based on the obtained data, we made the following observations. Bots do not make pointless movements (there are no Move logs). Bots always choose a partner (there are

Table 4. Teleport bot logs statistics for each event.

Event	M	SD	Total
Activated	18.5	5.6	1774
TakeOff	2.8	1.8	266
Saved	2.5	1.7	236
Move	0	0	0
Deactivate	7.1	2.9	677
Ask	7.0	2.9	676
Escaped	0	0	0
Thank	7.0	2.6	673

no Escaped logs). Bots are more likely to thank the partner and ask for help more often than people (the average values of the Thank and Ask logs for bots (7.01 and 7.04) are several times higher than the average values of the same logs for people (2.14 and 3.57)). Bots activate the platform for another player with the same frequency as people (the average of Activated logs is approximately the same for people and bots (21.70 and 18.48)).

Based on the obtained data, we made the following observations. Bots do not make pointless movements (there are no Move logs). Bots always choose a partner (there are no Escaped logs). Bots are more likely to thank the partner and ask for help more often than people (the average values of the Thank and Ask logs for bots (7.01 and 7.04) are several times higher than the average values of the same logs for people (2.14 and 3.57)). Bots activate the platform for another player with the same frequency as people (the average of Activated logs is approximately the same for people and bots (21.70 and 18.48)).

Based on the observations given above, the following conclusions can be made. The following characteristics can be attributed to bots: courage, sociability. Bots do not tend to show anxiety and lack of balance, which distinguishes them from people. Bots are not prone to betrayal, unless they are programmed to do so.

4   Discussion and Conclusions

We investigated the relationship between the personal factors of the experiment participants and their behavior during the game "Teleport", and also defined the degree of humanlike nature of the bots and formed their psychological portrait in the research paper.

The study showed that there is a connection between the behavior of the player controlled by the participant in the experiment and the psychological portrait of the participant. Based on the game data, we were able to attribute psychological characteristics of a person to a bot.

We also defined partner and emotional characteristics of bots. A psychological portrait of bots in the game "Teleport" was compiled. We attributed to bots such characteristics as courage, sociability, calmness, balance, and loyalty.

In more than 50% of all cases, the bot behavior could not be distinguished by participants from the human behavior.

This study is a continuation of our previous work (Tikhomirova et al. 2020), where the task was to study the social-emotional behavior model of virtual agents and the dynamics of human emotional states in the process of social interaction in a virtual environment.

Overall, the findings of this study suggest that intelligent virtual actors constructed based on the eBICA model can be considered possessing humanlike socially emotional intelligence applicable to the selected paradigm. Moreover, based on the behavioral data analysis using the approach developed in this work, human psychological characteristics can be confidently attributed to virtual actors possessing socially emotional intelligence. This finding and the developed method will be extended elsewhere and will be useful for a variety of practical domains.

Acknowledgements. This research was funded by the Russian Science Foundation Grant No. 18-11-00336. The authors are grateful to all NRNU MEPhI students who participated in the study, and to all anonymous Reviewers for their useful comments on the manuscript.

References

Adams, S., et al.: Mapping the landscape of human-level artificial general intelligence. AI Magazine **33**(1), 25–42 (2012)

Azarnov, D.A., Chubarov, A.A., Samsonovich, A.V.: Virtual actor with social-emotional intelligence. Procedia Comput. Sci. **123**, 76–85 (2018). https://doi.org/10.1016/j.procs.2018.01.013

Chubarov, A.A., Tikhomirova, D.V., Shirshova, A.V., Veselov, N.O., Samsonovich, A.V.: Virtual Listener: A Turing-like test for behavioral believability. Procedia Comput. Sci. **169**, 892–899 (2020). https://doi.org/10.1016/j.procs.2020.02.146

Ilyin, E.P.: Emotions and Feelings. Second Edition (Russian). Piter, St. Petersburg (2007)

Kapustina, A N.: Multivariate Personal Method of R. Catell (Russian). Speech, St. Petersburg (2004)

Karson, W., O'Dell, J.W.: A Guide to the Clinical Use of the 16PF. University of Michigan Press, Ann Arbor (1976)

Korukonda, A.R.: Taking stock of Turing test: a review, analysis, and appraisal of issues surrounding thinking machines. Int. J. Hum Comput Stud. **58**, 240–257 (2003)

Mueller, S.T.: A partial implementation of the BICA cognitive decathlon using the psychology experiment building language (PEBL). Int. J. Mach. Consciousness **2**(2), 273–288 (2010). https://doi.org/10.1142/S1793843010000497

Nass, C., Steuer, J., Tauber, E.R.: Computers are social actors. In: Adelson, B., Dumais, S., Olson, J. (eds.). Proceedings of the CHI'94 Conference on Human Factors in Computing Systems, pp. 72–78, ACM Press, New York (1994). ISBN: 978-020176557-1

Raygorodsky, D.Ya.: Practical psychodiagnostics. Methods and tests (Russian). Bakhrakh-M Publication, Moscow (2011)

Samsonovich, A.V.: On the semantic map as a key component in socially-emotional BICA. Biol. Inspired Cogn. Archi. **23**, 1–6 (2018a)

Samsonovich, A.V.: Schema formalism for the common model of cognition. Biol. Inspired Cogn. Archi. **26**, 1–19 (2018b)

Samsonovich, A.V.: Emotional biologically inspired cognitive architecture. Biol. Inspired Cogn. Archi. **6**, 109–125 (2013)

Samsonovich, A.V., Ascoli, G.A., De Jong, K.A.: Human-level psychometrics for cognitive architectures. In: Smith, L., Sporns, O., Yu, C., Gasser, M., Breazeal, C., Deak, G., Weng, J. (eds.) Fifth International Conference on Development and Learning ICDL 2006. Bloomington, IN, 2006: Department of Psychological and Brain Sciences, Indiana University. CD-ROM (2006). ISBN 0-9786456-0-X

Tikhomirova, D.V., Chubarov, A.A., Samsonovich, A.V.: Empirical and modeling study of emotional state dynamics in social videogame paradigms. Cogn. Syst. Res. **60**, 44–56 (2020)

Logical Probabilistic Biologically Inspired Cognitive Architecture

Evgenii E. Vityaev[1,2]([⊠]) [iD], Alexander V. Demin[3], and Yurii A. Kolonin[2]

[1] Sobolev Institute of Mathematics SD RAS, Novosibirsk, Russia
vityaev@math.nsc.ru
[2] Mathematics and Mechanics Department, Novosibirsk State University, Novosibirsk, Russia
[3] A. P. Ershov Institute of Informatics System, Novosibirsk, Russia

Abstract. We consider a task-oriented approach to AGI, when any cognitive problem, perhaps superior to human ability, has sense given a criterion of its solution. In the frame of this approach, we consider the task of purposeful behavior in a complex probabilistic environment, where behavior is organized through self-learning. For that purpose, we suggest cognitive architecture that relies on the theory of functional systems. The architecture is based on the main notions of this theory: goal, result, anticipation of the result. The logical structure of this theory was analyzed and used for the control system of purposeful behavior development. This control system contains a hierarchy of functional systems that organizes purposeful behavior. The control system was used for modeling agents to solve the foraging task.

Keywords: Architecture · Functional systems theory · Adaptive control system · Purposeful behavior · Goal-directed behavior

1 Introduction

At the moment there is a lack of a unitary approach to AGI development. Currently the most popular stance in the area are neural networks of different kind. While this approach is widespread and practically useful for some "intellectual" tasks, it still has its well-known disadvantages: huge amounts of data are needed for the network to become effective, high computational cost, the infamous "black box problem" are preventing us from understanding how the result of calculations was obtained. All these problems compel us to look for other approaches.

We consider a task-oriented approach to AGI, when any cognitive problem, perhaps superior to human ability, has sense given a criterion of its solution. In the frame of this approach, we consider the task of purposeful behavior in a complex probabilistic environment, where behavior is organized through self-learning.

Purposeful behavior was deeply studied in the USSR and Russia under the framework of the Theory of Functional Systems (TFS), which describes the organization of

The first author financially supported by the Russian Foundation for Basic Research # 18-29-13027.

B. Goertzel et al. (Eds.): AGI 2020, LNAI 12177, pp. 337–346, 2020.
https://doi.org/10.1007/978-3-030-52152-3_36

purposeful behavior aimed at satisfying a certain need [1]. In this theory the elaboration of an action plan to achieve the goal is carried out on the basis of existing experience by predicting the achievement of the goal and all its subgoals, organized hierarchically. This prediction, even before any action begins, is accompanied by the formation of a mechanism controlling the achievement of the goal and its subgoals by the corresponding groups of receptors responsible for recording the achievement of the subgoals and the goal. These groups of receptors form a certain complex receptor for achieving the subgoals and goals, which is called the acceptor of action results. Thus, TFS is quite consistent with the task-oriented approach to AGI and, in addition, it was worked out in detail and experimentally confirmed.

In this paper, we present a formalization of TFS based on logical-probabilistic learning driven by detecting the most specific rules of behavior. Prediction of achieving goals and subgoals is carried out by an inductive-statistical inference of predictions based on these most specific rules. Such rules have a number of important properties. Firstly, they can be detected by special logical-probabilistic neurons that satisfy the Hebb rule [2]. Secondly, their predictions in accordance with the inductive-statistical conclusion are consistent [3]. The preference of a particular actions plan is carried out taking into account the probability of predicting the goal achievement. This model may be implemented in the frame of probabilistic programming [4].

In our approach we can see some parallels to Jeff Hawkins's Hierarchical Temporal Memory (HTM), as it is also based on prediction and biologically inspired. But with regard to the organization of purposeful behavior, TFS has been worked out in much more detail. Our system is more structurally simple due to the difference in mathematical foundations and actions plan, based purely on a prediction with the highest probability of the goal achievement.

Another relatively close approach is SOAR [5], a classic architecture that solves multiple tasks including purposeful behavior. Its inference is also based on "if-then" rules, but not on probabilistic predictions.

Our architecture is not only plausible from a biological point of view, but is also quite effective: it learns to explore the environment and achieve goals in it much faster than reinforcement learning and neural networks. Also it can achieve more complex, two-stage goals in the same environment, the task that classic approaches cannot do much with. The results of experiments confirming this are presented in Sect. 5.

2   The Theory of Functional Systems of Brain Function

The theory of functional systems developed by P. K. Anokhin and many other distinguished scientists of his school, is, at the moment, one of the few known theories in which the concepts of goal, purpose, result, and goal-directed activity are principal ones and which exposes the physiological mechanisms that implement these concepts.

Desire is not passive. It makes no sense to desire if there is no possibility to get closer to satisfying the desire by some actions or activities. Desire is active, but meaningless without purposefulness – it causes the organism to be active and display some behavior in order to satisfy it. Thus the concept of goal emerges. Activity and actions are always goal-directed. If there is no goal for an action, it is unclear when it should be terminated. Let us define the goal as an activity or behavior that is aimed at satisfying a certain criterion. A goal cannot be attained without having a criterion of its attainment; otherwise we can always assume that the goal has already been attained. Such definition of goal allows us to define the result of attaining the goal as what we obtain by meeting the criterion and attaining the goal (fulfilling the desire). Between the concepts of goal and result, the following relationship is found: the result is obtained when the goal is attained and the criterion of its availability is "triggered". But when the goal is being set, we have the goal yet not the result.

The definition of goal is paradoxical since the activity/behavior of satisfying some criteria does not essentially presuppose knowledge of how to attain a goal; you can set a goal without defining either how it can be attained, or by what means, or when. This paradoxical nature of the goal concept we call the "goal paradox". For the paradox solution we need an experience. As will be seen later on, in the framework of the TFS, brain activity during goal-directed behavior is seen as being constantly occupied with solving the goal paradox, and determining by what means, when, and how to attain goals.

Let us proceed to outline the theory of functional systems, in which the concepts of goal, result, and goal-directed activity are principal one, analyzing the physiological mechanisms of these concepts.

The TFS is a theory of systems, whose function is to attain goals (satisfy needs) by solving the goal paradox. Therefore, we will outline the TFS as a theory of solving goal paradoxes, and describe how the brain determines by what means, when, and how goals can be attained.

As achieving results consists of satisfying some criteria, this achievement should be registered in some way. In the physiological sense, what constitutes a criterion for registering the attainment of a result? According to P.K. Anokhin, this is physiologically realized by a "special receptor apparatus" [6]. The signaling of this receptor apparatus about obtaining a result (i.e., on the lack of deviation from the optimal level of metabolism) and attaining the goal is called reverse afferentation.

Now we can explain, within the framework of TFS, how goals are being physiologically set by an organism. An organism needs to constitute a goal in TFS. The goal (and its attainment criterion) firstly signals by means of reverse afferentation that there is a lack of some sort; secondly, it sets a goal to wait for a signal, indicating that the results have been attained; and thirdly, it provides energy and forces the organism to attain the goal. Thus, the physiological mechanism of goal-setting consists of the emergence of a need.

The interaction of different goals and results is organized in several ways according to TFS: by the "principle of the dominant", "hierarchy of results" and "result models".

3   Central Mechanisms of Functional Systems

"According to P. K. Anokhin, the central mechanisms of functional systems that support goal-directed behavioral acts have a similar structure" [6]. Let us examine in detail the architecture of goal-directed activity, as well as the physiological mechanisms of solving the goal paradox.

Afferent Synthesis. The afferent synthesis, which includes the synthesis of motivational excitation, memory, contextual and triggering afferentation, constitutes the initial stage of the behavioral act of any complexity. *Motivational Excitation*. As we know, the goal is set by an emerging need. In case of goal-directed behavior, it transforms into a motivational excitation. However, a motivational stimulus does not consist of the excitation of receptors which stand "on guard" for some physiological constant – it is rather an excitation of "central brain structures" initiated by the arising need. It is the motivational stimulus that constitutes the goal set in the organism in case of goal-directed behavior. As in the case of needs, the motivational stimulus not only sets a goal but also energetically supports its attainment. *Memory*. The whole sequence of stimuli that has led to goal attainment is recorded during reinforcement, starting with the motivational stimulus. Motivational stimulus extracts all previous sequences of actions which have led to attaining the result from memory. *Situational Afferentation*. While recording a memory trace, the situation in which the result is attained is also being recorded. This situation is registered, along with the motivation, as a necessary precondition for attaining the result. Thus, the motivational stimulus in this situation extracts only those ways of attaining the goal that are possible in the given situation. *Triggering Afferentation*. The fourth component of afferent synthesis is the triggering afferentation. It is essentially the same as the situational afferentation with the difference that considers the time and place of attaining the result.

Consequently, the goal paradox is solved for the most part during afferent synthesis, as it is when the "what", "how", and "when" of goal attainment are determined. Therefore, taking experience and environment into account, the motivational excitation as a goal automatically solves the goal paradox and determines by what means, how, and when can the goal be attained.

Decision-Making. At the stage of afferent synthesis, motivational excitation can extract several ways of attaining the goal from memory. At the stage of decision making, only one of them is selected – thus forming the "program of actions".

Acceptor of Action Results. Suppose a program of actions is chosen. At that point, there is no guarantee yet that the final result will necessarily be attained, not even intermediate ones. The goal can only be attained if each of the intermediate results of the current program of actions will be attained. Motivational excitation extracts the entire sequence and the hierarchy of results that should be attained during the program of actions from memory. This sequence and hierarchy of results are defined in TFS as the *acceptor of action results*. Therefore, while being transformed into a particular goal, the motivational excitation extracts a particular criteria of this goal attainment. This consists of the whole sequence and the hierarchy of criteria of results which must be attained in the process of attaining the goal and performing the program of actions, i.e. the acceptor of action results. Thus, the acceptor of action results anticipates the particular criteria of attaining the goal.

Transforming motivational excitation as a goal into a particular goal shifts the original paradoxical goal – for which it is not determined by what means, how, and when it can be attained – into a non-paradoxical particular goal, for which the final goal (and result) is divided into subgoals (and sub-results), so that for each sugoal it is already known by what means, how, and when it can be attained.

4 Formal Model of TFS

Now let us assume that our model constitutes the control system of some animat that operates in discrete time $t = 0, 1, \ldots$ as it was done in [7]. Suppose the animat has a set of sensors $S_1, \ldots, S_n$ which characterize both the state of the animat itself and of external environment. Each sensor S_i has a set of possible indications VS_i. The animat also has a set of available actions in the environment $A = \{a_1, \ldots, a_m\}$. Any action that animat performs at a moment t_i may result at a moment t_i+1 in some changes in the environment, and, consequently, in its sensors indications. Since the animat "perceives" the world only through its sensors, then from its point of view the system's state at any given point in time can be written as a vector of all sensors indications $V(t) = (v_1, \ldots, v_n)$, where $v_i \in VS_i$ is the indications of the the i-th sensor at the moment t, and the states with same sensor indications are indistinguishable for it. The set of all possible states of the system is denoted by $S = (VS_1 \times VS_2 \times \ldots \times VS_n)$.

On a set of states of the system $S = (VS_1 \cup VS_2 \cup \ldots \cup VS_n)$ we define a set of predicates $PS = \{P_1, \ldots, P_k\}$ each of which is calculated on the basis of sensors indications. Each state of the system can thus be written as a vector $s = (p_1, \ldots, p_k)$, $p_i \in \{0, 1\}$ of predicates' values from PS where 1 means validity of a predicate and 0 – its falsity. The state may be described by a subset of predicates $s = (p^e_{i_1}, \ldots, p^e_{i_e})$, $p^e_{i_1}, \ldots, p^e_{i_e} \subseteq p_1, \ldots, p_k$. The animat's task is to attain a certain goal. Let us define a goal $Goal$ as a state of the system $s_{Goal} = (p^{goal}_{i_1}, \ldots, p^{goal}_{i_{goal}})$ which it is required to attain. A notation $(p^{goal}_{i_1}, \ldots, p^{goal}_{i_{goal}})$ means that predicates $p^{goal}_{i_1}, \ldots, p^{goal}_{i_{goal}}$ should be true when the goal is attained.

Let us clarify concepts of event and history. By an event $e = (s_0, s_e, a)$ we will understand a singular fact of transferring the system from the state $s_0 = (p^0_1, \ldots, p^0_k)$ into a state $s_e = (p^e_1, \ldots, p^e_k)$ as a result of an action a and by a history of events – a set of pairs (e_t, t) where $e_t = (s_t, s_{t+1}, a)$ is an event and t is a point in time when this event has occurred.

Let us define a rule R that predicts a change of a state(s) after the execution of an action a as a transformation $R = \left(s_0 \xrightarrow{a}_{p} s_e \right)$, where: s_0 – is the initial state of the system $(p^0_{i_1}, \ldots, p^0_{i_0})$; s_e – is the final state of the system $(p^e_{i_1}, \ldots, p^e_{i_e})$; a – is an action that transforms the initial state into the final one; p – in the probability of the rule, which calculated as follows: if n is the number of cases in which the initial state was s_0 and an action a was executed, and m is the number of those n cases, in which the action a transform the state s_0 into the state s_e, then $p = m/n$.

The rules may be discovered by neurons, which detect conditioned connections in accordance to the semantic probabilistic inference and formal model of neuron [2].

Let us first define a functional system $FSC = (s_{Goal}, R_1, \ldots, R_n, p_{FSC})$ that realizes one action. Functional system FSC performs transformations $s_0 \xrightarrow[R_1,\ldots,R_n]{p_{FSC}} s_{Goal}$, where $s_{Goal} = (p^{goal}_{i_1}, \ldots, p^{goal}_{i_{goal}})$ – is the target state of the functional system, $R_1, \ldots, R_n$ – are rules of the form $s_0 \xrightarrow{a}_{p} s_{Goal}$, using which the system can get to the target state s_{Goal} (Fig. 1) from various initial states s_0 by performing some action a. Functional system FSC chooses the most probable rule $s_0 \xrightarrow[p]{a} s_{Goal}$, which leads to attaining the goal. The chosen rule is rewarded if the goal s_{Goal} is attained (increase m in $p = m/n$) and penalized otherwise. An estimation of the probability of attaining a goal by a functional system can be calculated based on the statistics of attaining goals: if n is the number of cases in which a request to attain a goal s_{Goal} was received and m is the number of cases in which the selected rules and sequences/hierarchies of actions led to attaining the goal s_{Goal}, then $p_{FSC} = m/n$.

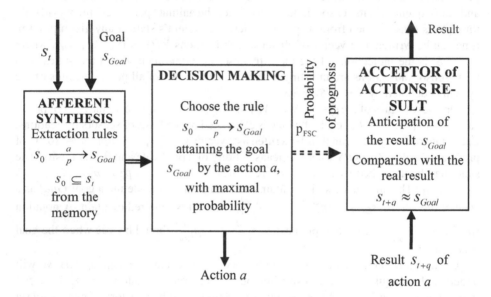

Fig. 1. Functional system that implements sensory corrections.

In general case functional systems are sequences and the hierarchies of the functional systems FSC. A functional system $FS = (s_{Goal}, \langle FSC_1, \ldots, FSC_n \rangle, p_{FS})$ that combines a sequence of functional systems of the form FSC is defined as:

$$FS = s_0 \xrightarrow[\to s_1 \to s_2 \to \ldots s_{goal}]{\substack{FSC_1, \ldots, FSC_n \\ p_{FS} = p_{FSC_1} \cdots p_{FSC_n}}} s_{goal}, \text{ where}$$

$$FSC_1 = \left(s_0 \xrightarrow[p_{FSC_1}]{R_1^1, \ldots, R_{v_1}^1} s_1 \right), FSC_2 = \left(s_1 \xrightarrow[p_{FSC_2}]{R_1^2, \ldots, R_{v_2}^2} s_2 \right) \ldots FSC_n = \left(s_{n-1} \xrightarrow[p_{FSC_n}]{R_1^n, \ldots, R_{v_n}^n} s_n \right)$$

are functional systems of the type FSC. The goal of the functional system FS is to successively attain goals $s_1 \to s_2 \to \ldots \to s_{goal}$ using functional systems $FSC_1, \ldots, FSC_n$ with a resulting probability $p_{FS} = p_{FSC_1} \cdot \ldots \cdot p_{FSC_n}$. If the goal s_{Goal} is not attained by some functional subsystem, then orienting-investigative reaction occurs, which selects another sequences/hierarchies of the functional systems to attain the goal, and the activated rule of the corresponding functional subsystem is penalized. If the goal s_{Goal} is attained and results for each functional subsystem are registered by the acceptor of action results, then all activated rules for each functional subsystem are rewarded.

5 Experiments

For investigation of the control system behavior two experiments were carried out. We explored the foraging task. In this task some agent explores the area and gathers pabulary objects. There are no subgoals in this task, so in the second phase we have complicated this task by introducing a "tablet" that is needed to eat the pabulary object. In this case the subgoal is eating the tablet before eating the pabulary object.

The virtual world was modeled in which the agent gathers the pabulary objects. This world includes the rectangular field with 25×25 cells. Each cell may be empty or include the "pabulary object" or "barrier" (the latter are placed strictly on the perimeter of the field). Agent is placed on one of the cells and may be oriented in one of the four directions. The possible actions $\{a_1, a_2, a_3\}$ of the agent are: step one cell forward, turn left, turn right.

In the first experiment some pabulary objects are placed randomly on the field. To eat the pabulary object agent needs to take a step on the cell where the pabulary object is located. In that case the pabulary object disappears from the cell and randomly appears on some other cell.

Agent has sensors $S_1, \ldots, S_9$, in which $S_1, \ldots, S_8$ stand for the area around the agent and inform the agent about the objects placed on these cells, and S_9 informs the agent about the object placed on the cell that agent occupies.

The second experiment is more complicated. In this experiment, apart from pabulary objects, "tablet" objects are randomly distributed over the cells of the field. To eat the pabulary object agent needs to have a "tablet" object, which he needs to gather on the field. When the agent eats a pabulary object the gathered "tablet" object disappears and for eating a new pabulary object the agent needs to gather a new "tablet" object. The agent gathers a "tablet" object if it occupies the cell with this object. The agent may gather only one "tablet" object. When agent gathers a "tablet" object the cell becomes empty and a new "tablet" object randomly appears on the field. In the second experiment agent has ten sensors $S_1, \ldots, S_9, S_{pill}$, where first nine are the same as in the first experiment and sensor S_{pill} informs the agent about availability of the "tablet" object.

For the estimation of the effectiveness of the control system we compared it with control systems based on reinforcement learning, described in the work [8]. For comparison we used two control systems based on Q-Learning. These algorithms consist in consecutive refinement of the estimation of the reward $Q(s_t, a_t)$ summary, if in the state s_t the system acts as a_t:

$$Q^{(i+1)}(s_t, a_t) = Q^{(i)}(s_t, a_t) + \alpha(r_t + \gamma \max_A Q^{(i)}(s_{t+1}, a) - Q^{(i)}(s_t, a_t)).$$

The first system (Q-Lookup Table) uses table, which includes Q-values of all possible states and acts. Initially, the table is fulfilled randomly. Then the system in each act specifies the Q-value.

The second system (Q-Neural Net) uses approximation of the function $Q(s_t, a_t)$ using neural networks. In that case for each act a_i a special neural network is used. In each time period the system chooses an action and neural network produces a greater value of the estimation Q-value. Then the action accomplishes, and weights of the neural nets are changed.

For the estimation of the systems the period of agent functioning was divided on stages for 1000 steps. The estimation consists of the volume of the pabulary objects gathered for a step of the work. After learning every system reaches some optimal value. During the experiment we can estimate the learning speed and corresponding optimal value.

6   Results of the First Experiment

In the first experiment there were 24 predicates for sensors – three predicates ($S_i = empty$), ($S_i = block$), ($S_i = food$) for each sensor S_i, $i = 1, \ldots, 8$. At the beginning the control system contained only one functional system with purpose $S_{Goal} = (S_9 = food)$, when sensor S_9 informs about pabulary objects in the central cell.

This experiment had no subgoals. The main task of this experiment is the estimation of the effectiveness of the functional system and its learning. In the Fig. 2 there are results of comparison for different control systems. For each control system the mean values for 20 experiments are presented. The duration of each experiment is 50,000 steps of the agent. The number of pabulary objects on the field is 100.

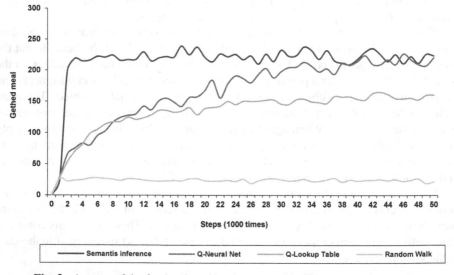

Fig. 2. Amount of the food gathered by the agent with different control systems.

It is seen from the figure that the control system based on the semantic probabilistic inference is fully learned during the 1000 steps. By comparison, control systems based on the neural nets (Q-Neural Net) learn more slowly and become fully learned after nearly 10,000 steps. Slow learning of the Q-Lookup Table follows from the huge number (2496) of states with three possible actions.

The results of this experiment demonstrate that the control system based on the semantic probabilistic inference works rather effectively and learns more effectively than systems based on the reinforcement learning.

7 Results of the Second Experiment

The following experiment is crucially different as the task may be divided in two parts: at first – to find a "tablet" object and then to find pabulary objects. The purpose of this experiment is to demonstrate the ability of automatic subgoals formation.

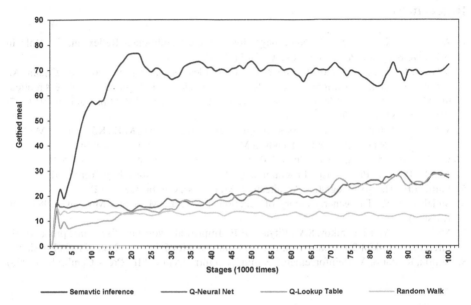

Fig. 3. Amount of food gathered by the agents in the presence of the "tablet" objects.

The agent now has 32 predicates – four predicates for each sensor S_i, $i = 1, \ldots, 8$: ($S_i = empty$), ($S_i = block$), ($S_i = food$) и ($S_i = pill$) and one predicate ($S_{pill} = yes$) for the state when the agent has a "tablet" object and one predicate ($S_9 = food$) for the state when the pabulary object is in the central cell under the agent.

At the beginning the control system of the agent has only one functional system with the purpose $S_{Goal} = (S_{pill} = yes)$ & ($S_9 = food$), when the agent has a "tablet" object and finds a pabulary object.

During the experiment the control system of the agent had always found the subgoal $S_{Goal}^2 = (S_{pill} = yes)$ and formed a corresponding functional system. When the agent had no tablet in possession, the control system passed the control to the subsystem for the search of a tablet, and, after finding the tablet and achieving the goal $S_{Goal}^2 = (S_{pill} = yes)$, the upper level control system started searching the pabulary objects.

The results of the experiment are presented in the Fig. 3. In the figure the mean values for 20 experiments are presented for each control system. In each experiment the agent had 100,000 steps. The number of pabulary objects and "tablet" objects on the field was 100 for each.

As seen from the figure, the control system based on the semantic probabilistic inference was working more effectively than systems based on reinforce-ment learning. Control systems based on reinforce-ment learning showed almost no learning ability and worked unstable. They cannot learn the need of the "tablet" objects for the goal achievement during the reasonable time and have passed by "tablet" objects after 100,000 steps of learning. Additional experiments demonstrated that control system (Q-Neural Net) can sometimes learn during the 300,000–500,000 steps.

References

1. Anokhin, P.K.: Biology and Neurophysiology of the Conditioned Reflex and its Role in Adaptive Behavior. Pergamon Press, Oxford (1974)
2. Vityaev, E.E.: A formal model of neuron that provides consistent predictions. In: Chella, A., Pirrone, R., Sorbello, R., Johannsdottir, K.R. (eds.) Biologically Inspired Cognitive Architectures 2012. AISC, vol. 196, pp. 339–344. Springer, Heidelberg (2013). https://doi.org/10.1007/978-3-642-34274-5_57
3. Vityaev, E., Odintsov, S.: How to predict consistently? In: Cornejo, M.E., Kóczy, L.T., Medina, J., De Barros Ruano, A.E. (eds.) Trends in Mathematics and Computational Intelligence. SCI, vol. 796, pp. 35–41. Springer, Cham (2019). https://doi.org/10.1007/978-3-030-00485-9_4
4. Avi, P.: Practical Probabilistic Programming. Manning Publications, New York (2016)
5. Laird, J.E.: The Soar Cognitive Architecture. MIT Press, Cambridge (2012)
6. Sudakov, K.V.: The general theory of functional systems. Medicine, Moscow (1984). (in Russian)
7. Muhortov, V.V., Khlebnikov, S.V., Vityaev, E.E.: Improved algorithm of semantic probabilistic inference in task of 2-dimention animat. Neuroinformatics 6(1), 50–62 (2012). (in Russian)
8. Sutton, R., Barto, A.: Reinforcement Learning: An Introduction. MIT Press, Cambridge (1998)

An Architecture for Real-Time Reasoning and Learning

Pei Wang[✉], Patrick Hammer, and Hongzheng Wang

Department of Computer and Information Sciences,
Temple University, Philadelphia, USA
{pei.wang,patrick.hammer,hongzheng.wang}@temple.edu

Abstract. This paper compares the various conceptions of "real-time" in the context of AI, as different ways of taking the processing time into consideration when problems are solved. An architecture of real-time reasoning and learning is introduced, which is one aspect of the AGI system NARS. The basic idea is to form problem-solving processes flexibly and dynamically at run time by using inference rules as building blocks and incrementally self-organizing the system's beliefs and skills, under the restriction of time requirements of the tasks. NARS is designed under the Assumption of Insufficient Knowledge and Resources, which leads to an inherent ability to deal with varying situations in a timely manner.

1 Various Versions of "Real-Time"

Roughly speaking, solving problems "in real-time" means there are time requirements on the problems to be solved, coming out of the needs or restrictions of the domain. This topic has both theoretical and practical significance, because traditional theories of computation do not take it into consideration, while many (if not all) practical applications have time requirements.

In computability theory [6], the time spent in a computation is not considered, as far as it is finite. In computational complexity theory [1], processing time is usually considered as an attribute of an algorithm (a solution of a problem), rather than of a problem itself. Furthermore, in algorithm analysis, the "time complexity" of an algorithm indicates how fast its processing time increases as the size of problem instances, but not the actual period of time costed by the process, since that not only depends on the algorithm, but also on the size and content of the instance, the processing speed of the (hardware and software) platform, etc.

Therefore, the above theories do not cover problems that have concrete time requirements as part of their specifications. The most common form of time requirement is a deadline, which is also called "hard real-time". The other form, "soft real-time", correspond to the situation where the utility of the solution is a decreasing function of time [10, 11, 15]. We can see the former as a special case of the latter, where a deadline is the point where the utility of the solution drops from 1 to 0.

B. Goertzel et al. (Eds.): AGI 2020, LNAI 12177, pp. 347–356, 2020.
https://doi.org/10.1007/978-3-030-52152-3_37

From the perspective of Artificial General Intelligence (AGI), "to work in real-time" can be taken in a more general form, including the following aspects:

- New problems can appear at arbitrary time, rather than only when the system is idly waiting for them.
- The time requirement of a problem instance can change in its different occurrences, that is, the same problem instance may have different urgency levels in different cases.
- The time requirement of a problem instance can change during its processing, that is, to become more or less urgent, rather than fully known at the beginning of the process.
- The relevant data or knowledge used in problem-solving comes incrementally after the solving process starts, partly due to the active learning and exploring of the system.
- It is desired for the best-so-far solutions to be reported whenever they are found, even though they may need to be revised or updated later.

Real-time problem-solving is not a new topic at all, though there is still no theory or technique that provides a general solution. The major approaches explored in artificial intelligence and computer science include the following:

- To find a problem-specific design by considering all software-hardware factors to meet specific time requirements in one concrete application, though parameters in the design allow flexibility of using the design in similar applications [9];
- To depend on a meta-level reasoning process to find a proper solution among the given candidates by considering their quality and time requirement, so as to get the best balance between them according to the current requirement [3,7,13];
- To use an "anytime algorithm", i.e., an interruptible procedure that incrementally updates the best-so-far solution, to achieve a flexible quality-time trade-off [2,22];
- To share processing power among multiple tasks as in an operating system, where tasks are prioritized to reflect their levels of [14]. Such a system can accept a new task in any moment (assuming sufficient memory), processes it with a speed according to its priority, while guaranteeing to avoid starvation.

Though each of the above techniques addresses certain forms of time requirements, and has its applicable domains, none of them has handled all the aspects of real-time in the AGI context as mentioned previously, so a new architecture is in demand. In the next section, we will introduce NARS and how it satisfies the relevant demands.

2   NARS as a Real-Time System

NARS, standing for Non-Axiomatic Reasoning System, is a general-purpose AI project [17,20]. Many of the topics addressed in the following have been described

in the previous publications [5, 16, 18, 19], though this paper is the first time when
the issue of real-time in NARS is comprehensively discussed.

NARS is designed according to the opinion that intelligence is adaptation
under AIKR (the Assumption of Insufficient Knowledge and Resources), meaning
that the system has finite information processing capability, while it has to work
in real-time, and be open to novel tasks [21]. On the other hand, as an AGI
system, NARS is supposed to deal with arbitrary problems which can occur at
arbitrary time. There is no guaranty that the system has enough data and an
appropriate algorithm, or can predict every possible variation of the situation.
So the AIKR principle is necessary and satisfactory. Therefore, "to work in real-
time" is a fundamental design requirement of NARS, and interpreted in a very
broad sense that covers all aspects listed in the previous section.

As a new task can show up at any moment with a time requirement, and
may be novel to the system, it means that the system cannot process it by
following an existing routine or algorithm, but has to construct a solution at
run time, in a case-by-case manner, for the problem (instance, not type) [18]. It
also means there is no way to guarantee solutions of a fixed quality. Instead, the
system simply does its best under the knowledge–resource restriction, evaluated
globally with respect to all the existing tasks.

Concretely speaking, a task for NARS to carry out may be a piece of new
knowledge to be absorbed into the system's beliefs, a question to be answered
according to the relevant beliefs, or a goal to be achieved by executing relevant operations of the system. Under AIKR, the system has no algorithm that
describes the complete process for a task, and nor can the system compare all
solutions then pick the best. Furthermore, as new tasks constantly come to the
system, the processing of a task may be interrupted or terminated at unanticipated moments by other more urgent tasks.

As a reasoning system, NARS processes tasks using its beliefs. In each inference step, a task interacts with a belief, and that may lead to a partial solution
for the task, and at the same time generates derived tasks. Given the assumption of insufficient knowledge, no task can be "fully resolved" in a predetermined
number of steps, though more steps usually lead to better solutions. On the other
hand, given the assumption of insufficient resources, normally no task can interact with all relevant beliefs in the system, so as to reach a "logical end" and no
better solution can be found.

Working in such a situation, the system is made to work in real-time by
making each inference rules to only cost a small constant time, and allowing the
processing of a task to stop after any number of inference steps.

This strategy can only be used with a logic that is fully compatible with
AIKR. The Non-Axiomatic Logic (NAL) used in NARS [20] satisfies this requirement. All inference rules of NAL are "local" in the sense that the conclusion
is only generated and justified with a small number of (usually one or two)
premises. All non-local effects in the system are produced by multi-step processes. Consequently, the time granularity of atomic (uninterruptible) activity
in NARS is very small (currently below millisecond).

In this way, the actual solution obtained for a task is by the beliefs interacting with it (which decides the inference rules triggered in a data-driven manner), as well as their order. All these decisions are made at run time when the task is processed, rather than planned in advance.

To achieve the overall efficiency in resource allocation, the selections of tasks and beliefs are made in a specially designed data structure called "bag" [16], which is basically a probabilistic priority queue with a *put* and *take* operation (see Fig. 1) for the adding of elements and their retrieval. Each data item in a bag has a *priority* value attached, which is positively correlated with the probability for the item to be selected (with *take*) in the next round. The priority also decides which element to remove when a new item is added via *put* at full capacity, namely the lowest priority item. This makes sure finite space constraints are maintained in the "bag".

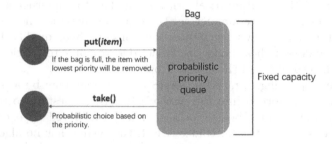

Fig. 1. The basic functions of a bag.

The priority of an item is a summary of a number of factors, including its quality, usefulness in history in similar contexts, relevance to the current situation, etc., and is dynamically adjusted according to the feedback of its usage and the change in the environment. There is also an across-the-board forgetting mechanism that decreases all priority values over time. Different items have different forgetting rate, which is indicated by a *durability* value. There is also a *quality* value, which shows the long-term significance of a data item to the system. This *priority–durability–quality* triple forms the "budget" of a task (or belief), which summarizes its relative competitiveness in the system's resource allocation at the moment.

When a user assigns a task to NARS, an initial budget can be provided, otherwise system defaults will be given according to the type and features of the task. After that, the system will adjust the budgets, as well as to decide the budget for each derived tasks and beliefs by taking the relevant factors into account.

From the viewpoint of the users, the system processes multiple tasks in a time-sharing manner, though here the mutual interference among the tasks is much stronger than that among the processes in an operating system. For a task, its processing path and results not only depend on its budget and the existing beliefs, but also on the budgets of the coexisting tasks, as well as their processing paths.

When the processing of a task stops, usually it is not because the process has reached its final state or the quality of the solution has reached a certain criterion, but because the task has lost in the resource competition, though the processing may be resumed at a future time.

Beside the above automatic resource-allocation mechanism, NARS also supports more complicated time management. For instance, the system can have knowledge about the execution time of an operation or operation sequence, and can use it in a planning process to decide whether to use the operation to reach a certain goal. For instance, to meet a specific deadline, careful planning and scheduling will be needed.

The above architecture and mechanism makes NARS capable of working in real-time, in a manner similar to that of a human in similar situations.

3   Examples

The following examples serve as an illustration of the discussed real-time aspects of NARS on what it means to operate in real-time. These examples can directly be tested with the current version of OpenNARS[1], an open-source implementation of NARS.

New Information Coming in While Solving a Problem

After a detective presents initial information and relevant background knowledge, the system changes its mind about who is the murder after newly presented evidence.

```
//It is known that the first suspected murder,
//Rambo is living in NYC and known to be aggressive
<{Rambo} --> (&,(/,liveIn,_,NYC),[aggressive])>.
//It is known that the other
//suspected murder lives in Philadelphia
<{Sam} --> (/,liveIn,_,Philadelphia)>.
//Also it is known from a psychological study that
//murder tend to be more aggressive to some degree
<murder --> [aggressive]>. %0.7%
//Who is the murder?
<{?who} --> murder>?
//System considers Rambo more likely to be the murder
Answer <{Rambo} --> murder>. %1.00;0.22%
//24 days later...
24000
//the detective got the information, that the
//murder surely must be from Philadelphia
<murder --> (/,liveIn,_,Philadelphia)>.
//Now the system thinks Sam is more likely the murder:
Answer <{Sam} --> murder>. %1.00;0.45%
```

The same order of finding solutions could possibly also have happened if the new information would have been known from the beginning. But due to the low

---

[1] http://opennars.org/.

truth-value obtained from the psychological study, and the control mechanism's tendency to pursue more truthful paths of reasoning, it is more likely that it would have found the right solution first. Note that the problem-solving process here is similar to that of an anytime algorithm, with the difference that in which order the solutions are found is not deterministic, and that not all information is demanded to be present at the beginning.

Event Sequences

OpenNARS' ability to stay responsive to new incoming event sequences

```
//A sequence of entities are observed
//a was observed
<{a} --> [observed]>. :|:
251
//b was observed
<{b} --> [observed]>. :|:
...
//g was observed
<{g} --> [observed]>. :|:
131
//h was observed
<{h} --> [observed]>. :|:
//What comes after c?
<(&/,<{c} --> [observed]>,?i) =/> <{?what} --> [observed]>>?
//d comes after c
Answer <(&/,<{c} --> [observed]>,+232) =/>
                   <{d} --> [observed]>>. :-1088: %1.00;0.44%
//What comes before f?
<(&/,<{?what} --> [observed]>,?i) =/> <{f} --> [observed]>>?
//e comes before f
Answer <(&/,<{e} --> [observed]>,+602) =/>
                   <{f} --> [observed]>>. :-239: %1.00;0.43%
```

This example illustrates the system's ability for event processing. The key here is that the processing time for a new event does not increase with the amount of events seen so far. This means the system is guaranteed to stay responsive to new input, while of course it cannot be guaranteed that every possible pattern will be extracted. The system's control mechanism tends to recognize patterns that span a relatively shorter time distance, are truthful, repeating, goal-relevant, conceptually important etc. (see [4] and [5] for more details). However, if relevant questions arise, the control mechanism can make question-driven inference, as to answer a specific question which answer otherwise would have less likely been generated by the system. Example:

```
//Does h come after a?
<(&/,<{a} --> [observed]>,?1) =/> <{h} --> [observed]>>?
//h comes after a
Answer <(&/,<{a} --> [observed]>,+1789) =/>
                   <{h} --> [observed]>>. %1.00;0.09%
```

Sensitivity on Elapsed Processing Time

This example shows the system's tracking capability of elapsed time.

```
//Lighting usually generates thunder in 5 seconds
<(&/,<lighting --> [seen]>,+500) =/>
                        <thunder --> [heard]>>. %1.0;0.45%
//Lighting is seen right now
<lighting --> [seen]>. :|:
//10 seconds later:
1000
//Do you hear thunder?
<thunder --> [heard]>? :|:
//I should have heard a thunder 5 seconds ago
Answer <thunder --> [heard]>. :-506: %1.00;0.40%
```

Many existing techniques, even when a deadline is taken into account, do not assume that the processing itself leads to the passing of problem-relevant time duration. In the above example we see that the answer to the question, which originally was a prediction, is already an event of the past. This is captured by the occurrence time of the prediction the system tracked, which in this example is, after the additional 10 s passed, already smaller than the current time. Generally, the system tries to find answers which are both more reliable and closer to the occurrence time of the question. Also, for decision making, the system tries to use procedure knowledge which preconditions were fulfilled more recently by events, these tend to be still valid to base a decision on. Here, both the occurrence time and truth-value are taken into account.

4 Comparisons and Discussions

Overall, there are the following possibilities for real-time problem solving:

- Using a single program specially designed to meet a predetermined time restriction under all circumstances.
- Selecting a program among an existing set of programs according to their running time and the current time demand.
- Constructing a program following a meta-algorithm according to the time requirement in the program specification.
- Running an interruptible program that has a repeatable path but unpredictable ending. It has no fixed complexity, but has a time–quality function.
- Building a one-time procedure according to time requirement of the problem and the context, without accurate predictability and repeatability.

One type of common and widely used real-time system is the programs used for the control in automation, e.g. the program for a mechanical arm to assemble a product. Such a program is relatively simpler than other kind of approaches because the environment of such program is always well defined and stable, and it is also customized for a single process. So the mechanism can run smoothly following the determined schedule. Obviously, such specifically designed program cannot deal with unexpected events, which appear in many situations.

Some other approaches are more flexible to deal with various types of deadline. Design-to-time [3] approach prepares multiple solutions and organizes the solution by making trade-offs between quality and time. An anytime algorithm

[2] can be interrupted at any moment to get the most satisfied solution within that deadline, so is closer to our expectations because it can still get a satisfactory solution even if the deadline is unexpectedly changed, assuming it already found a solution to be refined further. The control mechanism of NARS shares this property, which makes it possible for the system to operate without knowing relevant deadlines beforehand. Compare to anytime algorithms, the mechanism in NARS excludes not only the predetermined final states, but also the predetermined path of processing. As long as an approach is based on a predetermined algorithm, it cannot handle unexpected changes in the environment during its running.

A fundamental difference between NARS and many traditional theories of intelligence is the AIKR principle. Under AIKR, any belief can be changed according to new information. NARS does not assume any absolutely certain knowledge about the future, and it allows unexpected changes to occur at any time. Therefore, NARS is prepared to respond to new input during the process and adjust its beliefs and inference paths. In this paper, we regard "real-time" as a more general situation. We regard the time as a part of problem, so there is fundamental difference between the idea of "real-time" and computational complexity theory. Since we cannot guarantee the environment is always suitable for a prepared algorithm, AIKR makes the NARS approach necessary to handle such situations.

While some real-time systems have been designed to take insufficient resources into account (such as schedulers in operating systems), attacking both insufficient resources and knowledge raises additional challenges. The NARS approach is somehow like the student doing the programming question with limited memory and run time, but doesn't have the ability to deal with this question perfectly, then how to get the imperfect but proper result with such restriction.

The ability to work under AIKR is significant for a general purpose AI system, especially if real-time responses should be supported. There are also other AGI researches which apply similar principles. In the Anytime Bounded Rationality (ABR) model [12], knowledge is bounded within fixed memory budget and can be updated and revised based on the new experience, while the ABR model schedule inferences deterministically using objective time semantics. The Economic attention allocation (ECAN) model of OpenCog [8] also considers the space limitation and applies two key parameters, STI (short-term importance) and LTI (long-term importance), to manage the resource allocation. However, ECAN does not stress real-time operating conditions as the ones discussed in this paper.

In Sect. 2, we describe how NARS works in real-time. The system solves problems in a case-by-case manner using procedures composed at run-time, by taking many factors in the current context into account, rather than following a predetermined algorithm for that type of problem. Therefore, there is no specific requirement to the environment. NARS does not guarantee the quality and delivery time of solutions. If more knowledge and resource are provided, NARS may obtain a better solution. If the process is interrupted, NARS can still provide the best solution under existing knowledge and resources which was found, for instance by returning the highest-confident candidate solution found so far. Without the restriction of needing a predetermined algorithm for the problem to solve, NARS is more flexible in various situations, as also argued in [19].

It is however also clear that in some applications, flexibility is not the major factor under consideration. For instance in real-time operating systems, time requirements are sometimes known (example: let programs running on it respond to I/O within 1 ms, and under all circumstances), and can be taken into account by the corresponding specifically designed scheduling strategy. In this case, the specifically designed algorithm will of course be superior to NARS, but the algorithm cannot be used when time requirements are not known beforehand.

5 Conclusion

We have seen that "real time" has different interpretations, and that NARS fulfills multiple requirements typical for real-time systems, also going further in certain aspects. Some of the requirements we believe to be most relevant have been demonstrated with examples in Sect. 3: the ability to accept a new problem and new information while still working on previous ones (staying open), the resource demand for processing new events not being dependent on the amount of events seen so far (staying responsive), and the system's sensitivity to elapsed time while processing tasks, incorporating elapsed time in question answering and decision making.

Especially since the system does not assume the existence and knowing of deadlines, it fulfills more than certain common understandings of the term "real-time" would ask for. However, since it makes no guarantee about the quality of the solutions to be found, or even to find one at all, it is also in some sense "weaker" than the alternative techniques. This weakness, as argued, follows from the fundamental restriction of operating under Insufficient Knowledge and Resources. The requirement of real-time responses is often satisfiable only by the re-allocation of available resources, as a direct consequence of the often insufficient computational resource supply. Also, as argued, the system cannot make any guarantees about the quality of its solutions, also due to the often insufficient knowledge it has available to solve problems.

Aspects coming from AIKR shed some light on what we believe to be unavoidable properties of AGI systems, unless inherently different philosophies are followed. Philosophies with views like computational resources are infinite, and/or the system does always know the problem-relevant information, assume too much to be acceptable. As we argued, an AGI should work in any environment, including uncertain ones as well. Hence AIKR cannot be dropped, and leads to systems falling in its own subcategory of "real-time system" to be studied further.

Acknowledgement. This work is partially supported by a gift from the Cisco University Research Program Fund, a corporate advised fund of Silicon Valley Community Foundation.

References

1. Cormen, T.H., Leiserson, C.E., Rivest, R.L., Stein, C.: Introduction to Algorithms, 3rd edn. MIT Press, Cambridge (2009)
2. Dean, T., Boddy, M.: An analysis of time-dependent planning. In: Proceedings of AAAI-1988, pp. 49–54 (1988)
3. Garvey, A., Lesser, V.: Design-to-time real-time scheduling. IEEE Trans. Syst. Man Cybern. Special Issue Plan. Schedul. Control **23**(6), 1491–1502 (1993)
4. Hammer, P., Lofthouse, T.: Goal-directed procedure learning. In: Proceedings of the Eleventh Conference on Artificial General Intelligence, pp. 77–86 (2018)
5. Hammer, P., Lofthouse, T., Wang, P.: The OpenNARS implementation of the Non-Axiomatic reasoning system. In: Proceedings of the Ninth Conference on Artificial General Intelligence, pp. 160–170 (2016)
6. Hopcroft, J.E., Motwani, R., Ullman, J.D.: Introduction to Automata Theory, Languages, and Computation, 3rd edn. Addison-Wesley, Boston (2007)
7. Horvitz, E.J.: Reasoning about beliefs and actions under computational resource constraints. In: Kanal, L.N., Levitt, T.S., Lemmer, J.F. (eds.) Uncertainty in Artificial Intelligence 3, pp. 301–324. North-Holland, Amsterdam (1989)
8. Ikle, M., Pitt, J., Sellmann, G., Goertzel, B.: Economic attention networks: associative memory and resource allocation for general intelligence. In: Proceedings of the Second Conference on Artificial General Intelligence, pp. 73–78 (2009)
9. Korf, R.E.: Real-time heuristic search. Artif. Intell. **42**(2–3), 189–211 (1990)
10. Laffey, T.J., Cox, P.A., Schmidt, J.L., Kao, S.M., Read, J.Y.: Real-time knowledge-based systems. AI Magazine **9**, 27–45 (1988)
11. Musliner, D.J., Hendler, J.A., Agrawala, A.K., Durfee, E.H., Strosnider, J.K., Paul, C.J.: The challenges of real-time AI. Computer **28**(1), 58–66 (1995)
12. Nivel, E., Thórisson, K.R., Steunebrink, B., Schmidhuber, J.: Anytime bounded rationality. In: Proceedings of the Eighth Conference on Artificial General Intelligence. pp. 121–130. Springer, Cham (2015). https://doi.org/10.1007/978-3-319-21365-1_13
13. Russell, S., Wefald, E.H.: Principles of metareasoning. Artif. Intell. **49**, 361–395 (1991)
14. Silberschatz, A., Galvin, P.B., Gagne, G.: Operating System Concepts, 9th edn. Wiley, Hoboken (2012)
15. Stankovic, J.A.: Real-time computing systems: the next generation. Technical report 88–06, University of Massachusetts, Amherst (1988)
16. Wang, P.: Problem solving with insufficient resources. Int. J. Uncertainty, Fuzziness Knowl.-based Syst. **12**(5), 673–700 (2004)
17. Wang, P.: Rigid Flexibility: The Logic of Intelligence. Springer, Dordrecht (2006). https://doi.org/10.1007/1-4020-5045-3
18. Wang, P.: Case-by-case problem solving. In: Proceedings of the Second Conference on Artificial General Intelligence, pp. 180–185 (2009)
19. Wang, P.: Solving a problem with or without a program. J. Artif. General Intell. **3**(3), 43–73 (2012)
20. Wang, P.: Non-Axiomatic Logic: A Model of Intelligent Reasoning. World Scientific, Singapore (2013)
21. Wang, P.: On defining artificial intelligence. J. Artif. General Intell. **10**(2), 1–37 (2019)
22. Zilberstein, S.: Operational rationality through compilation of anytime algorithms. AI Magazine **16**(2), 79–80 (1995)

A Model for Artificial General Intelligence

Andy E. Williams[(⊠)] [iD]

Nobeah Foundation, Nairobi, Kenya
awilliams@nobeahfoundation.org
http://www.nobeahfoundation.org

Abstract. A recently developed Functional Modeling Framework suggests that all models of cognition can be represented by a minimally reducible set of functions, and proposes to define the criteria for a model of cognition to have the potential for the general problem solving ability commonly recognized as true human intelligence. This human-centric functional modeling approach is intended to enable different models of AGI to be more easily compared so research can reliably converge on a single understanding, enabling the possibility of massively collaborative interdisciplinary projects to research and implement models of consciousness or cognition where difficulty in communicating very different ideas, particularly in the case of new models without a significant following, has prevented such massive collaboration from in practice having proved possible before. This paper summarizes a model of cognition developed within this framework.

Keywords: Adaptive problem solving · Functional Modeling Framework · Human-centric

1 Background – The Problem of Cognition

In common usage the term "general problem solving ability" functions to mean "a human-like level of ability to solve general problems through abstract reasoning" . Furthermore, taking a functional view of reasoning or understanding as processes with inputs, and outputs, and taking a functional view of problems as a set of input concepts and a set of output concepts that are bridged by such cognitive processes, it can be agreed that general human problem solving ability requires a general reasoning process that solves a general problem, that is, a general problem which all problems in the cognitive system can be defined as belonging to, and that all reasoning processes solve. And the one general problem that can be intuitively seen as being shared by all humans, is the problem of achieving "well-being" , where the exact meaning of that term will be specified.

While others such as Bach [17], or Strannegård [18] address the issue of goals or motivation in a cognitive system, those approaches focus on defining a system that targets achieving specific outcomes like securing sufficient food.

© Springer Nature Switzerland AG 2020
B. Goertzel et al. (Eds.): AGI 2020, LNAI 12177, pp. 357–369, 2020.
https://doi.org/10.1007/978-3-030-52152-3_38

However, any system constrained to solve a specific problem fails to meet the definition of adaptive problem solving because the system can't adapt to solve different problems. On the other hand, solving the most general possible definable problem of well-being, which is proposed here to be the fitness of the system to execute all its functions, enables the system to adapt to solve any problem that impacts fitness in performing any function, even functions that adaptive processes such as evolution may not have created yet. In the same way, solving such a general problem of well-being might also enable the system to eliminate functions that evolution or other adaptive processes no longer see as necessary.

The approach to AGI described in this paper represents the human organism in terms of a hierarchy of adaptive processes that each function to achieve a generalized property of fitness in their respective domains. Human functions are categorized as belonging to a number of functional components that include four functional systems (body, emotions, mind, and consciousness) with each system having its own metric for fitness that may be intuitively understood as well-being in that system. Formalization of the concept of well-being in terms of a functional model allows processes of observation to be confined to well-defined state spaces. Processes of self-observation then become processes for observing changes from one well-defined state in a well-defined space to another state in that same space. Any process of observation can then be seen as attempting to transmit a well-defined signal (truthful information), with the result that the ability of such processes to reliably transmit truth (as opposed to transmitting the noise of groundless speculation based on beliefs or other cognitive biases) is governed by well-understood information theory. Where before such self-observation had to be discarded as "anecdotal evidence" , this formalism makes external verification of self-observation reliably achievable [16].

In this approach, cognitive well-being is the goal of the mind in the domain of adaptation through cognition. Defining well-being as a measure of the fitness of that system to exercise all its functions matches the intuitive way that human-beings assess well-being. In comparison, current AI models from this perspective might lack a sufficiently general definition of well-being, and therefore lack a problem to solve that is sufficiently general to achieve human-like general problem-solving ability.

2   Introduction

In the FMF each functional system or functional component in a human is represented by the minimal set of functions (functions meaning behaviors or things the component can do) that can be used to compose all its behaviors. All the states then form a "functional state space" to which the system or component is confined and within which it navigates a path. Each function is essentially a vector in that space. The FMF can then be used to represent and compare models of living systems in terms of how they implement those functions, and in terms of how those implementations govern the dynamics of the system through that functional state space. This paper focuses on only one adaptive domain, the domain of adapting through reasoning that is implemented by the cognitive system, where the cognitive system is represented as moving through a conceptual space. The problem of AGI addressed in this paper is how to define a functional model of cognition that is simple (general) enough to apply to all problems of cognition in an intuitively understandable way that can be implemented, and can be intuitively validated to be complete enough to have general problem solving ability, and be intuitively validated as having the potential to be human-like. Other cognitive architectures, such as SOAR [19], or LIDA [16], also might define a list of functions. However, such functions differ where they do not form a minimally reduced set, as required to maximize generalizability in modeling the functions of any cognitive architectures. And they may differ in not separating the definition of functional models from any implementations. Defining a minimal functional model and defining a metric for the fitness of each implementation of that model is one potential way to compare all AGI research in a fashion that reliably converges on the observed functionality of cognition. Lacking this generalizability, and lacking this simple comparability, current research approaches may lack the capacity to reliably converge on a single understanding. Novel approaches to AGI, for example, may simply be ignored because of lack of popular following [4].

3   The Components of an AGI in the Functional Modeling Framework

The FMF proposes that the individual mind's cognitive functions consist of a number of functional units that process neural signals into concepts, and a number of functional units that process concepts according to the functions involved in cognition. Three lower order cognitive functions represented by the functional units F1 to F3 map to and from signal space to the conceptual space. And the higher order cognitive functions F4 to F7 and FS consisting of storage (memory), recollection, recognition of patterns, recognition of sequences of patterns, and the cognitive awareness FS, receive concepts from the functional state space of the cognitive system ("conceptual space") as input, and produce other concepts as output to that "conceptual space". By executing reasoning processes defined in terms of these functions, the cognitive system navigates this conceptual space.

Assuming that any concept in the human cognitive system can be represented by specifying the state of each of N neurons, then any concept can potentially be represented by a function F1 that detects the distribution of neural signals over the array of N neurons, a function F2 that detects the sequence of signals distributed over time, and a function F3 that detects a pattern in those distributions that represents a concept. Assuming that all concepts can be expressed in terms of their relationship with other concepts, and assuming that these relationships can be expressed in terms of reasoning, then if concepts are represented as points in a conceptual space, all concepts are separated from other concepts by paths that represent reasoning processes. All reasoning is then a path from one point in conceptual space to another.

A minimal set of functions potentially capable of spanning the entire conceptual space begins with a function F4 that stores concepts into the conceptual space, a function F5 that retrieves concepts from the conceptual space, a function F6 that detects patterns in the concepts, and a function F7 that detects sequences in the patterns. The function F4 is intuitively recognizable as memorizing, the function F5 is intuitively recognizable as remembering, F6 is intuitively recognizable as understanding a pattern or employing a pattern in reasoning, and F7 is intuitively recognizable as understanding a sequence of patterns or as employing a sequence of patterns in reasoning. These functions form a minimally reducible set not just within the cognitive system but across the entire human organism, since the same functions F1 to F3 are required for the body to perceive sensory signals as sensations, for the emotional system to perceive emotions, and for the consciousness to perceive awarenesses. In addition, the same function F4 is represented in the FMF as occurring in the body to process sensations, the same functions F4 to F5 are represented as occurring in the emotional system as an evolutionary adaptation to process emotions, and all the same functions F4 to F7 are represented as occurring in the consciousness system as an evolutionary adaptation to process all these awarenesses. The cognitive system must have the capacity to conceptualize all these sensations, emotions, and awarenesses. In the FMF conceptualization is represented as the three functions F1 to F3 being used to map each point in sensory space (each sensory perception), each point in emotional space (each emotion), or each point in awareness space (each self-awareness), to a point in conceptual space (to a concept). The consciousness system must also have the capacity to be aware of all concepts. As consciousness evolved functionality F3 to F7 to navigate awarenesses, the FMF represents this functionality as becoming incorporated in the cognition as well.

The set of these cognitive functions occurs on both the input processing path (cognition of sensory or other input) as well as the output path (cognition driving sensory or other output). The set of these input cognitive functions are proposed to act to receive understanding in terms of concepts (understanding meaning the process that enables comprehension of the sentence "the quick brown fox jumped over the lazy dog"). On the output path (using cognition to drive reason towards conclusions) these cognitive functions are proposed to direct reasoning (reasoning meaning the process that enables answering the question "what fox jumped over what dog?").

These functional units have an evolutionary order in that functional unit FN-1 must exist before its output can be available to be used in functional unit FN. This paper proposes that representation of any reasoning or understanding processes in this way is possible because any thought can be represented in a functional model as a form of pattern detection in concepts (F6), and in terms of a sequence of those patterns (F7). And since the set of functions AND, OR, as well as NOT can represent all logic and is therefore Turing complete, this paper proposes that any logic, and therefore the logic in any rational methodical thought process, can be represented in a functional model in terms of a function to detect patterns representing a Turing complete set of logical operations on concepts, whether or not those operations are the functions AND, OR, and NOT, and in terms of a sequence of those patterns (F7) (Table 1).

Table 1. Functional units in a system of human-like cognition as defined by the Functional Modeling Framework (FMF).

Functional Units in Systems of Cognition		
Functional Unit	Input Function	Output Function
F1 to F3	Create Concept	Create Signals from Concept
F4	STORE (Store Concept)	DECOMPOSE STORAGE (Determine Concept in Storage Function)
F5	RECALL (Recall Concept)	DECOMPOSE RECALL (Determine Concept in Recall Function)
F6	DETECT PATTERN (Detect Pattern in Concept)	DECOMPOSE PATTERN (Detect Concept in Pattern)
F7	DETECT SEQUENCE (Detect Sequence of Patterns in Concept)	DECOMPOSE SEQUENCE (Detect Concept in Sequence of Patterns)
FS	COGNITIVE AWARENESS	

As an example, consider how the following sentence might be represented with the set of cognitive functions and other functional components defined by the framework: "The quick brown fox jumped over the lazy dog". The words in the diagram represent concepts. The relationships between concepts from a given perspective are proposed to define the position of concepts in the conceptual space that is defined by the Functional Modeling Framework (Fig. 1).

Constructs in Conceptual Space – Zoom In

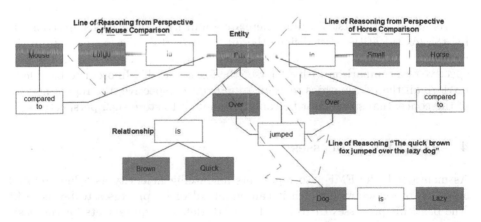

Fig. 1. Depiction of relationships in conceptual space.

The reasoning process that produces this natural language sequence can potentially be modeled in this case as beginning at a position on the diagram above representing a given perspective on the entity "fox", and then executing the RECALL function on the properties "quick" and "brown" and the DETECT PATTERN function to associate them with the "fox" to produce "the fox is quick" and "the fox is brown" . The process might then execute the DETECT SEQUENCE function to group "quick", "brown", and "fox" into "quick brown fox". The process might then execute the RECALL function on the relationship "jumped". And then might execute the RECALL function on the modifier "over". Finally, it might execute the RECALL function on "lazy dog", and then execute the DETECT SEQUENCE function to group "the quick brown fox", "jumped over", and "the lazy dog". Reasoning processes, such as those required to construct text or speech in natural language, then become a sequence of paths through the conceptual space. In this case, the first path P1 is "the fox is quick" (Fig. 2).

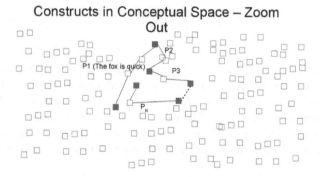

Constructs in Conceptual Space – Zoom Out

Fig. 2. High-level view of conceptual space.

As noted in the first diagram, there are a multitude of relationships connecting the fox to entities that define other of its properties. For example, from the perspective of a comparison with a "mouse" the fox is "large". From the perspective of a comparison with a "horse" the fox is "small". In order to be able to retrieve all the relationships relevant to a given perspective, the representation of the conceptual space must be complete enough to store such perspectives.

4   Adaptive Processes

As mentioned, the FMF also represents an intelligent entity as a hierarchy of adaptive processes with which it can adapt all of its processes to be more fit (the basic life processes L1 to L8). The FMF defines requirements for the basic life processes and the components that implement these processes, but leaves cognitive architectures to define their own implementations to ensure that the most fit component at executing any given required functionality can be taken from any other implementation suggested by any researchers, while ensuring the overall implementation model continues to become more fit at representing the functionality of cognition. The implementation model of AGI described in this paper serves as a reference implementation. The importance of representing intelligent entities in terms of a hierarchy of adaptive processes that together choose the optimal definition of any problem (optimum in terms of the choice that optimizes fitness), and that together choose the optimal solution to that problem, is that in order to increase problem solving fitness to the point that it is general enough to be human-like, nature's design process must remove the constraints against this optimization. And one of the constraints against optimization is whether and how functionality is segmented across components. The principles of intelligent cooperation between components (defined by the domain of adaptation through cooperation) dictate that systems must have the capacity to centralize decision-making where necessary to prioritize the function of a single component. And they must have the capacity to decentralize decision-making where necessary to maximize outcomes for all components. Centralization constrains the system from solving problems that are not aligned with the interests of the components in which decision-making is centralized. Functionality must be decentralized across all components to maximize impact on the problem as perceived by the entire system rather than becoming aligned with the interests of subset of components. To achieve this segmentation, nature must take a modular approach that separates adaptive processes into different domains and that chooses which adaptive functionality to put in each. This choice must be made according to the principles of intelligent cooperation between components if the set of domains is to have the capacity to maximize adaptive fitness across all domains. In other words, rather than defining an AGI as a single adaptive system, adaptive domains in an AGI must be limited in their functionality (modular and reuseable) so they can be adapted without having to change the entire system. As a result some of the constraints against problem definition and problem solving might exist in each adaptive domain. For example, each adaptive domain might lack the capacity to change its own adaptive functions. Therefore each adaptive domain must exist in a hierarchy of other adaptive domains if the constraints to its adaptability are to be removable.

5   An Algorithm for General Problem Solving Ability

General problem solving ability in the FMF is the ability to sustainably navigate the entire conceptual space so that it is potentially possible to navigate from any problem that can be defined within that conceptual space to any solution that can be formulated within that conceptual space. Where a non-intelligent system such as current computer programs solves the problem it's designers have chosen for it, a system with general human-like problem solving ability or true human intelligence, must have the ability to choose which problem to solve. The model of cognition described within this paper chooses which problem to solve through maintaining global stability in the dynamics with which it executes all reasoning processes, where that stability exists within a fitness space related to cognitive well-being.

The system of cognition is modeled as projecting the cognitive value minus cost of each activity being executed (its "fitness" in achieving its targeted outcome in terms of cognitive well-being) and either investing resources into the current reasoning activity until complete, or discontinuing the current reasoning activity to invest resources into the next (choosing to solve another problem) in a way that maintains stability in fitness to continue to execute these cognitive functions. In this way, investment of the cognitive system into each given reasoning process forms a kind of convection that is reflected in the motion of the cognitive system through fitness space. To implement this model, a system of equations capable of demonstrating this convection throughout a three dimensional fitness space (the Lorenz equations for convection) can then be used to define forces of selection of reasoning processes according to projected, targeted, and actual impact on cognitive well-being so that the path through fitness space might form this stable convection, despite the path through the conceptual space being potentially chaotic.

Having defined the equations governing this relationship, an algorithm for selecting the sequence of reasoning activities to be executed by the cognitive process in a way that approximates those dynamics has been defined. By executing reasoning activities in a sequence that keeps the state of cognitive well-being within a stable range, the cognitive system is proposed to gain the capacity to adaptively navigate the conceptual space as well as to gain the capacity to navigate the state space of the environment it conceptualizes. In this way, reasoning in the cognitive system is an adaptive process that enables the entity to find stability in greater regions of the external environment (to understand and reason about the external world). Where the parameters of the Lorenz equations can be chosen to form a globally stable dynamics (a strange attractor) in the cognitive well-being space, despite a chaotic path through the conceptual space. The same Lorenz equations can also be used to implement all the other functional components in the model so that their dynamics within their fitness spaces and state spaces obeys the same global stability despite local instability [2,3].

6   The Importance of an Intuitive Approach

From the standpoint that simple, ubiquitous patterns are intuitive, we would expect that human-beings should intuitively be able to describe their cognitive activities in terms of such a minimally reducible set of cognitive functions, that is, we would expect that such functions would then be consistent with the functions human beings could easily observe within their own self-awareness. In line with these expectations, while the majority of individuals might demonstrate the ability to reliably understand a cognitive process in terms of the FMF's functions (memorize, recall, recognize pattern, or recognize a sequence of patterns) through experiments that test the subject's consistency in using such labels in a wide range of circumstances, most individuals might fail to reliably label a thought in terms of the "perceptual associative memory" or other functions defined by other cognitive architectures. This is not a criticism of the usefulness of those cognitive architectures as potential implementations of AGI functionality, but instead is an illustration of the usefulness of defining simple and intuitive functional models of cognition, within which other cognitive architectures are implementations whose fitness in representing the observed functions of cognition can be measured and compared in order to reliably converge on the best working model of each element of functionality.

From this perspective of a minimal functional model, some functions that are commonly thought of as integral become mere details of some particular implementation of cognition. By analogy, a very simple functional model of computation might not make a distinction between long-term-storage on a hard drive and short-term storage in memory. But any effective implementation of the storage function would certainly identify the optimal implementation in each of those contexts. In the same way, this minimal functional model of the FMF identifies functions as having inputs, outputs, and separate information specifying the context of execution, and leaves other details to be a matter of choosing the optimal implementation of each function.

The approach to functional modeling used in this paper may be a radical departure in that it attempts to create a bridge between approaches for understanding the human system in terms of functions that can be observed in the individual's own self awareness, and approaches held to be "scientific" in restricting themselves to external measurements. Where the vast tradition of such observations has not before been readily accessible to the sciences, this human-centric approach formalizes the process of representing systems in terms of their functions that human beings already use intuitively, so that it is possible to leverage that vast understanding. Furthermore, rather than introducing jargon that forces researchers to adjust to an individual researcher's way of framing cognitive architectures, this human-centric formalization attempts to frame the general problem of cognition in a way that can be intuitively understood in natural language by anyone with a deep understanding of the problem.

The usefulness of the conceptual space defined for this domain of adaptation through cognition is that representing all cognitive processes as being confined to it (i.e. cognitive processes receive concepts as inputs and produce concepts as outputs) allows us to understand what the cognitive system can and cannot do. A cognitive process in the FMF cannot for example have an awareness as input or produce a physical movement as output. In discussions in which a researcher familiar with one cognitive architecture attempts to explain the implications of their model to a researcher versed in another cognitive architecture, any terms that can't be validated intuitively might easily be misinterpreted, making it too unclear what is being discussed for the discussion to be conclusive. This approach of confining behavior to an intuitively understandable functional state space means that a significant source of ambiguity is potentially removed. As a consequence, even when deducing the outcome of an unlimited number of reasoning operations resulting in very complicated patterns of behaviors of the cognitive system, like the patterns representing general problem solving ability, arriving at an answer becomes reliably achievable.

Breaking cognitive architectures down to a set of discrete, objectively defined functions that can be independently implemented by people from different disciplines might also facilitate massive interdisciplinary cooperation to do so, where such cooperation has not proven possible before. In fact, functional modeling approaches are commonly used in systems and software engineering to facilitate cooperation in the design of complex systems by removing the need for individuals in interdisciplinary teams to understand each other's approaches. A functional modeling approach that is also human-centric enables functional modeling to be extended to systems like consciousness or cognition for which functions can be observed within our innate human awareness, but for which the mechanisms of operation are unknown, and being unknown with no universally agreed upon models, researchers might propose models of those mechanisms from mathematics, neurology, physics, or a wide variety of other backgrounds that don't necessarily understand each other. Without this human-centric functional modeling to create the potential for massive interdisciplinary collaboration across disciplines, and between projects to implement poorly understood human functions like consciousness or cognition, the proliferation of models of cognition may tend to remain in silos, and their lessons remain unexplored wherever the complexity of translating between them remains too great to permit more than a tiny minority of models to be readily understood by people in different fields. With such a functional modeling approach, all work might be combined in a way that has the potential to reliably converge on the functions of a working model of AGI.

7   Conditions for an AGI to Be Valid in the FMF

In the FMF the ability to solve a specific problem, such as accomplished by narrow AI, is represented as the lack of a path from one concept to another concept, where that path is the solution. General problem solving ability is the ability to sustainably execute a library of reasoning processes, including reasoning processes that generate new reasoning, so that the cognitive system navigates the conceptual space in a sustainable way that creates the potential to navigate the entire cognitive space. That is, so it is potentially possible to navigate from any problem to any solution. In order to be a valid model of AGI, the FMF then requires this global stability in dynamics despite following a potentially locally chaotic path through the conceptual space. Models that don't explicitly define a maximally general fitness space and that don't explicitly constrain the dynamics in that fitness space to be globally stable, fail in this regard.

8 Implementation

Through defining every cognitive architecture as implementing one or more of these functions, the FMF aims to facilitate the use of best of breed implementations of each function to in turn facilitate convergence of all cognitive architectures into a single architecture that is more fit at representing cognition. Beginning by defining functional models of all rational methodical reasoning processes that can be catalogued (whether human deductive reasoning or reasoning defined in procedural software programs), and functional models of pattern based processes (whether human intuitive reasoning or AI pattern detection), the resulting library of reasoning might be used by all AGI implementations to increase their general problem-solving ability [14] where those implementations are compatible with such abstract functional models of reasoning. By defining the fitness of each reasoning process in achieving each of its outcomes, each implementation can gain the ability to reliably converge on the best reasoning process regardless of the number of such processes. By defining the domains (in terms of concepts) in which each implementation of each process is most fit in achieving those outcomes, each cognitive architecture can store or retrieve this information.

The FMF dictates that a number of functional components must be implemented in an AGI. However, having defined these functional components and their requirements, implementations of each component can proceed independently of each other, and in fact may have already existed for some time and might just need to be identified. Functional unit F3, for example, performs pattern detection, and since some form of pattern detection is general to all neural networks this has been demonstrated. In the case of position as in F1, sequence detection as in F2, storage as in F4, and the generalization involved in learning as in F7, we can show that each of these functions has been implemented as a neural network (position [5,6], sequence detection [7,8], storage [9–11], and the generalization [12,13]) and therefore that each mechanism has been explored in an actual implementation. The FMF suggests that nature follows precise principles of intelligent cooperation (the domain of adaptation through cooperation) that enable components of organisms to use decentralized cooperation to adapt any functions of the organism. Where AGI engineers experience the inability to coordinate and integrate the functions they create so those functions can cooperate, this may indicate that the interfaces defined by such efforts don't follow these specific principles by which the FMF suggests the implementation of such functions might be decoupled.

9 Conclusions

A model suggested to represent an AGI has been presented. Defining general human-like problem solving ability as a pattern of dynamical stability in cognitive well-being space (cognitive fitness space), and defining well-being or fitness more generally (the capacity to execute available cognitive functions) than might be the case with current cognitive architectures with more specific problem solving ability, this model is believed to be novel in identifying an equation which represents general human-like problem solving ability in satisfying those dynamics, and in identifying an algorithm for executing reasoning processes in a way that approximates that equation. As a result, this model is proposed to have the potential for general human-like problem solving ability. This model is also potentially new in defining a minimally reducible set of cognitive functions. While sophisticated AI implementations already exist, organization of all implementations by the same set of functional units enables problem solving reasoning to be constructed the same way for every implementation, so that the library of reasoning processes can steadily grow. Being able to compare the fitness of each implementation of a reasoning process or other element of functionality can also enable the fitness of all cognitive architectures to steadily improve in achieving the functionality required for cognition. Finally, to reiterate, human beings intuitively represent systems in terms of their functions. By formalizing this process of representation, this functional modeling approach enables AI researchers to access the vast traditions in which the functions of human cognition have been observed, where these observations have not been readily accessible to the sciences before. Since these traditions provide experientially verifiable definitions of terms that when defined intellectually are ambiguous, this in itself is a tremendous contribution to AGI research. In other words, intellectual reasoning has a capacity to arrive at truth that is finite (limited to problems in which adequate reasoning and the facts to plug into that reasoning exist) and potentially unreliable (reliable only where such reasoning is computationally reducible or simple enough to be accurately computed). Experiential reasoning has a capacity to arrive at truth that is infinite (the truth of an infinite number of observations can be experienced) and than can be reliable (experience can reliably be observed wherever awareness is practiced enough that an observation can be accurately identified as one's experience). The more experiential and less intellectual the discussion of cognition, potentially the more capable that discussion is of reliably converging on the truth.

References

1. Williams, A.E.: A Human-Centric Functional Modeling Framework for Defining and Comparing Models of Consciousness and Cognition, 16 April 2020. https://doi.org/10.31234/osf.io/94gw3
2. Williams, A.E.: Model for human: artificial 1& collective consciousness (Part I). J. Consciousness Explor. l Res. **10**(4), 250–269 (2019)
3. Williams, A.E.: Model for human artificial 1& collective consciousness (Part II). J. Consciousness Explor. l Res. **10**(4), 270–293 (2019)
4. Lucentini, D.F., Gudwin, R.R.: A comparison among cognitive architectures: a theoretical analysis. Procedia Comput. Sci. **71**, 56–61 (2015). https://doi.org/10.1016/j.procs.2015.12.198. ISSN 1877–0509
5. Bruyndonckx, P., Léonard, S., Tavernier, S.: Neural network-based position estimators for PET detectors using monolithic LSO blocks. IEEE Trans. Nuclear Sci. **51**, 2520–2525 (2004). ieeexplore.ieee.org

6. Ebong, I.E., Mazumder, P.: CMOS and Memristor-based neural network design for position detection. In: Proceedings of the IEEE (2012). ieeexplore.ieee.org
7. Sutskever, I., Vinyals, O.: Sequence to sequence learning with neural networks. In: QV Le - Advances in Neural Information Processing Systems 27 (NIPS 2014). papers.nips.cc
8. Houghton, G.: The problem of serial order: a neural network model of sequence learning and recall - Current research in natural language generation (1990). dl.acm.org
9. Nara, S., Davis, P., Totsuji, H.: Memory search using complex dynamics in a recurrent neural network model. Neural Netw. **6**, 963–973 (1993). Elsevier
10. Cohen, M.A., Grossberg, S.: Absolute stability of global pattern formation and parallel memory storage by competitive neural networks. IEEE Trans. Syst. Man Cybern. **42**, 288–308 (1983). ieeexplore.ieee.org
11. Yao, K., Peng, B., Zhang, Y., Yu, D.: Spoken language understanding using long short-term memory neural networks. In: 2014 IEEE Spoken Language Technology Workshop (SLT) (2014). ieeexplore.ieee.org
12. Aranson, I.S., Pikovsky, A., Rulkov, N.F.: Advances in Dynamics, Patterns, Cognition, LS Tsimring. Springer, Cham (2017). https://doi.org/10.1007/978-3-319-53673-6
13. Sietsma, J., Dow, R.J.F.: Creating artificial neural networks that generalize. Neural Netw. **4**, 67–79 (1991). Elsevier
14. Williams, A.E.: Defining Functional Models of Artificial Intelligence Solutions to Create a Library that an Artificial General Intelligence can use to Increase General Problem Solving Ability, 27 April 2020. http://www.osf.io/preprints/africarxiv/hpzb7
15. Williams, A.E. (n.d.): A Mathematical Model for Identifying Truth in Observations Made within Individual Human Self-Awareness. Retrieved from osf.io/preprints/africarxiv/4nsgk
16. Franklin, S., Madl, T., D'Mello, S., Snaider, J.: LIDA: a systems-level architecture for cognition, emotion, and learning. IEEE Trans. Autonom. Mental Dev. **6**(1), 19–41 (2014)
17. Bach J.: A motivational system for cognitive AI. In: Schmidhuber J., Thórisson K.R., Looks M. (eds.) Artificial General Intelligence. AGI 2011. Lecture Notes in Computer Science, vol 6830. Springer, Heidelberg (2011) https://doi.org/10.1007/978-3-642-22887-2_24
18. Strannegård, C., Svangård, N., Bach, J., Steunebrink, B.: Generic Animats. In: Everitt T., Goertzel B., Potapov A. (eds.) Artificial General Intelligence. AGI 2017. Lecture Notes in Computer Science, vol 10414. Springer, Cham (2017). https://doi.org/10.1007/978-3-319-63703-7_3
19. Laird, J.E.: The Soar Cognitive Architecture, MIT Press (2012) ISBN 0262300354, 9780262300353

Author Index